Jewish Messianism and the Cult of Christ

Jewish Messianism and the Cult of Christ

William Horbury

SCM PRESS LTD

0 334 02713 6

First published 1998 by
SCM Press Ltd
9–17 St Albans Place London N1 0NX

Typeset by Regent Typesetting, London
Printed in Great Britain by
Biddles Ltd, Guildford and King's Lynn

Contents

Introduction   1

I   Messianism and the Old Testament   5

   1. The word 'messiah'   7
   2. The origins of messianism   13
   3. The Old Testament as edited and collected   25
   4. Messianic prototypes   31

II   The Prevalence of Messianism in the
Second-Temple Period   36

   1. The kingdom of God and the kingdom of the messiah   37
   2. The LXX Pentateuch and royal messianism   46
   3. The Apocrypha of the Old Testament and contemporary
     sources   52
   4. The Qumran texts   59

III   The Coherence of Messianism   64

   1. Messianism and Israelite government   66
   2. Ruler-cult and messianism   68
   3. 'Not by the hand of an angel and not by the hand of a legate'   78
   4. Co-ordination of angelic and messianic deliverers   83
   5. A spiritual messiah   86

IV   Messianic Origins of the Cult of Christ   109

   1. The cult of Christ and the question of its origins   109
     (*a*)   Acclamation and hymnody   109
     (*b*)   Gentile or Jewish origins?   112
   2. Angel-christology and messianism   119

3. The praise of Jewish rulers and the worship of Christ   127
   (*a*)   Praises of Jewish rulers   127
   (*b*)   Titles of Christ and Jewish messianism   140

Bibliography   153

Notes   171

Index of References   204

Index of Authors   222

Subject Index   229

Introduction

'Our religion and law does not depend upon a messiah.' So Nahmanides, representing the Jewish community, claimed before King James I of Aragon, according to the Hebrew account of the Barcelona Disputation of 1263.[1] He went on to say that the root of Christian-Jewish disagreement lay rather in the Christian doctrine of the incarnation of the deity.

These weighty claims represent an important trend in opinion then and since. They point by implication to the importance of Torah in Judaism as well as that of the divine status of Christ in Christianity, and to the part played by the Torah as well as the messiah in the earliest Jewish-Christian debate. In their original context of controversy these claims did less than justice, however, to the place of messianic hope in Nahmanides's own environment, among Jews as well as Christians.[2]

The claims sponsored by Nahmanides posed, nevertheless, a genuine question to the New Testament and patristic belief that Jews and Christians did indeed differ only or mainly on the subject of the messiah. In the longer term, these claims have formed what is clearly a debatable interpretation of both Jewish and Christian tradition; thus the Christians' attitude to the Torah and their special honouring of Christ can both be connected with a distinctive messianic loyalty. Nevertheless, Nahmanides's indications of the importance of Torah among Jews and of the exalted Christ in Christianity possess enough intrinsic force to have influenced both Christians and Jews repeatedly towards assessing messianism as marginal.[3] The two claims seem also to be echoed in historical study of the subjects of this book, Jewish messianism during the Second-Temple period, and Jewish and Christian messianism in and at the time of the rise of Christianity.

Thus modern biblical study moves on lines which recall these influential assertions when messianism is judged to be marginal both to the Old Testament and to the New.[4] Similarly, in accord with the distinction drawn by Nahmanides between messianism and a doctrine of incarnation, discussion of messianism is commonly separated from the question of the divine status of Christ among the early Christians, even when the Jewish antecedents of christology are in view. Old Testament material which could be considered messianic is subsumed under headings such as kingship ideology or the rise of apocalyptic writing, and the significance of messianic hope in the Second-Temple period is often thought to be minimal;[5] this position is not, however, universally accepted.[6] Correspondingly, messianism is widely viewed as tangential to Jesus's ministry, and in the study of New Testament christology it has been possible to interpret the treatment of Jesus as messiah as mainly a consequence of belief in his resurrection, with Johannes Weiss and Rudolf Bultmann, and then to reckon it as but a brief phase or a minor aspect of the earliest communal Christian confession. The association of resurrection and messiahship at Acts 2. 36 (compare 10. 40–42, 13. 33) and Rom. 1. 3–4 has been widely taken to show that the resurrection made Jesus the messiah, although it is also likely that belief in the resurrection confirmed views of Jesus as messiah held before his death.[7] On the growth of christology it is urged, to quote the representative words of M. de Jonge, that Jewish hope took many forms, and chiefly involved a decisive intervention by God himself: 'God might employ one or more intermediary or redeemer figures – a messiah-king, a prophet, a new priest, angels or an archangel, etc. – or he might not'; any of these ways of envisaging the divine inception of a new era might be employed in christology.[8]

Then, however, there remain questions such as those considered below. How did the Old Testament come to offer so much material which could be interpreted messianically in the Septuagint, the Targums, the Qumran texts and rabbinic literature? How did early Christian christology, as represented in the New Testament, come to be so deeply imbued with messianic terms and concepts?

In the present study a different view of the historical development is advocated, with a view to two main topics. The first is the place of messianism in the Judaism of the Second-Temple period, roughly from Haggai to Josephus. Much recent work seems to the present writer to underrate the significance of messianic hope within the scripture and tradition of Jews in this period. It is urged below that a rich but largely consistent messianism grew up in pre-exilic and later Israel. In the Old Testament it forms an important theme, which was given clarity and impetus through the editing and collection of the Old Testament books. It cohered with the theme of the kingdom of God. Messianism was then correspondingly influential in the Judaism of the Greek and Roman periods, and the biblical passages which expressed it were at the heart of a vigorously developing interpretative tradition, with vivid details which formed a ramified but not incoherent messianic myth and expectation. Superhuman and spiritual traits regularly appeared in the messianic portraits.

This point leads to the second main topic. Perhaps the most prominent feature of early Christianity was the Christ-cult, but its origins are debated. It bore a close resemblance to contemporary gentile cults of heroes, sovereigns and divinities. This resemblance was noted in the ancient world, and in modern times has supported the view that the cult of Christ was essentially a gentilized manifestation of Christianity. Nevertheless, the Christ-cult has so many Jewish elements that it is more likely to originate from the Jewish or the Christian-Jewish community, but the process of its derivation remains unclear. Here it is argued that the flourishing messianism just mentioned formed the link between the Judaism of the Herodian period and the Christian cult of Christ. This view, it is urged, can also do justice to the resemblance between the Christ-cult and the gentile cults, for both in its earlier and its later developments messianism shared many of the characteristics of ruler-cult.

The interpretation presented here has taken shape over a long period. The writer has argued in earlier publications for the importance of messianism in the Second-Temple period, the messianic origins of the Christ-cult, and the influence of ruler-cult on Jewish messianism and the cult of Christ.[9] These arguments are now put forward in the framework of a fuller study of the development of messianism and its significance for the cult of Christ. This book is deeply indebted to constant patience and encouragement on the part of my wife, Katharine. It owes very much to teachers, friends, and pupils over many years, in Old Testament, New Testament, and Jewish studies. Warm thanks are due to Mr J. D. Lierman, who has compiled the indices. Recently, thought and writing on the subject have been aided by the privilege of spending a term as visiting scholar at the Tantur Ecumenical Institute, Jerusalem, and by library facilities and discussion at the École Biblique and the Hebrew University of Jerusalem. Among many seminars from which I have benefited, I should single out the Cambridge New Testament Seminar, led successively by Professor C. F. D. Moule and Professor M. D. Hooker, and minuted with unfailing wit, fidelity and perception by the Secretary, Mr G. M. Styler.

Perhaps one point of method deserves mention. The Targums and rabbinic literature are considered from time to time among the evidence which may shed light on Judaism at the time of Christian origins. Most of their wealth of material is later, but when viewed in conjunction with the Septuagint and the writings of the Second-Temple period they can be seen to preserve much exegesis and tradition which will have been current then. Moreover, traditions which are clearly later often indicate what biblical texts were customarily viewed together, and what lines of interpretation were gaining importance or had continuing vigour when Christianity arose.

Finally, third- and fourth-century rabbinic biblical interpretation from Galilee and Caesarea, which often plays a part in this study, belongs to the Greek-speaking as well as the Aramaic- and Hebrew-speaking world; it shares with the strongly biblical Christianity of Origen and Eusebius of Caesarea much Hellenic culture and thought, not only through its contemporary forms but also through an inheritance, common to Jews and Christians, from the Hellenically-influenced Judaism of the Second-Temple period.

The argument presented here has points of contact with the historic Christian argument from messianic prophecy, as that was developed in the first and second centuries, particularly in the assertion that there is a continuity between Jewish and early Christian treatments of the messiah. Of particular importance in the argument presented here is the continuity in homage to the messiah as attested in the LXX and in the targums and rabbinic texts. The literary deposit of early Christian homage to Christ to a great extent belongs within this continuum.

The growth of the cult of Christ is then envisaged here on the following lines. Recognition of Christ as messianic king, beginning in the ministry of Jesus and intensified in the earliest Christian comunity, shaped address to Christ according to the tradition of homage just noted, and led to the acclamations and titles preserved in the New Testament. Early Christianity also offers signs of continuity with the developed messianic expectation of ancient Judaism, especially in respect of conceptual links beween spirit and messiah, and those narratives of advent and reign which make up a kind of messianic myth. These developments of an inherited messianism were encouraged by its parallel continuation in the Jewish community throughout the period of Christian origins, and by the importance of ruler-cult under both Greek and Roman rule. Within Christianity the Christ-cult developed side by side with the cults of the angels and the saints.[10] For all three customs there were Greek and Roman counterparts, but the origins lay in Jewish practice which had already been influenced by the Greek and Roman world. In the case of the Christ-cult, messianism in particular formed the link between Judaism and the apparently gentilic acclamation of *Kyrios Iesous Christos*.

I

Messianism and the Old Testament

The Old Testament forms the backbone of any study of messianism in the Second-Temple period. The process of the composition and redaction of the Old Testament culminates in the first part of this period, the two centuries of Persian rule. Characteristic interests and emphases of these centuries govern the editorial process, and it is in these years that the impact of the Old Testament as a whole begins to be felt. Later in the Second-Temple period, correspondingly, in the years after Alexander the Great, Jewish tenets and customs take shape above all as part of a rolling interpretation of the Old Testament; the law and the prophets and other books are expounded, elaborated, supplemented, and rewritten with contemporary needs and interests in view. Messianism owes its own continuing influence throughout the Second-Temple period in large part to the convergence between its thematic importance in the Hebrew scriptures and the pressures of contemporary Jewish life.

Yet to call messianism an important Old Testament theme is immediately to encounter what John Sturdy called 'the impossibility of Old Testament theology'.[1] At least three questions arise. First, do the Hebrew scriptures attest messianism at all? Kingship ideology is plainly seen in the Old Testament, but messianic hope, in the sense of the expectation of an eschatological ruler and saviour, is much less obvious. Thus it is often observed that clear instances of the use of 'the Lord's anointed' for a future king are not, or not easily, found.[2] J. Becker is representative of many biblical students when he refers passages which might be considered messianic, rather, to the ideology of sacral kingship under the kings, or to restorative monarchism during and after the exile, and when he identifies a 'messianological vacuum' in many books of the Old Testament and its Apocrypha and pseudepigrapha.[3] What may be called a 'no hope list' – a list of books wherein it is thought that no messianic hope can be found – has long been a standard item in writings on messianism.[4]

Secondly, even if there is some messianic hope in the Old Testament, has it a place in Old Testament theology? To quote a summary of trends in modern research: 'The conception of a royal messiah represents only a narrow area within the Old Testament tradition, and is certainly not its centre.'[5] Hence, as R. E. Clements notes, many major works on Old Testament theology find little to say about messianic hope.[6] Messianism is indeed important in traditional interpretation of the Old Testament, Jewish as well as Christian; but in both traditions the messiah is linked with conceptions of future life, both national and individual, of a kind which are arguably marginal in the Old Testament itself. Moreover, Jewish tradition is divided on this subject; from the Middle Ages onwards, as already noted, Jews have claimed on occasion that the concept of a messiah is not essential to Judaism.

But then, thirdly, is messianism itself a unitary concept? As it is documented during the period of the Second Temple, roughly from Haggai to Josephus, it can seem patchily attested and diverse. Biblical students identify a wide range of mediators of salvation, including priestly, prophetic and angelic figures; and the depictions of God himself as deliverer are vivid and influential. Messianism in a special form was indeed central in primitive Christianity, but it can be argued that it has already become marginal in the New Testament writings, and in any case Christian messianism might be the exception that proves the rule – the rule that expectation of a messiah was not general or unified. If that is true, as many students of the subject think, the importance and even the existence of messianism is called into question.

These three questions may then suggest that there is not much messianism in the Old Testament, no place for messianism in Old Testament theology, and indeed probably no influential messianic expectation in the period of the Second Temple. Yet it is not clear that these questions should be answered in the way just outlined. Here a case is offered for a different set of answers: namely, that messianism grew up in Old Testament times; the Old Testament books, especially in their edited and collected form, offered what were understood in the post-exilic age and later as a series of messianic prophecies; and this series formed the heart of a coherent set of expectations, which profoundly influenced ancient Judaism and early Christianity.

Are these alternative answers reached simply by some convenient redefinition of messianism? Messianism has long been an elusive word 'chargé de vibration et peu définissable', in A. Gelin's phrase — one of those words, he adds, 'dont on use et abuse aujourd'hui'.[7] Writers on messianism indeed usually try to clarify the term. S. Mowinckel, for example, distinguished between eschatological and political messianism, and restricted himself to the former. Here both are included, in the tradition of writers such as H. Gressmann. Messianism is taken in the broad sense of the expectation of a coming pre-eminent ruler – coming, whether at the end, as strictly implied by the word 'eschatology', or simply at some time in the future. The future in question is often conceived as very near, and consequently messianism here covers the treatment of a present leader in a messianic way, as seems to have happened with Zerubbabel, John Hyrcanus, Bar Kokhba, and Jesus of Nazareth. Hence in what follows some evidence appears which others would classify simply under kingship ideology, but an attempt has been made to be true to the kind of working definition of messianism which is suggested, not least, by ancient usage of the term messiah itself.

1. The word 'messiah'

To turn now to historical inquiry, the word messiah itself attests a special accepted notion current at the end of the Old Testament period, in the second century BC and later. By this time it seems that the Old Testament description of the king as 'the LORD's Anointed', *mᵉshiah YHWH* (I Sam. 24. 6, etc.; cf. 'the anointed of the God of Israel', II Sam. 23. 2, and 'his anointed', I Sam. 2. 10; Ps. 2. 2, etc.), a phrase reflecting the importance of anointing in Israelite and Judaean coronations (II Sam. 2. 4, 5. 3; I Kings 1. 34, 45; II Kings 9. 3, 6; 11. 12; 23. 30),[8] had been commonly abbreviated to '(the) Anointed', (*ha-*) *mashiah*. The abbreviated description still referred to a divinely-approved ruler, but this ruler now included the high priest, whose anointing is prominent in Exodus and Leviticus, and the term acquired an increasing emphasis on the future.

The anointing of the tabernacle and its vessels, also described in Exodus and Leviticus, was likewise remembered in later times, as is suggested by Dan. 9. 24 'to anoint the holy of holies'; but the anointing of the sanctuary is unlikely to be the origin of the Christian usage of the term messiah, as argued by Martin Karrer, for uses of the term often recall the royal context. Biblical references to the anointing of the sanctuary could indeed be linked with or assimilated to the anointing of the messiah in ancient Jewish and Christian interpretation (as in Targum Ps.-Jonathan on Exod. 40. 9–11, or the Peshitta of Dan. 9. 24); but this indicates the strength of the association of the word 'anointed' with the messiah rather than the source of that association. There are much rarer biblical references to the anointing of prophets, as well as kings and priests (I Kings 19. 16; Isa. 61. 1; cf. Ps. 105. 15 = I Chron. 16. 22, but here the patriarchs are probably viewed as kings); these were also developed in the later Second-Temple period, for instance in the Qumran War Scroll (1QM xi 8, 'by the hand of thine anointed ones, seers of things ordained'), but neither is this development likely to have led directly to the special usage of the term for a coming ruler.[9] The persistent use of the abbreviated form '(the) Anointed' from the second century BC onwards suggests that it corresponded to a familiar notion which needed no special explanation.

Some detail is needed to bring out this point, which is somewhat neglected because on the whole it has been taken for granted in the intensive study devoted to the vocabulary of messianism.[10] The New Testament Greek word *messias* (John 1. 42, 4. 25), which provides the term messiah and its equivalents in Western European languages, represents Aramaic *mᵉshiḥa*, '(the) Anointed', corresponding to Hebrew (*ha-*)*mashiah*. The Greek represents an Aramaic rather than a Hebrew word: a word, therefore, which was current in the vernacular (Aramaic), but was also sufficiently technical to be transliterated into Greek, not simply translated – although a translation is also attested, the familiar *christos*.

Messias is of course just one of a number of Greek transliterations of significant Jewish Aramaic terms. A comparable form is Greek *geioras*, 'proselyte', found in the LXX and elsewhere, representing Aramaic *gᵉyora*, corresponding to Hebrew *ger*. In this case too Greek translations (*proselytos*, *paroikos*) were current as well as the transliteration. Hence the attestation of the Greek *messias* suggests that in the Jewish vernacular of the first century AD the term *mᵉshiḥa*, 'the Anointed', was current in a technical sense.

The force of this suggestion is strengthened by the occurrence of the Hebrew term with very little additional explanation in Dan. 9. 25–6, which may be rendered as follows:[11]

> Know therefore and understand that from the going forth of the word to restore and to build Jerusalem to governor messiah (*mashiah nagid*) shall be seven weeks: and for threescore and two weeks it shall be built again, with broad place and moat, and that in troublous times. And after threescore and two weeks shall messiah (*mashiah*) be cut off.

In this prediction seven weeks of years will elapse before 'governor messiah', and then after sixty-two weeks 'messiah will be cut off'. Here the Hebrew past participle 'anointed' is qualified on the first occurrence by *nagid*, 'governor' (for this noun as a qualifier compare Jer. 20. 1, *paqid nagid*); but it is used without the article on both occasions, and has evidently become a technical term, either for the rightful ruler of Israel in general or for the high priest in particular.

Here in v. 25 it probably refers to Zerubbabel or his contemporary Joshua the high priest, and in v. 26 to a high priest, possibly the Onias who was ousted by his brother Jason near the beginning of the reign of

Antiochus Epiphanes (II Maccabees 4. 10, compare chapters 3 and 15). The anointing of the chief priest is described in Lev. 8. 12, among other places. He could be called in general 'the anointed priest', as in Lev. 4. 3–5, and his anointing implied his special governing authority; compare II Macc. 2. 10, 'Aristobulus, king Ptolemy's tutor, from the stock of the anointed priests' (Num. 3. 3, 'the anointed priests', seems ambiguous). The Old Greek translation of Daniel 9 either presupposes a somewhat different text or attests reinterpretation, or both, but it seems to retain a trace of the same usage in its rendering of v. 26, as attested by P967 as well as other witnesses (*meta tou christou*).

Daniel 9, therefore, probably from the early second century BC, gives a relatively early instance of Hebrew corresponding to the special Aramaic and Greek terms already noted, here applying messiah to the anointed priest who governs the nation, and perhaps to the rightful ruler in general. For this broader sense, compare an earlier text, Ps. 105. 15, cited above; here Abraham, Isaac and Jacob are called God's 'anointed' as well as his prophets, and are probably being envisaged as the rightful rulers of Israel, as noted already.

The idiomatic and vernacular use of messiah without any further explanation is often indicated in literature after Daniel, despite the currency of other names like 'branch' or 'son of David', and despite the scholarly instinct which in ancient as in modern times longed for clarity, and so produced more precise descriptions like 'prince of the congregation' in some Qumran writings, or 'king messiah' (a better rendering would be 'the king, the messiah'[12]) in many rabbinic and targumic texts (compare Luke 23. 2, χριστὸς βασιλεύς, 'messiah-king').

Some examples will illustrate the widespread currency of the unexplained technical term. For this purpose they may include occurrences either with or without the article, as regards Hebrew and Greek, and in either the emphatic or the absolute state, as regards Aramaic, because this degree of determination still leaves the sense unexplained; but examples embodying fuller explanatory qualification, such as 'his messiah' in the Qumran 'messianic apocalypse' (4Q 521, fragment 2, ii 1), have been deliberately excluded. Despite this necessary selectivity, the earlier among the examples may also serve to give a first impression of the vivid image of the messiah, including detail not immediately obvious from biblical texts, which was current at the end of the Second-Temple period and in early rabbinic tradition.

First, however, it should be noted that some fuller designations imply the currency of the abbreviated form. Thus the persistence of unqualified 'messiah', in the sense of 'the Lord's anointed', is implied by the Qumran designations 'messiah of Aaron' and 'messiah of Israel', and the rabbinic phrases 'messiah son of Joseph', 'messiah son of David', 'messiah son of Epraim'. Some occurrences of these phrases which imply the shorter designation may be noted here:

(a) 1QS 9. 11, 'until there shall come the prophet and the messiahs of Aaron and Israel'; 1QSa ii 20–1, 'the messiah of Israel shall stretch out his hand towards the bread'; CD xii 23–xiii 1, 'during the epoch of wickedness until there shall arise the messiah of Aaron and Israel'; 4Q266, fragment 10 i, line 12, 'until there shall arise the messiah of Aaron and Israel' (a text parallel with, and more fully preserved than, CD xiv 19);[13]

(b) Babylonian Talmud, Sukkah 52a, 'Messiah son of Joseph' (on the mourning for the pierced one in Zech. 12. 10–14); Targum Cant. 4. 5, 'your two redeemers who will redeem you, messiah son of David and messiah son of Ephraim'.

The unqualified form '(the) messiah' itself is directly attested in Hebrew in the Qumran rule literature, and indirectly attested in some translated texts from the end of the Second-Temple period, notably II Baruch and II Esdras, and probably also the Psalms of Solomon; and it is similarly reflected in the New Testament, sometimes possibly in translation Greek, but often probably in original Greek. Relevant passages may be noted as follows:

(a) in Qumran rule literature: 1QSa ii 11–12, 'until God engenders the messiah' (the verb is discussed in chapter III, section 5, below, but the occurrence of 'the messiah' (*ha-mashiah*) is uncontroversial);[14]

(b) in translated Jewish texts: Syriac Apocalypse of Baruch 29. 3, 'Messiah shall then begin to be revealed'; II Esdras 12. 32, 'Messiah (*unctus*), whom the Highest has kept to the end'; and probably Ps. Sol. 17. 32 (36), 'all shall be holy, and their king, messiah (*Christos*) the lord' (cf. Ps. 110. 1, 'my lord'; Lam. 4. 20 LXX and Luke 2. 11, '*christos* the lord'');

(c) in New Testament Greek: *messias*, John 1. 42; 4. 25; (*ho*) *christos*, e.g. Mark 8. 29; 12. 35 (on Ps. 110. 1); John 7. 41–42 (where to be born?); Acts 2. 36; 9. 22 (true messiah); 26. 33 (messiah must suffer); I John 2. 22.

Finally, unqualified 'messiah' is often directly attested in Hebrew or Aramaic in rabbinic literature and the Targums. Here we meet what look like current phrases – 'days of messiah', 'footprints of messiah', 'tribulation of messiah' – that is, tribulation in the times of the messiah – as well as 'messiah' on its own, for instance in the Targumic rendering of Gen. 49. 10 as 'until messiah shall come'. A few examples from a large number of occurrences may be noted as follows:

(*a*) Mishnah, Ber. 1. 5 'days of messiah', Sotah 9. 15 'footprints of messiah' (Aramaic, cf. Ps. 89. 52); these are the sole direct references to the messiah in the Mishnah, although its treatment of the king, high priest and sanctuary suggests expectation of a restored Israelite monarchy and high priesthood, but in both instances the context suggests that current usage needing no explanation is taken over;

(*b*) Jerusalem Talmud, Kil. 32b and Ket. 35a (Aramaic), 'so, when messiah comes, I shall be ready' (R. Jeremiah [fourth century] gives instructions for his burial); Babylonian Talmud, Sanh. 97a (Hebrew), 'for it is taught, Three come unexpectedly: messiah, a discovery, and a scorpion'; 98b (Hebrew), 'and it is taught: the disciples of R. Eleazar asked, What shall a man do to escape the tribulation of messiah?'

(*c*) Targum: Gen. 49. 10 MT, 'until Shiloh come' (Targum Onkelos, 'until Messiah come'); Isa. 52. 13, 'my servant shall prosper' (Targum, 'my servant messiah shall prosper'); Zech. 6. 12, 'a man whose name is branch' (Targum, a man whose name is messiah).

From these instances various qualified occurrences of 'messiah' have been deliberately excluded. Among early examples are 'his messiah' in the Parables of Enoch (48. 10; 52. 4) and in 4Q 521 (cited above), or 'messiah of righteousness' in 4Q Patriarchal Blessings, on Gen. 49. 10 (compare the Fourteenth Benediction of the Amidah, which in one version has the phrase 'the kingdom of David, messiah of thy righteousness', referring either to the past or to the future David). These qualified occurrences confirm that 'messiah' is indeed short for 'God's messiah', and some of them help to show that the term is rooted in the Old Testament vocabulary of kingship, as noted already. Nevertheless, such instances of messiah with some explanatory qualification have been excluded here in the interests of showing the persistence from the second century BC onwards of the quite unexplained word 'messiah', which made its way as a technical term into the vernacular languages, Aramaic and Greek, and designated a rightful ruler of Israel, above all the coming Davidic king.

This short study of 'messiah' has now thrown into relief the continuous use of this technical term from the second century BC onwards, through the era of Christian origins and the Jewish revolts against Rome, and into the rabbinic period. The appearance of unqualified 'messiah' in both Hebrew and the main Jewish vernaculars, and in a wide range of sources – the Qumran rule literature, apocalypses of the late first century AD, the Mishnah about AD 200, and the Targums – indicate that the uses of *messias* and *christos* in the New Testament are less likely to attest an independent Christian development paralleled by a slighter later independent Jewish development, as is suggested by M. Casey, than a participation in a Jewish usage which was already familiar in the time of Jesus.[15] Early examples quoted, from II Baruch and II Esdras, incidentally illustrate the development of a myth of the messiah; as these apocalypses show, by the end of the Second-Temple period the expectation of the revelation of the messiah from obscurity was developed considerably beyond what might be immediately suggested by biblical passages such as I Sam. 16. 1–13. This development had no doubt taken place well before the destruction of Jerusalem, as is suggested by Isa. 32. 1–2 LXX, 'a righteous king shall reign . . . and a man shall be hiding his words, and shall be hidden as from rushing water, but shall appear in Sion like a glorious rushing river in a thirsty land'.[16]

These phenomena suggest at least four considerations which implicitly question the view that messianism was insignificant.

(i) The usages reviewed occasionally allow a glimpse behind the literary evidence into common parlance, notably in the case of the Greek form *messias*, with its reflection of a vernacular, and perhaps too with phrases like 'days of messiah'. This point suggests that the relatively sparse *literary* attestation of the term messiah need not, as is often inferred, signify a correspondingly patchy interest in the subject.[17]

(ii) Moreover, the consistent use of this word will have been among the factors making for unity and coherence, and it sets a query against the equally widespread assertion that conceptions of the messiah were disparate and inconsistent.[18]

(iii) Expectations of the messiah gave rise to relatively detailed narratives of his advent, wars and reign.

(iv) Lastly, the term which became so persistent is derived from the Old Testament vocabulary and is found in contexts which are also shaped by Old Testament vocabulary and thought. This suggests that, despite doubts on the presence of messianism in the Old Testament, we should look to the Old Testament for the main lines of the notions which the term messiah evoked.

In what follows four aspects of the Old Testament are considered. First, to what extent can Old Testament material be correlated with the origins and development of messianism in Israel and Judah? Reconsideration of some earlier work on origins suggests that movements of life and thought which can be called messianic can properly be envisaged during the period of the composition of the Old Testament books.

Secondly, irrespective of this historical question, some features and tendencies belonging to messianism become apparent in the editorial arrangement of material within individual books. Similarly, some such features were enhanced when the books were collected together. These editorial and collective features had an immediate influence on later messianic vocabulary and thought, from the end of the Persian period onwards, including the vocabulary just noticed in review of the term 'messiah'.

Thirdly, some passages from the earlier stages of the composition of the Old Testament became important during the Second-Temple period as presenting messianic prototypes.

Lastly, this phenomenon is one of the indications that there was a set of expectations, flexible and various but sufficiently coherent to be called a narrative or myth of the messiah. Such a myth was probably already current in the time of the Davidic monarchy, as already proposed in the study of origins.

On this basis it will be suggested that messianism can be envisaged both before and after the exile; moreover, the stamp which it left on the Old Testament as finally edited and collected will have been such as to encourage the continuation and enrichment of messianic hope in the Jewish community of the Greek and Roman periods.

2. *The origins of messianism*

Old Testament material on a coming king has been assigned to various historical settings, especially in exilic and post-exilic times. The currency of messianic hopes during and after the exile is widely recognized, but a judgment on their importance in this later period involves attention to the vexed question of their antecedents during the monarchy. In this context the problem of the dating of what appear to be messianic Old Testament passages is bound up with the broader discussion of the content and setting of messianic hope.

Three questions which constantly recur in study of the content and context of early messianism are important also for the later developments considered below. First, how are the praises of a present king in the royal psalms related to messianic hope? This question anticipates the question of the relationship between royal praises and Jewish messianism in the Greek and Roman periods, discussed below.

Secondly, how far is hope for a messianic king consistent with the assertion of Israel's God as king? This assertion is met especially, but not solely, in the 'enthronement psalms'. Was the emphasis on the kingship of God which appears in these psalms sometimes linked with opposition to the very idea of an Israelite king? Such opposition seems to be implied in passages like I Sam. 8. 7, 'The LORD said to Samuel . . . They have rejected me from being king over them'. The recognition of God alone as governor recurs in the Roman period as the watchword of Josephus's 'Fourth Philosophy' (*Ant.* 18, 23), and in connection, accordingly, with opposition to the existing government. The question whether hope for a messianic kingdom is needed, or even permissible, in the light of the doctrine of the kingdom of God recurs in arguments for the importance of restoration hopes without a messiah, and for a so-called 'messianological vacuum', in the later period.

Lastly, and not least importantly, was there a messianic myth, an account of the coming deliverer which would offer an outline of his person and work? This question was heralded, in the quest of the historical Jesus, by Bruno Bauer's doubt concerning the detailed expectation of the messiah's achievement which D. F. Strauss assumed;[19] but it came to be central in discussion of the origins as well as the development of messianism.

These questions can be approached through review of some landmarks in study of the origins of messianism.[20] Critical scholars at the end of the nineteenth century were ready, as is also the case at present, to envisage the emergence of messianic hopes during the period of the Israelite monarchy. Thus J. Wellhausen dated their appearance after the decay of the kingdom of David and Solomon, when the Assyrian threat was paramount. He justly stressed, however, that messianic prophecies are not simply predictions of deliverance, but affirmations of the ideal of the Israelite state as it should be. This perception would in principle leave some room for understanding the depictions of ideal government in royal psalms like 72 or 110 as expressions of hope, but Wellhausen dated these psalms in the Greek period or later, and understood them as addresses to Ptolemaic or Hasmonaean kings. He recognized, therefore, their resemblances to the literature of ruler-cult in the Greek period, but he set them far apart from pre-exilic messianic prophecy.

On the second question noted above, Wellhausen added that the messianic hopes of the later monarchical period involved no conflict between the divine and the earthly kingship, for the human king was regarded as the Lord's representative. 'The earthly ruler is not in the way of the heavenly: even the glorious kingdom of the future cannot dispense with him.'[21] Here Wellhausen is not referring to the enthronement psalms, but to the notion of a 'theocracy', a divinely-governed nation, as already present in the pre-exilic period and eventually, in an altered form, to be enshrined in the Pentateuch. (He regarded the enthronement psalms as expressions of national hope, moulded by the notion of the theocracy, from the time of Alexander the Great.[22])

On the third question, the growth of a messianic myth, he was ready to see a Jewish mythology behind Rev. 12 and in other apocalypses, but he was more interested in relating such material to an historical setting than in studying its development for its own sake.

Wellhausen's comment on the indispensability of the earthly ruler introduced a quotation of Isa. 32. 1–2, 'A king shall reign in righteousness', a passage which in the LXX has been affected by the notion of the hidden messiah, as mentioned above. The Hebrew text, in some studies since Wellhausen, has been assessed as an idealized picture of a reigning king, probably Josiah.[23] Whether this assessment is correct or not, it suggests a consideration which came to the fore after Wellhausen, in the work of H. Gunkel and the *religionsgeschichtliche Schule*, especially H. Gressmann, and in the related but in many ways distinct position of S. Mowinckel. Was messianic hope simply a response to the decline of the pre-exilic kingdoms, as might be inferred from Wellhausen's treatment, or was it in some sense given together with the circle of ideas surrounding the institution of monarchy – ideas which Gunkel's work had connected with a mass of ancient Near Eastern mythology?

Gunkel and his followers came to be particularly associated with the view that biblical myth reflects external influence, notably from a common fund of ancient oriental mythology; but Gunkel also threw light on the internal Jewish development of a myth of the messiah, in 'the great book which both made and unmade his name', *Schöpfung und Chaos in Urzeit und Endzeit* (1898).[24] Here, in his study of the passage in Rev. 12 on the woman clothed with the sun, Gunkel urged that Babylonian mythology is the ultimate source of this account; but another element of his interpretation was a reconstruction of the development of the underlying tradition within the Jewish community. He argued that the rabbinically-transmitted story of a messianic child who is snatched away by the wind (Lam. R. 1. 51, on 1. 16; Talmud Yerushalmi, Ber. 2. 3, 5a) was a fragment of a tradition related to, and in part more original than, the narrative in the Revelation.[25] The reconstruction to which this argument belonged influenced Wilhelm Bousset in his own attempt to reconstitute a tradition concerning Antichrist.[26]

Gressmann and Mowinckel both firmly distinguished royal psalms, praising a present king, from messianic oracles of the future, and they reserved the term 'messianic' for the latter. Here, although they differed from Wellhausen on the dating of the psalms, they retained much of his separation between psalms and prophetic oracles. Nevertheless, following Gunkel, they both affirmed that mythological connections between the king and the divine realm, paradise and a golden age provide important themes in Old Testament monarchical literature, and in some way influenced the expression of messianic hopes.

Gressmann and Mowinckel built on this basis in closely similar yet different ways. The influence of non-Israelite mythology was far more important in the eyes of Gressmann, who was close to Gunkel on this point. He argued that 'the messiah derives from the outside world'; the earliest messianic hopes, with the strong mythological traits exemplified in the portrait of an 'eschatological demi-god' in Isa. 9. 5, belonged to a circle of ideas, including the expectation of a divine king of the end-time, which went back ultimately to the neighbouring kingdoms of the Near East. In a non-eschatological form these myths also shaped the 'court style' (*Hofstil*) of the royal psalms, with their idealized and divinized king. In the royal praises of Israel, as in ancient Mesopotamia, Syria and Egypt, the righteous king brings divinely-blessed peace and prosperity. As the eschatological messianic hopes of Israel developed, their mythological elements began to drop away, and the eschatological hero-king, who originally had the divine traits which can still be observed in Isa. 9 and Micah 5, was humanized and subordinated to the heavenly king under the influence of the Yahwistic zeal attested in the enthronement psalms. On the other hand, the divinized depiction of the present king in the royal psalms, with their mythological *Hofstil*, also began to affect the portrait of the eschatological messianic king; and mythology fully reclaimed the messiah in the end, as seen especially in the treatment of the Son of man in Daniel, Enoch and II Esdras.[27]

This argument was pungently expressed in the brief, vivid chapters of Gressmann's *Der Ursprung der israelitisch-jüdischen Eschatologie* (1905), which soon found an English echo in the work of W. O. E. Oesterley, *Evolution of the Messianic Idea* (1908).[28] Gressmann rewrote and supplemented *Der Ursprung* as *Der Messias* (1929); in this second book, which he left unfinished at his untimely death in 1927, he gave fuller attention to the inner-Israelite setting of messianism, but he stuck to a non-Israelite derivation for it, because of the eschatological rather than merely future orientation which he discerned in messianic oracles: the messiah is the king of the last days (*Endzeit*). He now urged that Israel took over messianic hope from Egypt in particular. Herein, like H. Lietzmann (see below), he followed

Eduard Meyer's suggestion that Israelite prophecy owed much to its Egyptian counterpart,[29] and he pointed out that the notion of primaeval kingship and the production of dynastic oracles were both clearly attested in Egypt at an early date.[30] These oracles of a coming king were broadly comparable with those of Israel, as Gressmann stressed with his phrase 'the Egyptian messianic hope' ('die ägyptische Messiashoffnung').[31]

Mowinckel, however, derived eschatology not directly from non-Israelite sources, but from the expectations connected with 'the enthronement festival of Yahweh' (*das Thronbesteigungsfest Jahwäs*), the great autumn festival which became the feast of Tabernacles. He criticized Gressmann accordingly in *Das Thronbesteigungsfest Jahwäs und der Ursprung der Eschatologie* – the second volume of his *Psalmenstudien* (1922) –, and then again in *He That Cometh* (*Han son kommer*, 1951; ET of revised text, 1956). Gressmann held that existing non-Israelite myths of a coming deliverer, which had already long been current in Israelite popular religion, were reflected in the earliest messianic prophecies. Mowinckel urged, however, that mythology influenced messianism only in the later stages of a complex development, especially in the post-exilic period.

The essential source for messianism, Mowinckel argued, was the royal ideology of the early monarchical period. This was indeed pervasively mythological, especially in the divinization of the king attested in passages from the royal psalms like 2. 7 and 110. 3, but prophetic Yahwism drastically undermined any high doctrine of kingship. Correspondingly, when messianic hopes are first attested, in the pre-exilic period, they are hopes for a human descendant of David, not for a divine figure. Mythological influence on messianism can, however, be envisaged with caution before the exile, under the influence of the concept of a divinized king which has shaped the royal psalms; but it appears in force only in apocalypses like I Enoch and II Esdras, where the messiah has indeed become 'a second-rank god or a first-rate angel'.

This reconstruction recalls Wellhausen in so far as messianism is envisaged as a secondary development, not an original element in the hopes of the monarchical period. On the other hand, Mowinckel made an important criticism of Wellhausen: messianism, in Mowinckel's view, was not a response to the decline of the pre-exilic kingdoms, but a natural offshoot of belief in a divinely-blessed monarchy. This offshoot was encouraged, he urged, by the 'enthronement festival of Yahweh', which he posited as the setting of the enthronement psalms; for every year on this occasion the earthly king was enthroned as a vassal of the heavenly king, and hope for the ideal king portrayed in Ps. 72 was repeatedly renewed. Hence the acclamation and expectation of the enthronement of God was from very early times accompanied by hope for God's representative, the righteous earthly king – however inconsistent this hope might be with the stress of the enthronement psalms on the kingship of God alone.[32]

To return to the three questions set out above, on the relation of the royal psalms to messianic hope Gressmann and Mowinckel were largely in agreement, as noted already. They both separated the royal psalms, on the present king, from the literature of messianism, on a coming king; but they also both conceded that royal psalms had helped to shape the portrait of the coming king at a late period.

On the second question, however, they both followed Gunkel in viewing God's kingship and messianic kingship as mutually incompatible – a point which, as already noted, had not been accepted by Wellhausen. Gressmann quoted with approval Gunkel's dictum that 'where the Lord is king, there is no messiah; the messiah has no place in the kingdom of the Lord'.[33] Mowinckel similarly endorsed Franz Delitzsch's observation that the 'theocratic' psalms, on the kingdom of God, seem in principle inconsistent with the 'christocratic' psalms, on the kingdom of the messiah; the God of the enthronement psalms 'needs no co-regent or representative'.[34] Gressmann and Mowinckel agreed, moreover, in supposing that the 'theocratic' principle, as expressed in the enthronement psalms, had tended to cut the Israelite image of the messiah down to human size. Nevertheless, they both admitted that, however inconsistently, pre-exilic Israelites had already hoped for a coming king manifesting the divine attributes ascribed to the earthly monarch in the royal psalms. This admission suggests that the seeming inconsistency between theocracy and messianism should be treated with caution, especially in view of the association in other cultures between king-like deities and monarchs here below. On this point in particular, H. W. Wolff showed that the messianic kingdom is more truly a representative than a rival of the kingdom of God.[35]

On the third question, concerning a myth of the messiah, Gressmann and Mowinckel agreed in recognizing such a myth, and in giving it high importance. They differed, however, when Gressmann found that the pre-exilic (originally non-Israelite) expectation of an eschatological hero-king was there at the start as well as the close of the whole development, whereas Mowinckel saw it as a secondary, if early, offshoot of the celebration of earthly as well as heavenly kingship involved in the 'enthronement festival of Yahweh'. Yet Mowinckel looked for its origins not to the decline of the monarchy, but to the circle of ideas connected with Israelite kingship at its height. Unlike Gressmann, therefore, he rated external culture as only a secondary influence, mediated through Israelite royal ideology. Nevertheless, he allowed that messianic hope obtained a central place in connection with the monarchy in Israelite life and thought, and developed the myth of a figure like a demi-god or angel.

To move from these particular questions to the general evaluation of messianism, Gressmann and Mowinckel jointly showed that messianism must be treated not just as a reaction to bad times, but as an abiding element in the circle of ideas which surrounded Israelite kingship and reflected foreign culture, including that of Egypt with its high monarchical doctrines. Both scholars recognized a myth of the messiah formed under external influence; Gressmann's position in principle did more justice to this influence than Mowinckel's. Their common identification of the *Hofstil* of the royal psalms as the medium through which non-Israelite court theology influenced messianism remains influential in recent study.[36] Both also recognized the formidable force of the acclamation of God as king, and saw it, perhaps questionably, as a deterrent to development of the messianic theme.

Their dating of messianism in the time when the monarchy still flourished was attacked in an influential criticism by A. von Gall. He regarded Persian rather than ancient Near Eastern influence as primary in the shaping of eschatology, and he also thought that the hope for a coming kingdom of God first arose at the time of the exile – occasionally in connection with hope for a Davidic king, although generally the king of the realm was God himself, who was envisaged in Deutero-Isaiah as the national saviour and redeemer; these hopes were influenced by Persian thought.[37] Von Gall's thesis as a whole will receive further notice in the following chapter. His seeming disregard of the ideas surrounding the pre-exilic institution of the Israelite monarchy must be viewed in the light of his conviction that pre-exilic datings of messianism unduly neglected the mainly post-exilic appearance of Old Testament hopes for a golden age.[38] This point has repeatedly recurred in subsequent discussion of the date of the enthronement psalms, for perhaps the strongest argument for dating them late is drawn not from their points of contact with Deutero-Isaiah alone, but from the widespread attestation of the theme of God as king in material from the exilic or post-exilic periods.[39]

Similarly, the external derivation of mythology sponsored by Gressmann was widely criticized. Thus, when he and others envisaged an 'Egyptian messianic hope', they were considered by von Gall to neglect the differences between the Egyptian literature and Israelite prophecy; similarly, H. Gross later concluded that Gressmann had looked in vain for the origins of a religious concept in writings which were fundamentally political propaganda.[40] Yet some points in these criticisms rest on premises which are themselves questionable, notably as regards the dating of Old

Testament texts (von Gall) and the separation of messianism from political publicity (Gross).

Moreover, Gressmann drew attention to comparative material of lasting importance. The relevance of royal titles and court praise from the ancient Near East becomes apparent especially when Mowinckel's sharp distinction between eschatology and future hope is questioned, and Mowinckel himself readily admitted that mythological conceptions known from non-Israelite as well as Israelite sources, such as the association of the king with paradise, came to the fore in messianic hopes as expressed in Isa. 9. 1–6; 11. 6–8.[41] Again, Gressmann's derivation of Israelite messianism simply from Egypt seems dubious in principle, given the wide geographical range of ancient Near Eastern texts on kingship and the gods; but doubt on this point does not affect the significance of the Egyptian material to which he pointed. Archaeological finds continue to indicate that, although Egyptian political power in Canaan declined during the period of the Israelite monarchy, the cultural and artistic influence of Egypt remained strong.[42]

It is true that, as von Gall stressed, in manner the Egyptian writings classified as messianic by Gressmann are closer to apocalyptic compositions such as Daniel and the Sibyllines than to earlier Israelite prophecies – although the close links between these compositions and the prophetic corpus should not be forgotten.[43] Ptolemaic and later Egyptian works of this kind like the Oracle of the Lamb and the Potter's Oracle have justifiably been used, accordingly, to illustrate messianic prophecy near the time of Christian origins. Earlier Egyptian works, however, like the prophecies of Neferti (twentieth century BC, but exhibiting motifs which still recur in the Potter's Oracle), or the Papyrus Westcar story (seventeenth century BC) of the divinely-assisted births of the three first rulers of the Fifth Dynasty, can appropriately be considered among the antecedents of Israelite oracles like Isa. 9. 1–6.[44] To quote from the prophecies of Neferti, which legitimize the founder of the Twelfth Dynasty,

> I will show you the land in turmoil,
> The weak-armed is strong-armed,
> One salutes him who saluted . . .
> Gone from the earth is the nome of On,
> The birthplace of every god.
> Then a king will come from the south,
> Ameny, the justified, by name,
> Son of a woman of Ta-Seti, child of Upper Egypt . . .
> Rejoice, O people of his time . . .

Asiatics will fall to his sword,
Libyans will fall to his flame . . .
Then Order will return to its seat,
While chaos is driven away.

The messianic oracles of the Israelites therefore followed comparable productions which had long been familiar among their influential Egyptian
neighbours. Lastly, Gressmann's less-debated discussion of the inner-
Israelite development of messianism, in *Der Messias*, included the proposal
that the figure of Josiah formed a focus for messianic hope from the time of
his death onwards, as might be suggested by the Chronicler's notice of the
long survival of lamentation for him (II Chron. 35. 25). This proposal is
close to the more recent suggestion, mentioned above, that Josiah formed
the model for passages in the book of Isaiah on an ideal king. Moreover, it
has been taken up in the work of A. Laato (1992), who finds the figure of
Josiah at the heart of messianic expectations in the exilic and early post-
exilic periods. Gressmann's suggestion is important, irrespective of its
revival in recent study, because it indicates a messianic prototype who is
defeated and slain, rather than continually victorious.

In the mid-twentieth century Gressmann and Mowinckel both aroused
among many of the succeeding generation of Old Testament students,
especially in Germany, what P. Welten calls 'a certain horror at parental
audacity'.[45] By contrast, in Scandinavia, in the period roughly from 1935 to
1960, many of their interests were intensively pursued in an efflorescence of
work on divine kingship and mythology in the ancient Near East. This
work ran parallel, especially in the 1930s, with anthropologically-inspired
work in Britain on the Israelite cult by S. H. Hooke and other members of
the so-called Myth and Ritual School.[46] In both cases impetus was added to
these studies by the discovery of the Ugaritic texts at Ras Shamra in 1929,
for the attestation in these texts of a Syrian mythology evincing links with
the information on Syrian deities in Philo of Byblos shed much light on
Canaanite influence on the Old Testament. These movements in Scandinavian and British Old Testament study led to widespread awareness of the
importance of kingship as a focal point in cult, mythology and national
hope; they issued after the Second World War in important publications
specifically on messianism by A. Bentzen and H. Riesenfeld, with emphasis
on the Old and the New Testament, respectively, and by two scholars
familiar yet not fully one with these movements in their countries,
Mowinckel in Norway (in a new comprehensive study of messianic hope)
and A. R. Johnson in Britain.[47] Mowinckel's view of the enthronement
psalms in his earlier work exercised strong influence in the English-speak-

ing world,[48] and his insistence on the Israelite origins of messianism fitted better than Gressmann's position into the widespread mid-century assertion of the distinctiveness of biblical tradition. Thus in a 1952 treatment of eschatology and messianism S. B. Frost followed Mowinckel rather than Gressmann, holding that Israelite eschatology is essentially unparalleled in ancient Near Eastern sources; but Frost departed from Mowinckel as well as Gressmann in concluding that expressions of messianic hope can best be dated from the beginning of the exile onwards. He held that messianism then went underground until its revival about the end of the third century BC, as an 'eschatologizing of the enthronement cult'; and he singled out for disagreement S. H. Hooke's declaration that the messianic element was central in the apocalypses of the later Second-Temple period, although he laid stress on the importance of the transcendental messianic figure of the Parables of Enoch for the christology of John, Ephesians and Colossians.[49]

At just the same time, however, A. R. Johnson, who also had much in common with Mowinckel, was formulating the view that – by contrast with Mowinckel's identification of the emergence of messianic hope as a separate stage in development – the royal psalms as used at the autumn festival in the time of the monarchy themselves always implied hope, and were indeed messianic in the eschatological sense; 'and in that case' (he wrote) 'the Messianic Hope, in its association with the House of David, is much earlier than is commonly thought'.[50] Johnson's view was associated with his conception of a ritual drama performed by the king at the festival, first put forward in 1935, but it retains its force irrespective of acceptance of his reconstruction of the role of the king in the cult. It rests on the inference that psalms such as 2; 18; 72; 110; and 118, when applied to the reigning king in communal use, were always partly unfulfilled promises of deliverance, peace and righteousness, and implied a future hope. Mowinckel had come near to saying this, but had preferred to envisage the emergence of messianism as a definite new stage. Johnson's change in the total picture appropriately recognizes the future as well as present dimension which the common prayer and hymnody connected with the institution of the monarchy is always likely to have had. A pre-exilic messianism could therefore be identified not only in special oracles reflecting times of crisis (as probably in Isa. 9. 1–6; Micah 5. 1–4), but also in the recurrent yet ever-hopeful praise of the reigning king.

A second notable contribution by Johnson was his special emphasis on the close links of the Zion psalms like 46; 48; and 76 with the role of the king, so that in his reconstruction the royal psalms, the enthronement psalms and the Zion psalms are all brought together in a way that foreshadows the later conjunction of their themes in messianic texts like the Psalms of Solomon, the Parables of Enoch, II Esdras and the Amidah.[51]

A final landmark which can be appropriately noted in the setting of the 1950s is formed by the renewed impact of the Ugaritic texts on the question of messianic origins.[52] Through studies from the 1930s onwards, notably by O. Eissfeldt, it had become clear that a Canaanite pantheon comparable with that attested in Ugaritic sources and Philo of Byblos had left traces in the Old Testament books. El presided over this pantheon, and its members included Baal. The Ugaritic texts confirmed the likelihood that El and Yahweh had been two separate deities. Moreover, Yahweh appeared in biblical texts with the attributes of a storm-god, like those assigned to Baal in the Ugaritic texts. Hence, whereas the origins of the demigod-like messianic Son of man in the Parables of Enoch and II Esdras had been traced through Dan. 7 back to a very ancient myth (Gunkel, Gressmann), and in particular to variations on Iranian conceptions of a Primal Man (*Urmensch*) current in the Persian and Greek periods (Mowinckel), it became possible for A. Bentzen to recognize the revival of old mythology in these apocalypses, recognized in different ways by Gunkel, Gressmann and Mowinckel, as a 'renaissance' of specifically Canaanite mythology.[53] J. A. Emerton argued convincingly that the Ancient of Days and the Son of man in Dan. 7 represent a tradition of two divine beings originating in Israelite-Canaanite contact. The two were understood in the Greek and Roman periods as the God of Israel and an angelic figure, who was identified in the Parables of Enoch and II Esdras with the messiah.[54] With regard to the royal psalms, Bentzen again represents those who, especially in Scandinavia, saw the ideas surrounding the Israelite divine king as a modified form of Canaanite royal ideology, and an important early stage in the development of messianism.[55]

Later chapters in this book will take up some contributions from this long period of intensive work on pre-exilic and later messianism, from about 1880 to 1960. These include Wellhausen's broad view of the political background of messianic praise; the argument for long-term continuity in mythical aspects of the messianic figure which was advanced in different ways by Gunkel, Gressmann, Bentzen and Emerton; the discussions of the coherence of post-exilic and later messianism by Wolff, Mowinckel and Riesenfeld; and above all, perhaps, the perception of the centrality of the institution of kingship as a focus of myth and hope which marked much Scandinavian and British biblical study of the mid-twentieth century, for instance the work of Bentzen and Johnson. This perception can be applied, *mutatis mutandis*, to later Jewish kingship and messianism, and to sovereignty in the Greek and Roman world.

In the present discussion of the origins of messianism, however, this review of landmarks prompts some observations on the nature of pre-exilic messianism, with reference first of all to the three particular questions noted above. First, in the studies just noticed an increasingly close connection has been discerned between the royal psalms and messianic hope. Wellhausen set them apart, although he rightly discerned the kinship between these psalms and the Greek literature of ruler cult; Gressmann and Mowinckel both viewed the psalms as the medium whereby ancient oriental kingship influenced Jewish messianism; but Johnson identified an element of messianic hope as always present when these psalms were addressed to the reigning monarch. One should perhaps go one step further, and affirm, on the lines sketched by Bentzen, that the praises of the king will always have been messianic in character, irrespective of any hint of non-fulfilment, for in hymns of praise the present king becomes for the moment the godlike figure of the ideal king.

Secondly, whereas Gressmann and Mowinckel strongly contrasted the kingdom of God with the kingdom of the messiah – a view which has found many adherents – they allowed that the two were combined in messianic hope, as Wellhausen had noted and H. W. Wolff and H. Riesenfeld re-emphasized. The admission by Gressmann and Mowinckel itself suggests that the contrast should not be pressed, despite the emphasis laid on it in much recent study.

Thirdly, Gunkel, followed by both Gressmann and Mowinckel, brought out the ramification and development of a myth of the messiah, best seen in apocalypses like II Esdras and Revelation, but also to be discerned behind other material preserving vestiges of legendary motifs. As Gressmann especially stressed, the myth seen most clearly in relatively late sources is likely to be very much older – a point underlined by Isa. 9 and Micah 5. Another element in the myth, likely to go back in Israelite form to David's capture of Jerusalem, was given by the messianic associations of the Zion psalms which Johnson noted.

Lastly, to return from these specific points to messianism in general, widely varying views of its inception have been current. For Wellhausen it arose when the Israelite monarchy declined, for Gunkel and Gressmann it was 'that which was from the beginning', for Mowinckel it was a relatively late addition from ancient kingship to pre-exilic Israelite religion, for von Gall and Frost it came in with eschatological hope under Persian rule. Gressmann supported his case that messianism is essentially very old by his indication of comparable Egyptian material, but he also allowed for its specifically Israelite development at the end of the period of the monarchy by his suggestion that the figure of Josiah was influential. These variations have been affected by definitions of messianism, and especially by its association with future hope or eschatology, as opposed to existing kingship. Johnson's special contribution was to point clearly to its association with kingship from the beginning – an association supported by the perception of kingship as a focal point of religion and myth which was a strength of the 'Myth and Ritual' and 'Scandinavian' approaches, and which also justifies the claims of Gunkel and Gressmann for the great age of a broadly defined messianism in the Ancient Near East.

Messianism can therefore be regarded as a deep-rooted and long-standing influence in the community at the beginning of the Second-Temple period. The core of its literary tradition consisted of royal psalms of praise and oracles of good hope, reflecting often fragmentarily the myth of a saviour king. This material was strongly marked by ascription to the monarch of superhuman and divine characteristics and titles. The expectations embodied in this myth and its literary reflections had been bound up with Israelite kingship from its inception, and the tradition as it survives is marked by Davidic dynastic loyalty and the exaltation of Zion. Expectations will have been renewed with each king, and probably each year, but they could also be developed in special hopes for a coming deliverer and in connection with particular persons.

Perhaps the clearest example of a leader who attracted messianic prophecy is the Davidically-descended Zerubbabel in the sixth century; the oracles concerning him in the books of Haggai and Zechariah are more naturally interpreted in this way than as simple endorsements of his position as Persian governor (see especially Haggai 2. 20–23; Zech. 3. 8; 4. 6–10; 6. 12, and chapter II below). The hopes for a coming David or a descendant of David which are widely attested in the prophetic books as now preserved (notably Deutero-Isaiah, Jeremiah, Ezekiel, Hosea, Amos and Zechariah), and are probably also reflected at Gen. 49. 10, will sometimes likewise have been focussed on particular members of the royal family.[56] The tradition nevertheless had an impetus and a literary embodiment which were independent of such special applications.

3. *The Old Testament as edited and collected*

The editing and collecting of the Hebrew scriptures culminated in Judah under Persian and Greek government. Two aspects of this external political setting are reflected within the Israelite literature, and contribute to the shaping of messianism. First, monarchy was a familiar form of government, and Judah was in the middle of large-scale conflicts between kings, first between the great king of Persia and the Pharaoh of Egypt, and then in the

Greek period between the Seleucid king and the Ptolemaic Pharaohs; the vision of wars between 'the king of the north' and 'the king of the south' in Dan. 11 suits the whole post-exilic period, not just the second century. It is not surprising that, within the Israelite community, the native ancestral traditions of monarchy are important in the books composed after the exile, notably the prophecies in Haggai and both parts of Zechariah, the histories of the kings in Chronicles, and the meditations of king Solomon in Ecclesiastes. (To some extent we may compare the impact of the Persian monarchy on the fifth-century Greek city-states; in Aristophanes's *Birds* the divine bride whom the hero hopes to win is called Basileia, 'kingdom'.)

Secondly, the Persian and Greek empires were the scene of non-Israelite prophecy expressing national hopes and fears, best known from the late Egyptian examples mentioned above, notably the so-called Potter's Oracle reflecting hostility to Alexandria under the Ptolemies. Gressmann brought out their importance as comparative material for Israelite messianism. The oracles of Hystaspes quoted by early Christian writers form a tenuous reminder of comparable Persian material. Analogous prophecies in the Greek literary tradition are the Sibylline Oracles, foretelling the rise and fall of cities and kingdoms through the mouth of sibyls who are themselves sometimes Eastern prophetesses; these oracles were adopted by Jews in the Greek period and enriched by messianic prophecy, and have ever since been closely linked with the Old Testament. The prophecies concerning the four kingdoms in Daniel, and earlier post-exilic prophecies such as those in favour of Zerubbabel and Joshua in Haggai and Zechariah, are Israelite instances of a more widespread expression of national hopes, often focussed as in Israel on national traditions of kingship.

The external setting of the Hebrew scriptures therefore suggests that national aspirations connected with kingship may have left their mark on the processes of editing and collecting the books. These processes will have been to some extent contemporaneous. What is called in Ezra and Nehemiah 'the book of Moses' or 'the law of Moses' will already in the fifth century have been known together with much of the corpus of the Prophets and much of the Psalms and other books, although the composition of new books and the editing and enlargement of these existing bodies of literature was still in progress. For convenience we may notice first the effect of *collecting* the books, with special reference to the effect of viewing the Pentateuch, the Prophets and the Psalms together.

These three bodies of literature, once they are viewed together, integrate the mainly Davidic oracles of the prophets and psalms with the more general prophecies and prescriptions concerning an Israelite monarch in the Pentateuch. Pentateuch, Prophets and Psalms then together offer a single striking series of oracles expressing national aspiration in the form of hopes for a coming king. In the Pentateuch these prophecies are uttered by Jacob and Balaam, especially in the form of the Shiloh oracle and the star oracle (Gen. 49. 10; Num. 24. 17), both of which foretell a specifically Israelite ruler and are introduced as relating to 'the latter days' (*aharit ha-yamim*). These oracles of an Israelite king alternate in the Pentateuch with the prophecies of the kingdom of God and the blessings of Israel in the two songs of Moses and the blessing of Moses (Exod. 15; Deut. 32–33), and this alternation encourages the hearer to fit the prophecies of a coming king into the Mosaic prophecies of the coming divine kingdom and the felicity of Israel.

When the prophets are read after the Pentateuch, this series of Penta-teuchal prophecies appears as taken up and continued by another series which primarily express the specifically Davidic covenant and hope. Such oracles are interspersed in the Former Prophets, notably in the Song of Hannah (I Sam. 2. 10) and the song and last words of David in II Sam. 22 (Ps. 18), and 23. 1–7, on God's mercy to his anointed, David and his seed, for ever.

In the latter prophets, Isa. 7; 9 and 11 are reinforced within Isaiah by 16. 5, on the throne set up in mercy in the tabernacle of David (the beginning of this chapter is also taken messianically in the Targum, cited in chapter II, section 4, and chapter IV, section 4, below); 32. 1–3, on the king to reign in righteousness; and 55. 3–5, on the sure mercies of David. This last oracle comes in the midst of prophecies of a restored Jerusalem. Jeremiah includes expectations of Israel's return 'to the Lord their God, and to David their king' (23. 5; 30. 9, etc.). Ezekiel expresses this expectation in the setting of restoration, war, and a new city and temple (34. 24; 37. 24). Finally, the Book of the Twelve Prophets, brought to its completion probably at the end of the Persian period, is punctuated by similar oracles, notably Hosea 3. 5, on return to David again 'in the latter days'; Amos 9. 11, on the tabernacle of David; and Micah 5, on the ruler from Bethlehem.

In the psalter, therefore, the royal psalms, when heard in this context of the Pentateuch and prophets, can readily be understood as oracles of the future; especially notable are 89 and 132, on David's line and throne as never-failing; 2 and 110, ascribed to David in the title; and 72, ascribed to Solomon.

It is possible to read many of these Pentateuchal and other oracles as prophecies of the kingdom of David and Solomon, but their context some-times points to the horizon of 'the latter days' and to restoration yet to come, as already noted. This suggests that they were read as unfulfilled or only partly fulfilled prophecy in the Persian period, as certainly happened later on. The production of oracles in favour of Zerubbabel and Joshua the high priest in the late sixth century (see Haggai and Zech. 3 and 6, further discussed in the following chapter) confirms the likelihood that such an understanding was current. Thus Zech. 3. 6 and 6. 12, on the man whose name is branch, appear to take up the phrase 'righteous branch' used in the Davidic oracles of Jer. 23. 5 and 33. 15. The long biblical series of prophecies of a coming king would then be comparable with the non-Israelite prophecies which have already been mentioned.

This point is further confirmed by the interest in national redemption and eschatology evident in the editing of some individual books. Thus Genesis interrupts the Joseph narrative with the tale of the birth of Judah's son Perez, the forefather of David (Gen. 38);[57] and it ends with the prophetic last blessing of Jacob, as noted already, and the last words of Joseph, predicting exodus and divine visitation (Gen. 49; 50. 24–26). In both Leviticus and Deuteronomy, the bodies of law end with blessings and curses which comprise predictions of the national future (Lev. 26; Deut. 27–28). Deuteronomy as a whole in its completed form has an eschatological stamp, as G. von Rad noted, a stamp given partly by its projection of the occupation of the land into the future, and partly by the substantially prophetic character of the close; the blessings and curses already mentioned are followed by further warnings and prophecies from Moses, speaking of exile and ingathering (see especially 30. 3–5), and including the oracular song and blessing of Moses mentioned already. The linguistic links visible not only between Deuteronomy and the historical books as far as II Kings, but also between Deuteronomy and Jeremiah, have suggested that Jeremiah was edited by a Deuteronomistic redactor or redactors. This suggestion has been extended to other parts of the prophetic corpus, in the form of surmises that the Deuteronomistic redactors had some collection of prophetic writings, and in an argument for Deuteronomistic redaction of Zech. 9–14.[58] My impression is that the links in vocabulary are stronger for Zechariah 12–14 than for the other chapters, but this and other questions about possible Deuteronomistic redaction need not be settled here. However these proposals of Deuteronomic editing may be viewed, one observation which has given them impetus remains valid and important in the present connection – the observation, namely, that Deuteronomy shares an eschatological interest with the prophetic books in their later forms.

There is thus a genuine thematic link between the Pentateuch and the Prophets. So Isaiah ends with a great eschatological scene of the exaltation of Jerusalem and divine judgment, which came to be associated with specifically messianic hope.[59] Ezekiel ends with the oracles which have shaped later articulation of the eschatological events: from chapter 36 onwards the book successively mentions the outpouring of the spirit, the revival of the dry bones, the new kingdom of David, the wars of Gog of the land of Magog, and the building of the new Jerusalem. Among the minor prophets, Hosea has an eschatological ending, Amos a Davidic ending, and Zechariah a conclusion which, for all its obscurity, is plainly and in succession messianic, royal, Davidic, Zion-centred and eschatological. The whole Book of the Twelve ends at the close of Malachi with the announcement of the day of the Lord and the sending of Elijah the prophet. Once again, just as in the case of the Pentateuch noted already, it is natural to read the specifically messianic prophecies, like those in Ezekiel, Amos and Zechariah, in the context of the more general prophecies of the future among which they are interspersed.

The collection of the books, therefore, and the editing of the individual books, produces a series of what can be properly called messianic prophecies, envisaging the future – sometimes evidently the immediate future. This occurs within the period of the growth of the Old Testament, and accords with a major Old Testament theme, the eschatological interest of Deuteronomy and parts of the prophetic corpus. It was also momentous for the later development of messianism. The prominence of a coherent series of prophecies will have been among the factors which led to the interpretation of still further oracles as messianic, and to still greater specificity in conceptions of the work of the expected ruler or rulers.

Now a brief illustration of these two developments can also draw attention to the conception of two messianic figures, and link the collection of the books in the sixth and fifth centuries with the messianism of the second century BC and later. First, the interpretation of further oracles as messianic is evident in the LXX, despite the possibility of reluctance to include material which would depict Jews as disloyal. Thus Num. 24. 7 LXX, 'there shall come forth a man', probably from the third century BC, illustrates not only the addition of messianic value but also, with the word 'Gog', the effect of combining Pentateuch and prophets; the 'man' is implicitly identified as the victor over Ezekiel's Gog, the great opponent of the last days. Another influential example, probably later in date, is Hab. 2. 3, LXX, 'the one who is coming shall come and not tarry'.

Secondly, the tendency to specify the works of the coming king has just been seen in Num. 24. 7 LXX. Its further development through the combination of Pentateuch and Prophets can be seen in the well-known Qumran text 4Q 285, on the slaying of the last enemy by 'the prince of the congregation, the branch of David'. The fragment begins with a quotation of Isa. 10. 34–11. 1, so that the Isaianic promise of a rod from the stem of Jesse is illustrated by one title derived from the Pentateuch – 'prince of the congregation' – and another which comes from Jeremiah – 'branch of David'.

More than one messianic figure is envisaged in this Qumran text. No doubt is left that the prince of the congregation is indeed the Davidic messiah, the 'messiah of Israel' in Qumran terms. The mention of a priest reminds one, however, that probably a priestly 'messiah of Aaron' is envisaged as well. The carefully composed title prince of the congregation in fact itself implies this. It appears to derive from the title of the office to which Joshua was ordained, that of a 'man over the congregation' (Num. 27. 16); in the same passage Eleazar the priest is to decree the times when Joshua, the man over the congregation, shall lead the congregation to war. The title prince, *nasi'*, was used in Qumran texts for the king, as happens with the coming Davidic king in the book of Ezekiel; and in this Qumran title it probably also recalls Lev. 4. 22, where the prince – probably a tribal prince, but sometimes understood as the ruling prince of all the congregation – is mentioned not long after the anointed priest.[60] The joint government of prince and priest was already seen in the sixth century, as mentioned above, in the case of Zerubbabel and Joshua; reflected as it is in the Pentateuchal prescription in Numbers, and to some extent also in the joint government of Moses and Aaron, this constitutional arrangement had much influence.[61] It is reflected in the messianism of the Testaments of the Twelve Patriarchs (probably contemporary with the Qumran writings), is regarded by Josephus as the genuine Jewish constitution, and seems to have had some revival in practice in Bar Kokhba's revolt, as coins indicate. It also leaves a deposit in rabbinic expectations.

What is remarkable, perhaps, is not so much the occurrence of a dual messianism, given the view that this was the true Mosaic constitution, but rather the failure of dual messianism to exert a still more obvious influence. In the Septuagintal texts just considered the royal messiah is the single messianic focus of attention, the same is true of the Sibylline Oracles and the single clear messianic reference in Philo (a quotation of Num. 24. 7 LXX), and the same applies to the Psalms of Solomon, the apocalypses of Baruch and Ezra, the Amidah (Eighteen Benedictions), and the New Testament, rabbinic and Targumic instances of Messiah used without qualification exemplified on pp. 10–11 above. Even in Qumran texts, where two messiahs are sometimes clearly mentioned, there appears the ambiguous phrase 'messiah of Aaron and Israel' (4Q266, quoted above), which could also be understood of just one messianic figure, and the single phrase 'the messiah' (1QSa = 1Q28 ii, line 12). The development of the technical term messiah would indeed hardly have been possible if two figures had normally been in view.

Why did things turn out in this way? Two factors noted already may have contributed to this surprising result. First, the great Pentateuchal and prophetic series of prophecies speaks almost entirely of a single coming ruler. Secondly, the comparable non-Jewish prophecies and expectations also envisaged a single coming king. Perhaps these gentile expectations are in mind when LXX renders Gen. 49. 11 *He* – that is, the coming Israelite king – is the expectation of the nations.

The development from the collected Old Testament in the sixth and fifth centuries to the messianism of the late Second Temple period has now been briefly sketched. Some further detail from the Persian period and later will be added in the following chapter. Here it remains to notice, within the Old Testament books, five figures not considered so far which can be called messianic prototypes.

4. *Messianic prototypes*

(*a*) Moses is represented as a king in Ezekiel the Tragedian (probably second century BC), Philo, and much rabbinic tradition. This interpretation is of course suited by his activity as leader of the exodus and lawgiver. It has been convincingly argued by J. R. Porter that the biblical narratives of Moses, which are likely to have been formed to a considerable extent in Jerusalem during the monarchy, were in fact shaped according to the model of the Israelite king.[62] Deut. 33. 5 can be translated 'and he was king in Jeshurun', so as to present Moses as king in Jeshurun; and this is perhaps the most natural rendering, although other translations cannot be ruled out. A royal interpretation of Moses seems to appear in any case in Isa. 63. 11, where Moses is the shepherd of the flock, and Exod. 4. 20 LXX, where he receives his sceptre from God. In the same chapter the LXX comparably enhances a messianic aspect of Moses presented already elsewhere in the Hebrew text: the congregation believe in Moses. (See Exod. 14. 31 [they believed in the Lord and in Moses], with Exod. 4. 1–9 LXX, where by comparison with the Hebrew, 'in you', referring to Moses, is added after 'believe' in vv. 5, 8 and 9.)[63] At the heart of the Pentateuch, then, is a figure which could be and was interpreted as that of a royal deliverer.[64] Note that his pleading for his people (e.g. Exod. 32. 11, 32) and his rebuttal by them introduce an element of suffering into this royal picture.

(*b*) David has of course been mentioned above, but without specific reference to his profile as a whole in the Hebrew Bible. When the Psalms and their titles are considered together with the historical books, a step which was already being taken in the editing of II Samuel (see II Sam. 22

= Ps. 18), David emerges as a suffering and humiliated yet ultimately victorious king, notably in Ps. 18 = II Sam. 22; Pss. 21–22, and the psalms associated in their titles with his flights from Saul and from Absalom into the wilderness (3; 54; 57; 59; 62; 142); he prays for divine help in his battles (e.g. in Ps. 60, title; Pss. 20, 68, 86) and sings the praise of the kingdom of God (Pss. 22; 145); he receives the divine pattern of the temple and its vessels, and he ordains the levitical singing and the observance of the festivals (I Chron. 16; 18–29); he is an exorcist (I Sam. 16. 14–23) and an inspired prophet (II Sam. 23. 1–7; cf. I Chron. 28. 12, 19). The Lord's anointed suffers as David himself had, but the oath to David is recalled on his behalf, Ps. 89. Prophecies already mentioned expect a coming David to govern a united kingdom for ever (Jer. 30. 9; Ezek. 34. 23; 37. 25; Hos. 3. 5). The divine choice of David receives continual emphasis; see Ps. 78. 68; Ps. 89. 20–21 (LXX ἐκλεκτός); I Kings 8. 16; I Chron. 28. 4; II Chron. 6. 5–6; and Ps. 151. 6–7 (11QPsᵃ col. 27), LXX vv. 4–5.

The prophetic and therapeutic aspect of this biblical profile emerges in the list of David's poems in the Psalms scroll from Qumran Cave 11, immediately following a transcription of his last words from II Sam. 23. 1–7: 'And David son of Jesse was a wise man, and a light like the light of the sun, a scribe'; he wrote 4050 canticles, including four 'songs to sing over the stricken' for exorcism (one of these will have been Ps. 91, which has a Davidic title in the LXX); and 'all these he spoke in prophecy' (11QPsᵃ, col. 27). A psalm generally resembling Ps. 151 and a psalm of exorcism are accordingly put in David's mouth in the paraphrase of I Sam. 16 in Ps.-Philo's *Biblical Antiquities* (59. 4; 60. 2). In the New Testament, correspondingly, David is regularly cited as a prophet, sometimes with emphasis on his status as the great king who prophesies his yet greater messianic descendant (Matt. 22. 43 and parallels, on Ps. 110 1; Acts 2. 30, on Ps. 16. 8–11); but New Testament writings also reflect an expectation of the messianic kingdom as a renewed kingdom of David (Mark 11. 10 and parallels; Luke 1. 32, 69; John 7. 42). This emerges likewise in such non-Christian Jewish texts as the Psalms of Solomon (17. 4, 21, echoing Jer. 30. 9), the Dead Sea Scrolls (for instance in the title 'branch of David' quoted above from 4Q 285, echoing Jer. 23. 5), and Pseudo-Philo's *Biblical Antiquities* (63, 9, where David's kingdom is in this age, but from him is also the beginning of a kingdom to come). The suffering aspect of the royal figure of David goes unmentioned for the most part in sources from the time of Christian origins, but its biblical prominence in the histories and psalms will have kept it in view, as is suggested by the reference to David's flight in Mark 2. 25–26 and parallels. This aspect of the figure of David will then have contributed, together with the suffering of Moses noted above, to the messianic interpretation of the suffering servant of Isaiah and the smitten shepherd of Zechariah.

(*c*) The servant of Isa. 53 is interpreted as messiah in the Targum, but as victorious rather than suffering. This interpretation is not unnatural, for the passage is preceded by a prophecy of the redemption of Jerusalem (52. 1–12), begins with a reference to a root growing out of the dry ground which recalls Isa. 11, and is followed by a vision of the city's restoration, and a reference to the sure mercies of David (54; 55. 1–5). The chapter was linked with this sequel by Justin Martyr, who also gives a messianic interpretation, here including suffering, and says that Trypho the Jew agreed with it (*Dial.* 13. 2–9; 18. 2–90. 1). The Israelite king appears as a suffering servant in Ps. 89. 39, and the messiah is God's servant in Zech. 3. 8. It is likely, however, that this messianic interpretation of Isa. 53 was not invariable, for the Ethiopian in the Acts of the Apostles (8. 32–33) is represented as asking whether the prophet speaks about himself, or about some other. The LXX can be read in accordance with a messianic interpretation, but does not clearly indicate it. The chapter is echoed in the pre-Christian period in contexts dealing not with the messiah, but with the lowly and afflicted righteous (Dan.12. 3; Wisdom 2 and 5; Ecclus. 11. 12–13).[65] In the New Testament it is cited relatively sparingly, but in connection with Jesus, notably in depicting him as a martyr for others (Mark 10. 45). It was perhaps originally formed on the model of the suffering king, and a messianic interpretation was probably current in the Second-Temple period, but the passage was not then regarded as obviously messianic.

(*d*) The smitten shepherd of Zech. 13. 7 forms part of a series of prophecies in Zechariah, beginning with the advent of the lowly king in 9. 9, which find a messianic interpretation both in the New Testament and in rabbinic literature.[66] In the latter they are associated with Messiah ben Joseph or ben Ephraim, who fights Gog and Magog and dies in battle.[67] The death of a messiah is already envisaged in II Esdras 7, at the end of the messianic age, and the cutting off of a rightful ruler called messiah is foretold in Dan. 9. 26, quoted already. The notion of a slain messiah is then likely to have been current in the Second-Temple period, partly on the basis of Zechariah, although it seems clearly to have been less prominent than the expectation of a great and glorious king. The objections of the disciples to Christ's expectation of suffering, as depicted in the Gospels, might then be ascribed not to their total ignorance of the notion of a humiliated messiah, but to their unwillingness to accept that it might apply in this case.

(*e*) The Son of man in Dan. 7 is viewed messianically in the earliest interpretation, ranging from the middle of the first century BC to the middle of the second century AD in the Parables of Enoch, II Esdras, the Fifth Sibylline Book, a saying attributed to R. Akiba, and Justin Martyr's *Dialogue*. In its setting in Daniel, however, it is widely taken at present to represent an angelic deliverer, probably Michael, the patron of Israel, who is mentioned as such in 12. 1. (See the survey of interpretation in Collins, *Daniel*, 310.) This is an attractive view, because human figures often represent angels, in Daniel and elsewhere, and the importance of angels as regulating terrestrial affairs is clear not only in Daniel but also in the Qumran War Scroll. Nevertheless, the early messianic interpretation seems more likely to be right. Both angelic and human leaders functioned in the Exodus, both are mentioned in the War Scroll, and both can be envisaged without difficulty in Daniel. In Daniel 2, the coming of the kingdom of God, represented by the stone which breaks the image, can naturally be associated with a messianic figure, just as in the War Scroll the kingdom is said to belong to God pre-eminently at the moments when Israel is delivered by David, the kings of his line, or the messiah. In Dan. 7 the beasts represent kings or kingdoms (7. 17, 23–24), not the angel-princes who are the expected foes of Israel's angel-patron (10. 13, 20–21). Finally, the designation 'Son of man' is close to the use of various words signifying 'man' in pre-Danielic messianic oracles, including Num. 24. 17; II Sam. 23. 1 and Zech. 6. 12, quoted above, and Ps. 80. 18, which has *ben adam*.

Of these five figures, then, Moses, David, the smitten shepherd and the Son of man will have influenced the growth of messianism from the first. In each case they fitted well into the royal messianism which we have seen to predominate, despite the importance of dual messianism. In the end the servant of Isa. 53 also contributed to the picture of the messianic king. The presupposition of a broader picture than the relatively fragmentary messianic passages individually reflect is an important aspect of messianic passages in general, from the pre-exilic period onwards. The process of the incorporation of these figures itself suggests the pre-existence of what may be called a messianic narrative or myth, as suggested especially by the passages on the wonderful birth of the messiah in Isa. 9; Micah 5 and Ps. 110. G. S. Oegema has drawn attention, in the manner of Wellhausen, to the likely influence of external political figures on messianic conceptions; thus the Son of man in Daniel might mirror, he suggests, a Ptolemaic governor, while the universal judge and avenger of II Esdras and similar works reflects none other than the Roman emperor.[68] This proposal rings true in general, but external politics should probably be reckoned as just one important factor in the formation of messianic conceptions; they interacted with an existing myth, and, flexible as it was, it had its own coherence and impetus.

Yet although the lengthy development of messianism *from* the Old Testament is obvious, not least when the influence of messianic proto-types is considered, it has also become clear that messianism is important *within* the Old Testament. It flourished especially in the period of the collecting and editing of the books, it deeply influenced the ancient versions, notably the Septuagint and the Targums, but within the corpus of Hebrew scriptures it was integrally linked with the future hopes which form a great theme both of the Pentateuch and of the Prophets, and from the inception of Davidic monarchy and the Israelite capture of Jerusalem it was bound up with the traditions of kingship in Zion.

II

The Prevalence of Messianism in the
Second-Temple Period

The study of the Old Testament itself draws attention to the Second Temple period; the six centuries beginning with the rebuilding of 'the house of God at Jerusalem' embrace, as noted in the last chapter, the later stages of the composition, editing and collecting of the Old Testament books, and early stages in their development and interpretation through further writings. Nevertheless, the literature of the period, although so much of it stands in relation with the biblical tradition, also needs separate consideration if some justice is to be done to its individuality. The literary sources belonging to this period have been crucial in the discussion of messianic hope.

Differing assessments of the nature and significance of messianism in the Second-Temple period in particular were sketched in the introduction. They represent a divergence of opinion which is of long standing in modern biblical study. In publications in 1841 and later Bruno Bauer, as has been noted already, concluded that Jewish messianism had almost died out in the Greek and early Roman periods; in Bauer's view, therefore, so far from messianism constituting a factor in Christian origins, the rise of Christianity was itself the leading factor in the renaissance among Jews of a messianism which had been moribund or defunct. From 1867 onwards a modified version of Bauer's argument for the near-extinction of messianic hope before the time of Christian origins was expounded by the New Testament scholar H. J. Holtzmann, whose work in this area was saluted and rebutted by E. Schürer.[1] The sources do not encourage acceptance of any strong form of the view that messianic hope had almost disappeared in early Roman Judaea; but they have often been judged to support the emphasis on variety and the doubts concerning significance which have already been illustrated, as emerges from M. Karrer's analysis of the history of biblical and theological work on the topic.[2] The strength and continuity of the opinion that messianic hopes in the Second-Temple period were ill-defined and possibly marginal can be evoked simply by the names of two notable British scholars who held this view at the beginning and in the middle of the twentieth century, R. H. Charles and C. H. Dodd.[3] More particularly, a 'messianological vacuum' has been identified between the early fifth and the late second century, a period picked out to this effect by S. B. Frost and J. J. Collins.[4] This judgment seems to leave out of account the implications of the LXX Pentateuch, discussed below.

The long-standing debate just sketched on its negative side is of course related to a broader and equally continuous discussion of unity and diversity in ancient Judaism. The question of the coherence of messianism, in some ways a microcosm of the question raised concerning the coherence of ancient Judaism in general, will be considered in the following chapter. The present chapter, however, deals with the related but prior question of the prevalence of messianism. The evidence for messianic hope in the Second Temple period is reviewed. An attempt is made to show, through the study of literature from the earlier and later years of the Second Temple period, that messianic hope was more continuously vigorous and more widespread than has been allowed in the influential body of modern opinion just outlined.

1. The kingdom of God and the kingdom of the messiah

During the two centuries of Persian rule, from the conquest of Babylon by Cyrus in 539 to Darius III's defeat by Alexander the Great in the years 333–331, the literary tradition of Jewish messianism received its most lastingly authoritative embodiment. Some aspects of this development were picked out in the previous chapter. The Old Testament books were so edited that they emerge collectively as a messianic document. Within the Pentateuch and the books of Joshua and Chronicles, royal and messianic themes were developed especially in the portraits of Moses, Joshua, David, Solomon and the righteous kings. Messianic hope was prominent in the prophetic books of Haggai and Zechariah. These messianic elements in the composition and interpretation of the biblical books were then reflected and developed at the end of the Persian period, not long after Alexander the Great, in the messianism of the Septuagint Pentateuch.

Yet the biblical literature of the Persian period also reflects an intense concentration on God as king and the kingdom of God, which can be expressed without any overt reference to a messianic figure. In this period and later, particular influence will have been exerted by the two Songs of Moses, where the Lord is a man of war who takes vengeance on his enemies (Exod. 15. 1–18; Deut. 32. 36–43). Further striking examples of concentration on the deity himself as king and saviour are offered by Ps. 145, on the kingdom of God, and by the vividly anthropomorphic depiction of God as a warrior king in Trito-Isaiah (59. 16–18; 63. 1–6) and the Isaiah apocalypse (Isa. 24–27, especially 24. 21–3; 35. 6–12; 26. 21–27. 1). Comparable emphasis on God himself as saviour is found in Deutero-Isaiah, and in passages placed significantly near the conclusions of some of the Twelve Prophets (as at Obad. 18–21; Zeph. 3. 14–20; and Zech. 14. 1–9). Many have linked the enthronement psalms with this theocentric material. The anthropomorphic theocentrism of passages like these can readily be understood as an alternative to the often more reserved messianism which has just been noted, and then linked in turn with the silences on messianic hope in many books of the Apocrypha and some of the pseudepigrapha. If God himself saves, the messianic figure may be unnecessary.

Attention was drawn in this connection to Isa. 24–25, together with the enthronement psalms by Hugo Gressmann. In *Der Ursprung*, discussed in the previous chapter, he urged that the God of the enthronement psalms is the deity who goes up (Ps. 47. 8), is crowned and holds a coronation feast (Isa. 24. 23; 25. 6), and is also depicted elsewhere as an earthly king and warrior; he is, so to speak, the double of the messiah, and his portrait in the Isaiah apocalypse perhaps preserves features of the hero-messiah which have not survived in specifically messianic passages of the Old Testament.[5]

This observation of Gressmann is underlined by texts from the later Second-Temple period. Thus the importance of the highly anthropomorphic depictions of the Lord as a victorious king in the Isaiah apocalypse and comparable material (for example Zech. 9. 14–17; 14. 1–9), in continuity with poetic passages of probably earlier date describing warlike theophanies (notably Exod. 15. 1–18; Deut. 32. 36–43; Ps. 28 and Hab. 3), is confirmed by the traces they have left in Qumran texts, for example in the hymns to the divine warrior in the War Scroll (e.g. 1QM xii 11–12), despite the superexaltation of the deity in the War Scroll and other Qumran texts as a king of angels. The continuing vigour of the theophany texts from the Hebrew Bible appears in another way in Wisdom 5. 16–23, where the portrait of the divine warrior armed with righteousness and jealousy in Isa. 59. 16–18 is retained, but it is shown that the creation supplies his weapons (vv. 17, 20–23).

The influence of these biblical depictions can be traced further in the bold anthropomorphisms of rabbinic interpretation, which were later pilloried by Karaite and Christian critics of the Talmud. These anthropomorphisms are exemplified in early piyyutim, as when Zech. 9. 14 is employed as an address to God – 'Thou shalt blow the trumpet' – in the *Shofaroth* of Yose ben Yose, perhaps from the fifth century.[6] Their better-known appearances in the rabbinic haggadah can be illustrated from Pesikta de-Rab Kahana on the Lord as the man of war (Exod. 15. 3), and on the garments of glory, righteousness and vengeance worn by the Holy One to create the world, give the law, and requite his foes (PRK 5. 17; 22. 5, and Supplement 6. 5). Another element in this picture is the boldness of rabbinic speech on the divine grief and anger. Cries of 'woe' and lion-like roars of sorrow are envisaged, for example, in sayings in the names of Eliezer b. Hyrcanus (end of first century) and Rab (early third century) transmitted in Babylonian Talmud, Ber. 3a; and these bold sayings are in continuity with the anthropomorphic grief, anger and vengeance depicted in such biblical passages as Isa. 62, cited above; Ps. 78. 40, 49–50, 65; and Ps. 95. 10–11; Jer. 10. 19; 25. 30; Hos. 11. 10.[7] It is clear from these rabbinic extensions of the theophanic biblical passages that an anthropomorphically conceived royal warrior-deity lived on in Jewish imagination at the end of the Second-Temple period; and in principle his image is indeed very close to that of the messiah. This way of envisaging the deity is an important element in the background of the Septuagintal and rabbinic 'no mediator' slogans discussed in chapter III, below. Rabbinic and targumic passages on national redemption, like earlier material, can be analysed into those which do or do not include explicit reference to a messiah; Paul Billerbeck and Raphael Loewe are among those who from varying viewpoints have emphasized the importance of the apparently non-messianic references to redemption by God himself.[8]

Moreover, it can be argued that the depictions of angelic deliverers should also be credited to the importance of the notion of redemption by the deity alone. Thus Bousset and his pupil W. Lueken suggested that Michael in Daniel in effect fills the place of a messianic figure, and many since have urged that angels are similarly envisaged in other texts, notably the Qumran War Scroll. In particular instances this interpretation is often questionable, as is argued below; but part of the strength of this widely-held view is its congruence with the passages just noted on God himself as deliverer. The angel can be plausibly understood as representing the deity, and as in a sense continuing the line of depictions of deliverance by God himself. A probably post-exilic biblical passage which could support such an interpretation is Ps. 35. 1–6, where the Lord himself is petitioned to make war, stand up, take the shield and draw the sword, in a fashion which recalls the two Songs of Moses; but it is the *angel* or *messenger* of the Lord who is expected to be thrusting down and pursuing the enemy.

The notion that the kingdom of a God envisaged in this way excludes a kingdom of the messiah, as Gunkel and others had suggested, was developed with regard to the whole Second-Temple period by A. von Gall in 1926, in his book on the kingdom of God already cited in the previous chapter. Von Gall set the Old Testament and later material on the kingship of God and the messianic kingdom almost entirely in exilic and post-exilic times; the relevant Old Testament passages, including the enthronement psalms, were in his view largely from the Persian period, and subsequent material belonged to the Greek and early Roman periods, but the literature in question throughout reflected a sense of oppression by alien rule, and the relevant material from the Hebrew Bible is not far removed in time or setting from that in the Apocrypha and Pseudepigrapha. Von Gall regarded Persian rather than ancient Near Eastern influence as primary in the shaping of eschatology, but although this view has not found general favour many would still agree for other reasons with von Gall's placing of Old Testament material on the kingship of God and the messianic kingdom in the exilic and post-exilic periods.

Von Gall thought that the hope for a coming kingdom of God first arose at the time of the exile – occasionally in connection with hope for a Davidic king, although generally the king of the realm was God himself; thus the heavenly king, not an earthly Jewish leader, was envisaged in Deutero-Isaiah as the national saviour and redeemer.[9] In the post-exilic period the hope for the kingdom of God was intensified and developed, with emphasis on his coming reign and judgment in Zion, as in Zech. 14; and some in Israel, especially from the time of Zerubbabel onwards, added to this expectation of God's kingdom a specifically messianic hope, although the hope for God's own kingdom was primary and more widespread.

Accordingly, the messiah played only a subordinate role in the eschatology of Judaism at the end of the Second-Temple period, for God himself was to rule in the kingdom of the last days. Specifically messianic hopes were cherished only by strong nationalists – in fact von Gall calls them (374) 'out-and-out chauvinists' (*die ausgesprochene Chauvinisten*). The greater part of the Jewish leadership, however, emphasized the kingdom of God rather than the messiah. That is why the messiah is often unmentioned in the writings of the period. The only genuine attestations of messianic hope, in von Gall's view, are found in Jubilees 31, the Testaments of the Twelve Patriarchs, the Gospels, Psalms of Solomon 17–18, the Targums and Jewish prayers.[10] Thus in von Gall's reconstruction the Apocrypha and Pseudepigrapha, roughly speaking non-messianic and sometimes messianic respectively, would correspond to the dual Old Testament emphasis on the kingdom of God and the kingdom of the messiah, respectively; and in the Greek and Roman periods, just as under the Persians, the theme of the kingdom of God would have been the more important.

Many elements of von Gall's view recur in later study, notably in German and French dating of the enthronement psalms and allied material, and his contrast between the kingdoms of God and the messiah criticized by Wolff (p. 18, above). Von Gall's evidence as a whole was surveyed from differing points of view in the later studies of messianic hope by H. Gressmann (1929) and S. Mowinckel (1951). Older works by these two writers had already been criticized by von Gall, but they both returned to the subject after he had written. Thus Gressmann agreed with von Gall in contrasting the kingdom of the messiah and the kingdom of God, and in stressing the importance of the latter, especially with regard to the enthronement psalms; but, unlike von Gall, he regarded messianic hope as very ancient, saw it as revitalized by late pre-exilic hopes for a returning Josiah, and viewed the Servant of Isa. 53 and the Son of man in Dan. 7 as messianic figures. Mowinckel, on the other hand, despite his assignment of the enthronement psalms to a pre-exilic festal setting in which the heavenly king and the earthly king were both exalted together, remained close to von Gall in many other ways; he differed from him in viewing messianic hope as pre-exilic, although not as old as Gressmann held, but he agreed with von Gall in classifying the Deutero-Isaianic Servant and the Danielic Son of man as fundamentally non-messianic, and in holding that, during the Second Temple period, messianism was exceptional by contrast with the regular hope for the kingdom of God himself.

Von Gall and Mowinckel, especially, show that the 'no hope list' mentioned at the beginning of chapter I – the list of books thought to lack any expression of messianic hope – links the Hebrew Bible with the Apocrypha. The silences on messianism in both bodies of literature can be plausibly interpreted as arising from the primacy of hope for the kingdom of God himself, a primacy continuing throughout the whole period of the Second Temple, from the exile onwards. This broadly-based argument against any over-estimation of messianism considerably reinforces those presentations of a similar case which have been made simply with the literature of the Hebrew Bible or of the Second-Temple period in view. Thus J. J. Collins endorses (with some caution, as just noted) the view that messianism was virtually dormant from the fifth century to the second, and E.P. Sanders has contended that in Jewish hopes during the century leading up to the First Revolt against Rome 'the expectation of a messiah was not the rule'.[11]

In reply, it is urged in the present work that messianic expectation was far stronger and more continuous throughout the Second-Temple period than the arguments just considered would allow. The later Second-Temple period, from Alexander the Great onwards, receives a more extended treatment here and in the following chapters; but the messianism evident under Greek and Roman rule is most naturally viewed as a continuation and development, under new but not wholly dissimilar political conditions, of tendencies already prominent under the Persians.

This earlier part of the Second-Temple period, from Cyrus to Alexander, has already been sketched as the great epoch of editing which made the Hebrew Bible into what may be called a messianic document. It was also, as noted at the beginning of this chapter, an age of concentration on royal and potentially messianic themes, especially in the portraits of Moses, Joshua, David and the kings in the Hexateuch and Chronicles.[12] By contrast, however, some more recent study of the Jews under Persian rule has tended to squeeze further the minimization of post-exilic messianism which had been suggested by von Gall and Mowinckel. Thus R. Albertz, as noted already, understands the visions of Trito-Isaiah, especially the Zion prophecies of 60–62, to follow Deutero-Isaiah in eschewing any hopes for restoration of royal or priestly rule; he sets them in the aftermath of the explosive nationalism surrounding Zerubbabel.[13] This interpretation of their emphasis on the deity and the city as excluding messianism neverthe-less remains debatable. It requires Isa. 61. 1 to be taken as the transfer of a royal formula to Zion, and it was not followed in the collection of these oracles, where 60–62 are now immediately preceded by the promise of a redeemer for Zion (59. 20, discussed below); similarly, 62. 11 was taken in the LXX interpretation to refer to a specific saviour (see below). In another recent approach to messianism under the Persians, the post-exilic emphasis on the kingdom of God is linked again by A. Moenikes with earlier opposition to the very idea of a king in Israel (as reflected in I Sam. 8. 6, quoted in chapter I); he argues that ancient anarchic traditions, show-ing esteem for the non-monarchical society reflected in the closing chapters of Judges, ultimately influenced, through exilic editing of narratives in Judg. 8–9 and I Sam. 8; 10; and 12, those theocratic assertions (for example in Trito-Isaiah) which can be understood as having relativized and limited messianic hope.[14] It may be added that the criticism of Israelite kings and kingship embodied in Judges and I Samuel was indeed powerful enough to leave a deposit in rabbinic and early Christian interpretation, notably in the Pseudo-Clementines; I Sam. 8. 20 shows that the Israelites only sought a king so that they could follow idolatry (R. Nehorai, according to Sifre Deut. 156, on Deut. 17. 14), and the early monarchs were 'tyrants rather than kings' (*Rec. Clem.* 1, 38).[15] Yet, as Moenikes also points out, in the post-exilic period the preaching of God as king had already been used to legitimize earthly Israelite kingship. This aspect of the kingship of God continued to be formative, as emerges especially in Chronicles, further dis-cussed below. Moreover, it should be noted that a great strength of the Davidic tradition taken up in messianism was its own firm link with the age of Samuel and the tradition of leaders seemingly chosen and sent at need by God alone (Judg. 2. 16–18; I Sam. 12. 6–11); as noted already in chapter I, the incalculable divine choice of the shepherd David to save and govern Israel (I Sam. 16–17) was repeatedly emphasized, for example in Ps. 151.

Messianism in the Persian period has been minimized somewhat comparably in the suggestion that the lowly king of Zech. 9. 9 is God rather than a messianic king, an interpretation permitted by the vitality of the anthropomorphic depictions of the deity which have just been considered. The balance of probability seems, however, to incline the other way, in the light of the royal oracles which this passage resembles.[16] Again, the hopes clustering round Zerubbabel, attested in Haggai and Zechariah, have been interpreted as something less than messianic; the relevant oracles would then simply express divine ratification of a Persian governor. A more far-reaching suggestion of succession to the pre-exilic Davidic kings seems to be reflected, however, in the links between the oracles in both Haggai and Zechariah and those in Jeremiah concerning Jehoiachin and the branch of David, viewed together with the claim later reflected in Chronicles that Zerubbabel was of Davidic descent.[17] Finally, many of the numerous Davidic traditions current in the Persian period have been interpreted by K. E. Pomykala as non-dynastic and non-messianic; but this argument seems not to reckon with the impact of earlier passages on the understanding of later ones. Thus passages which Pomykala interprets in this way, such as the prophecies of Isa. 55. 3–5; Amos 9. 11–12 or the Davidic genealogy of I Chron. 3, will have been viewed against the background of the Davidic oracles in Isa. 11; Jer. 30. 8–9; Ezek. 34. 23–24 and 37. 23–25; Hos. 3. 5; and Pss. 89; 132.[18]

On the other hand, the vitality of messianic ideas in the same period is suggested not only by the Davidic texts just noted, and the oracles discussed above from Haggai, Zechariah 1–8, and Zechariah 9–14, but also by one or two passages on the coming of 'a saviour', 'a redeemer' or 'saviours' (Isa. 19. 20; 59. 10; Obad. 21; cf. Isa. 62. 11 LXX σωτήρ). The hope reflected in these passages seems to correspond to the contemporary identification of a series of 'saviours' sent by God in the past, notably at the time of the judges (Neh. 9. 27; cf. Judg. 3. 9, 15; I Sam. 12. 6–11). To these texts we should probably add 'my messenger' (Mal. 3. 1), and the 'man' of the LXX Num. 24. 7 – for the interpretation here attested in the LXX, early in the Greek period, no doubt represents expectations already current under Persian rule. An important element in the background of these texts is corporate recollection of the exodus, as exhibited in a prayer current in the Persian period, Isa. 63. 7–64. 11 (12), especially at 63. 11–14; here emphasis is laid on God's deliverance by means of the shepherd or shepherds of his flock (Moses, or Moses and Aaron) and his holy spirit, probably the angel of the exodus and conquest (cf. Neh. 9. 20). Hope therefore dwelt on a past pattern manifestation of joint angelic and human leadership.

Much of this material has been examined by A. Rofé.[19] He is ready to allow that earthly kings will have been depreciated because of emphasis on the kingship of God himself; on the basis of the LXX (see chapter IV, below) he suggests that there was a recension of the Hebrew text of the Pentateuch in which, from this cause, *nasi*, 'prince', has been substituted for *melekh*, 'king'.[20] He envisages a succession of overlapping and sometimes contradictory expectations. In the sixth century a hope for 'saviours', probably non-Davidic since the expression recalls contexts expressing hostility to an earthly king in Judges and I Samuel, could co-exist with expectations based on divine election of Cyrus and with a Davidic messianism focussed on Zerubbabel. After Zerubbabel, the apparently bleak prospects for Jewish independence evoked a new and eschatological hope for ultimate divine intervention;[21] this was reflected in the Trito-Isaianic emphasis on God's own miraculous victory, especially strong in the anthropomorphic descriptions of the divine warrior in Isa. 59. 16–18; 63. 1–6. Yet the new hope seems to have included expectation of a divinely-sent envoy on earth, the 'redeemer' who will come to Zion (59. 19–20).[22] Then, however, the Davidic line became central in this hope. The oracles on the people's future under 'David their king', cited above from Jeremiah, Ezekiel and Hosea, are set in the fifth century by Rofé; he understands them of a king envisaged as David *redivivus*, and connects with them the present form of the story of David and Goliath in I Sam. 17.[23]

This reconstruction convincingly identifies a cluster of differing but related messianic concepts. The particular dates and settings suggested are inevitably debatable, but there is little doubt that the passages concerned all belong to the Persian period. If, as seems likely, some of the references to unspecified 'saviours' originally allowed for deliverers of non-Davidic descent, they will attest the expectation of a deliverer in a variety of settings. A wide spread geographically for such expectation is suggested by the association of some of the material with Egypt (Isa. 19. 20 in the Hebrew and the LXX; Num. 24. 7 LXX; Isa. 62. 11 LXX). When the relative oracles came to be incorporated into the prophetic books, especially Isaiah and the Twelve Prophets, it became possible at will to associate them with the specifically Davidic prophecies, as noted in the previous chapter. This move will have been facilitated by the centrality of divine choice in the Davidic tradition itself, as noted already. The same association was possible in the case of the enormously influential Pentateuchal oracles of an unspecified 'man' or 'star' in Balaam's prophecies (Num. 24. 17; Num. 24. 7 LXX); and in LXX Isaiah the oracle of a 'saviour' in 19. 20 has been expansively rendered with the words 'a man who shall save them' (ἄνθρωπος ὃς σώσει αὐτούς), and so linked with the 'man' (ἄνθρωπος) of Num. 24. 7 LXX.

In the light of this material from the Hebrew Bible, and of the messianic expansions found soon after the end of the Persian period in the LXX Pentateuch, the Chronicler is best understood not only as royalist, but also as tinged with messianism.[24] An antecedent of the dual messianism of the Qumran texts has indeed been discerned with some justice in the stress on the temple as well as the kingdom found in Chronicles; the high priest is mentioned as well as the king, and the Aaronic priesthood as well as the Davidic line, for example in the anointing of both Solomon and Zadok or in Abijah's assertion of Judaean rectitude (see I Chron. 29. 22; II Chron. 13. 8–11).[25] This dual emphasis is outweighed, however, by the persistent assertion in Chronicles of 'the kingdom of the Lord in the hand of the sons of David'. Chronicles is thereby also one of the sources which contributed to the prevalence of a single messianic figure, despite the popularity of the dual constitution. The Chronicler lays heavy stress on the divine choice of David and Solomon, making one of the most intense statements of the tradition of David as chosen which was sketched in the previous chapter; and equally heavy stress is laid on the committal of the kingdom of God to David and his line (see I Chron. 5. 2 on the ruler from Judah [interpreting the genealogy in I Chron. 2. 3–15 and the oracle in Gen. 49. 10]; I Chron. 14. 2 [on David's kingdom, echoing Balaam's oracle in Num. 24. 7]; 28. 5 [David and Solomon on 'the throne of the kingdom of the Lord']; 29. 23; II Chron. 6. 5–6; 9. 8; 13. 8). These points recall the Danielic view of the gentile king as the deity's chosen earthly representative (Dan. 4. 32), a view which implies great royal power as well as responsibility. Gentile ruler-cult, when depicted in Dan. 6. 7 as forbidding petition to any mortal or deity other than the king, was no more than a further emphasis on this royal mediation of divine power. Within the biblical portrait of David, the presentation in Chronicles recalls the praise of the kingdom of God in psalms ascribed to David, especially Ps. 145. 13 = Dan. 4. 34; in the light of Chronicles it can be seen that this praise uttered by the chosen king also implicitly celebrates his own great power.

Chronicles therefore teaches a very high doctrine of Davidic kingship. The chosen dynasty is sure of the divine ratification forfeited by Nebuchadnezzar and Belshazzar, and mediates God's power here below. This doctrine reappears later on in messianic contexts. Thus, in the Parables of Enoch and in Luke–Acts, the messiah receives the title

'Chosen', and is God's representative in giving judgment; 'for the Chosen One stands before the Lord of Spirits, and his glory is for ever and ever, and his power for all generations . . . and he will judge the things that are secret' (I Enoch 49. 2–4, compare Luke 23. 35; Acts 10. 42).[26] Identification of a messianic element in Chronicles does not depend, however, on these chronologically more distant echoes of the Chronicler's Davidic doctrine. Rather, it is suggested by the combination of this doctrine in Chronicles with an insistence on the continuance of David's line, and by the attestation of messianic hopes in other sources from the Persian and early Greek periods. Particularly notable among these are the oracles of a David *redivivus* in Jeremiah, Ezekiel and Hosea, the oracles in favour of Zerubbabel, and the oracles of saviours, all discussed above. The choice of Hebrew rather than Aramaic as the medium of the books of Chronicles might also indicate a certain nationalism.[27] There seems to be no clear case for identifying any Jewish resistance in Judah to Persian rule in the fourth century comparable with the resistance of Sidon to Artaxerxes Ochus, or Tyre to Alexander the Great;[28] but it is likely enough that the spirit of Phoenician independence which helped to sustain these ill-starred ventures had its counterpart among the Jews nearby.

Against this background the period after Alexander the Great will now be considered. The aim will be to show that messianic hope continued to be prevalent and broadly consistent. Attention will be concentrated first on a series of literary evidences which extend over the period from Alexander to Domitian: the LXX Pentateuch, from the third century; the biblical Apocrypha, mainly from the third and second centuries, but including a much later pendant, II Esdras, from the end of the Herodian period; and the Dead Sea Scrolls, compositions which often date from the Hasmonaean period, but were still being copied under the Herodian kings. Some contemporary material from the Old Testament Pseudepigrapha and the LXX is considered in conjunction with the Apocrypha and the Scrolls. This survey of bodies of literature in sequence is followed in the next chapter by synoptic studies, on the significance of silence about messianism in some sources from this period, and on the appearance of variety in expressed messianic hopes.

2. *The LXX Pentateuch and royal messianism*

The LXX Pentateuch attests Jewish interpretation current in the Diaspora, and is especially connected with Ptolemaic Egypt; but according to legend it was translated by Judaeans, and it is not without significance for Judaean views. Thus, links between Egypt and Palestine were close, and in the third century, the period of the Pentateuchal translation, both were under Ptolemaic rule. Later on it appears that this translation was used by Judaeans and in Judaea, as Josephus and the Pentateuchal LXX fragments from Qumran Cave 4 attest; and a number of the interpretations discussed below are also found in Hebrew and Aramaic sources. In the present argument the LXX Pentateuch is important in two ways. First, as a witness to messianism in the third century it attests the tendencies which will have been strong at the end of the Persian period, and it illustrates the situation before the time of Ben Sira and the more frequently discussed Hasmonaean and Herodian evidence for messianism. Secondly, it shows that, not long after Alexander the Great, messianism was sufficiently prominent in communal Jewish understanding of the scriptures to find its place in interpretation of the Pentateuch, the 'book of Moses' which was central and universally revered in the Jewish community.

The topic of messianism in the LXX Pentateuch overlaps with the topic of monarchy.[29] Among the Jews themselves at this period the high priest was the greatest authority, and Pentateuchal interpretation might have been expected to turn in the direction of affirming priestly prestige. So in part it did, but it also continued to reflect the importance of kingship in the biblical literature. One factor contributing to this fidelity will have been the general importance of kingship in the Greek world. After Alexander the Great, monarchy became the principal form of Greek government, and the subject-matter of philosophers, historians and poets whose work was influential at the time when the Roman republic, transferred 'to a single pilot' (Philo, *Leg. ad Gaium* 149), itself became a monarchy in all but name.

This Greek preoccupation with kingship is mirrored in Jewish literature of the Greek and early Roman periods. The philosophy of monarchy has left monuments in the Letter of Aristeas, Philo's *Life of Moses*, and the interpretations of the Deuteronomic law of the king in the Temple Scroll (cols. lvii 1–lix 21) and in Josephus (*Ant.* 4), who was proud of his own royal as well as priestly descent (*Vita* 2);[30] monarchical history appears in the third-century history of the Judaean kings by Demetrius, roughly contemporary with the LXX Pentateuch, and later on in the Herodian writings of Nicolas of Damascus and Justus of Tiberias's lost work on the Jewish kings; and the poetry of monarchy is exemplified by passages from the Jewish Sibyllines, I Maccabees, the Testaments of Judah and Levi, and the Psalms of Solomon, and by the portraits of Solomon in Ecclesiastes and the book of Wisdom. These works alone indicate an environment favourable to royal messianism, continuing throughout the period from Alexander the Great to the time of Christian origins.

Still more indicative of communal Jewish thought than all these, however, is the understanding of the Pentateuch itself in the Greek period as a document of Jewish monarchy as well as priesthood. This understanding of the Pentateuch has strong antecedents in earlier Israelite history, as suggested in the previous chapter;[31] but tendencies to play down Jewish royal and messianic claims have long been traced in the LXX, and have seemed natural in a version in the language of the overlords, and one made when the Jews' own indigenous governors were not kings but high priests.[32] It is all the more striking that Jewish monarchy, both past and future, remains important in the Greek Pentateuch, and forms a theme which shows signs of messianic development by comparison with the Hebrew text. Z. Frankel, indeed, regarded the LXX as showing that messianism was more strongly developed in Alexandria than in Judaea at the time of the translation of the Pentateuch.[33] He justly recognized the remarkable messianic intensity of the LXX Pentateuch, but it seems likely that here too the Greek translation bears out his own observation that the LXX often reflects the exegesis of Jewish Palestine. Similar messianic Pentateuchal interpretation from the homeland is later found in the Dead Sea Scrolls, the Targums and rabbinic literature.

Thus, although in the LXX the Hebrew *melekh*, 'king', is rendered in the law of the king and elsewhere by the more comprehensive Greek *archon*, 'ruler', and although it is possible that this rendering reflects a recension of the Hebrew text in which *melekh*, 'king', has been replaced by *nasi*, 'prince',[34] Jewish hearers would still readily refer the texts in question, in revised Hebrew or in Greek, to the succession of Israelite kings. What in the Septuagintal Greek becomes the 'law of the ruler' in Deut. 17. 14–20 remains in the LXX an emphatic commandment to set up a ruler who shall be both divinely-chosen and Israelite (v. 15).[35]

This commandment is strengthened, however, by the Septuagintal renderings of three Pentateuchal prophecies, in the mouths of Jacob, Balaam and Moses. These renderings form fundamental but often neglected documents of Jewish kingship and messianism. Their importance for Jewish views of kingship in the Greek period lies especially in their guarantee of a succession of rulers out of Israel. Jacob, looking with far sight to 'the latter days' (Gen. 49. 1), prophesies that a ruler and governor shall never be lacking from Judah, until the things that are laid up for him shall come (Gen. 49. 10 LXX); Balaam foresees that 'the glories of rulers' shall be in Israel (Num. 23. 21 LXX, for Hebrew 'the shout of a king'); finally, according to the Blessing of Moses, 'there shall be a ruler in the Beloved, when the rulers of the nations [plural, against MT singular] are gathered together at one time with the tribes of Israel' (Deut. 33. 4–5 LXX). These three oracular passages are made to refer, more clearly than in the Hebrew, to the Israelite succession of rulers, and the use of *archon* in all three binds them more closely than in the Hebrew to the Israelite ruler ordained in Deuteronomy.[36] The Jews' own indigenous ruler, therefore, is now yet more clearly the subject of prophetic promise bound up with the Davidic line descended from Judah (Gen. 49.10), and the Deuteronomic ordinance (Deut. 17. 14–20) is yet more readily taken as a commandment to set up such a ruler.[37]

The exaltation of Jewish monarchy in the LXX Pentateuch is not of course restricted to these passages. Thus, in addition – here with use of βασιλεύς and related words – Abraham was a king (βασιλεύς) from the side of God (Gen. 23. 6 LXX, discussed below); kings shall come forth from Jacob (Gen. 35. 11, a forerunner of the final Blessing of Jacob in Gen. 49); and, most strikingly, at Mount Sinai Israel was divinely established as a kingdom as well as a priesthood: 'you shall be to me a kingdom, a priesthood and a holy nation' (Exod. 19. 6 and 23. 22 LXX).[38] This third passage was particularly influential. In the LXX it occurs twice, as noted above. Its second occurrence is just after the promise of the divinely-sent messenger who will bring Israel to the holy place. It can be readily heard as another oracular promise, for the Greek future tense is used. This appears to have been the case when it is echoed in II Macc. 2. 17–18 with the words 'even as he promised through the law'.

Pentateuchal interpretation on these monarchical lines continued into the Roman period, embracing the recognition of Moses himself as king which was noted in the previous chapter. This view is probably implied in the Hebrew Pentateuch (Deut. 33. 5), as noted above, and is brought out in a different way in the LXX, where Moses receives his sceptre (*rabdos*)[39] from God (Exod. 4. 20 LXX, similarly interpreted in the midrash), and is named with God as object of the faith of the congregation (Exod. 14. 31, cf. Exod. 4. 1–9 LXX, where by comparison with MT 'in you' [i.e. Moses] is added after 'believe' in vv. 5, 8, and 9); it is clearly attested in Greek Jewish literature from the second century BC onwards, in Ezekiel the Tragedian and Philo, and then in rabbinic interpretation.[40]

After Alexander the Great, therefore, Jews participated in the Graeco-Roman production of monarchical philosophy, history and poetry; and the fundamental document of their own ancestral literature, the Pentateuch, retained its monarchical dimension in developed form, and was read as including a connected series of oracles and ordinances on Jewish kingship. Among these oracles, in the LXX, were three extended messianic prophecies, uttered respectively by Jacob, Balaam and Moses himself. Their prediction of Israelite rulers has been illustrated, and their specifically messianic aspect will now be noticed.

(*a*) In the first two verses on Judah in the Blessing of Jacob (Gen. 49. 9–10), the LXX renders v. 9 'Judah is a lion's whelp; from the shoot, my son, you came up (ἀνέβης)'. The second part of this rendering recalls Isa. 11. 1 LXX, 'a bloom shall come up (ἀναβήσεται) from the root'. Verse 10 in LXX, quoted above, has 'ruler' and 'governor' for the Hebrew 'sceptre' and 'staff'; they will not fail from Judah until the things that are laid up for him come – 'and he is the expectation of the nations'. LXX therefore seems to presuppose the connection between this oracle and the Davidic Isa. 11. 1 which is probably also assumed in I Chron. 5. 2, 'of him' (Judah) 'is the prince', and is found in Qumran texts. So an interpretation of Gen. 49. 10 in a fragment from Cave 4 has it that kings of David's line will never fail 'until the messiah of righteousness comes, the branch of David' (4Q 252, fragment 2). A link between the lion's whelp of Judah and Isaiah 11. 1, as found in the LXX Gen. 49. 9, has shaped Rev. 5. 5, 'the lion of the tribe of Judah, the root of David, has conquered'.[41] The glowing description of the royal figure in Gen. 49. 11–12 LXX will be considered in the discussion of messianic acclamation in chapter IV, below.

(*b*) The oracle of Balaam in the LXX foretells the glories of rulers in Israel (Num. 23. 21, quoted above). Then at Num. 24. 7 (Hebrew 'water shall flow from his buckets') it predicts, as already noted in chapter I, that 'there shall come forth a man from his seed, and he shall be lord over many nations, and his kingdom shall be exalted above Gog', the adversary of the last days. This 'man' who shall rule an empire is then naturally identified, when Balaam returns to his prophecy and speaks of 'the latter days' (Num. 24. 14), with the star of Jacob. 'A star shall rise out of Jacob, and a man (Hebrew 'sceptre') shall rise up out of Israel' (Num. 24. 17 LXX). The messianic value of the title 'man' appears among other places at Isa. 19. 20 LXX, 'a man who shall save us', quoted above, where the 'saviour' of Egyptian Jews is evidently identified with the star-man of Balaam's prophecy.[42] The pattern of the oracles in their LXX form, from Num. 23. 21 to 24. 17, is that already given in the Blessing of Jacob: a succession of rulers from Israel culminates in the advent of the great king who will crush the final adversary.

(*c*) Moses says in his final blessing, according to the LXX, 'and there shall be a ruler in the Beloved, when the rulers of the nations are gathered together at one time with the tribes of Israel' (Deut. 33. 4–5 LXX). The 'Beloved' (rendering the name Jeshurun) is Israel. The future 'there shall be' contrasts with the past indicated in the Massoretic pointing and in rabbinic interpretation, where the ruler can be Moses himself (as in Targum Ps.-Jonathan here, or Midrash Tehillim i 2, on Ps. 1. 1); and the plural 'nations' contrasts with MT singular. The LXX interpretation thus makes Moses here predict either the rule of God himself (the Greek can be rendered 'and he shall be ruler . . .') or an emperor-like ruler in Israel, a figure at the centre of the unity of Israel and the nations. The latter interpretation seems preferable, for it accords with the emphasis laid in Gen. 49. 11 and in Num. 23. 21 LXX on the future presence of rulers in Israel. This messianic interpretation is found also in Targum Neofiti and the Fragmentary Targum here ('a king from the house of Jacob shall arise . . .').[43] The ruler to come would then naturally be identified with Balaam's star of Jacob in the latter days, lord over many nations, and with the final ruler whom the nations expect, according to the Blessing of Jacob. He is in fact, as is most clear in the blessing of Jacob, the supreme Davidic king of the latter days.

This understanding of Deut. 33. 5 LXX involves a slight adjustment in the relative weight ascribed to royal and priestly authorities in these texts in the Hebrew Bible. In the Blessing of Jacob Judah has an extensive dynastic promise, but Levi only a rebuke; the oracles of Balaam in the LXX allude to a line of rulers and then a single great ruler from Israel, and are most naturally understood, in the LXX and the Hebrew alike, simply of royal messianism; but the Blessing of Moses has only brief words for Judah, and by contrast a rich promise to Levi, further developed in the LXX. The messianic interpretation of Deut. 33. 5 found in the LXX and in Neofiti and the Fragmentary Targum then adds much strength to the relatively attenuated royal messianic aspect of the Blessing of Moses, and enhances the predominantly royal messianism of these Pentateuchal oracles as a whole. Here then in the LXX Pentateuch, as in Chronicles perhaps about a century earlier, the force of the expectation of a single messianic king still predominates in a context which is also much affected by the prestige of the priesthood.

These oracles in their LXX form belong to the third century. They presuppose, already at that time, a developed messianic interpretation which has given rise to a chain of exegetical interconnections, between these great prophecies within the Pentateuch and also between the Pentateuch and the books of the Prophets. The LXX interpretation attests the reading of these oracles as a series, in the manner which, it was urged above, the formation of the biblical canon naturally commended. At the same time these LXX passages point to a consistent set of messianic hopes, constituting an expectation centred on a royal messiah which was sufficiently central and widespread among Jews of the third century to be included in the interpretation of the Pentateuch.

3. The Apocrypha of the Old Testament and contemporary sources

The third century is also the probable date of some of the earlier material in the Apocrypha. The Apocrypha are those writings outside the Hebrew canon but associated with the Old Testament, especially in the LXX collection of books, which early Christian tradition approved; the Pseudepigrapha are, for the most part, those writings associated with the Old Testament or attributed to biblical authors which early Christian tradition doubted or disapproved. This early Christian judgment of these books probably reflects contemporary and earlier Jewish opinion. All these books are affected in varying degrees by the great stream of early biblical interpretation which was already moving in the Persian period, and has just been met in force in the LXX Pentateuch. Broadly speaking, however, the Apocrypha give but a sparse attestation of messianic hope, whereas much material contemporary with the Apocrypha in the Pseudepigrapha and in the Old Greek translations of the Prophets and Psalms is outspokenly messianic.

The largely non-messianic aspect of the Apocrypha may help to support the view that the early Christian approval of these books simply reflects contemporary and earlier Jewish approval; the Christians of themselves might have favoured more obviously messianic writings.[44] In the present argument on messianism, however, the silence of many of these books on a messiah raises again the question of interpreting a so-called 'messianological vacuum'. A representative list would include at least Baruch, Tobit, Judith, I–II Maccabees and the Wisdom of Solomon as writings from the Apocrypha where mention of a messiah might be expected, but is absent. Thus C. W. Emmet wrote in 1915: 'In the eschatology of the Apocrypha, with the exception of II Esdras, the Messianic hope is practically ignored.'[45]

The inclusion of the Apocrypha in this summary review therefore helps to ensure that material which might be thought to speak against the argument is given due consideration. The Apocrypha and Pseudepigrapha overlap in date, but the Apocrypha have a greater proportion of writings which can be securely assigned to the Greek period. Thus pre-Maccabaean works in the Apocrypha include, together with Ecclesiasticus, probably also I Esdras, Tobit, Judith, the Greek adjuncts to Esther, and at least the first part of Baruch (1. 1–3. 8); coeval with these books or earlier, but within the Hebrew canon, is the older part of Daniel, a pre-Maccabaean work given its present form in the Maccabaean period. To return to the Apocrypha, a second-century date is likely for the Epistle of Jeremy, the Greek adjuncts to Daniel, and II Maccabees, while I Maccabees and probably also Wisdom can be assigned to the early years of the first century BC. The short Prayer of Manasses, handed down in the LXX book of Odes, is probably pre-Christian. II Esdras = IV Ezra, from the end of the first century AD, is probably the latest of all the books in the Apocrypha; but it teeters on the very edge of this class of approved books because of its comparatively weak ecclesiastical support, as its relegation to an appendix in the Vulgate attests. The works from the Apocrypha represented in discoveries from the western shore of the Dead Sea are Tobit in Hebrew and Aramaic, the Epistle of Jeremy in Greek, and Ecclesiasticus in Hebrew. Also attested at Qumran in Hebrew is a pseudepigraphon which through the LXX came near to gaining apocryphal status, Ps. 151. All four texts represented in Dead Sea discoveries are probably from the older material in the Apocrypha.

On these datings the relatively non-messianic Apocrypha are contemporary with other more strongly messianic texts, notably the LXX Pentateuch in the third century; Jubilees, the Testaments of the Twelve Patriarchs and the LXX Isaiah, Jeremiah, Ezekiel, Twelve Prophets and Psalms in the second; and the Messianic Apocalypse, the Psalms of Solomon and relevant parts of the Third Sibylline book in the first century BC. Messianism is then important, from the time of Herod the Great onwards, in the series of apocalypses beginning with the Parables of Enoch (I Enoch 37–71, not attested at Qumran) and including, after the destruction of Jerusalem by Titus, the Syriac Apocalypse of Baruch and II Esdras; the Fifth Sibylline book and the Christian Revelation of St John the Divine should be viewed together with this series.

Silence on messianism is especially noticeable in the substantial group of mainly prose and mainly narrative books in the Apocrypha. This group comprises I Esdras, the Greek adjuncts to Esther and Daniel, Tobit, Judith, I–II Maccabees, and (with a smaller proportion of prose) Baruch and the Epistle of Jeremy. Their silence on messianism is indeed qualified by their wealth of material on kingship and priesthood, to be noticed presently. Moreover, it is true that we should not expect messianic expectations to be straightforwardly mentioned in prose historical narrative following the biblical model, for in biblical prose directly messianic material is mainly found in prophecies or psalms inserted into the narrative, as is the case with the Song of Hannah or the Pentateuchal prophecies just surveyed. It turns out, however, that even the poems and prayers in the apocryphal narratives, although they do indeed express hopes for national redemption, normally lay emphasis on the kingdom of God, not the kingdom of the messiah.

The narrative books give occasion for the expression of redemptive hopes above all because they have many prophetic and martyr-like heroes: Daniel and the Three Children, Eleazar the scribe and the seven brethren and their mother in II Macc. 6–7, and also Tobit – who flees from persecution and suffers the loss of all his goods, but returns when times improve (1. 19–20; 2. 8), and before his death prophesies the glorification of Jerusalem. Baruch speaks comparably of the consolation of Jerusalem at the ingathering. Mordecai and Esther can to some extent be associated with the martyrs, for in the Greek Esther his perilous refusal to bow to Haman is explained as a Zealot-like refusal to honour man rather than God (13. 12–14), and she risks her life and endures a mortal agony of fear (14–15). Martyr-themes also appear in Judith, where the nation expects the destruction of the temple and the forcible imposition of the ruler-cult (3. 8; 6. 2). The distinctive treatment of martyrdom in Wisdom, where the horizon seems to be dominated by internal rather than external enemies, will be noted separately below.

The prophecy associated with these themes in the narrative books concerns above all the ingathering and the divine vengeance, considered as a victory over idols and over earthly enemies. Thus in Esther, Judith, Tobit and I–II Maccabees stress is laid on the overthrow of Israel's enemies – Persian, Assyrian or Greek. The prayers and prophecies in the narratives follow suit. In the Greek Esther, Mordecai and Esther pray to God as king and victor over idols, in words which echo the enthronement psalms and the greater song of Moses in Deut. 32, see 13. 9, 15 (Lord, thou God, king, God of Abraham, cf. Ps. 47. 6–9); 14. 3, 8–12 (king of the gods, cf. Ps. 95. 3), 17 (nor have I drunk the wine of the drink offerings, cf. Deut. 32. 38). Similarly, in the thanksgiving of Judith (16. 2–17) the thought that the battle is the Lord's, associated with the victories of David over Goliath and Jehoshaphat over the Moabites (I Sam. 17. 47; II Chron. 20. 15) and taken up repeatedly in the Qumran War Scroll, leads to a passage echoing Ps. 96 and Exod. 15 which ends with a woe to the nations, for 'the Lord almighty will take vengeance of them in the day of judgment, to put fire and worms in their flesh' (compare Deut. 32. 41–3; Isa. 66. 14–16, 24). Judith's thanksgiving is immediately followed by a dedication of the spoils of Holofernes in Jerusalem (Judith 16. 18–20), and this scene crowns an important series of allusions to the biblical Zion theme; Judith prays for the defence of the sanctuary (9. 8, 13) and stands for 'the exaltation of Jerusalem' (10. 8; 13. 4; 15. 9). Tobit prophesies the ingathering and the end of idolatry (13–14), again with repeated emphasis on the kingdom of God in his prayer (13. 1, 6, 7, 10, 11, 15), and now with an address to Jerusalem (13. 9 onwards). Baruch 4–5 combines echoes of Deut. 32, on Israel's idolatry and the coming punishment of the nations, with an apostrophe to Jerusalem on the ingathering, echoing Isa. 60. Finally, ingathering to the holy place (Exod. 15. 17) and vengeance on the oppressor-nations are the main themes of the

Jerusalem prayer in II Macc. 1. 25–29 which reads like an antecedent of the Eighteen Benedictions.

Ingathering to Zion and vengeance on oppressors can naturally imply a messianic leader and a 'gathering together to him', in a phrase applied by Christians to messianic advent and vengeance (II Thess. 2. 1); compare the explicitly messianic ingatherings of Ps. Sol. 17. 26, 42–44; II Esdras 13. 39–40, in each case with an emphasis on this as the work of God. Is such a leader deliberately ruled out by the sole stress on the kingship of God in these passages from the Apocrypha, with their echoes of the enthronement psalms, Trito-Isaiah on Zion, and Deut. 32? This understanding might be suggested on the line of interpretation described at the beginning of this chapter, in which a conflict is identified between the notions of a kingdom of God and a kingdom of the messiah. The positing of such a conflict behind literature of the Second-Temple period will be questioned from various angles in the synoptic studies in the following chapter. In the case of these narrative Apocrypha, however, it is already thrown into doubt by the fact that the Pentateuchal and prophetic passages mainly echoed were themselves subject to messianic interpretation from the Persian period onwards, as noticed above. Thus, the prediction of divine vengeance at the end of the greater Song of Moses in Deut. 32 was immediately followed by the Blessing of Moses, which was messianically interpreted by the third century, as the LXX Pentateuch shows (Deut. 33. 5 LXX, discussed in the previous section). Similarly, the Trito-Isaianic prophecies of Zion included during the Persian period the oracle of a redeemer for Zion and, by the second century, the oracle of a saviour (Isa. 59. 20; Isa. 62. 11 LXX, both discussed in the first section of this chapter, above). It is worth adding that, in the introduction to the judgment scene at the end of Trito-Isaiah, the man-child of Isa. 66. 7 was understood in the Targum as a messianic king; this interpretation of the passage was probably current towards the end of the Second-Temple period, for it seems to be presupposed in Rev. 12. 5, and perhaps also in the use of *zakhar*, 'man-child', in the early lines of 1QH col. xi (iii). Moreover, as just noted from the Psalms of Solomon and II Esdras, mention of a messianic leader was not thought incompatible with heavy emphasis on the deliverance as the work of God himself. It is therefore by no means clear that the silence of the prayers and predictions in the narrative Apocrypha which echo these Pentateuchal and prophetic passages should be understood to exclude a messianic interpretation.

This conclusion can claim support from a second observation, about kingship and priesthood in the books of the Apocrypha in general. Although, leaving aside II Esdras, there is little explicitly messianic material in the books of the Apocrypha themselves, there is much illustration of the prestige of Jewish priests and rulers. Ben Sira glorifies Moses, Aaron and Phinehas, without forgetting David (45. 1–26), and Simon the high priest in his own days (50. 1–21). Similarly, I Esdras glorifies Ezra 'the high priest' (9. 40) as well as the Davidic Josiah and Zerubbabel. The *éclat* of the high priest reappears in Judith, where she is honoured by the high priest Joakim, but he is clearly the supreme authority and has a central role (4. 6–15; 15. 8). Similarly but more vividly, II Maccabees gives a saint-like depiction of the high priest Onias (see chapters 3 and 15). The Wisdom of Solomon develops the figure of Solomon as the young prince endued with celestial knowledge and virtue, and of Aaron as the blameless high priest who stayed the plague (see Wisdom 7–9; 18. 20–25).[46]

The books of the Maccabees illustrate the overlap between kingship and messianism. II Maccabees 2. 17–18, a prayer mentioned in the previous section as an early witness to the widespread LXX understanding of Exod. 19. 6 as 'a kingdom and a priesthood', refers to God as having 'restored the heritage to all, and the kingdom, and the priesthood, and the hallowing', as he promised in the law. The strength with which this view was put forward at the Hasmonaean court is illustrated by the tradition that John Hyrcanus I had the threefold gift of sovereignty, priesthood and prophecy (Josephus, *Ant.* 13, 299–300). The Maccabaean recovery of the temple was thought to have brought in a true recovery of the ancient constitution. Thus the Maccabaean house is surrounded by court praise as 'the seed of those by whose hand salvation (*soteria*) was given to Israel' (I Macc. 5. 62); areta-logical poems honour Judas Maccabaeus as a veritable lion of Judah, 'saving Israel' (I Macc.3. 3–9; 9. 21), and Simon Maccabaeus in 'his authority and glory' (14. 4–15). These admiring, almost hagiographical presentations of kings and high priests do not in themselves attest a messianic future hope, but they surround contemporary rulers with a messianic atmosphere, and show how messianic expectation would be imaginatively filled out. Their illustration of Jewish court praise will be considered further in the dis-cussion of messianic acclamation in chapter IV below. Yet, despite their creation of a messianic atmosphere at court, the prayer of II Macc. 2. 17–18, where kingdom and priesthood and hallowing are restored but the future ingathering into the holy place is still looked for, confirms that the Hasmonaean polity was not regarded as the total fulfilment of the divine promises. Judas Maccabaeus was a saviour of Israel, and *soteria* was in the hand of his seed; but he still prayed to God as saviour of Israel (I Macc. 4. 30), and the hymns in praise of Judas and Simon still leave room for divine deliverance to come.

This point is underlined by the Davidic as well as priestly reference in the last words of Mattathias the priest, the patriarch of the Hasmonaeans, according to I Maccabees (2. 49–70). His list of examples for his sons includes not only 'Phinehas our father', as might be expected of a priest, but also David, who 'by his mercy inherited a throne of kingdom for ever' (2. 57). 'Mercy' here seems to be David's own good deeds, as probably in the appeal to his 'mercies' at the end of Solomon's prayer in II Chronicles (6. 42). A specifically Davidic messianic element should not therefore be excluded from the Maccabaean future hopes which have just been sketched. The hagiographical stress here laid on David's good deeds strikingly assimilates the past David to the expected future son of David; in the LXX Isaiah, perhaps also from the Maccabaean age, the Davidic messiah's role as a king of peace is further underlined (Isa. 9. 5–6 LXX, further discussed in the next chapter); and in the Psalms of Solomon, at the end of the Hasmonaean period, the virtue of the coming son of David is vividly emphasized (Ps. Sol. 17. 32–37, also further discussed in the next chapter).[47]

The two principal wisdom books of the Apocrypha add something to this messianic material. In the Wisdom of Solomon the righteous sufferer of 3–5 is hardly the messiah, since he is not said to be or to have been a ruler, although the messiah indeed embodies righteousness. On the other hand, the inspiration of king Solomon and of a series of Israelite leaders by wisdom, according to chapters 7–10, is implicitly messianic in so far as it suggests that the holy people may still be similarly blessed in the future. Ecclesiasticus at first sight looks non-messianic, particularly because the prayer for Israel's redemption in 36 anticipates the Eighteen Benedictions in almost every respect save a reference to the messiah. Yet it is significant that although Ben Sira envisages the dual constitution, and is a fervent upholder of the high priest's honour, he does not fail to mention the kingdom of David. In the praise of the fathers he puts Moses before Aaron, then goes on as one would expect to Phinehas, but then significantly (45. 25) he fits a reference to the covenant with David in after his reference to the covenant with Levi, and before he goes on to Joshua. This placing is possibly influenced by Jer. 33. 17–22, but in any case its presence when the context did not demand it suggests the abiding importance of the Davidic tradition and hope even when the high priest is the supreme contemporary figure. Comparably, the passage devoted to David in the praise of the fathers (47. 1–11) ends with a reference to his royal covenant and his throne, once again emphasizing David's line, not just David's own achievement. In the background may be envisaged not only the rich biblical material on David current in the Persian period, but also its development, outside the Hebrew canon, in Ps. 151.

One may compare these passages in Ecclesiasticus with the reference to

David's throne for ever made perhaps nearly a century later in I Macc. 2. 57, as noted above. On each occasion a writer who appears to be a staunch upholder of the current authorities in Judaea finds it natural to allude not just to David, but to the promises concerning his throne and line. These relatively slight references are therefore an impressive testimony to the strength of messianism as part of the biblical tradition. A similar inference can be drawn from the messianism of the LXX Pentateuch, Prophets and Psalms, books used in settings where Jews were acutely conscious of the importance of loyalty to rulers.

Much later than the bulk of the Apocrypha is the strongly messianic apocalypse of Ezra (II Esdras 3–14), probably completed in its present form under Domitian, and so standing near the end of a series of apocalypses from the Herodian period noted above. Like the Parables of Enoch and the Fifth Sibylline book, it reflects the integration of Daniel, especially the vision of one like a son of man, with the traditions of a Davidic messiah in the Pentateuch, Prophets and Psalms. So in II Esdras the messiah is symbolized by a lion, clearly the lion of Judah's blessing in Gen. 49. 10, who destroys an eagle, said to represent the fourth kingdom which appeared to Daniel (II Esdras 12. 11); he is to bring joy to his own for four hundred years in a messianic kingdom, but then to die before the last judgment (II Esdras 12. 34; cf. 7. 33); and he is symbolized again by a man flying with the clouds of heaven, who recalls by his form the man-like figure of Dan. 7, but whose deeds of judgment and redemption, including victory over the multitude of the heathen, are those expected of the Davidic messiah in Isaiah 11 and Psalms 2 and 110 (II Esdras 13. 1–53).

The passages outlined here strikingly attest the rich development of messianic expectation by the end of the Herodian period. The Danielic Son of man is understood as the Davidic messiah, on an interpretation already attested in the Parables of Enoch, perhaps to be dated near the beginning of the Herodian period.[48] This understanding implies the pre-existence and revelation of the messiah, notions already suggested by such biblical passages as Micah 5. 1 and Ps. 110. 3. As II Esdras shows in its present form, heavenly origins were not held to be inconsistent with an earthly reign of fixed length. The messiah rules from the top of mount Zion (13. 35). The specification of four hundred years itself implies that the thought of a messianic reign is already familiar, and its length a known topic of speculation. The length favoured in II Esdras 7 is one of a number suggested in rabbinic interpretation on the principle that the time of comfort and joy should correspond to the years of affliction, as Moses prayed (Ps. 90. 15); in this case it corresponds to the four hundred years of affliction prophesied in the vision between the pieces (Gen. 15. 13).[49]

Among factors contributing to expectation of the death of the messiah at the end of his reign is perhaps the influence of Dan. 9. 26 (compare the discussion of the smitten shepherd at the end of the previous chapter), and of the view exemplified in the Apocalypse of Weeks (I Enoch 91. 14) that this world is entirely dissolved before the new creation. The expectation attested in the apocalypse of Ezra is therefore rich, but by no means unparalleled.

4. *The Qumran texts*

Messianic expectation is reflected over a wide range of the writings attested in copies discovered at Qumran.[50] It marks the Qumran rule literature: the Damascus Document, not only in the Cairo Genizah MSS but also in the ancient fragments from Qumran Cave 4, cited in the previous chapter; and the Rule of the Community and the Rule of the Congregation, and the Blessings which immediately follow these two Rules, in the copy of them found in Cave 1. Messianic hope has likewise left traces in the War Scroll and associated material. It is also more widely attested in Qumran biblical interpretation, most famously in the Florilegium and Testimonia from Cave 4, but also in the expositions of Genesis and Isaiah. Lastly, it is reflected in some documents which recall psalmody and prophecy, notably the Hymns, 11Q Melchizedek and the so-called Messianic Apocalypse.

Doubtful attestations, not considered here, include the Aramaic 'Son of God' text (4Q246), perhaps directed against the figure of an evil king (see chapter IV, below), and the hymn concerning exaltation to a heavenly seat in 4Q491, fragment 11.[51] Again, a prayer from a fragmentary Genesis paraphrase from Cave 4 has been taken to allude to a ruler as God's son, but a reference to Israel seems more probable, and the passage (4Q369, Fragment 1, col. ii) is not discussed below.[52] Likewise excluded is the 'King Jonathan' fragment (4Q448), which has been interpreted as prayer for a Hasmonaean king; but the proper name 'Jonathan' is probably not to be read in the relevant passages (see chapter IV below, n. 95). This fragmentary text probably expresses hope for the future establishment of God's kingdom in Jerusalem, and coheres with messianism without being explicitly messianic.

In the present argument for the prevalence of messianism, the Qumran material deserves special notice for a number of reasons. First, the compositions in question can mostly be ascribed to the Hasmonaean period, although some, such as the War Scroll, are probably Herodian in their present form. They therefore in general antedate the Psalms of Solomon and the Herodian apocalypses, which are the most strongly messianic texts in the Apocrypha and Pseudepigrapha, and offer Hebrew-language material roughly contemporary with I Maccabees and the LXX Prophets and Psalms, considered in the previous section.

Secondly, they show that under the Hasmonaean monarchs 'messiah' was well on the way to becoming a technical term. Thus the form 'messiah(s) of Aaron and Israel', in the Rule literature, stands out as implying shorter forms such as 'his messiah', in the Messianic Apocalypse (see the previous chapter).

Thirdly, Qumran material indicates that a dual priestly and royal messianic concept did not exclude the special development of the notion of the Davidic messiah, and the inclination towards envisaging a single figure. Herein the Qumran evidence continues the tendencies already noted in Chronicles and the LXX Pentateuch. Thus, the Rule of the Community in its Cave 1 copy includes the clause 'until the coming of the prophet and the messiahs of Aaron and Israel' (9. 11). In its duality this clause seems to be consistent with references to 'the messiah of Israel' and 'the priest' in the Rule of the congregation, and with blessings for the prince of the congregation and for a figure likely to be the high priest in the collection of Blessings. On the other hand, the Damascus Document presents the singular form 'Messiah of Aaron and Israel'. This also can be interpreted as a reference to two figures, but it need not be. Moreover, the particularly elaborate development of the Davidic figure is evident in the Rule literature already cited, and in Qumran biblical interpretation.

Fourthly, in this development the Qumran material shows at the same time its close connection with messianic biblical interpretation in earlier and later sources preserved elsewhere, for example the LXX Pentateuch and the Herodian apocalypses, and the richness of contemporary expectation, amounting to a 'messianic myth'.

Thus, messianic expectations of the later Herodian period included a judgment scene in which the messiah condemned and executed his great adversary.[53] This scene was associated with an exegesis of Isa. 11. 4: 'but with righteousness shall he judge the poor, and reprove with equity for the meek of the earth: and he shall smite the earth with the rod of his mouth, and with the breath of his lips he shall slay the wicked'. In the LXX, the Hebrew of the second part of the verse is rendered, 'he shall smite the earth with the word of his mouth, and with a breath through the lips shall he remove the impious'. In the context of chapter 10 the wicked one in question can readily be understood as a threatening king, Sennacherib in Isaiah's time or the great foe of the messiah yet to come. This scene appears in slightly differing forms in II Thessalonians, II Baruch, II Esdras and the Fifth Sibylline book, but all are based on Isa. 11. 4.

Further attestations of this messianic judgment scene are found in the

Dead Sea Scrolls. First, in a fragment which has been attributed to the Rule of War (4Q 285, fragment 5), in the course of a continuous exegesis of Isa. 10. 34–11. 5, it is said that 'there shall slay him the prince of the congregation, the branch of David'. The foe to be slain by the Davidic messiah is unnamed because of lacunae, but will be connected with the Kittim mentioned in a surviving phrase; probably he is 'the king of the Kittim' who leads the enemy army in the War Scroll (15. 2).[54] The scene imagined then corresponds exactly with that described in II (Syriac) Baruch 40. Comparably, the Blessing of the Prince of the Congregation mentioned above prays, once again taking up Isa. 11. 4, that with the breath of his lips he may slay the wicked (1QSb col. v, lines 24–25). This slaying is mentioned yet again in the fragmentary commentary on Isa. 10. 33–11. 5 in 4Q 161.[55] Here the 'high ones of stature' (10. 33) are 'the mighty men of the Kittim' (line 5), and 'Lebanon' in 10. 34 seems likely again to be their chief or king, although the relevant text is lacking (beginning of line 8); later in this fragment (lines 16–18) 'he shall slay the wicked' is interpreted of the branch of David who will slay 'his [en]emy' (singular).[56] The description of his rule and judgment includes a mention of Magog (line 20), which recalls the role of Gog and Magog as the foe of the messiah.

This is already illustrated in the LXX Pentateuch, as noted above with reference to Balaam's prophecy in Numbers. Thus in the third century BC Num. 24. 7 is rendered in the LXX (presupposing *mg(w)g* for MT *m'gg*) 'there shall come forth a man . . . his kingdom shall be higher than Gog'. Here Gog is already the messianic opponent. In the prophets, the end of Amos 7. 1 is rendered 'behold, one locust was king Gog' (presupposing *gwg* where MT has *gzy*). This oracle could be understood of Sennacherib's invasion (so Jerome), but in the light of Num. 24. 7 LXX it seems likely that the translator took it of a future adversary. Comparably, Amos 4. 13 LXX includes the words, discussed further in the following chapter, 'creating the spirit and announcing to men his messiah' (presupposing the consonants *mshw*, cf. MT *mhshw*). Both these Septuagintal renderings in Amos fit the messianic close of the book (9. 11–15).[57] On a distinct but closely related line of interpretation, the third Sibylline book, in a passage reflecting Jewish Egypt perhaps during the second century BC, locates 'the land of Gog and Magog' in Ethiopia (cf. Ezek. 38. 5) and predicts its doom as a 'house of judgment' drenched in blood (Sib. 3. 319–21).

The wide early circulation of the understanding of Gog and Magog as the enemy to be destroyed by the messiah is further confirmed by its occurrence in the prophecy of Eldad and Medad according to the Targum: 'Gog-and-Magog and his forces go up to Jerusalem and fall into the hand of king messiah' (Num. 11. 26 in Neofiti and the Fragment Targum). 4Q 161, if rightly restored, similarly says that the Kittim or their leaders 'will be given into the hand of his great one' (fragments 8–10, line 8).

Still other biblical passages were probably drawn into this scene of the messianic judgment of the great adversary. An example is Ps. 68. 30–31 on the gifts brought by kings and the rebuke administered to 'the beast of the reeds', who seems to be linked with the Kittim in a fragmentary commentary on Ps. 68 (1Q 16).[58] In midrash and piyyut this beast is Rome; so, in a poetic account of the succession of the four Danielic kingdoms, 'to the beast of the reeds then he sold the land' (Yose ben Yose, *'anusah le'ezrah*, line 23).[59] Now in an exegesis of Ps. 68. 30–31 attributed to the early third-century Ishmael b. Jose b. Halafta (who himself is said to have repeated it as something that 'my father said'), Rome is rebuked by or in the presence of the messiah – who has accepted gifts from the other gentile monarchies (Exod. R. 35. 5, on Exod. 26. 15; Babylonian Talmud, Pes. 118b). In this probably tannaitic interpretation the judgment scene considered above seems to have been linked with the old and widely-attested scene in which the messiah receives gifts from the nations; for the latter see Ps. Sol. 18. 31; II Esdras 13. 13; cf. Ps. 72. 10–11; Isa. 66. 20; Ber. R. 78. 12, on Gen. 33. 11 (quoting Ps.72. 10); Midrash Tehillim 87. 6, on verse 4 (quoting Isa. 66. 20); Targ. Isa. 16. 1 (no doubt encouraged by v. 5, on the throne in the tabernacle of David). In the dream-vision of II Esdras 13. 1–13 the two scenes are already connected, through a messianic interpretation of Isa. 66. 5–24; and with the Qumran material in view it may be suggested that they were also linked in the Second-Temple period on the basis of Ps. 68. 30–31.

A scene of the messianic judgment of 'the wicked one' is therefore shared by some Hebrew texts discovered at Qumran with Jewish prophecies known through Christian transmission, and with early Christian and rabbinic texts. In the exegesis represented in the first three Qumran texts, Isa. 11. 4 was regularly interpreted of the execution of 'the wicked', probably the ruler of the Kittim, by the branch of David. This interpretation was also connected with other scriptural passages, including the prophecy of Gog and probably also Ps. 68, as suggested by 1Q 16 in the light of II Esdras and the midrash. This understanding of Isa. 11. 4 will therefore have been familiar among Jews at the beginning of the Herodian period. It will have influenced both the Christian and the Jewish texts from the end of this period which have been mentioned – II Thessalonians, Revelation, and the apocalypses of Ezra and Baruch. Moreover, it had already helped to shape an imagined scene of messianic judgment, found again in the fifth Sibylline book, which can properly be called an element in a myth of the messiah and his arch-enemy. This story could also be attached to other biblical texts, and from the Second-Temple period onwards it was sometimes linked with the related scene in which the messiah receives tribute from the nations.

To summarize: consideration of the biblical writings of the Persian period, and then of three bodies of Jewish literature from the time of Alexander the Great onwards, has led to some conclusions which suggest the prevalence of messianism throughout the Second-Temple period. They may be briefly tabulated as follows.

(*a*) Biblical texts of the Persian period evince a rich complex of messianic hopes. Their impetus and influence were enhanced by the editing and collection of the Old Testament in this period.

(*b*) Particularly good signs of the centrality and widespread importance of messianic hopes soon after Alexander the Great are the messianic interpretations of the Pentateuch in the LXX, extending this element in the Hebrew text, linking the Pentateuch with the Prophets, and showing that messianic prophecy was thought to be part and parcel of the supremely authoritative book of Moses; there is then an abundance of such interpretation in the LXX Prophets and Psalms.[60]

(*c*) The silence of many probably second-century books of the Apocrypha on messianic hope, during a period when such hope is being expressed in other writings, should not be interpreted as excluding messianism. The strength of Davidic expectation is impressively attested in Ecclesiasticus and I Maccabees. The richness of the expectation attested later on in the Psalms of Solomon and in apocalypses from the end of the Herodian period, including II Esdras, is not unprecedented.

(*d*) The Qumran texts, mainly reflecting the Hasmonaean period, confirm this point, and illustrate the elaborate development of a messianic narrative or myth. This development is already attested in the LXX Pentateuch and, after the period of most of the Qumran material, in the apocalypses just mentioned.

III

The Coherence of Messianism

Even if messianic hope was more prevalent and continuous throughout the Second-Temple period than is often held, was it sufficiently coherent to exert strong influence? In view of what can appear to be a great variety of hopes in the Greek and Roman periods, is it legitimate to envisage messianic expectation after Alexander the Great primarily as the expectation of a Jewish *king*? Texts which could broadly be called messianic deal with such apparently disparate figures as Enoch, Melchizedek, Moses, Joshua and Kenaz, with priests as well as lay Israelites, and with angelic as well as human beings; moreover, texts continue to appear in which emphasis is laid on deliverance by none other than God himself. In the attempt to do justice to this variety, distinctions have been drawn between heavenly and earthly messiahs (so Bousset, cited below), or messianism has been restricted to explicit expectation of an anointed king, while other evidence which could be called messianic in a broader sense has been associated with individual non-messianic divine agents or intermediary figures. Hence, even if the presence of messianic hope is admitted, against the background of the Hebrew Bible, the LXX Pentateuch and other texts studied in the previous chapter, is there not too much variety for kingship to be regarded as central in messianism, or for royal messianism to be regarded as central in hope for the restoration of Israel?

In reply one may say, first, that the Greek and Roman periods also comprehend much material from the Targums, the rabbinic literature, and Hebrew and Aramaic prayer and liturgical poetry; in this large body of writings messianic hope is important, and is focussed above all on expectation of a 'king messiah'. This literature is later than the period of Christian origins, but it includes some material in close touch with the Second-Temple period, and is of manifold significance for the understanding of pre-rabbinic messianic expectation. At this point, however, this Hebrew and Aramaic literature is noted simply because it reflects a widespread *royal* messianic expectation; it shows that, after the rise of Christianity, non-Christian Jews in Judaea, Galilee, Syria and Mesopotamia very generally understood the Hebrew scriptures as prophesying a messianic king, and it suggests that this interpretation of the scriptures was a natural one. It is in fact the interpretation which has already been encountered in the previous chapter in the Septuagint version of the oracles of Jacob and Balaam, and in the remarkably constant strength of Davidic messianism in the Seleucid, Hasmonaean and Herodian periods.

Secondly, however, the appearance of variety in the pre-rabbinic sources on messianism may be deceptive. It owes something to modern categorization of the figures in question. The material acquires a good measure of order and unity as soon as the centrality of monarchy in the various presentations is recognized, and the biblical background is remembered.

Some of these considerations have been brought forward in critical reviews of Bousset's vivid reconstruction of a diverse messianic expectation; in Bousset's view, messianism would have had a striking but by no means consistently central role in a chaotically diverse Judaism.[1] Thus the centrality of the Israelite monarchy, as perceived in the 'Myth and Ritual' and the contemporary 'Scandinavian' movements in Old Testament study, was justly underlined by H. Riesenfeld in 1947; one should not search for an abstract unifying principle of messianic hope, but should recognize that the various concepts surrounding the messianic figure are essentially those which surrounded the Davidic king.[2] Again, the importance of the biblical tradition for the coherence of messianism was brought out by M. A. Chevallier in 1958. In a survey of messianic texts associated with the diaspora and the homeland, he was able to speak of a Jewish messianic tradition, and to give a coherent general description of the person and work of the messiah; noting diverse and sometimes even apparently contradictory developments of the underlying tradition of biblical passages, he concluded that 'the essential point is that, underneath the luxuriance of the offshoots, the tree-stump of scriptural texts lives on'.[3] This point is illustrated by the varied yet broadly consistent development of a messianic judgment scene based on Isa. 11. 4 which was sketched at the end of the last chapter. Although since Chevallier's work the main scholarly emphasis has fallen on the luxuriance and potential rivalry of the offshoots, his evocation of their dependence on the living unity of a single tree-stump is still worthy of notice.[4]

In this chapter, first, two elements making for coherence are considered in turn: the connection of expressions of messianic hope with the succession of Jewish kings and rulers, and the links between messianic interpretation of Jewish rule, and gentile ruler-cult. Then an approach is made to three aspects of Jewish hope which have been seen as breaking the inner cohesion of messianism: the expressions of hope for deliverance by God himself; the prominence of angelic deliverers; and the description of transcendent or spiritual messianic figures which have sometimes been treated as a distinct category, contrasting with more earthly depictions of a messianic king. In each case, it is argued, further examination shows that coherence can still be discerned.

1. Messianism and Israelite government

A first approach towards the perceiving of some unity in the expressions of messianic hope can be made through those biblical and post-biblical passages in which the messiah is connected with the series of Jewish kings and rulers. Within the Hebrew scriptures, a particularly important instance is Gen. 49. 10, already considered; Jacob, speaking of the latter days, foresees a succession of princes and rulers from Judah, who shall never fail until he comes, to whom the kingdom pertains. This is the interpretation underlying Peshitta ('whose it (fem.) is'), Targum Onkelos ('the messiah, whose is the kingdom'), Targum Neofiti and Fragment Targum (both 'the king messiah, whose is the kingdom'), part of the LXX tradition ('until he comes for whom it is laid up', ἕως ἐὰν ἔλθῃ ᾧ ἀπόκειται), perhaps followed by Symmachus, and 4QPBless ('the messiah of righteousness, the seed of David, for to him and to his seed was given the covenant of the kingdom of his people'); the emphasis of the main LXX ('until the things laid up for him come') is on the coming of the kingdom to Judah, and the following clause 'and he is the expectation of the nations' then refers back, without full clarity, to the never-failing ruler of the first half-verse in the LXX.[5]

Comparably, a prayer in the War Scroll (1QM xi 1–7) envisages divine deliverance as given successively through David and the kings of Israel, by the God who promised the star from Jacob and the sceptre from Israel (Num. 24. 17); here the messianic sceptre is the climax of the series of royal deliverers. Probably, as in CD vii 19, the 'star' is the priest who will interpret the law as Eleazar did, and the 'sceptre' the prince of the congregation, who will fight the battles as Joshua did.[6] The exalted and representative place of the prince of the congregation in the War Scroll is evident in the passage on his shield (v 1), which is to bear his name, and the names of Israel, Levi, Aaron, the twelve tribes and their leaders.

Towards the end of the first century AD the interpretation of the cloud-vision in the Syriac Apocalypse of Baruch makes the messiah sit on the throne of his kingdom (chapters 70–73) at the climax of the series of good rulers – David, Solomon, Hezekiah and Josiah (61; 63; 66). The connection of the messiah not just with David, but with the line of good kings, emerges in a different way in the famous last words ascribed to Johanan b. Zaccai,

'Set a throne for Hezekiah, king of Judah, who is coming' (Ber. 28b); the messiah can be envisaged not only as David, as in Ezek. 37. 24–26, but also as one of David's great reforming heirs, the king in whose days Assyria was smitten. The more straightforward presentation of a royal succession leading up to the messiah, as in Gen. 49. 10, reappears in Pseudo-Philo's *Biblical Antiquities*, where Kenaz is presented as one of the kings and rulers mentioned in the prophecy (25. 2 and 5, quoting and echoing Gen. 49. 10). The pattern is repeated in a Christian source at the end of the first century, with recollection of the priestly as well as the royal line, when Jacob's blessings of all the tribes are summarized in I Clement 32. 2: from Jacob come the priests and Levites (Levi), the Lord Jesus according to the flesh (Judah, compare Heb. 7. 14), 'kings and rulers and governors according to the line of Judah', and the seed as the stars of heaven in the other tribes. Here the Christian messiah seems to be presented as the climax of both priestly and royal succession, but the thought of the royal sucession as leading up to the messiah retains an important place. In a Jewish apocalypse of the later Roman period, somewhat comparably, David appears with all the kings of his house and the kings of Israel when enthroned as the messianic king in heaven.[7]

In passages such as these the messiah emerges clearly as the expected Jewish monarch. In disputation with Christians it was indeed regularly urged that prophecies referred to one of the past Jewish kings rather than to the Christians' messiah (so, for example, Trypho in Justin's *Dialogue*, 33–34, on Psalms 110 and 72). Such arguments confirm the connection of 'messianic' prophecy with monarchy, but in the light of the passages just considered it can also be seen that reference of a passage to one of the kings of old would not rule out a further reference to the still awaited messianic king; he would form the climax of the line of good kings, and could be envisaged as David, Solomon or Hezekiah come again.[8]

Secondly, messianic expectation was linked with the royal line and the Jewish constitution not as they *were* according to modern historical reconstruction, but as they were *envisaged* from time to time in the Greek and Roman world. This means that material which now looks multifarious, for it includes messianic treatment of priests, judges and patriarchs, in the Greek and Roman periods would have naturally associated itself with the single succession of legitimate Jewish rulers. Thus the constitutional co-ordination of high-priest and king, as envisaged in the Pentateuchal portrait of Eleazar and Joshua (Num. 27. 15–23) and in Josephus, is reflected in the dual messianism of the Testaments of the Twelve Patriarchs, the Qumran texts, and the coins of the Bar Kokhba revolt. This political theory could evidently cover what was noticed, in an oracular survey of history preserved in a Qumran Hebrew text, as the change of government between the days of the kingdom of Israel and the (post-exilic) time when 'the sons of Aaron shall rule over them' (4Q 390 [Pseudo-Moses Apocalypse*] fragment 1, lines 2–5).[9]

Furthermore, the succession of rulers is traced back beyond David to the judges (Kenaz in Pseudo-Philo) and Moses. So Moses is king, probably in the book of Deuteronomy (33. 5), and the LXX Pentateuch (pp. 31, 49, above), and certainly in Ezekiel the Tragedian, Philo and the midrash;[10] Justus of Tiberias, already mentioned as a Jewish contributor to the literature of monarchy, began his history of the Jewish kings with Moses. Further back still, Abraham was a king from the side of God, βασίλευς παρὰ θεοῦ (Gen.23. 6 LXX, for נשיא אלהים); as in the case of Moses's kingship, this is a pre-Christian interpretation which also influenced rabbinic exegesis (e.g. Ber.R. 55. 7, on Gen. 22. 1), נשיא being regularly understood as 'king' in the second-temple period.[11] Melchizedek, king of Jerusalem and king of righteousness (Genesis Apocryphon, Josephus and the Targums on Gen. 14. 18), is linked with David by Ps. 110. 3, and in this psalm in the LXX the ruler begotten before the daystar is also to be a priest after the order of Melchizedek.[12] Lastly, Adam's descendants before the flood begin the Davidic ancestry (I Chron. 1. 1–4, Luke 3. 36–38), and are enumerated as rulers in Josephus (*Ant.* 1, 80, 83–88); Enoch, the seventh from Adam (Jude 14), is outstanding among them. The messianic treatment of patriarchs, judges and priests can accordingly be seen as an aspect of the tendency to associate all the relevant figures with the series of legitimate rulers of Israel.

2. *Ruler-cult and messianism*

The strong monarchical thread in messianic hope is therefore also an important clue to the coherence of messianism. The strength and importance of this thread can only be fully appreciated, however, through separate notice of its connection with contemporary ruler-cult. Jewish attitudes to ruler-cult are perhaps most familiar in the form of opposition. Influence from ruler-cult on Jewish and Christian messianism has therefore been doubted.[13] The Christ-cult was indeed criticized in language which recalled earlier criticisms of ruler-cult, both Greek and Jewish (see chapter 4, part 1, below). Yet opposition was not the only Jewish attitude. Ruler-cult inevitably attracted attention and imitation because it symbolized the focus of power. Moreover, although it could challenge traditional piety, Greek and Roman as well as Jewish, it could be interpreted in ways which upheld ancestral religion. Among Jews, accordingly, it must be reckoned with as an influence on views of kingship and messianism, as has sometimes been recognized.[14] The importance of messianic hope under Greek and Roman rule derives not only from its roots in biblical tradition, but also, to a considerable extent, from the function of messianism as a counterpart to contemporary ruler-cult and the ideas surrounding it.[15] The probable links between the two have been recognized by a number of scholars, but were perhaps shown most succinctly when Bousset included Greek and Roman ruler-cult within his treatment of messianism.[16]

Three aspects of ruler-cult deserve notice in this connection here: its capacity for integration with ancestral religion, its characteristically exuberant forms of praise and prayer, and the variegated pattern of Jewish reaction to it, through participation as well as opposition. First, the capacity of ruler-cult for integration with ancestral piety is notable not only because of the potentially disruptive and even impious character of its homage to the monarch here below, but also because of the vast social, political and religious significance of the cults of Greek and Roman rulers; they might seem apt to overwhelm rather than to coalesce with ancestral religion. These cults can be more narrowly conceived simply as the acts of worship offered to a ruler as to a god, but more broadly they embrace the people's perceptions of the role of the sovereign, in relation to the whole mundane and supra-mundane order of things.[17] Their religious as well as political importance was brought out in the past by writers such as P. Wendland and W. Bousset, but it has often also been minimized in view of the links of ruler-cult with benefaction and flattery. More recently it has won recognition through anthropological comment on the significance of ritual (compare the earlier anthropological influence on the study of Hebrew kingship, noticed above). Rites and ceremonies which might have been dismissed by some inquirers as the trappings of power have been seen rather as belonging to its very substance.[18]

Ruler-cult was of course a thoroughly political phenomenon, and divine honours were indeed widely held among Greeks to form an appropriate recognition of exceptional benefactions.[19] A. D. Nock's epigrammatic description of these honours as 'an expression of gratitude which did not involve any theological implications' seems nevertheless to need the qualification that ruler-cult was also religion.[20] In accord with a broader view of cult, in this review its manifestations are taken to include writings which reflect royal ideology, especially court poetry. 'The rhetoric of poets and sycophants offers no evidence of cult' (E. Bickerman);[21] but it may indicate the shape and ethos of contemporary ruler-cult known from other sources, especially through its witness to praise and petition.[22]

Warnings against viewing ruler-cult through the lens of Christian criticism are salutary up to a point.[23] Nevertheless, Christian objections to ruler-cult as servile and impious continued the terms of non-Christian Greek criticism (see below); and both the pagan and the Christian phases of this criticism, not least the Christian-influenced historiographical treatment of ruler-cult as a rival to Christianity, bring out the force of ruler-cult as religion.[24] In any case, the degree of detachment as well as sympathy which warnings against a Christianized reading of ruler-cult desiderate should not obscure the common theological ground between pagans, Jews and Christians in antiquity, especially in the Platonic tradition. Apotheosis raised the monarch into the company of spirits and divinities themselves subordinate to transcendent divine majesty; Jews and Christians, whatever their attitude to the honour, could readily share the view of the cosmos within which it was envisaged.

Divine honours to rulers could thus be accommodated within the framework of due honour to the gods. Although Greek piety after Alexander still upheld a strict distinction between the blessed immortals and humankind, as in the insistence that the alleged tomb of Zeus in Crete was empty (Callimachus, *Hymn* 1, 8–9; *Iambi* 12, 16 [Fragment 202]), in Greek mythology the heroes or demigods, above all Heracles and Dionysus, had gained the ranks of the immortals. The Olympian gods themselves could be perceived as king-like and the protectors of kings (so Zeus, with Apollo at his right hand, in Callimachus, *Hymns* 1, 165–89; 2, 26–28). Monarchs were accordingly, in an important aspect of ruler-cult, linked with and assimilated to particular gods, and such association was often reflected in the praises of both gods and kings offered by court poets. Examples are the links forged between Ptolemy II Philadelphus and Zeus (Theocritus *Id.* 17, 130), an unnamed Ptolemy (perhaps III) and Apollo (Callimachus, *Hymn* 2, 26–27, cited below), and Ptolemy IV Philopator and Dionysus (compare III Macc. 2. 29); Julius Caesar and Augustus were comparably linked with both Jupiter and Apollo.[25] Alternatively, the monarch could attain heaven as heroes had done, in the capacity of a supremely virtuous benefactor (so Augustus, in Horace, *Od.* 3, 3, 9–12; 4, 5, 31–36; compare *Ep.* 2, 1, 5–17). In these literary presentations, supremely exemplified by the invocation of Augustus after the ancient gods of the countryside at the beginning of Virgil's *Georgics*, the cult of the monarch here below fits into, depends on, and in turn upholds due reverence for the gods above.

Such links between gods and kings could also appeal, however, to the rationalizing interpreter. When Euhemerus in the early third century, following earlier explanations of some gods as deified rulers, claimed that Zeus had once been an outstandingly benevolent earthly king, he was not just a sceptic who outraged the traditionally pious, but also the most influential sponsor of a theological system into which deified monarchs fitted perfectly.[26] Ruler-cult should probably not be linked with an assumed but debatable decline in Greek faith and piety;[27] it was compatible, however, with widely differing philosophical positions on the nature of the gods. For its impact on messianism, its capacity for integration with Greek piety in a traditional form is particularly notable. Its counterpart in glowing messianic depiction, such as is discussed later on in this chapter (section 5, below), could likewise be integrated with ancestral Jewish reverence for the King of heaven.

The second element of ruler-cult to be viewed in connection with messianism is formed by prayer and praise. These exuberant manifestations of ruler-cult placard its aspect as piety or impiety. The charge of impiety in the Greek world seems to have emerged paradigmatically, however, in debate over posture rather than language. This is suggested by Arrian's presentation of the court discussion of Alexander the Great's request for obeisance (*proskynesis*).[28] The motives of the request itself are not transparent.[29] In Arrian, however, both sides understand it as a request for divine honours. Obeisance is defended by Anaxarchus, whose speech includes the argument that Alexander would certainly be honoured as a god after death, and in all justice should receive this token of gratitude in his lifetime; but on the other side Callisthenes urges that the king – whose surpassing merits are admitted by all – is confounding the due distinction between mortals and gods by requiring reverence deeper than a mortal should claim. This charge of impiety could of course be used to make a political point.[30] Moreover, later Greek objections appear to presuppose not that the rendering of divine honours would be sacrilegious in itself, but that the particular recipient in view is unworthy.[31] Nevertheless, it is significant that the charge of impiety could be made. Spoken prayer and praise confirm that it could seem not inappropriate.

The sometimes strained relationship between ruler-cult and other pieties, Greek as well as Jewish, emerges clearly in attitudes to petition. This was a fundamental activity of subjects in an ancient monarchy, as is attested through the Ptolemaic examples classified as *enteuxeis*, 'intercessions', cf. II Macc. 4. 8 (a Jewish Seleucid instance); I Tim. 2. 1; and Tiberius Julius Alexander's edict of AD 68 (chapter IV, section 1, below).[32] Ruler-cult seems therefore naturally to have involved petition as well as praise, although this point is sometimes questioned.[33] Thus the Athenian hymn to the Macedonian king Demetrius I Poliorcetes, son of Alexander the Great's general Antigonus, includes 'we pray you, first of all, make peace, most dear one; for you are lord' (Athenaeus, *Deip.* 6. 253e).[34] In Rome, Horace predicts that Augustus shall be honoured with 'much prayer' (Horace, *Od.* 4. 5, 33). Martial, in an epigram addressed to Jupiter, states that prayer to the gods for anything other than Caesar's health is otiose; for everything else, Caesar himself should be petitioned: 'For Caesar, I should ask You; for myself, I should ask Caesar.' Indeed (he says elsewhere) it is petition, rather than a statue, that really makes a god.[35] When Dan. 6. 8–10 (7–9) envisages a decree that Darius should be sole recipient of all petitions, the writer seems to be slightly exaggerating, but not otherwise misrepresenting, an element of ruler-cult which is well attested in Greek and Roman sources.[36]

An instance in which poetic praise at court closely reflects cultic petition in a form known to have been familiar to Jews is the treatment of Augustus as god of the sea, which was expressed monumentally in the great Alexandrian Augusteum opposite the harbours, admiringly described by Philo as a 'saving hope' (ἐλπίς . . . σωτήριος) to seafarers (Philo, *Leg. Gai.* 151). A corresponding hymn was sung in an Alexandrian ship off Puteoli when Augustus sailed by, according to Suetonius; and the theme was taken up in literary verse by Virgil, who asks (*Geo.* 1, 29–30, in Dryden's version):

> 'Or wilt thou, Caesar, choose the wat'ry reign,
> To smooth the surges, and correct the main?
> Then mariners in storms to thee shall pray . . .'.[37]

('*an deus immensi venias maris ac tua nautae | numina sola colant*'). In Judaea, the Augusteum built by Herod opposite the harbour-mouth at Caesarea (Josephus, *BJ* 1, 414) will also have recalled this attribute of the emperor.

The ruler, then, like other divinities, could be asked for those benefits which lay within his particular power, and in the nature of the cult it would be stressed that his power was extensive and effectual – more effectual, as has just been noticed, than that of the gods above.

The charge of impiety seems not to be absent in the Roman period, even though divine honours are most obviously criticized as flattery. In such criticism it might be allowed that outstanding benefactors deserved exceptional honours, but the point at which laudation became excessive was often perceived as the point at which a king received the honour due to a god. Thus in language which had become formulaic Claudius, writing to the Alexandrians after the upheavals under Caligula, declines a high-priest and temples, judging that these have always been considered as set apart for the gods alone (P. Lond. 1912, col. iii, lines 50–51, in *CPJ* II, no. 153, p. 40).[38] Plutarch, a believer in monarchy and also a man of piety, takes it that royal titles like Philadelphus are justifiable, but that 'god' or 'son of god' would be mendacious and empty (Plutarch, *De Laude ipsius*, 12, 543 D–E).[39]

Royal praises at their most exuberant could indeed involve impiety in the form of insults or near-insults to the gods. In this shameless praise the natural force and impetus of ruler-cult comes out most clearly. Thus a long discourse on flattery in Athenaeus includes two Hellenistic instances in which monarchs, as true and living gods, are contrasted with lifeless and unprofitable deities. In the first to be mentioned, when Sicilians were following their custom of dancing round the statues of the nymphs, Democles, parasite of the tyrant Dionysius the Younger, danced round Dionysius's statue instead, with the words 'one should pay no attention to lifeless divinities (ἀψύχοις θεοῖς)'. The second is the Athenians' hymn to Demetrius Poliorcetes, quoted already for its prayer for peace. It also includes the famous Elijah-like boast that 'other gods are far away, or have no ears, or do not exist, or pay no attention to us at all, but we see You here present, not made of wood or stone, but true'.[40]

Such praise of the 'present god', by contrast with the gods above, was a court commonplace. Under the Roman principate, within a literature inspired especially by Greek exemplars, it reappears dramatically in Horace:

Dread Jove in Thunder speaks his just domain;
On Earth a present God shall Caesar reign

(Philip Francis, rendering *Od.* 3, 5, 1–3, '*caelo tonantem credidimus Iovem | regnare; praesens divus habebitur | Augustus*'). It is hard not to hear the sequence as climactic. Similarly, in a dedicatory passage in his *Epistles*, cited above (2, 1, 5–17), Horace leads up to Augustus through a series of great heroes and benefactors who attained divine status – Romulus, Bacchus, Castor, Pollux and Hercules – and then addresses his own patron and ruler with an implied contrast: 'to you, *present as you are*, we bring our fullest honours' ('*praesenti tibi maturos largimur honores*'). Augustus has therefore attained divinity like Pollux and Hercules – between whom he reclines to quaff the nectar of the gods, as Horace says elsewhere (*Od.* 3, 3, 9–12); but unlike them he has remained present on earth, where he wields the sovereignty of Jupiter himself.

This bold yet tradition-derived depiction of Augustus as present divine vicegerent of Jupiter will have been one of the many precedents for the treatment of Nero as Zeus in the court poetry of Leonides of Alexandria; Poppaea is hailed as 'wife of Zeus'.[41] Horace's point recurs in the passages of Martial noted above, and was made less subtly by Statius when he hailed Domitian as the god who, '*propior Iove*', 'nearer than Jupiter', directs human actions (*Silvae* 5, 1, 37–38).[42] In prose the topos is used under

Augustus by Valerius Maximus, and again in Pliny's panegyric to Trajan, and later on in a panegyric to Maximian.[43] In the Hellenistic instances the royal praises verge still more closely on impiety, but they were adduced in Athenaeus as instances of gross flattery. Nevertheless, as the Augustan refusal formula and Plutarch confirm, impiety is evidently still implicitly an element in the predominantly political and ethical critique of the rendering of divine honours to kings. The praise and prayer which attracted this charge from both Greeks and Jews also attest the vigour and glamour of ruler-cult. A corresponding vigour and exuberance emerge in messianic praise.

The third aspect of ruler-cult to be considered in connection with messianism is the pattern of Jewish opposition and participation. To begin with, the opposition, famous and important as it is, must receive some assessment. Its significance in Jewish writings of the Greek period can be summarily outlined as follows.[44] Royal oppression by imposition of pagan worship is important in the Jewish sources, above all in the Maccabaean tradition, but within the tale of this oppression ruler-cult itself plays at most a minor part; Hebrew oracles on Antiochus IV in Daniel hint at it, but in the historical narratives in Greek its failure to be specified in the comparatively detailed indictments of a hostile Ptolemy (III Maccabees) and of Antiochus Epiphanes (I, II and IV Maccabees) is striking.[45]

This impression is comparable, however, with that left later by the acts of the Christian martyrs, in which, similarly, imperially-imposed idolatry is far more prominent than the cult of the emperors themselves.[46] It is also consistent with what Samuel Krauss called the 'surprisingly unconstrained tone' of the extensive later rabbinic references to the imperial cult, in which hymnody and acclamation addressed to the emperor are constantly mentioned without any expression of criticism.[47] The cult is nevertheless attacked from the beginning of the Greek period onwards, in sources surviving in Aramaic (Daniel) and Hebrew (Ben Sira) as well as Greek (Judith, the Greek Esther, Wisdom); and it was important enough to gain a place in interpretation when not explicit in the biblical text (LXX Dan. 3, and perhaps 4Q246).

On the other hand, Jewish loyalty to gentile rulers is also prominent, especially but not only in III Maccabees, and their divinely-ordained status is underlined (Daniel, the Greek Esther, Wisdom). With regard to gentile rulers, accordingly, Jews were able to use those honorific formulae which were worded to allow for Greek or other reservations, notably the phrase ὑπέρ, 'on behalf of', the monarch which occurs in the earliest surviving dedications of *proseuchae*, from the reign of Ptolemy III Euergetes II and so not far from the time of Callimachus's hymns.[48] Under Roman rule, correspondingly, the Alexandrian *proseuchae* could be presented as centres of Jewish homage to the emperor, in virtue of the shields, crowns, stelae and inscriptions set up there in his honour (Philo, *Leg. ad Gaium* 133). Finally, Jewish thought on indigenous monarchy sometimes comes into view in contrast with gentile ruler-cult; a great Jewish leader can be pictured over against the gentile ruler (Ben Sira, Daniel) as receiving exceptional homage and honour (Dan. 2. 46), in continuity with the Jewish royal honours in Psalms and Chronicles, and with the commandment and the oracles of the law of Moses as understood in the Greek period. A Jewish pendant to the debate in Arrian was provided by the legend that Alexander himself did obeisance (not to a mortal, but) to the divine Name on the high priest's mitre, and also highly honoured the high priest – a formulation sensitive to zealous Jewish as well as Greek reservations on ruler-cult (Josephus, *Ant.* 11, 331–9). Compare, without explicit reference to ruler-cult, the presentation of Moses as king, by contrast with Pharaoh, in Ezekiel the Tragedian. In the Greek period, therefore, conditions under which influence may readily be envisaged are present; ruler-cult is universally known to Jews, refused if imposed absolutely (Daniel 6, Judith, Greek Esther, Daniel 3 LXX), but normally shared, as part of Jewish loyalty to the overlord, in the ways which ancestral custom permit; and it can be connected and contrasted with Jewish monarchy in an exaltation of Jewish rulers.

This pattern can still be recognized in the Roman period. The divine claims of Gaius Caligula came after seventy years of Jewish familiarity with the imperial cult, as recounted and interpreted in some detail by Philo and Josephus. A great focus of Jewish opposition was the Second Commandment; the statues in the temples of Augustus and Rome built by Herod the Great at Caesarea, Paneas and Samaria, the images of Caesar on legionary standards in the time of Pilate, the likenesses and statues of Gaius which the Alexandrians intruded into Jewish *proseuchae*, and finally the statue of himself as Zeus Epiphanes Neos which Gaius sought to place in the Jerusalem temple, are all said to have been opposed on the basis of the ancestral Jewish law (Josephus, *Ant.* 15, 329–30; 18, 55 [*BJ* 2, 169–71], 264–7 [*BJ* 2, 195] [Jews forbidden any image of God, much more of man]), 271; Philo, *Leg. ad Gaium* 134–7, 346). The theological interpretation of the Second Commandment which these passages imply is more fully expressed elsewhere. Philo comments that changing a man into a god and pretending that corruptible nature is incorruptible is the most grievous impiety towards the true divine benefactor (so, keeping the language of ruler-cult, Philo, *Leg. ad Gaium* 118; cf. *Dec.* 6–9, 66–76, on images; Rom. 1. 23); this impiety is no real honour to the emperor, for the Alexandrians, involved as they are in

Egyptian animal-worship, think nothing of conferring divine titles on mortal creatures, as they did in the case of the Ptolemies (*Leg. ad Gaium* 139, 162–4; cf. *Dec.* 76–80). The address of 'god' required by Caligula (θεὸν προσαγορεύειν αὐτόν) is correspondingly represented as the Jews' legitimate sticking-point in the version of Claudius's edict to Alexandria and Syria in favour of the Jews in Josephus, *Ant.* 19, 284.

The Decalogue was linked also to the commandment to destroy alien altars in the holy land (Exod. 34. 13; Deut. 12. 2–3), for the latter is paraphrased in Josephus (*Ant.* 4. 201) with the explanation 'for God is one'.[49] This prohibition of altars will have encouraged the Jewish destruction of the altar to Gaius provocatively set up by the Greeks of Jamnia (Philo, *Leg. ad Gaium* 200–203). The link between the Decalogue, its theological interpretation, and reservations about imperial cult is seen most clearly in a passage in Josephus where Moses is said to have forbidden the making of the image of any being, above all of God, as a practice which profits neither man nor God, *not* as a prophetic prohibition of due honour to the power of the Romans (Josephus, *Ap.* 2, 74–75). This explanation confirms that opposition based on the Second Commandment was well-known to gentiles. Apion is said elsewhere in Josephus to have claimed before Gaius that the Jews alone scorned to honour the emperor with statues and to swear by his name, a sequence probably implying successive reference to the Second and Third Commandments (*Ant.* 18, 258).[50] Such an understanding of the Decalogue is likely to be reflected already in Wisdom 14, where the royal statues play their part in the origins of idolatry. Similarly, the Decalogue was probably taken to enjoin the tradition of affirming God's sole rule, adumbrated in biblical sources such as Psalms 146 and 149, noted above, and followed by the Sicarii who refused to acknowledge Vespasian as δεσπότης at Alexandria (Josephus, *BJ* 7, 418–19), and by Mordecai as envisaged in Targum Sheni on Esther (he will not bow down to a mortal, but only to the Creator).

The literary deposit of debate in the early Roman period, therefore, brings out the links forged between opposition and the ancestral laws, the Decalogue above all. This exegesis probably arose before Alexander the Great, for in a less extreme form it is likely to have been presupposed in the Ptolemaic allowance for Jewish aniconic custom, and to have been bound up with post-exilic development of thought on the kingdom of God.

Nevertheless, the desire to affirm Jewish loyalty evident in literature from the Greek period also reappears. Restraining interpretations of texts relating to gentile statues and altars continued to be current. Examples are the precepts 'Do not revile the gods', Exod. 22. 27 LXX, linked with respect for temples by Josephus *Ant.* 4, 207; and 'Do not destroy their high places', a comment in the name of Johanan b. Zaccai connected with Deut. 12. 2–3 (*ARN* B 31). It was emphasized that Jews were eager to offer all the permitted honours in their prayer-houses and (especially by daily sacrifices for the emperor) in their temple at Jerusalem (Josephus *Ap.* 2, 76–77 [continual sacrifices for the emperors and the Roman people]; Philo, *Leg. ad Gaium* 133 [honours in the *proseuchae*, as noted above]).

Correspondingly, despite Apion's allegation noted above, Jews at least sometimes took an oath by the king or emperor.[51] Examples include Gen. 42. 15 LXX, 'by the health of Pharaoh', suggesting that swearing by the king was acceptable among Jews in the third century BC; Josephus, *Ant.* 13, 76 (Jews and Samaritans in Ptolemaic Alexandria are said to swear by God and the king); and BGU 1068 = CPJ II, no. 427, of AD 101 (oath by the emperor Trajan); in Roman Arabia, Babatha's oath and the oath of an unknown 'son of Levi', both by the Fortune (*tyche*) of Trajan, in two documents of AD 127 (P. Yadin 16; XHev/Se 61). To quote H. M. Cotton's comment on the last-named document, after discussion of parallels: 'It would seem that the Jews of the period were less conscious – even oblivious – of the religious implications, from the standpoint of a monotheistic Jewish theology, of an oath by the emperor or by his *tyche*. It is not necessary to assume that they felt coerced into using the formula.'[52]

Lastly, in this later period the celebration of Jewish leaders over against the kings who receive cult appears most clearly in the glorious messianic figures of II Baruch (where the Roman leader is put to death, as noted in chapter II, section 4, above), II Esdras, and the Fifth Sibylline book (discussed in section 5, below). The earlier pattern of both opposition and loyalty, together with exaltation of Jewish rulers, remains perceptible despite the strength of opposition.

In sum, therefore, gentile and Jewish reactions overlapped considerably, and Jewish reactions were not uniformly hostile, but varied. Jewish writings are not so strongly marked by opposition specifically to ruler-cult as might have been expected; it is clear that often its forms were taken for granted without objection.

To summarize this brief review as a whole, it may be said that ruler-cult presented a vigorous challenge to traditional Greek and Roman piety, but also had a capacity for integration with it. As the focus of governmental power it attracted attention and imitation; among Jews, such imitation influenced the praise of their rulers and the depictions of their messianic king. Ruler-cult was therefore an important factor in the continuing vigour and centrality of monarchy and monarchic ideas in the messianism of the Greek and Roman periods.

3. 'Not by the hand of an angel and not by the hand of a legate'

Sometimes, however, this central monarchical strain in Jewish thought on redemption seems to lead to a non-messianic concentration on the kingship of God himself, in the manner considered in the previous chapter. There are consequently those slogans, attested from the time of the LXX Isaiah onwards into rabbinic tradition of the later Roman empire, which seem to contend for a 'God without mediators', in M. Pesce's phrase.[53] They can lead to contrasts between God and his agents, in favour of hope for lasting redemption by God himself. E. P. Sanders views specifically messianic expectation as likely to be diminished, particularly in the face of Roman might, by the conviction that the Lord himself will fight for Israel; 'once God is thought of as doing the main fighting anyway, the need for a warrior-king is reduced'.[54] Although Rome was indeed in the end too mighty for any Israelite leader, it is (paradoxically, on Sanders's argument) against Rome that specifically messianic figures were invoked in II Esdras, II Baruch and Sib. 5 (just beyond the period covered by Sanders in the book quoted above). On the other, an argument on Sanders's lines with regard to the Jews of the later Roman empire might appeal to a saying current in third-century Tiberias, in the name of R. Johanan. Israel are imagined as praying, after their experience under the four kingdoms of Daniel's vision: 'We are wearied of being enslaved, and redeemed, and again enslaved. Now we are not asking for redemption by flesh and blood, but (Isa.54. 5) our redeemer – "the Lord Sabaoth is his name, the holy one of Israel". From now on we do not ask that flesh and blood should shine upon us, but that the Holy One, blessed be he, should shine upon us, as it is said, For with thee is the well of life, in thy light shall we see light (Ps. 36. 6), and it is written, The Lord is God, and he has shone upon us (Ps. 118. 27).'[55] This saying takes up the Deutero-Isaianic emphasis on God himself as redeemer, and could be understood as a warning against specifically messianic hope, perhaps comparable with other sayings attributed to R. Johanan which have been thought to suggest that he had little enthusiasm for messianism[56] – although teachings attributed to him, his contemporaries and pupils suggest that it was an important topic in their circle (see this section, p. 81, and section 5, below).[57] Do the slogans on redemption by God himself, not an agent, imply that messianic deliverance is not envisaged?

The argument has already encountered texts thought to be silent about a messiah, especially in discussion of the Apocrypha in the previous chapter. As noted there, the implications of this silence need not be negative. It should also be remembered, however, that the claimed silences are sometimes themselves questionable. Thus a recent list of books with no attestation of messianic hope includes Trito-Isaiah, Chronicles, Jubilees and the War Scroll, but each of these has passages discussed above which were or could be understood as messianic.[58] Moreover, in books where the silence itself is more clearly established, its likely significance varies. The argument from silence seems strongest, as noted already, in books or passages where hopes for the future are expressed, but the sole explicit reference is to divine deliverance. Examples would be the consolation of Israel and Jerusalem in the poems of Baruch 4–5 and Tobit 13, the briefer reference to divine vengeance at the end of the thanksgiving of Judith (16. 17, developing Deut. 32. 35–36, 41–43), and the prayer for ingathering which is among the antecedents of the Eighteen Benedictions, in II Macc. 1. 24–29. Yet in Baruch, Tobit, Judith and II Maccabees, as argued already, the messianic overtones which had come to attach to the Pentateuchal and prophetic passages being used make it unlikely that the sole emphasis on divine deliverance should be taken negatively.

The question arises from material extending beyond the apocryphal books already reviewed. Thus it is regularly considered with regard to the near-silence of the Mishnah on the messiah, noticed in chapter I, section 1, above.[59] In this case it has been argued that messianic hope was given prominence in Jewish compilations of tradition only after the time of the Mishnah; Christian messianism impinged strongly on the Jewish community in the age of Constantine, and gave the subject an importance in rabbinic Judaism which it had not had before.[60] It is indeed likely that Jewish statements on messianism came to be affected in various ways by Christian hopes, even before Constantine. Thus Christian messianism could lead to counter-assertion among Jews (see section 5, below), and could also be among the factors contributing to reserve on messianic hope in literature reflecting the position of Jewish communal teachers and guides. On the other hand, another factor contributing to reserve will have been the continuing importance of messianism within the Jewish community itself. Traditions preserved in the Talmud and midrash suggest that messianic hope flourished among the body of interpreters who are cited in the Mishnah. The continuing importance of messianism in the community in general is further shown by its place in the LXX, the revised Jewish Greek biblical versions and the Targums and in common prayer such as the Amidah. From another point of view, it is indicated by the great uprisings in the Diaspora under Trajan and in Judaea, led by Bar Kokhba, under Hadrian.[61] The near-silence of the Mishnah – significantly broken by use of a current phrase 'days of messiah' (Ber. 1, 5) – is therefore likely to be a paradoxical sign of the vigour of messianism and its potential danger to the community.

It is then an open question whether silences on messianism in passages which stress divine deliverance exclude any specifically messianic expectation among those responsible for the poems and prayers in question. Yes seems at first a possible answer, because of the distinction expressly drawn, from the time of the LXX Isaiah onwards, between deliverance by an angelic or human legate and deliverance by God himself. Yet the Yes seems to be qualified by the most famous instance of this distinction, the assertion that precisely in the exodus Israel was saved by God himself, not an agent.

So, in the LXX Isaiah, 'Not an envoy nor a messenger, but the Lord himself saved them' (LXX Isa. 63. 9, οὐ πρέσβυς οὐδὲ ἄγγελος, ἀλλ' αὐτὸς Κύριος ἔσωσεν αὐτούς). Similarly, in the same Septuagintal book, the promise of divine vengeance and salvation in Isa. 35. 4 is further clarified in this sense: 'behold, our God shall requite, he himself shall come and save us (ἰδοὺ ὁ θεὸς ἡμῶν . . . ἀνταποδώσει, αὐτὸς ἥξει καὶ σώσει ἡμᾶς)'. Comparably, at a later date, the Passover Haggadah interprets Deut. 26. 8, 'The LORD brought us forth', with the comment 'not by the hand of an angel and not by the hand of a seraph and not by the hand of a legate' (לא על ידי מלאך ולא על ידי שרף ולא על ידי שליח).

In the case of the exodus, angelic and human emissaries are clearly attested in the biblical narrative, and this 'no agent' assertion is not a denial of their existence, but a claim that no less than God himself was the Israelites' true deliverer; it is supported in the Passover Haggadah by quotation of Exod. 12. 12, on the Lord himself as smiting the first-born and the gods of Egypt. This visitation was indeed ascribed also to God's 'word', in the Wisdom of Solomon and the Targum (Wisdom 18. 14–16; Targum Neofiti Exod. 11. 4; 12. 12), or to angelic destroyers (Jub. 49. 2–4; cf. Exod. 12. 23; Heb. 11. 28); but in rabbinic thought it came to be emphasized as a decisive revelation of God himself, in addition to the mediation of Moses, Aaron and the angel.[62]

The pre-Christian 'no agent' formula was widely used in rabbinic exegesis, being applied not only to the exodus but also to other acts of God, including (of special interest here) his future vengeance as prophesied in the song of Moses in Deut. 32. 35–36: 'Vengeance is mine, and recompense . . . for the LORD shall judge his people' (see Sifre Deut. 325, ad loc.).[63] A heavy emphasis on God's *own* action characterizes the verses which follow in Deuteronomy, and their analogues in the prophets and psalms: Isa. 59. 16–18; 63. 3–5 (see pp. 38, 44 and 55, above); Nahum 1. 2–8; Ps. 94; Isa. 35. 4 LXX, 'Behold, our God shall requite . . . he himself shall come and save us (Greek text quoted above)'. Hence this whole passage in Deuteronomy gains the emphasis on God's own action evident when it is quoted at Heb. 10. 30 with the comment 'it is a fearful thing to fall into the hands of the living God'; but, once again, this emphasis did not exclude a divine emissary, as appears in the development of Deut. 32 in the Assumption of Moses, with its 'messenger' (9. 7–10. 7; cf. Deut. 32. 43), and in the messianic understanding of Isa. 59. 16–20 on a 'redeemer' (Rom. 11. 26; Sanh. 98b, in the name of R. Johanan; PRK Supplement VI 5).

Comparably, on the 'day of vengeance for our God' mentioned in Isa. 61. 2, not God himself but 'Melchizedek will execute the vengeance of the judgments of G[od]', according to a Qumran text (11Q Melch ii 13). This indication of a messianic figure of course follows the tenor of the Hebrew text of Isa. 61. 1–2, in which God's day is announced by one who is anointed and upon whom is the spirit of the Lord. Similarly, in Hebrews itself the quotation of Deut. 32. 35–36 (Heb. 10. 30–31) is quickly followed by quotation of Hab. 2. 3–4 with the words 'he who is coming shall come and shall not tarry', implying that God's own judgment will be carried out by the coming Christ, who will bring those who endure their great reward (Heb. 10. 35–39).[64] Again, at the beginning of Hebrews (1. 6), Deut. 32. 43 LXX has been quoted as attesting angelic homage to the Son.

In Romans, Paul's quotation of 'rejoice, O gentiles, with his people' from the same verse (Deut. 32. 43) is particularly natural if he too takes it as prophesying homage to the messiah (Rom. 15. 11). Earlier in Romans, then, the execution of God's own vengeance by Christ is probably envisaged when 'vengeance is mine' is quoted from Deut. 32. 35 (Rom. 12. 19). Probably the same passage from the end of the Song of Moses, especially verses 41–43, lies behind the expectation of the revelation of the Lord Jesus with his angels for vengeance attested at II Thess. 1. 7–8.

These widespread early Christian interpretations of the Song of Moses, viewed together with the Assumption of Moses and the Qumran and rabbinic texts cited above, show that the prophecy of God's own vengeance could be understood as to be fulfilled by an emissary. This point confirms that when the thanksgiving of Judith takes up Deut. 32. 43 on divine vengeance (pp. 54–5, above), silence on a messiah should not be taken to rule out messianic hope.

Thus, even when Israel is distinctly said to be saved by God, not by one of his agents, the activity of angelic and messianic emissaries is not ruled out. This conclusion is consistent with Pesce's judgment that the 'no agent' slogans represent a tendency always in competition with others.[65] This is particularly clear in the exodus pattern, which repeatedly moulded messianic hope. Thus, in addition to Exod. 12. 12, the exodus narrative includes an express statement that God himself will fight Israel's battle: 'The Lord shall fight for you, and you shall hold your peace' (Exod. 14. 14).

This verse forms, in combination with its analogue in the Deuteronomic speech of the priest before battle (Deut. 20. 4), perhaps the most influential expression of a conviction which in its later manifestations has been judged sometimes to overshadow or replace hope for a messianic king. Once again, however, as the Pentateuchal contexts show, it does not exclude, and indeed is closely bound up with, the parts played by Moses and the angel and Israel's military leader(s); so the Deuteronomic speech was understood in Josephus's time to mean that Israel should go to war, 'taking God as supreme commander (στρατηγός), and electing as his lieutenant (ὑποστράτηγος) one man pre-eminent in valour' (Deut. 20. 1, 4, 9, as paraphrased in Josephus, *Ant.* 4, 297). The shift in this interpretation of Deuteronomy from the plural 'officers' of the Hebrew text and the LXX to one general under God suggests how readily the thought of God as general could combine with the thought of a messianic leader here below.

Similarly, when the thought of God as fighting the battle is taken up in biblical and post-biblical narratives of war and defence, it does not exclude the figures of Joshua, Ahijah, Jehoshaphat, Nehemiah, the king, or Judas Maccabaeus with an angel (Josh. 10. 14, 42; II Chron. 13. 3–4, 12; 20. 15, 29; Neh. 4. 20; Ps. 20. 7–9; II Macc. 11. 8–10). Likewise, the hand and arm of the Lord, which stand for the divine initiative and power in particular (e.g. Exod. 15. 6, 16), are considered as sustaining Moses and the king (Isa. 63. 12; Ps. 89. 22). Josephus, accordingly, envisages that the people of Jerusalem under Roman siege expected *both* heavenly aid *and* messianic deliverance.

Moreover, in another biblically-derived line of thought, the activity of the emissary can itself be described as God's own act. So in the divine vengeance as conceived in Lev. 26. 24–25, 'I, even I, will smite you' (v. 24), but will also bring 'the *sword* which executes the vengeance of the covenant' (v. 25, quoted in CD i 17, and again [here connected with the slaying of backsliders when the messiah of Aaron and Israel comes] in 19. 13). A comparable view of the redemptive work of the messiah as the work of God himself has already been noted at 1QM xi 1–7, cited above. This too has biblical antecedents. '*I* will pasture my flock and *I* will make them lie down' (italics represent the emphatic personal pronouns in the Hebrew), but also 'I will raise up over them one shepherd, and he shall shepherd them, my servant David' (Ezek. 34. 15 and 23); the coming Davidic reign will be God's own rule. Similarly, at the end of Obadiah, it is precisely when the saviours come up on mount Zion that 'the kingdom shall be the Lord's' (Obadiah 21). Comparably again, but with regard to past kingship, in Chronicles, the reign of the Israelite monarch manifests God's reign, for Solomon sits upon 'the throne of the kingdom of the Lord over Israel'

(I Chron. 28. 5), and enemies have to fight no less than 'the kingdom of the Lord in the hand of the sons of David' (II Chron. 13. 8). In the Pentateuch itself the people arrive at trust in God concurrently with trust in Moses as leader ('they believed in the Lord, and in his servant Moses'), and Moses then proclaims that the Lord is conqueror and king (Exod. 14. 31–15. 18).

This biblical pattern is followed in two thematically related messianic poems of the first century BC: the description of the coming righteous king of Israel in Ps. Sol. 17 leads up to the cry 'The Lord is our king for ever and ever' (Ps. Sol. 17. 46 [51]), and in Sib. 3. 47–49 (probably not long after the battle of Actium, at the time of an accumulation of divine honours to Octavian) the manifestation to humankind of the reign of the divine king corresponds to the dominion of a 'holy lord' (ἁγνὸς ἄναξ) on earth. Similarly, towards the end of the first century AD, the Man from the Sea in the apocalypse of Ezra is 'he whom the Highest, who by himself will deliver his creation, keeps a great while'; the ultimate sending of the messianic redeemer kept in heaven is God's own redemption of his creation, 'when the Highest begins to deliver those who are upon the earth' (II Esdras 13. 26, 29). Similarly again, later in the Roman period, a Hebrew apocalypse contrasts God's own action with human delay, and envisages that the arm of the Lord will be revealed (Isa. 51. 9; 53. 2), and then Messiah will appear.[66]

Silence, then, need not always be non-messianic, for a heavy emphasis on God's own action was fully compatible with recognition of the activity of a king or messiah. This point emerges with particular force from the biblical material, in which both are held together. In the examples of silence given above, there is no need to assume that messianic expectation is absent, as already noted with regard to Judith 16. 17. On the contrary, the pre-eminent importance of the exodus narrative, viewed as it was together with the long series of Pentateuchal and prophetic promises of a coming king, suggests that expectation of future deliverance would normally include expectation of leadership by a divinely appointed king. The Septuagint and Targums of the Pentateuch are among the most important witnesses to the widespread character of this specifically messianic hope.

4. Co-ordination of angelic and messianic deliverers

Yet, could the angelic figures who were envisaged as heaven-sent deliverers have been readily associated with earthly leaders? The answer seems to be Yes, given the exodus pattern of combined earthly, angelic and divine leadership, the prophecies of God's help for the messianic king, and the current beliefs in correspondence and association between human and angelic beings (see for example 'their angels' in Matt. 18. 10, and Peter's angel – thought to look like Peter – in Acts 12. 15); but it should be noted first that the deliverers considered in contemporary discussion of divine agents are not always unambiguously angelic. Some of the relevant figures are human beings who gained angelic status: Moses in Philo, Melchizedek in Philo and Qumran literature, Enoch in I Enoch.[67] In the biblical tradition a monarch is of course at least potentially angelic (II Sam. 14. 17, 20; 19. 28 [as the angel of God for insight]; Isa. 9. 5 [6] LXX 'angel of great counsel' [μεγάλης βουλῆς ἄγγελος]). This line of thought will be considered further in the following section.

In other cases the biblical language is and was ambiguous. The one like a son of man in Daniel, and the heaven-sent messengers of Exod. 23. 20; Mal. 3 and the Assumption of Moses, can all be interpreted as either human or angelic. The one like a son of man has been identified with Michael or Gabriel by some modern interpreters,[68] but was regularly understood as the messianic king at the end of the Second-Temple period (in I Enoch, II Esdras, Sib. 5. 414–33, discussed below); this royal messianic exegesis is related to the whole scene in Dan. 7 in the saying in the name of Akiba explaining the 'thrones' of v. 9 as two, 'one for him [the Almighty], and one for David' (baraitha in Hag. 14a, Sanh. 38b).[69] Secondly, Exod. 23. 20–21, on the angel or messenger sent before Israel, was understood in rabbinic exegesis as referring to an angel, sometimes identified as Metatron;[70] but it could also be applied to John the Baptist, probably in his capacity as Elijah (Mark 1. 2), and to Joshua (Justin, *Dialogue*, 75. 1–2), the latter being Moses's successor and a model of the royal deliverer. Thirdly, in Ass. Mos. 10. 2 the messenger (*nuntius*), consecrated and appointed in the highest to deliver the Israelites from their enemies, may be Michael, but is more probably Elijah or a priestly messiah; Moses himself in this work is 'holy and sacrosanct spirit', *sanctus et sacer spiritus*, and 'great messenger', *magnus nuntius* (11. 16–17).[71] In some important instances, therefore, the possibly angelic figures were or could be interpreted as human deliverers linked with the line of Israelite kings and rulers.

Nevertheless, it has already been made clear that in the Greek and Roman periods the thought of an angelic deliverer played a part in Jewish hopes, as is widely emphasized by commentators.[72] Particularly striking is Dan. 12. 1, where it can seem that 'Michael stands in the place of the messiah' (Lueken).[73] What seems to be less often noted is the degree of co-ordination between angelic and earthly deliverers, a co-ordination which had received particularly influential emphasis in the Hexateuch.[74] There the exodus is under the patronage of an angelic guide (Exod. 3. 2; 14. 19; 32. 34; 33. 2; perhaps also Num. 20. 16;[75] cf. Isa. 63. 9–11), naturally identified with 'the prince of the Lord's host' (ἀρχιστράτηγος) seen by Joshua (Josh. 5. 13–15); the emissary in Exod. 23. 20–21 can also be interpreted as angelic in the context of this series of references, as noted above.

The angel-guide, however, does not cancel the figures of Moses and Aaron, Eleazar and Joshua, but is viewed together and co-ordinated with them. Thus Moses and Aaron are commissioned by the angel who appeared in the burning bush (Exod. 3. 2). Accordingly, 'Moses and Aaron arose by the hand of the Prince of Lights' (CD v 17–18).[76] Likewise, 'God sent forth [Moses] as ruler and redeemer, with the hand of the angel who appeared to him in the bush' (Acts 7. 35). Similarly, Moses is to lead the people, but the angel is to precede him (Exod. 32. 34; 33. 2), and Joshua leads the army, but receives information from the angel-captain (Josh. 5. 13–6. 2). So in prayer incorporated into late prophecy the angelic and human leaders are mentioned together as the shepherds of the flock and the angel or spirit (on a probable interpretation of Isa. 63. 10–11, pp. 43–4, above).

Philo seems to presuppose this exodus pattern of both human and angelic guidance when he speaks of the Israelites in their time of future blessing as following a human leader, the great king of Num. 24. 7 LXX (discussed above), but also (a little later) as following a divine vision like that of the cloud in the wilderness (Philo, *Praem.* 95 and 165).[77] Similarly, the War Scroll exults in the assurance of angelic aid, above all from 'the Prince of Light', probably Michael; but it also hopes for priestly and royal deliverers (xi 1–7; cf. v 1), with reference to Num. 24. 17, as already noted.

The War Scroll is probably also influenced by a second biblical pattern noted above, that given by the prophecies of God's help to the messianic king. The Psalter is rich in examples, for instance 2. 4–9; 18. 50; 21. 1–7, 13; 22. 21; the execution of divine vengeance by an angel already noted in Ps. 35. 5–6 is requested in a prayer of David, and accordingly suggests that the messianic king can count on angelic aid. This pattern seems to be followed when, in Pseudo-Philo's *Biblical Antiquities*, Kenaz is appointed as ruler under angelic guidance, and defeats the Amorites with angelic aid (25, 2; 27, 10–12). This angelic dimension of the pattern of deliverance illuminates the belief in angelic and human correspondence also met in Daniel; in the War Scroll the God of angelic aid and messianic promise acts 'to raise up amongst the gods the princedom of Michael, and the dominion of Israel amongst all flesh' (xvii 7). It is evident that trust in patron angels did not exclude hope for messianic rulers; the two were co-ordinated, on the lines memorably sketched in the exodus narratives of the Torah. 'The dominion of Israel' in the War Scroll, in the light of xi 1–7, would have implied an Israelite king. Accordingly, the messianic interpretations of Dan.7 noted above would have been compatible with full acceptance of the importance of Michael in Dan. 12; conversely, by contrast with the exegesis of Lueken and others, the importance of Michael in Dan. 12 did not mean that there was no place for a messiah. Rather, as in the Christian messianism of the Revelation of John, the victory of Michael could bring in 'the kingdom of our God and the power of his messiah' (Rev. 12. 7–12 [10]).

The angelic deliverers, therefore, can be associated with the line of Israelite rulers which is central to messianic expectation. To sum up, not every passage now taken to attest the thought of such an angel will have been clearly so interpreted in the Greek and Roman world. Some angelic deliverers are human messianic figures who gained angelic status without losing their association with the line of Israelite rulers. Early interpretation of Dan. 7 is messianic, not angelic, and it is questionable whether a solely angelic figure was originally in view. Other passages refer to emissaries who could be either angelic or messianic. Nevertheless, the thought of angelic guidance was undoubtedly important. Characteristically, however, it was co-ordinated with the expectation of human messianic leaders, as in the influential pattern offered by the biblical exodus narratives and the prophecies of divine help for the messianic king. Messianic prototypes like Moses, Aaron and Joshua were guided by a patron angel. This pattern reappears in Philo and (combined with the prophecies of help to the king) in the War Scroll and Pseudo-Philo's *Biblical Antiquities*. Consequently, passages like Dan. 12. 1 which solely stress angelic deliverance should not be taken to exclude hope for messianic rulers of Israel. Rather, it is likely that angelic victory on high would have been expected to correspond to a messianic kingdom here below.

5. *A spiritual messiah*

Lastly, as suggested at the beginning of the previous section, some material which can be classified as angel-speculation can also properly be called messianic, for the messiah could be understood as the embodiment of an angel-like spirit. It is here that a particularly deep division between types of messianic hope has often been perceived. The view presented below can be summarized as follows. In much study of this subject, texts like II Esdras in which the messiah has angelic and superhuman traits have been viewed as exceptional, and as standing in contrast with a more wide-spread ancient Jewish perception of the messianic figure as thoroughly human; Christianity, it has been suggested, took up and developed the exceptional superhuman depiction, but in non-Christian Judaism, so far as a messianic figure was of concern, the more widespread human portrayal was continued.[78] Here, however, it is urged that spiritual and superhuman portrayals were more customary than has been commonly allowed; they take up the exalted characteristics of many messianic passages in the Hebrew scriptures, are widely attested in biblical interpretation from the time of the LXX Pentateuch onwards, and continue to be influential in rabbinic tradition. Their background is the view of God as lord of angels and spirits which emerges clearly in the LXX, and the messiah seems often to be envisaged as an embodied spirit. In its relation to earlier work on the subject, the argument presented here can appeal especially to elements in the surveys of messianism by E. Schürer and S. Mowinckel. Schürer noted that the Herodian apocalypses stand in the tradition of the messianism of the Hebrew Bible; and Mowinckel, although he distinguished in principle a this-worldly from a transcendental messianic conception, stressed that in practice some combination of the two is always met, and that widespread interest in messianic figures portrayed with this range of traits is attested by the LXX and Targum.[79] Comparably, H. Riesenfeld, in an argument noted at the beginning of this chapter, urged that the superhuman and transcendent as well as the earthly traits of the messiah are among the characteristics of the pre-exilic Davidic king inherited by the messianic king.[80]

Yet, although such portrayals were widespread in the Second-Temple period, they will have sometimes have run contrary to the emphasis on God's sole rule and human transience which likewise has biblical roots, came to characterize Zealot thought, and was evinced in the slogans on redemption without agents considered above. To judge from Christian sources, in the second century this emphasis marked statements of Jewish messianic belief viewed in contrast with Christian messianism. Thus, the Jews' messiah would be 'of merely human origin' (Trypho in Justin, *Dial.* 49, 1), 'from the race of David, but not from a virgin and from holy spirit, but from a woman and a man, as it is ordained for all to be begotten from seed'; in the war at the end of his reign in Jerusalem 'he would fall by the sword' (Hippolytus, *Ref.* 9, 30, 7–8, on Jewish messianic expectation).[81] It is likely that various internal and external factors contributed to attempts by Jewish communal authorities to divert attention from angelology and messianism in this period, or to shift the emphasis of messianic hope (compare the discussion of the Mishnah in this chapter, section 3, above). Nevertheless, the biblically-rooted and widespread depictions of a spiritual messiah continued to be lively, as is suggested by the apocalypses current at the beginning of the second century and the rabbinic traditions of the third century. These portrayals were not in principle incompatible with the humanity of the messiah, or inconsistent with depictions of the messiah as a conquering king; but they assumed the importance of the spirit in the human make-up, and continued the notion of a foreordained spiritual messiah known to God.

In these depictions the spirit is pre-existent in the sense of having existed before birth, or before the world, not necessarily from all eternity; but this point seems not to divide Jewish sources from otherwise comparable early Christian christological material so sharply as is often suggested.[82] Thus Origen's development of the Pauline phrase 'the image of the invisible God, the first-born of all creation' (Col. 1. 15) still left Christ in a lower realm than that of the unqualified transcendence of God the Father.[83] Moreover, Christian insistence on the pre-eminence of Christ did not make him a solitary celestial figure or take away a general resemblance between Christian and Jewish conceptions of pre-existence. In both communities, the messiah was one of a number of pre-existent entities. The pre-existence of the sanctuary is already important in the LXX (Exod. 15. 17 and else-where).[84] In rabbinic tradition the name of the messiah, or the messiah, is on a list of six or seven things that preceded the world or came into God's mind before the world: '. . . the throne of glory, the sanctuary, the name of the messiah' (baraitha in Pes. 54a); 'the throne of glory, king messiah, the law, Israel . . .' (Mid. Teh. 93, on Ps. 93. 3 [2] 'thy throne is ready from of old').[85] In Christian interpretation, Origen's statement of the eternal generation of the Son as a spirit who is the 'breath of the power of God', based on Wisdom 7. 22, 25–26 together with Prov. 8. 22 understood as 'the Lord created me as the beginning of his ways', is accompanied by the state-ment that there must always have been a creation for the Son to rule (*Princ.* 1, 2, 9–10). Compare the perhaps roughly contemporary Christian Sibylline statement that Adam and Eve saw Christ when he had first shone forth (Sib. 6, 18–19). With similarity as well as difference, at an earlier date, the church was imagined as pre-existing together with Christ, the 'female' created like Christ the 'male' (Gen. 1. 27, as interpreted in II Clem. 14. 1–2; for a pre-existent church see also Hermas *Vis.* 1, 3, 4; 2, 4, 1; Iren. *Haer.* 1, 1, 1, on the aeon-pair Man and Church in the thought of Ptolemy the Valentinian). Rabbinic emphasis on the ante-mundane creation even of the Torah can perhaps be opposed with some justice to the polemical emphasis which fourth-century Christians came to place on the eternal generation of the Son in forms of teaching directed against Arian views.[86] There is also, however, a considerable extent of common ground, especially in the period from the first century to the fourth, between ancient Jewish conceptions of a pre-existent messiah, among other pre-existent entities, and contem-porary Christian conceptions of the pre-existent Christ reigning over the church or creation.[87]

The shared background of all these ancient Jewish and early Christian sources, illustrated further in the discussion of angel-christology in chapter IV, below, is the conception of God as lord of godlike angels and spirits: 'God of the spirits', 'God of powers', 'king of gods', 'father of the spirits', 'lord' of the 'hosts' of heaven and earth (Num. 16. 22 LXX; Ps. 80 [79]. 5 LXX; Esther 4. 17r LXX = Rest of Esther 14. 12; and 4Q 400 2, 5; Heb. 12. 9; Exod. R. 15. 6, on 12. 2).[88] Angels might represent or inspire or become identified with individuals, as noted in the previous section, for example from Ass. Mos. 11. 16. 'The souls (spirits) of the righteous' are regularly envisaged as a group (I Enoch 22. 9; Dan. 3. 86 LXX; Wisdom 3. 1; Heb. 12. 23; II Esdras 7. 99; Sifre Deut. 344), a notion which seems already to be familiar in the third century BC, when Balaam is made to ask that his soul may die ἐν ψυχαῖς δικαίων (Num 23.10 LXX).[89]

Emphasis has often been laid on the closeness of the relationship between body and soul envisaged in biblical tradition, but the relative independence of souls or spirits is implied in many of these passages, and beliefs in the pre-existence and transmigration of souls have left an impression on ancient Judaism. Thus, in the apocryphal Prayer of Joseph quoted by Origen, Jacob is the embodiment of the archangel and ruling spirit named Israel (Origen, *Jo.* 2, 188–90 [31]). Again, Josephus on the transmigration of souls, in his description of the Pharisees and in the speech which he presents himself as having made at Jotapata against suicide (*BJ* 2, 163; 3, 374; cf. *Ap.* 2, 218), can be compared with the expectation of the return of eminent figures of the past under new names reflected in the Gospels (Mark 6. 14–16; 8. 28).[90] Philo was therefore probably not far from widely-held opinion when he imagined Moses praying 'Lord, lord, king of the gods' (Deut. 10. 17 as paraphrased in *Conf.* 173, on the heavenly 'powers'), and when he presented in Platonic fashion the view that angels are disembodied 'souls' which can also enter into mortals (*Gig.* 6–18; *Conf.* 174). So, in the book of Wisdom, Solomon inherited a good soul, or could rather say that he was a good pre-existent being who came accordingly into an undefiled body (Wisdom 8. 19–20). Compare the successive references, in Pauline discussion of prophecy in the congregation, to 'spirits', 'my spirit' (praying through glossolalia), and 'the spirits of the prophets' (I Cor. 14. 12, 14, 32); a distinction between the 'spirits' of the Christians and the angelic 'spirits' which inspire them is not clearly drawn.

Pre-existence, then, is suggested by biblical oracles such as Isa. 9. 5 (6) and Micah 5. 1 (2), as noted in the previous chapter; and it characterizes the glorious messianic figure depicted with traits of the Danielic Son of man in the Parables of Enoch, II Esdras and the Fifth Sibylline book, sketched above (chapter II, section 3) with special reference to II Esdras. This material has often been interpreted as presenting an angel-like messiah, with reference also to Septuagintal renderings including 'angel of great counsel' at Isa. 9. 5 (6).[91] The conception of an angelic messiah has sometimes been identified almost exclusively with the Jewish apocalypses; but the apocalyptic sources themselves show that the Danielic figure of the Son of man coming with the clouds of heaven had come to be associated closely with the series of messianic oracles in the Pentateuch, Prophets and Psalms.[92] Bousset urged that the royal title 'angel of great counsel' in the LXX Isaiah is only one of a number of indications, in the LXX and elsewhere, that the messiah of the biblical oracles was envisaged as a pre-existent angelic figure.[93]

An explanation on these lines is commended by convergence between a number of different sources: the LXX Pentateuch, Prophets and Psalms, the Psalms of Solomon, apocalypses of the late Herodian period, the Fifth Sibylline book, and rabbinic material. Together they suggest that the messianic king, a human figure endued with heavenly virtue and might, can be regarded as the manifestation and embodiment of a spirit sent by God. In the context of the LXX and rabbinic biblical exegesis, the exalted messianic figures of the apocalypses can be seen as arising from existing traditional interpretation of the Pentateuch, Prophets and Psalms.

Some instances of this interpretation should now be presented more fully, beginning from the Septuagint.

(a) In the LXX Isaiah, Hebrew which can be translated 'wonderful counsellor, mighty god' (9. 5) and presents the royal child as 'a kind of demi-god' (G. Buchanan Gray)[94] is rendered by 'angel of great counsel' (9. 6 LXX μεγάλης βουλῆς ἄγγελος). This phrase gains pictorial force from the possibility of identifying the child with the 'great light' (φῶς μέγα) announced at the beginning of the oracle, to shine on those who sit in darkness and in the land and shadow of death (9. 1 [2] LXX). The association of this 'light' with the messiah derives naturally from the immediate context in Isaiah, as is evident when 9. 1 (2) is quoted in Matt. 4. 16 (on Christ's preaching specifically in Capernaum) and Luke 1. 79 (from the canticle *Benedictus*). The association probably appears again when apocryphal additions to Matt. 3. 16 attest a 'great light' at the moment of Christ's baptism.[95]

The Septuagintal rendering of the whole passage in Isaiah was linked by R. Hanhart with Davidic hopes at the beginning of the Maccabaean age, as noted in chapter II, section 3, above;[96] but it also forms part of a broader Septuagintal interpretation of Isaianic messianic oracles, displaying a consistent emphasis on spiritual gifts which led I. L. Seeligmann to comment on 11. 2–4 LXX: 'Evidently, to the translator's mind, the figure of the prophetic Messiah dissolves itself into his image of the Hellenistic ecstatic.'[97] Within this broader interpretation the title 'angel' of Isa. 9. 5 (6) LXX seems consistent with 11. 2–4 LXX, 'a spirit of God shall rest upon him . . . a spirit of the fear of God shall fill him', and 61. 1, 'the spirit of the Lord is upon me, because he has anointed me'. This depiction has probably been influenced by the angelic and spirit-inspired biblical image of David himself (see chapter I, section 4 [b], above). According to II Samuel, David was as the angel of God for insight (II Sam. [LXX II Kgdms] 14. 17, 20; 19. 28 [27]); in his 'last words', embellished in the LXX with laudatory epithets, and including a reference to light and sunrise, he said that the spirit of God spoke by him, and God's word (λόγος) was upon his tongue (II Kgdms 23. 2–4). Isa. 11. 4 LXX recalls this passage in its rendering 'he shall strike the earth by the *word* of his mouth'. In the Qumran Psalms Scroll, as already noted (chapter I, section 4 [b], above), his last words lead to the statement that in his wisdom he was 'a light like the light of the sun, a scribe' who 'spoke in prophecy' (11QPs^a, col. 27). In some contrast as well as continuity with these passages on David, however, is the still stronger and repeated emphasis in Isaiah on the coming of a spirit. The title 'angel of great counsel' can then readily be taken as an acknowledgment of the spirit of wisdom upon and within the child.

(*b*) Elsewhere in the prophetic corpus the LXX renderings suggest that the messianic king has been associated with divinely-sent spirit. Amos 4. 13 LXX, quoted in chapter II, section 4, above, speaks of God as 'creating spirit, and announcing to men his Christ' (κτίζων πνεῦμα καὶ ἀπαγγέλλων εἰς ἀνθρώπους τὸν χριστὸν αὐτοῦ). As noted above, the reference to 'his Christ' fits the messianic development of the 'tabernacle of David' in Amos 9. 11, and is matched by a reference to the messianic adversary 'king Gog' in Amos 7. 1 LXX. The conquering messianic king implied in the two passages of LXX Amos last-mentioned is perceived here at 4. 13 in a passage on creation. The messiah is announced from the time of creation, and is mentioned just after the thunder and the 'wind' or 'spirit', which in this context recalls the spirit upon the face of the waters in Gen. 1. 2 (compare the rabbinic interpretation of this as 'the spirit of the messiah', discussed below).

Secondly, a remarkable court and constutional phrase in the Hebrew Bible occurs at Lam. 4. 20, where the king is spoken of as 'the breath of our nostrils', the breath of national life. The Hebrew (*ruah*) rendered here by 'breath' in English versions (so RV, REB, NRSV) can also be rendered 'spirit': 'The spirit of our nostrils, the anointed of the Lord, was caught in their pits.' In LXX, 'the spirit of our countenance, Christ the Lord (p. 145, below), was caught in their works of ruin' (πνεῦμα προσώπου ἡμῶν χριστὸς κυρίου συνελήμφθη ἐν ταῖς διαφθοραῖς αὐτῶν). This Greek is a straightforward rendering of the Hebrew, but within the larger biblical context of the translators and hearers or readers the Lord's Anointed is associated once again with creation and the breathing of life into newly-created humanity, in a passage which in the Greek speaks of the coming king himself as 'spirit'.

These two verses should not be over-pressed into a systematic doctrine of the person of the messiah, but they can properly be taken to show that the messianic king was associated with creation and divinely sent spirit(s), and could himself be understood as a spiritual messiah, in touch with or embodying a spirit sent from God. This understanding was expressed in terms of an angelic spirit in Isa. 9. 5 (6) LXX, considered above. With this approach to the messiah, attested in Greek translations probably current in the Hasmonaean period, there may be compared the view of Moses as a 'holy spirit' or 'mediator spirit' expressed in the Herodian period in the Assumption of Moses (11. 15, *sanctus et sacer spiritus*) and Ps.-Philo's *Biblical Antiquities* (9. 8, *mediator spiritus*, in a quotation from Gen. 6. 3).[98]

(*c*) Already in the LXX Pentateuch, the angelic character of the messiah was also suggested by Balaam's prophecy that 'a star has marched forth from Jacob, and a sceptre shall arise out of Israel' (Num. 24. 17), since the stars belonged to the angelic 'host of heaven' (Deut. 4. 19; cf. I Kings 22. 19). In the LXX rendering, discussed in chapter II, section 2, above, 'a star shall spring out of Jacob, and a man shall rise up out of Israel'. The impression of a man linked with a star left by this oracle emerges again in the reign of Hadrian from Aramaic-speaking Judaean circles in the nickname Bar Kokhba, 'son of the star', playing on the patronymic of Simeon ben Koseba[99] (*Barchochebas*, Justin Martyr, *I Apol.* 31, and Eusebius, *HE* 4, 6, 2); for Akiba's application of Num. 24. 17 to him see Talmud Yerushalmi, Taanith 2, 8, 69d (baraitha in the name of R. Simeon b. Johai). The assertion that the Jewish leader claimed to be a 'luminary come down from heaven to shine upon those in distress' (Eusebius, *HE* 4, 6, 2) has a clear polemical ring, but its explanation of the nickname need not be far astray. A probably later midrash comparably envisages an angel- or star-like messiah as standing radiant on the temple-roof and proclaiming, 'Meek ones (cf. Isa. 61. 1), the time for your redemption has come; and if you do not believe in me, look at my light which shines upon you' (Pes. R. 36. 12, with reference to Isa. 60. 1–3, 'thy light').[100] The angelic associations of the star-verse recall the function of stars as signs of the celestial position and attributes of sovereigns in ruler-cults.[101]

The influence of the star-prophecy, and its close association with Davidic hope, is illustrated by its combination with Isa. 11. 1–2, on the pattern of the Pentateuchal-prophetic links noted already in the LXX Pentateuch in the previous chapter. Early Christian instances are Rev. 22. 16, 'the root and offspring of David, and the bright and morning star'; Justin Martyr, *I Apol.* 32. 12–13, 'a star shall rise out of Jacob, and a flower shall come up from the root of Jesse'; compare Commodian, *Carm. apol.* 291, 'a man shall rise up in Israel from the root of Jesse'.[102] With this series there should be noted the looser link between Num. 24. 17 and Isa. 11. 1–2 in Test. Judah 24, where the star will come forth and a man will arise like the sun of righteousness (v. 1, linking Num. 24. 17 and Mal. 3. 20 [4. 2] with a hint at *anatolé* [see below] in the sense of sunrise; compare the similar development of the star-verse in the priestly context of Test. Levi 18. 3–4, cited above); and the man shall be shoot, fountain, sceptre, and stem (vv. 4–5, including titles from Isa. 11). The present form of Test. Judah 24 will have been valued by Justin Martyr's Christian predecessors and contemporaries, but is likely to preserve non-Christian Jewish material.

To turn to sources transmitted in the Jewish community, in the targums Targ. Isa. 11. 1, 'And a king shall come forth from the sons of Jesse, and a Messiah from his sons' sons shall grow up', recalls Num. 24. 17 in Targum Onkelos, 'when a king shall arise from Jacob, and there shall grow up a Messiah from Israel', and in Targum Ps.-Jonathan, 'when a mighty king shall reign from the house of Jacob, and there shall grow up a messiah and mighty sceptre from Israel'. In each verse the same interpretation 'king . . . messiah' is given, representing 'shoot . . . branch' in Isaiah, and 'star . . . sceptre' in Numbers, respectively; and the second part of each verse has 'there shall grow up', a rendering which corresponds closely to 'shall grow' in Isaiah, but is much freer as a translation of 'shall rise' in Numbers. It seems likely that in the targumic tradition these verses from Isaiah and Numbers have been mutually influential, the Pentateuchal versions accepting 'shall grow' from Isaiah, and Isaiah receiving the formulaic interpretation 'king . . . messiah' from the Pentateuch.

Finally, to turn to writings from Hasmonaean or Herodian times, Ps. Sol. 17 draws on both Num. 24. 17 and Isa. 11. 4 in its evocation of the longed-for son of David (see vv. 23–24, 27 [21–22, 24]); and the blessing of the Prince of the Congregation (1QSb = 1Q28b, col. v) follows Isa. 11, but then echoes Num. 24. 17 as well as Gen. 49. 10, as J. T. Milik has shown.[103] Probably both the Targums and the early Christian combinations of the two prophecies are influenced by a long-standing association of the star-oracle in Numbers with the Jesse-oracle in Isaiah, already current in the Second-Temple period, as is suggested by its emergence in Ps. Sol. 17; 1QSb; Test. Judah 24; and Rev. 22. 16.

(*d*) To return to the LXX Prophets, the Davidic royal title *ṣemaḥ*, 'shoot' or 'branch', considered already for its links with Jehoiachin and Zerubbabel (see chapter II, section 1, above), was rendered in the LXX by *anatolé*, 'springing up' (Jer. 23. 5; Zech. 3. 9 [8]; 6. 12), a noun used not only for growth but also for sunrise or star-rise. It is understood in the latter sense, and identified with the 'great light' in the Isaianic oracle of the 'angel of great counsel', in the canticle *Benedictus* (Luke 1. 78–79): 'because of the bowels of mercy of our God, whereby the dayspring from on high shall visit us, to "shine on those who sit in darkness and the shadow of death"' (see Isa. 9. 1 [2]). This understanding will have influenced the sequential quotation of Num. 24. 17 (star and man) and Zech. 6. 12 (man called *anatolé*) by Justin Martyr, *Dial.* 106. 4. Association of these two texts was facilitated by the Septuagintal form of Num. 24. 17, in which ἀνατέλλω, 'spring up', the verb cognate with the noun *anatolé*, renders Hebrew *darakh*, 'march forth'; this translation probably already attests the currency of the title *anatolé* understood as 'dayspring'.

The angelic implications of this title come out clearly in Philo's discussion of 'rising' (*anatolé*) in connection with the move *'from* the sunrising' (Gen. 11. 2 LXX) by the founders of the Tower of Babel (Philo, *Conf.* 60–3). Quoting 'Behold, a man whose name is *anatolé*' (Zech. 6. 12), Philo says that *anatolé* would be a strange name for a 'man' of body and soul, and rather denotes the 'man' as the incorporeal first-born who fully conforms to the divine image, the eldest son whom the Father of all 'raised up' (ἀνέτειλε). This is the figure whom Philo later in this treatise calls 'the Man according to the image' – the heavenly man from the double creation of heavenly and earthly man indicated by the pair of verses Gen. 1. 27; 2. 7 (*Qu. Gen.* 1. 4) – the Logos, 'the eldest of the angels, as it were Archangel' (Philo, *Conf.* 146).[104] *Anatolé* therefore forms another of the Septuagintal titles which were associated with an understanding of the messianic figure as a luminary and a heavenly being.

(*e*) A similar understanding of the LXX Psalter emerges in the Christian testimony-tradition of the second century, and probably derives from pre-Christian Jewish interpretation. The testimonies in the second century included proofs of Christ's glorious pre-existence in quotations, sometimes conflated, from Psalms 72 (71) and 110 (109). Thus Christ was 'before day-star and moon', with allusion to Ps. 110 (109). 3 and Ps. 72 (71). 5 (Justin, *Dial.* 45, 4); and 'David proclaimed that "before sun and moon" he should be "begotten of the womb" according to the "counsel" of the Father', with allusion also to Ps. 72 (71). 17, 'before the sun', and Isa. 9. 6 (5) LXX, 'angel of great counsel', discussed above (Justin, *Dial.* 76. 7).[105] The Greek text of Ps. 72 (71). 17 accordingly came to include in some copies reference to moon as well as sun.[106] Do these two LXX psalms witness to an opinion current in the Second-Temple period, that the messiah existed in glory before the world?

This testimony-cluster is old, and its christological interpretation draws on psalms linked by title and content with Davidic kingship.[107] With all allowance for innovation, therefore, the Christian testimonies might be expected to have some contact with Jewish interpretation.[108] Such contact is evident in the case of Ps. 72. 17, where Hebrew which can be rendered 'before the sun his name shall endure' or 'before the sun *Yinnon* is his name' was applied in rabbinic interpretation to the existence of the messiah's name 'before the sun' (baraitha in Pes. 54a; the name of the messiah is one of the seven things created before the world, as shown by this text; Targ. Ps. 72. 17, 'before the sun was, his [king messiah's] name was appointed').[109] This widely attested application of v. 17 in turn suggests that by the end of the Second-Temple period 'before the moon' in v. 5 and 'before the sun' in v. 17, verses which in the LXX are both applied to the lasting continuance of the glorious king, had come to be taken temporally, even though they can be understood as indications of place rather than time.[110] Verse 5 is linked with the messianic reign in a calculation of the length of the reign attributed to R. Jose ha-Gelili, from the years before Bar Kokhba; in this exegesis 'from generation to generations' is interpreted as three generations, that is sixty years (Midrash Tehillim 90, 17, on Ps. 90. 15; cf. Babylonian Talmud, Sanh. 99b). This is little in comparison with other such calculations, but by the same token it may reflect a lively and relatively realistic hope, and it attests the established messianic associations of v. 5. It seems likely, as A. M. Goldberg holds, that the temporal interpretation of Ps. 72. 5, 17 on the king and his name has influenced the Parables of Enoch on the royal Son of man: 'And before the sun and the signs [cf. Gen. 1. 14] were created, before the stars of the heavens were made, his name was named before the Lord of spirits' (I Enoch 48. 3).[111] The view that the psalm was already interpreted in this way before the end of the Second-Temple period is further supported by Ps. Sol. 17, discussed below, and by the similar Septuagintal and Targumic understanding of Micah 5. 1, noted above, which arises very naturally from the Hebrew of Micah.

This view in turn bears on assessment of Ps. 110 (109). 3 LXX. Here a divine oracle of the enthronement and dominion of 'my lord', 'on the day of your power, in the brightness of the holy ones', is understood to declare: 'From the womb before the daystar (πρὸ ἑωσφόρου) I have begotten you.' The verse has evidently been associated with Ps. 2. 8 (7), 'This day have I begotten you'; 'before' renders Hebrew which has been understood as a form of the preposition *min*, 'from' (this is the interpretation followed in the transcription of the Hebrew in Origen's Hexapla), and taken probably in the sense of 'earlier than'. P. Volz, cited above, followed and developed in a fresh review of the passage by J. L. W. Schaper, found here a messiah depicted as pre-existent and angel-like, and comparable in both respects with the messianic figure of the Parables of Enoch (46. 1; 48. 6; 62. 7).[112] The Anointed of the apocalypse of Ezra in II Esdras dies at the end of his four-hundred-year reign, but is also pre-existent (7. 26–29; cf. 12. 31–32; 13. 25–16). In Ps. 110. 3 the Targum is messianic, but follows an interpretation of the Hebrew in which, by contrast with the LXX, there is no association with Ps. 2 on begetting, no discernment of the preposition *min*, and consequently no opening for a temporal reference to origin. In the LXX version here, therefore, there is not the contact with targumic interpretation of the same verse which appeared in Ps. 72, but rabbinic interpretation of Ps. 72 comes together with the Parables of Enoch to suggest that the LXX interpretation, understood on the lines sketched above, would not have been isolated. In Ps. 110 (109). 3 the LXX translator probably used 'before' in a temporal sense; this could have been taken just as 'before dawn', an interpretation found in some Christian application of the text to Christ's nativity (so Tert. *Marc.* 5, 9, 7), but it would lend itself at least as naturally to the sense 'before the daystar came to be'. Taken in this sense, as seems likely to have occurred in the Second-Temple period, at the same time it juxtaposed the messianic king with a star, an angelic power.

In the LXX Psalter, therefore, Ps. 72 (71), and probably also Ps. 110, were texts taken in the Second-Temple period as prophecies attesting the view that the messianic king is a glorious pre-existent figure; Ps. 110 sets him beside a star in a way which recalls Num. 24. 17.

A series of Septuagintal texts has now been surveyed, from the Pentateuch, Prophets, and Psalms: Isa. 9. 1 (2); 9. 5 (6); Amos 4. 13; Lam. 4. 20; Num. 24. 17, regularly linked with Isa. 11. 1–2; Zech. 6. 12, with other occurrences of *anatolé*; Ps. 72 (71). 5, 17; Ps. 110 (109). 3. From these it can be seen that the messianic king was envisaged, variously yet consistently, as an angel-like spirit waiting to appear and be embodied; the shining of a 'great light' corresponds to the birth of a child who is 'angel of great counsel', and the rising of a 'star' to the coming of a 'man', the man whose very name is 'dayspring', and who was before sun, moon and daystar.

These expectations, which are also found in other sources noted in discussion of each text above, can be compared with expectations concerning the heavenly sanctuary which waits above to be revealed, the 'ready dwelling' in the LXX. Hopes for a sanctuary which has already been divinely prepared are widely attested among Jews from the third century BC onwards, as noted already (Exod. 15. 17 LXX; Isa. 54. 11 LXX; Wisdom 9. 8).[113] They can also be compared with the depiction of the great enemy of the messianic king as the embodiment of an evil spirit, the archdemon Beliar; this appears in Sib. 3, 63–74, a Jewish text probably from the Hasmonaean or Herodian period, and its early Christian counterpart Asc. Isa. 4. 1–18.[114]

(*f*) Against this broad background it is possible to discern traces of a notion of pre-existence in lines on God's foreknowledge of the messianic king in Ps. Sol. 17. 23 (21), 47 (42):

> 'Behold, Lord, and raise up for them their king, the son of David
> > at the time which thou knowest, O God . . .
> This is the beauty of the king of Israel, of which God has knowledge,
> > to raise him up over Israel, to instruct him.'

God knows the time when the king is to be raised up, as in Ps. Sol. 18. 6 (5), where the time is the 'day of choice', the day chosen by God; God also knows the king's 'beauty' or 'majesty' (εὐπρέπεια). This noun is one of those used to describe the king's beauty in Greek versions of Ps. 45 (44). 4, 'in your glory and beauty' (LXX variant recorded by Origen in the Hexapla) and 110 (109). 3, 'in the beauty of the holy one' (Theodotion).[115] These textual witnesses both represent translations which could have come into being later than the Psalms of Solomon, although this is not necessarily so; attempts to revise LXX passages will have been made in the first century BC, and some forms or antecedents of the second-century version ascribed to Theodotion will certainly have circulated in the Herodian period.[116] In any case, however, the occurrence of εὐπρέπεια in Greek versions of these royal psalms is a pointer to contexts likely to be important for interpretation of the psalmodic portrait of a coming king in Ps. Sol. 17. Both the passages concerned in the Psalms of David are exalted in style. Ps. 45 is a hymn to the king, considered further in its Greek form in the following chapter as an instance of Jewish royal praise; its lines on the king's beauty played an important part in second- and third-century Christian concepts of Christ.[117] In Ps. 110 (109). 3, which has just been discussed, according to Theodotion, 'in the beauty of the holy one' immediately follows 'with you is the rule in the day of your power', and precedes 'from the womb before the daystar I have begotten you'; it is therefore associated both with the king's epiphany on the day of his power, and with his origin 'before the daystar'.

It seems likely, then, that in Ps. Sol. 17. 47 (42) the king's beauty is considered to be known to God beforehand. It can have been envisaged as in heaven ready to be revealed, on the lines of the expectations about the revelation of the heavenly sanctuary – the 'ready dwelling' in the LXX – which are widely attested among Jews from the third century BC onwards, as just noted. This way of thinking is applied to a messianic figure in passages including the Lucan canticle *Nunc Dimittis*: 'thy salvation, that which thou hast prepared' (Luke 2. 30–31); II Esdras 12. 42, 'the anointed whom thou hast kept' (compare I Peter 1. 4, 'kept in heaven'); and II (Syriac) Baruch 29. 3; 30. 1 ('the messiah shall begin to be revealed . . . shall return in glory'). Schürer and his revisers regarded the Psalms of Solomon as contrasting with the Parables of Enoch and II Esdras precisely in the presentation of a thoroughly human and non-pre-existent messianic figure.[118] Nevertheless, expectation of the kind just discerned in Ps. Sol. 17 is within the range of ideas independently suggested by Ps. Sol. 18. 6 (5), cited above, on the day chosen by God for the 'raising up' or 'bringing back' (ἄναξις) of the anointed, or (on T. W. Manson's conjecture) his 'showing' (ἀνάδειξις, cf. Luke 1. 80).[119] In Ps. Sol. 17–18, then, it seems likely that the glory and beauty of the Davidic king are known to God, waiting in heaven for the appointed time when the son of David is to be raised up.

(*g*) It then seems probable that at least some clouds of glory trail about the messianic figures of the 'Messianic Rule' of 1QSa, where they are presented in what can appear a this-worldly manner as presiding over the corporate dinner of bread and new wine (1QSa = 1Q28, ii 11–22). This takes place 'when God engenders the messiah' (lines 11–12). The translation 'engenders', now adopted by G. Vermes, follows the text *yôlîd* read by D. Barthélemy, rather than the emendation *yôlîk*, 'leads forth', which was suggested by J. T. Milik and followed by Barthélemy in his translation in the first edition, by Vermes in his earlier translations, and by others, including J. H. Charlesworth and L. T. Stuckenbruck in their edition.[120] 'Engenders' should probably be understood in the sense 'causes to be born', with the implication that God brings the pre-existent spirit of the messiah to birth. For the present purpose it is unnecessary to decide whether 'the messiah' here (*ha-mashiah*) is royal (so F. M. Cross) or priestly (so G. Vermes); it is enough to note that this precise and almost matter-of-fact description of the messiahs at dinner seems to reflect, in what is said about 'the messiah', the notions of divine origin and pre-existence traced above in the LXX and the Psalms of Solomon, probably here with an echo of the use of the same verb *yld* in Ps. 2. 7, 'I, on this day, have begotten you.'[121] Among the texts made known for the first time through Qumran discoveries, it can be more generally compared with 1QH xi (formerly iii) lines 7–10, on the birth of a man child, where Isa. 66. 7 is echoed in association with titles from Isa. 9. 5 (6) (as noted in connection with the book of Isaiah in chapter I, section 3, above). Here the echo of Isa. 9. 5 (6), discussed in its LXX form in this section, above, suggests the wonderful birth of a superhuman figure.

(*h*) Lastly, two further messianic themes which contribute to the figure of a spiritual messiah are common to non-rabbinic and rabbinic Jewish literature, but emerge most clearly in the latter.

First, the messiah is light, or connected with light. This theme has already been noticed in several biblical passages which certainly or probably received a messianic interpretation in the Second-Temple period: the 'great light' of Isa. 9. 1 (2), Balaam's star, *anatolé* as the rising of a luminary, and the association of the messianic king with sun, moon and daystar in Pss. 72 and 110. It is particularly closely connected with the Davidic king, 'the lamp of Israel' (II Sam. 21. 17).[122] The theme emerges again in rabbinic sources. Thus *Nehora*, 'light', is a name of the messiah, on the basis of Dan. 2. 22, 'He reveals the deep and secret things: he knows what is in the darkness, and the light (*nehira*) dwells with him.' This teaching, found in different forms at Ber. R. 1, 6, on 1. 1, and Lam. R. 1. 16, 51, was probably current in fourth-century Tiberias.[123] It is an interpretation of a Danielic text, 2. 22, which is often cited to confirm that God is the revealer surrounded by light (e.g. Cant. R. 8. 6, 1) who perceives the hidden things of darkness (Num. R. 16. 8, on 13. 2); the importance of Dan. 2. 22 is already apparent in Paul (I Cor. 2. 10; 4. 5). This messianic interpretation of the Danielic verse presupposes that God will reveal the messiah, who dwells in heaven with him as a being of light.

This comment on Daniel stands beside much other rabbinic treatment of the light of the messiah, for example in connection with Ps. 132. 17, 'I have prepared a lamp for mine anointed'.[124] By virtue of the perpetual light prepared by Aaron (Lev. 24. 1–4), Israel will be counted worthy to greet the light of king messiah, as it says, 'There will I make the horn of David to flourish, I have prepared a lamp for my anointed', and (from Ps. 122. 1), 'I was glad when they said unto me, We will go into the house of the Lord' (Lev. R. 31. 11, in the name of R. Hanin, active in early fourth-century Sepphoris). Here it seems likely that the light of the messiah is 'prepared' in the heavenly Jerusalem sanctuary, into which Israel will rejoice to enter when it is revealed (Ps. 122. 3 is referred to the heavenly Jerusalem in the Targum). The angel-like aspect of the messiah accordingly continued to be vivid, as in his appearance on the temple-roof in Pes. R. 36. 12, quoted above. As is noted below, when he comes, the radiance which Adam lost will be restored.

Secondly, an overlapping series of rabbinic interpretations treat of the soul of the messiah and his links with the, or a, spirit of God. Three examples are offered by teachings probably current in third-century Tiberias. Thus, when Joseph had been sold and he and the other tribal patriarchs were preoccupied with their own concerns, God was preoccupied with creating 'the light of the messiah', probably understood here to be his soul – for 'it came to pass at that time that Judah went down' and became the father of Perez (Ber. R. 85. 1, on Gen. 38. 1, in the name of Samuel bar Nahman, who taught in Tiberias in the later third century).[125] The birth of Jesse's ancestor Perez was regarded as the beginning of messianic redemption, a view which has significant antecedents in the books of Chronicles (I Chron. 2. 3–15, noted in discussion of the Chronicler in the previous chapter, section 1; cf. Ruth 4. 18–22), and probably also in the placing of Gen. 38 within the Joseph narrative (chapter I, section 3, above), and has perhaps influenced the naming of Tamar as well as Judah in the Matthaean genealogy of Christ.[126] So, again in the name of Samuel bar Nahman, in a teaching recalling patristic thought on recapitulation, it was said that the created things marred by Adam's sin will not return to perfection until the son of Perez comes (Ber. R. 12. 6, linking Gen. 2. 4, 'these are the generations of heaven and earth in their creation', with Ruth 4. 18, 'these are the generations of Perez').[127] The first of these things is the radiant light of Adam, to be restored in the days of the messiah.[128]

Somewhat comparably, the messiah seems to be envisaged as a spirit waiting in heaven to come forth in an exegesis of Isa. 57. 16 attributed to contemporaries of Samuel b. Nahman in Tiberias: R. Assi, pupil of R. Johanan (Yeb. 63b), or Tanhum bar Hiyya (Ber. R. 24. 4), or a number of teachers in common. The prophetic passage is used in this instance as a proof-text for the belief that the messiah would not come until the appointed number of souls had been accomplished. A reference to the number of souls could be discerned at the end of Isa. 57. 16, which can be rendered 'For I will not contend for ever . . . for the spirit shall be faint before me, and the souls which I have made.' In the midrash the argument is presented as follows. 'King messiah will never come, until all the souls which were envisaged for creation have been created. What is the proof? "And the souls which I have made" (Isa. 57. 16)' (Ber. R. 24. 4, on Gen. 5. 1).[129] Here 'the spirit' detained in weakness before God is probably the spirit of the messiah, waiting for the full number of 'the souls which I have made' – the souls written in 'the book of the generations of Adam' (Gen. 5. 1).

This proof, current in a milieu in which Greek was known, perhaps builds on Isa. 57. 16 LXX, or the interpretation attested in it.[130] 'King messiah will never come' (*'eyn . . . ba*) recalls the second part of this verse in the LXX translation: 'for the spirit shall come forth from me, and I made all breath'. 'Shall come forth' (ἐξελεύσεται) has been used of 'the law' and 'salvation' in 51. 4–5, and of the rod from the stem of Jesse in 11. 1, here recalling the same Greek in the LXX rendering of the messianic prophecy Num. 24. 7, 'a man shall come forth'. In the specifically Isaianic context, the understanding of this verse as a prophecy that the spirit shall come forth links it with the past prophecy that 'the spirit of the Lord shall rest upon him' (Isa. 11. 1) and the shortly ensuing declaration that 'the spirit of the Lord is upon me' (Isa. 61. 1). The LXX rendering with its context therefore suggests the possibility that the spirit here is messianic, although it does not compel this interpretation; but in any case it makes the verse into a definite oracle of a spirit which 'shall come forth' from God.[131] In the rabbinic proof, based on the Hebrew text, it is assumed that the spirit of the messiah 'shall come forth', as the LXX rendering suggests – in the end; but that it must 'be faint', as the Hebrew suggests – for the time being.

A third example of a link between the spirit of the messiah and a spirit of God is formed by two interpretations ascribed to Simeon b. Laqish (Resh Laqish), an earlier Tiberian teacher of the third century. In the first of these, the spirit of God (Targums 'from before the Lord') upon the waters (Gen. 1. 2) is 'the spirit of king messiah, as you read [in Isa. 11. 2], And the spirit of the Lord shall rest upon him' (Ber. R. 1. 4, on Gen. 1. 2). Here the train of thought seems close to one which is suggested by Amos 4. 13 LXX, quoted already in this section, above: 'creating the spirit, and announcing to men his messiah' (κτίζων πνεῦμα καὶ ἀπαγγέλλων εἰς ἀνθρώπους τὸν χριστὸν αὐτοῦ). Resh Laqish is also said, however, to have identified the spirit of Gen. 1. 2 with the spirit of Adam, in connection with the words in Ps. 139. 5 ascribed to Adam, 'Thou hast fashioned me after and before' (Tanhuma Buber, Leviticus, 16b, Tazria 2, on Lev. 12. 1–2).[132] In these two comments the same God-sent spirit seems to be envisaged as the spirit of the first man and of the messiah. When viewed together, these interpretations recall Philo on the heavenly 'man according to the image' (Gen. 1. 26–27) who is also the dayspring-man of messianic prophecy (Philo, *Conf.* 62, 146, discussed above), and the view held by some Ebionites that Christ came again 'as he once came in Adam' (Epiphanius, *Pan.* 30, 3); not dissimilarly, and with special closeness to the two interpretations in the name of Resh Laqish, the Clementine Homilies teach that 'the man fashioned by the hands of God had the holy spirit of Christ' (ἐὰν τῷ ὑπὸ χειρῶν θεοῦ κυοφορηθέντι ἀνθρώπῳ τὸ ἅγιον Χριστοῦ μὴ δῷ τις ἔχειν πνεῦμα . . ., *Hom. Clem.* 3, 20, 1).[133] The resemblances of these third-century rabbinic interpretations to features of Septuagintal, Philonic and early Christian teaching suggest a common dependence on Hellenically-influenced Jewish thought.[134]

The Psalms of Solomon and these later Galilaean rabbinic interpretations have now been added to the mainly Septuagintal material considered above. The whole series of passages indicates that, from the Greek period of Jewish history to the later Roman empire, the messianic king was continuously taken to have what may be called a spiritual aspect. He was a star-like being of light, an angelic spirit hidden with God from of old in celestial beauty until the day when he should come forth as the conquering king of Israel. The continuity of this view is fostered by a continuously lively sense of 'the spirits' as impinging on 'all flesh' (Num. 16. 22 LXX).

It is within this long-standing and continuously attested tendency in interpretation of messianic prophecy that the pre-existent and angel-like messiah of late Herodian apocalyptic and Sibylline writing should be located, as suggested above. To the sketch based especially on II Esdras given in the previous chapter, where the integration of Danielic with Pentateuchal and prophetic oracles was brought out, there should be added here a reference to the series of passages on pre-existence in these sources.[135] In the apocalypse of Ezra, the glorious messiah has been 'kept by the Most High for the end', hidden with 'those who are with him' (II Esdras 12. 32; 14. 52; cf. 13. 26; 14. 9). In the Parables of Enoch, his name was uttered before the Lord of spirits before the sun and signs (I Enoch 48. 3, discussed in connection with Ps. 72 in this section, above); he was chosen and hidden by God from the beginning (48. 6; 62. 7), and was seen by Enoch in heaven, with his countenance full of graciousness, like a holy angel (I Enoch 39. 6–7; 46. 1–4); the glory of the Chosen One is for ever and ever, for he is indwelt by the spirit of wisdom and the spirit of the righteous who have fallen asleep (I Enoch 49. 2–4, discussed in connection with the election of David in Chronicles in chapter II, section 1, above).

The Fifth Sibylline book, compiled after the destruction of Jerusalem by Titus, and probably at the end of the first century or in the early years of the second, is close in time to the apocalypse of Ezra which forms the bulk of II Esdras; it probably represents hopes current among the Jews of Alexandria and Egypt. Among the prophecies likely to be important in their background are Num. 24. 7, 17 LXX on the 'man' and the 'star', and Isa. 19. 20 LXX on 'the man who shall save' the Jews of Egypt. In this book of the Sibyllines the pre-existence of the expected deliverer is implied by an oracle of the advent of the 'blessed man', sceptre in hand, 'from the expanses of the skies' (Sib. 5. 414–5, ἦλθε γὰρ οὐρανίων νώτων . . .); the link of the messianic figure with light appears when the Sibyl foretells that he will rebuild the city and the sanctuary with a brightness exceeding sun, moon and stars, so that the faithful and righteous behold and hymn the longed-for appearance of the glory of God (420–8; cf. Isa. 60. 1–3, 19–20). The combination of prophetic and Danielic allusions in the passage confirms that this is indeed the messianic 'man'.[136] Elsewhere in this Sibylline book the expected king, comparably, is 'sent from God' (108, θεόθεν . . . πεμφθείς);[137] and it is not improbable that a deliverer is also intended when the Sibyl foretells that 'a great star shall come from heaven' to burn up the sea, 'Babylon' and Italy (158, ἥξει δ'οὐρανόθεν ἀστὴρ μέγας).[138] The four lines on a 'pre-eminent man from the sky' (256, ἀπ' αἰθέρος ἔξοχος ἀνήρ) should not, however, be included in this list, as they are probably one of the Christian oracles added to the Jewish Sibyllines; but they begin with a further instance of a spiritual deliverer appearing from heaven, and as a whole they show how straightforwardly Christians could continue the depiction of a heavenly and spiritual messiah which has just been outlined from non-Christian Jewish sources, a point considered further in the following chapter.[139] The three non-Christian Jewish oracles cited here are of course veiled in Sibylline fashion. There is a fair probability that Sib. 5. 158 takes up the widespread conception of the messiah as a star, illustrated above, a good probability that Sib. 5. 108 refers to a king coming from heaven, and in Sib. 5. 414–15 a clear implication that the king was in heaven before his advent.

The Fifth Sibylline book thus stands together with the Parables of Enoch and the apocalypse of Ezra as a witness to hopes for a messianic deliverer who is already pre-existent with God in heaven.

Finally, in the Parables of Enoch and II Esdras, biblical theophany passages relating to God himself are sometimes strikingly applied to a messianic figure. Examples are Parables of Enoch 52. 6, where the hills melt like wax (Ps. 97. 5; Micah 1. 3–4) before the presence of the Chosen One; II Esdras 13. 3–4, where when the man from the sea turned his countenance to look, all things trembled (Ps. 104. 32), and those who heard his voice burned up like wax (Ps. 97. 5 again, probably in combination with the royal prophecy Isa. 11. 4).[140] Outside these books, Isa. 66. 18–20, 'they shall see my glory . . . they shall bring your brethren . . . as a gift to the Lord', are significantly adapted in Ps. Sol. 17. 34–35 (31–32), giving 'to see his glory' [the king's] as well as 'to see the glory of the Lord'.[141] This development may be compared with the hint at pre-existence in this source discussed under (*f*), above.

Such uses of the biblical theophany passages indicate a messiah endued with divine traits, which in the outlook of the Second-Temple period would have been classified as angelic characteristics; but they also suggest that some biblical theophanies could be understood to speak of an angelic messiah acting on behalf of God himself. These passages may then form an antecedent for the familiar New Testament phenomenon of the application to Christ of biblical texts which in their own contexts appear to refer to God.[142] An instance in Hebrews, and probably also in Paul, from the greater Song of Moses was noted earlier in this chapter (section 3, above, on Deut. 32. 43 in Heb. 1. 6; Rom. 15. 11). At the same time, this understanding of biblical theophanies would cohere with and prepare for the famous systematic interpretation of the Old Testament theophanies as christophanies in Justin Martyr, Origen and Eusebius (see the following chapter, section 2). To return to the three non-Christian Jewish texts considered here, this feature of their messianic depictions agrees with their references to pre-existence, noted above, and confirms that these sources reflect hopes for a heaven-sent deliverer with markedly angelic characteristics.

In the presentation by Schürer, followed in this instance by his revisers, these hopes are associated especially with the growth of apocalyptic imaginings; but they are also set against the background of a development of Old Testament conceptions.[143] In the present study it is urged that this development of the Old Testament was primary. The hopes expressed in the apocalyptic and Sibylline passages on pre-existence had already marked the tradition of biblical interpretation, from the Greek period onwards, as appears from the series of Septuagintal and other related passages considered above; and the apocalypses and the Sibyllines themselves stand in this tradition, which was common to the homeland and the diaspora.

Does a messianic figure exhibiting this spiritual aspect cohere well with messianic hope in general, as expressed in the Greek and early Roman periods? Any attempt to answer this question is affected by the variation in assessment of the material just considered. Schürer and his revisers, in the carefully balanced estimate cited above, pointed out that both before and after the rise of Christianity the messianic figure was envisaged among Jews as fully human, but that the speculation reflected in II Esdras and the Parables of Enoch had moved in the direction of a supra-mundane figure, whose appearance is raised to the level of the supernatural. This depiction of the messiah might seem at first sight to reflect Christian influence, but can in fact be fully explained as an inner-Jewish development of Old Testament ideas. It has just been urged here, in agreement with Schürer's indication of a biblical background but in some contrast with his concentration on II Esdras and the Parables of Enoch, that this line of development was not restricted to the late Herodian apocalypses, but is attested both earlier and later, and more widely and continuously.

On the other hand, an important trend in scholarly opinion departs in a different way from the assessment of the apocalypses represented by Schürer, and minimizes the significance of any indications of a superhuman figure. This trend is exemplified in the criticism noted at the beginning of this section from P. Billerbeck, G. F. Moore and G. Vermes. Each laid emphasis on the point that, however exalted the description, the messianic figure remained human. Billerbeck and Moore both kept in view non-rabbinic as well as rabbinic material, but both judged the latter to be more far-reaching in importance. Billerbeck stressed that expectation of a pre-existent messiah was not clearly attested in rabbinic teaching in the home-land until the middle of the third century. He urged in any case, with the exegesis of the prologue of St John's Gospel in view, that no form of pre-existence ascribed to the messiah in rabbinic texts exceeded what could be said of a human being. Rabbinic sources confirm, in Billerbeck's judgment, that Justin's Trypho rightly represented Jewish opinion, in a passage cited also by Schürer and his revisers to attest a continuing emphasis on the humanity of the messiah in post-Christian Judaism: 'all of us expect that the Christ will be human and of human origin' (πάντες ἡμεῖς τὸν Χριστὸν ἄνθρωπον ἐξ ἀνθρώπων προσδοκῶμεν γενήσεσθαι, *Dial.* 49, 1). Biller-beck concluded that 'the synagogue never allowed its messiah to exceed the common measure of humanity', whereas 'the pre-existence of the New Testament messiah is inextricably linked with his divine being'.[144] Moore, on the other hand, relating the apocalypses more closely to the rabbinic texts than Billerbeck had done, judged that the authors of the apocalypses of Ezra and Baruch were probably not unrepresentative of the thought of the early rabbinic movement in their time; but he similarly and charac-teristically concluded, in his case without appeal to Trypho, that 'for demi-gods Jewish monotheism had no room'.[145] Vermes, finally, stressed briefly but pointedly that, although these apocalypses take heavenly pre-existence for granted, the apocalypse of Ezra plainly foretells the death of the messiah at the end of his four-hundred-year reign ('and it shall be after these years that my son the Christ shall die', II Esdras 7. 29); Vermes held that this mortal messiah (despite his antediluvian span of years) should not be hastily likened to the Christ of the New Testament.[146]

This trend in opinion throws light on the question of coherence, and is also important for the question of the origins of the cult of Christ, to be considered in the following chapter. With regard to coherence, it is clear from II Esdras, as Vermes noted, that a markedly superhuman presentation of the pre-existence and advent of the messiah did not prevent his reign from being understood as that of a glorious but ultimately mortal king – exceptional though the reference to his death in II Esdras 7. 29 appears to be among messianic depictions.[147] The coherence in principle of super-human portraiture with mortality is underlined by the Sibylline oracles, where the king from heaven is depicted in a fashion which could also readily be applied to Ptolemaic or Roman rulers, as is evident in modern exegetical debate over the application of particular oracles. In the Syriac Apocalypse of Baruch (II Baruch), similarly again, the superhuman presen-tation is extended to the end of the messianic reign, which is concluded by the return of the messiah in glory to heaven rather than by a baldly-stated death (II Baruch 30. 1, probably expressing what is implied in I Cor. 15. 24–28); but the messianic advent is also considered as the climax of a series of good dispositions of affairs by past patriarchs and kings of Israel, as noted in section 1 of this chapter, above (see II Baruch 56–74). These super-human depictions accordingly seem to cohere with other depictions of a messianic figure more readily than might at first sight seem likely.[148] They come from the same stock of biblical expectations of a coming king which can also issue in seemingly less elevated presentations of a messianic reign, such as the relatively matter-of-fact description of 'the messiah' at the dinner of bread and new wine in the 'Messianic Rule' of 1QSa, or the glorious but 'entirely human king' of the Psalms of Solomon.[149] Even in these instances, however, there are traces of a concept of pre-existence, as has just been argued above; and it is important to recall that humanity as envisaged in all these sources was itself strongly spiritual, so that a leading part in the human being was thought to be played by the soul or spirit, which could in turn be affected by or even identified with an angelic spirit.

The spiritual messiah as outlined above then seems, in the light of the emphasis laid by Billerbeck, Moore and Vermes on the abiding humanity of the exalted figures, not to be incoherent with expressions of messianic hope in which superhuman features may appear less prominent – although it may be often be a question whether they are not implied. Yet, as this qualification suggests, the review of further sources undertaken here leads also to proposals for some modifications of this body of modern interpreta-tion. These bear on the discussion of the origins of the cult of Christ about to be undertaken, and can be summarized in the three concluding para-graphs of this chapter.

First, concentration on the late Herodian apocalypses in which an exalted messianic figure is most obvious led in the past to the view that here there was a distinct, transcendent messianic figure, contrasting with a more widespread attestation of a more human messiah. This view has played a big part in the discussion of the origins of messianism outlined in chapter I, and in New Testament investigation of the phrase 'the Son of man'. Yet, when the material just summarized is considered, it seems rather that the depiction which had been judged exceptional is relatively widespread. It is true that the superhuman and spiritual aspects of the descriptions do not abolish the humanity of the messiah; but it is also true that the messiah is widely, not just exceptionally, depicted with emphasis on his superhuman and spiritual aspect. The mainstream character of this depiction is indicated by its place in both scripture and tradition. This aspect of the messiah presents itself strikingly in the Hebrew Pentateuch, Prophets and Psalms, especially the royal psalms and oracles which were central to the discussion of messianic development outlined in chapter I, section 2, above; and this same superhuman aspect was perpetuated and developed in the interpretative tradition of the Hebrew scriptures, as witnessed above from the LXX, the apocalypses and the Jewish Sibyllines, the Targums and the midrash.

Secondly, this point suggests, especially when titles of the God of Israel such as 'God of powers' and 'king of gods' are recalled, that a dictum such as Moore's dismissal of 'demigods' needs qualification. Buchanan Gray's deliberate choice of this term to do justice to the Hebrew text of Isa. 9. 5 (6), in his comment quoted above, seems nearer the truth for the interpretation of messianic prophecy current in the Greek and Roman periods as well. Justin represents Trypho as conceding, with all his emphasis on the human origin of the messiah, that Daniel 7 and like scriptures constrain him to await 'one great and glorious', who takes over the everlasting kingdom as Son of man from the Ancient of Days (*Dial.* 32. 1). This concession is true to the interpretation of Daniel current in the second century in the apocalypse of Ezra and the Fifth Sibylline book. The messiah as king is close to the 'gods' in the form of angels, as is repeatedly shown by the 'spiritual' strand in the messianic depictions just noted, including the messianic understanding of biblical theophanies. This biblical and inherited strand in Jewish messianism was close in turn, as the Sibylline oracles show, to the court praise of the surrounding Greek and Roman world.

Lastly, the conception of the God of Israel as king of gods and powers was shared by the early Christian heirs of Jewish biblical tradition. This is one of the points which indicates, as suggested already, that the contrast between Jewish messianic depictions and early Christian messianism is overdrawn in the body of critical opinion just outlined. The emphasis on the divine being of Christ in the New Testament writings, which Billerbeck underlined at the end of his treatise-comment on the divine Logos in the Johannine Prologue, must be viewed against this background, common to Jews, Christians and pagans, of a cosmos with a range of divine beings.[150]

Similarly, as noted already, conceptions of pre-existence, whether Christian or Jewish, did not leave the messiah in solitary state. Ancient Jewish presentation of the messiah as a glorious mortal king with spiritual and superhuman aspects is then not necessarily far removed from the contemporary New Testament and early Christian depictions of a crucified but spiritual and glorious 'Christ'. Moreover, the Christian messianic depictions were influenced by the same interpretative tradition of the scriptures which has just been illustrated, and had some biblically-inspired elements which to later Christians looked archaic or even heretical, above all in the presentation of a pre-eminent yet still subordinate Christ.[151] This aspect of early Christian thought is brought out particularly clearly by the later condemnation of Origen's christological exegesis, illustrated above. The modification of an influential scholarly contrast between Judaism and Christianity which is being suggested here would allow more weight to be placed on apparent resemblances between ancient Jewish and early Christian messianism. Some of these are explored in the following chapter, in consideration of the rise of the cult of Christ.

IV

Messianic Origins of the Cult of Christ

1. The cult of Christ and the question of its origins

(a) Acclamation and hymnody

Christ was what a Greek would have called *euhymnos*, copiously praised in hymns, at least from the end of the first century. About the year 112 Pliny wrote to Trajan that former Christians under questioning declared that their custom had been to recite an antiphonal hymn 'to Christ, as to a god' at their early morning meetings (*'ante lucem convenire carmenque Christo, quasi deo, dicere secum invicem'*, Pliny, *Ep.* 10, 96, 7).[1] This testimony exacted by Pliny is indirectly confirmed by Christian writings from an earlier date, preserved in the New Testament. Thus the Gospels relate the hymn-like acclamation of Christ as he entered Jerusalem (Mark 11. 9–10 and parallels) and the temple (Matt. 21. 15). Comparably, the book of Revelation describes angelic and universal hymns to God, and the Lamb (especially Rev. 5. 9–14; 7. 9–12); also, the martyrs in heaven sing 'the song of Moses the servant of God and the song of the Lamb' (Rev. 15. 3).

The light shed by these passages picks out some phrases in the Pauline corpus as acclamations of Christ. The most famous of these is 'Jesus is lord' (I Cor. 12. 3; cf. Rom. 10. 9; Phil. 2. 11). Moreover, the use of such hymnody and acclamation seems to be inculcated by St John's Gospel, where a speech of Christ includes the claim that the Father has committed all judgment to the Son, 'that all may honour the Son as they honour the Father. He who does not honour the Son, does not honour the Father who sent him' (John 5. 22–23). Charles Wesley was probably right when, in a hymn recalling the cry of praise uttered by the servants of God in Rev. 7. 10, he interpreted 'honour' in this gospel passage as 'acclaim':

> ' "Salvation to God who sits on the throne",
> Let all cry aloud, and honour the Son.'[2]

Christ was therefore honoured by hymns and acclamations in the Christian usage reflected by Paul, the Synoptic Gospels, John and Revelation, irrespective of the question whether hymn-like New Testament passages such as Phil. 2. 6–11 do in fact reproduce current hymns.

Hymns to Christ have flourished ever since in the church. Noble ancient examples are formed by the evening hymn 'Hail gladdening light', Clement of Alexandria's hymn 'Bridle of colts untamed, wing of unwandering birds', and the second sections of both *Gloria in excelsis* and *Te Deum*. In the third century the long-standing currency of such hymns written by 'faithful brethren' was invoked in opposition to a low doctrine of Christ held by some in Rome; and on the other hand Paul of Samosata, whose doctrine was also taken to be of this kind, was said to have disused psalms in honour of Christ at Antioch on the ground that they were merely the product of more recent authors (Eusebius, *HE* 5, 28, 5–6; 7, 30, 10–11).[3] It is easy to see that both claims about hymnody to Christ could be justified; the tradition of addressing hymns and psalms to Christ went back to apostolic times, but new compositions were continually being added to it. Moreover, this tradition as a whole was more recent than the psalmody of David, wherein Christ was indeed praised, as the Christians held, but his praise was set in the context of praise addressed to God.

As the objection ascribed to Paul of Samosata suggests, hymnody and acclamation addressed to Christ have sometimes drawn criticism, in both ancient and modern times, as trenching on the honour due to the Father. 'They gave this man the title *son of God* not because they honour God greatly, but because they exalt (or "increase", ὅτι . . . αὔξουσιν) this man greatly', wrote Celsus against the Christians in the later second century.[4] Origen made a biblically-grounded reply, which would in later years offend for its subordinationism, but was intended to vindicate Christian reverence for God; stressing that God himself 'greatly exalted' his Son, who was no rebel, Origen admitted that some Christians might hastily affirm the Saviour to be the most great God over all (compare Rom. 9. 5) and forget that 'the Father is greater than I' (John 14. 28) (Origen, *c. Cels.* 8. 14).[5] In 1904 the revisers of *Hymns Ancient and Modern* envisaged a not wholly dissimilar criticism when they remarked: 'It is often urged as an objection to Christian hymn books, that so great a proportion of the hymns contained in them are addressed to our blessed Redeemer, rather than to the Father to whom he brings us. The defect lies largely with the composers of our hymns, and not with the compilers of the collections.'[6] In the setting of the Greek and Roman world the early Christian hymnody and acclamation addressed to Christ, when viewed together with the customs of being baptized 'into Christ Jesus' and eating 'the Lord's supper', and the invocation and confession of Christ and his name, all attested in Paul (Rom. 6. 3;

10. 9; I Cor. 1. 2; 11. 20; 16. 22), forms the clearest justification for calling one element in early Christian worship a cult of Christ, comparable with the cults of Graeco-Roman heroes, sovereigns and divinities.[7]

In the New Testament books traces of the Christ-cult appear in the Gospels, in narratives such as those of the entry into Jerusalem and the Last Supper and in allusions to prophecy and healing in the name of Christ; moreover, in the literary development which led up to the Gospels, the cult – from beginnings probably to be located in messianic praise, prophecy and healing offered by followers during the ministry of Jesus – will have been an important factor in the formation of the connected passion narrative and the assembly of testimonies to Christ from the scriptures.[8] 'Here' – in the Jewish scriptures – 'was to be found the portrait and the story of the *Kyrios* of the cult' (G. Bertram).[9]

This insight is amply confirmed by the Christian and Jewish messianic elaboration of the royal portraits in the blessing of Judah (Gen. 49. 8–12) and in psalms such as 45; 72 and 110. The biblical testimonies, together with Gospel narratives such as those of the transfiguration, mockery and crucifixion, evince an interest in Christ's external appearance, of beauty as well as humiliation. Such near-pictorial interest forms a further point of resemblance both to Graeco-Roman cults and to Jewish messianism. So in Rome a court poet thinks how Augustus, drinking with the gods, 'quaffs nectar with empurpled lips' (Horace, *Od.* 3, 3, 12, *'purpureo bibit ore nectar')*; compare the Septuagintal portrait of the king to arise from Judah with wine-drenched clothing, shining eyes, and white teeth (Gen. 49. 11–12 LXX), and the more general development of it in the Targum, 'how fair is king messiah who will arise from among those of the house of Judah' (cf. Ps. 45. 3) (Targum Ps. Jon. Gen. 49. 11). From the end of the Hasmonaean period, compare again Ps. Sol. 17. 42, 'this is the beauty (εὐπρέπεια) of the king of Israel', perhaps with allusion to Isa. 33. 17; Ps. 45 (44). 2–3, discussed with reference to pre-existence in chapter III, section 5, above. The importance of such royal beauty and majesty in practical politics is acknowledged by Josephus. He writes sadly and admiringly in the case of the young Hasmonaean prince and high-priest Aristobulus, whose form (*morphe*, cf. Phil. 2. 6) declared his nobility and attracted acclamation (*Ant.*, 15. 51); but there is mockery in his comment that after the death of Herod Simon the royal slave assumed the diadem in Peraea, 'relying on the beauty (*eumorphia*) and stature of his body' (*BJ* 2. 57). Among Christians, this theme was strongly developed in the second century, through testimonies which were probably important earlier;[10] but it already emerges in the first century, as just indicated. Christ as king is announced by 'his star' (Matt. 2. 2), and appears robed in purple and crowned with thorns (John 19. 5,

'Behold the man'), and Christian writings speak of the glittering garments of the transfigured Christ (Mark 9. 3; Luke 9. 29), and the glory of Christ, transfigured or exalted (Luke 9. 34; II Cor. 3. 18; 4. 6). Some early literary traces of a cult can therefore be set beside the hymnody and the other customs mentioned above; but the customs in themselves constitute honour to Christ sufficiently widespread and organized to be called a cult.

(b) Gentile or Jewish origins?

How did this cult arise? Its origins have been sought in Graeco-Roman religion, in Judaism and in Christianity itself. Here it is urged that, despite its combination of Graeco-Roman and specifically Christian features, it is best explained as a development of Jewish messianism; Jews before the rise of Christianity had customarily praised their kings and their expected future king in vocabulary which was biblically-derived but shared with that of gentile courts and sanctuaries, and Christians will have developed this Jewish usage against the background of the Herodian and Roman ruler-cult with which they were contemporary.

Jewish messianism is not widely regarded as an obvious antecedent of the Christian cult. In the first place, the doubts concerning the prevalence of messianism considered here in earlier chapters are strongly echoed by students of Christian origins such as E. P. Sanders and R. E. Brown, cited in the Introduction, above. Perhaps particular influence has been exercised by Morton Smith's identification of an inconsistent and unreconciled diversity of messianic expectation, and M. de Jonge on the 'remarkably few' references to the term 'anointed' found in Jewish literature of the time of Jesus.[11] Both these points were noticed in the study of the term 'messiah' in chapter I, section 1, above, and it was urged there that the inconsistencies are not such as to rule out a broad unity and coherence, and that the literary evidence in fact strikingly suggests the familiarity of the term 'messiah' in common parlance. The succeeding chapters have then argued for the prevalence and broad coherence of messianism throughout the Second-Temple period. The view sponsored by Sanders and Brown has many supporters and a long history, but reasons have been suggested in chapters I–III for holding, rather, that a varied yet coherent messianic expectation was widespread among Jews at the time of Christian origins.

Secondly, however, messianism is sometimes thought too restricted in its scope to lead to the great range of New Testament and early Christian praise of Christ. So E. P. Sanders, who is again representative, argues that Paul in his christology could not proceed on the basis of widespread Jewish messianic expectations surrounded by a developed theology of the messiah;

thus the designation of Christ as Son of God in power by the resurrection (Rom. 1. 4) and the claim that before his human appearance 'he was in the form of God' (Phil. 2. 6) constitute two apparently contrasting christological statements, but 'no known form of Jewish messianic expectation explains them. The hope for a Davidic king, or for an Aaronic priest, for example, does not lead easily and naturally to either of these passages.'[12]

Yet, to sketch a different view very briefly, 'Son of God' can be associated with widespread Jewish messianic application of biblical verses on the Davidic king as God's son: II Sam. 7. 14 (see 4Q174 [Florilegium] line 11), its analogue in Ps. 89. 26–27, and especially Ps. 2. 7, from a psalm which came to be called 'the chapter of Gog and Magog' – the great foe(s) of the messiah.[13]

Similarly, the pre-existent angel-like figure of Phil. 2 recalls (see chapter III, section 5, above) the lord begotten before the daystar in Ps. 110 (109). 3 LXX, the messianic title 'angel of great counsel' (Isa. 9. 5 LXX), the Philonic link beween the heavenly Adam and the dayspring-man, and the pre-existent 'spirit of the messiah' in rabbinic exegesis from third-century Tiberias (Ber. R. 2. 4, on Gen. 1. 2, in the name of Resh Laqish); when compared with detailed messianic descriptions from the end of the Second-Temple period, the pre-existent figure can be linked with the assertion in the Psalms of Solomon that the beauty of the coming Davidic king of Israel is known (beforehand) to God (Ps. Sol. 17. 42, cited above), and seems particularly close to the exalted messiah described, with traits taken from Dan. 7, in the Parables of Enoch, II Esdras 13 and Sib. 5. 414–33.[14] The depiction of the messiah in Ps. 110 and II Esdras 13 finds correspondence elsewhere in Paul.[15]

Paul's two statements, accordingly, reflect the presence of antecedents for both in psalms and prophecies which were messianically interpreted by Jews. These texts were woven into narratives of messianic victory and judgment like those illustrated in chapter II, above, notably in the combination of Pss. 2 and 110 with Dan. 7 in II Esdras 13; and probably, therefore, they were not thought to be mutually incompatible.

It can then reasonably be asked, without definite expectation of the answer No, whether Jewish messianism leads naturally to the hymns and acclamations to Christ which have just been illustrated. First, however, further attention should be given to the broader context of this inquiry, namely, the proposed derivation of the cult of Christ from Jewish rather than gentile usages. How has it been possible to derive this cult in the past, with considerable plausibility in each case, either from gentile or Jewish or from specifically Christian origins?

The gentile derivation, first, has the merit of a certain straightforwardness. On this view, the Christian cult can be understood simply as a product of the Graeco-Roman world, in which cults of heroes and rulers were familiar, and among them the cult of the Roman emperor was being developed at the time of Christian origins. So, in the classical presentation of a gentile derivation, Wilhelm Bousset's *Kyrios Christos* (1913, ²1921, reprinted 1967), the Christ-cult is held to correspond to the cult of a divinity – a classification in which, for Bousset, ancient ruler-cults were firmly to be included.[16]

Some of the support for this view can be seen in the one or two New Testament passages already quoted in the initial sketch of the cult. Thus the hymn was a staple of Greek and Roman praise of heroes, rulers and divinities, exemplified in the hymns of the Salian priests in Rome; in 28 BC the Roman senate resolved that Octavian 'should be inscribed, on a par with the gods, in the hymns' (ἐς τοὺς ὕμνους αὐτὸν ἐξ ἴσου τοῖς θεοῖς ἐσγράφεσθαι, Cassius Dio 51, 20, 1). Correspondingly, when the Greek *hymnos* is taken over into rabbinic Hebrew as *hymnon* or *ymnon*, it occurs in connection with the ruler-cult as well as praise of the God of Israel. So in the midrash, a king went out, and everyone came 'to sing a hymn to him', *lomar lo ymnon* (Tanhuma Buber, Exodus, 30b, Beshallah 13, on Exod. 15. 1).[17] Then, individual acclamations like 'Jesus is Lord' regularly occur in connection with deities – the most famous example is 'Great is Diana of the Ephesians', which was the cry for two hours in the theatre at Ephesus, according to Acts 19. 34 – and they are also particularly characteristic of the court and the ruler cult. An ironical rabbinic explanation of the Mishnaic phrase 'Herodian doves' suggests that they sit in rows in their cote, cooing like a claque the acclamatory invocation *kyrie, kyrie*.[18] Compare, from an earlier date, the emphatic *kyrie kyrie* in the Q saying Matt. 7. 21; Luke 6. 46, in its present forms probably shaped by the Christ-cult as well as the messianism of Jesus's ministry: 'Not everyone that says to me *kyrie kyrie* . . .', 'Why do you call me *kyrie kyrie* . . . ?'[19]

The title 'lord' itself could be given to a king, as these quotations show, but it was also the current word for a hero or deity who (like a king) received cult, and Paul uses it in this sense of gentile divinities (I Cor. 8. 5); accordingly, it was at the very heart of Bousset's case, as he indicated in his book-title *Kyrios Christos*. Similarly, the title 'son of God', justly associated by early Christians with biblical tradition but mocked as inflatory by Celsus, as noted above, was regularly applied to monarchs; Plutarch had classed it with 'god' as one of the royal titles which he regarded as excessive (Plutarch, *De Laude ipsius*, 12, 543 D–E, quoted in the previous chapter). Bousset accordingly underlined his point, with occasional reservations, from the substantial overlap in vocabulary between the New Testament and the cults of rulers noted by A. Deissmann.[20] Thus the adjective *kyriakos*, 'dominical', used of two institutions of the Christ-cult, 'the Lord's Supper' and 'the Lord's Day' (I Cor. 11. 20, Rev. 1. 10), was characteristic of the imperial administration, as when it was used of 'dominical' (imperial) revenue in an edict of Tiberius Julius Alexander, prefect of Egypt and Philo's nephew, from the year 68.[21] In this edict contemporary New Testament vocabulary is further recalled by an artistic passage of praise to the emperor Galba, 'who has shone upon us (ἐπιλάμψαντος ἡμεῖν) for the salvation of every race of men' with hope for a new era (lines 6–10).[22] Similar remarks could be made about the court setting of such New Testament terms as 'advent' and 'epiphany', *parousia* and *epiphaneia* (I Thess. 2. 19; II Thess. 2. 8, etc.).[23] To move from individual words, the themes of Phil. 2. 5–11 are illustrated by literature in honour of rulers, in the shape of Plutarch's description of Alexander the Great as a pre-existent soul who refuses plunder and fashions himself to show that all are one (Plut. *Alex. Virt.* 1. 8).[24] Outside the Pauline corpus Bousset drew attention to the importance of cult focussed on the title Son of God in John (1. 49; 10. 36; 11. 27; 19. 7; 20. 31; cf. 5. 18), manifest for instance in the call to honour the Son in 5. 22–23, quoted above.[25] It may be added that the commitment of all judgment to the Son, affirmed in this passage, recalls the central commonplace of ruler-cult that the supreme deity has transferred his powers to the earthly king, who now exercises god-like government and receives petition and praise as a 'present god' (see chapter III, section 2, above).[26]

Bousset's view is further supported by the many references to resemblance between Christianity and such cults met in early criticism and defence of Christianity during the first three centuries, beginning with Paul's comparison and contrast between the 'gods many and lords many' of the gentiles, and the 'one god . . . and one lord' of the Christians (I Cor. 8. 6). Ancient Christian apologists characteristically accepted that the resemblance was strong; *ad hominem*, they could defend the worship of Christ precisely because it would be fully justified on the analogy of pagan honours to deified mortals (so Justin Martyr, *I Apol.* 21–22; Arnobius, *Adversus Gentes*, 1. 36–42 [especially 38]), although at the same time they differentiated it firmly from non-Christian cults (so, without defence on the ground of analogy, Origen, *contra Celsum* 3, 22–44, 8, 12–15).[27] A similar double-sided defence was adopted in the case of the cult of martyrs and saints, which had comparable resemblances to pagan usage.[28] Despite the disadvantages of undifferentiated comparison with paganism, from the second century onwards Christians treasured the legend that Tiberius or Pilate had recommended Christ to the senate as a candidate for apotheosis (*consecratio*).[29]

Bousset, followed by R. Bultmann, accordingly traced the origins of the Christian cult to gentile influence on early gentile Christianity, specifically at Antioch.[30] Bousset's early critics, such as J. Weiss, L. Cerfaux, Eduard Meyer, W. Foerster, F. C. Burkitt and A. D. Nock, have nevertheless received a considerable measure of acceptance in later study. A weakness of Bousset's position was the Aramaic phrase Maranatha, probably to be rendered 'Our lord, come', preserved in Greek transliteration at I Cor. 16. 22. This suggests that Christian Jews, not only Christian gentiles, participated in the Christ-cult, and a Jewish context of course raises the question whether *lord* may not refer primarily, as in biblical usage, to the king of Israel or the God of Israel.[31]

Many have therefore agreed, against Bousset, that the title *Kyrios* was ascribed to Christ in the earliest Judaean Christian community, envisaged as a mainly Jewish body.[32] The Jewish background of christological vocabulary and the diversity of pre-Christian Jewish monotheism have been explored, with special reference to divine intermediaries;[33] and Jewish origins for the cult of Christ have been widely canvassed, usually with some stress also on specifically Christian factors in the origins. In these studies emphasis has sometimes fallen on subjects particularly relevant to cult, such as the titles and epithets of Christ;[34] but sometimes the question of the origins of the cult has been considered within the broader question of the rise of early Christian views of Christ. A notable instance is C. F. D. Moule, *The Origin of Christology* (1977), a book which envisages the growth of Christian views of Jesus as the unfolding of the impression left by Jesus on the disciples, within the context of ancient Judaism. Somewhat comparably, the personality of Jesus had been an important factor in the rise of the Christ-cult for Bousset's early critic Johannes Weiss.[35] More recently, Jewish and specifically Christian factors have been similarly primary in J. D. G. Dunn, and in M. de Jonge, who presents christological development as a continuing reaction to Jesus.[36]

The cult has therefore been envisaged as congruous with the outlook of Christian Jews. So O. Cullmann, M. Hengel, R. J. Bauckham and L. W. Hurtado have found the cultic veneration of Christ in the first-century Judaean congregations of Christian Jews. Bauckham laid stress on the influence of Jewish and Christian apocalypses as forming the atmosphere in which the cult flourished, and Hurtado argued that the Christ-cult arose in the first decade after the crucifixion among Jews under the influence of Christian religious experiences, notably the visions of the risen Christ; he understood it as a mutation of non-Christian Jewish conceptions of an exalted divine agent.[37]

It has been increasingly accepted, therefore, that the Christ to whom hymns were sung as to a god in the reign of Trajan was already honoured in essentially the same way seventy years earlier among Galilaean and Judaean Christian Jews. At the same time it has been increasingly stressed that this cult of Christ was never thought by its participants to impair their loyalty to the one God, although second-century critics like Celsus and Justin's Trypho could seize on its apparent inconsistency with monotheism (Origen, *contra Celsum* 8, 12; Justin Martyr, *Dial.* 8, 3, 38, 1). Bauckham emphasized that the apocalypses which contribute to the atmosphere of the cult also characteristically stress the sole sovereignty of God, whose angels are regularly said to disapprove obeisance offered to them by mortals.[38]

The derivation of the cult and its associated doctrines from Judaism has nonetheless evoked a dissent which seems at least partly justified when the admitted resemblances to pagan practice are brought once again to the fore.

A preliminary objection felt by some is voiced by Jonathan Z. Smith. He urges that the explanation of pagan-like features of early Christianity by ascribing them to Jewish ancestry is often an apologetic device. Such flights to Jewish origins not only, in his view, ignore the priority which the work of comparison should enjoy over speculative derivation, but in practice they also artificially restrict Judaism, without allowing for the possible breadth of Jewish thought and custom in the Greek world. Here his target is especially the suggestion that Christian language recalling the vocabulary of the mystery religions derives from the Septuagint rather than the mysteries themselves, and he selects A. D. Nock's work for criticism, but his general objection would apply equally to Jewish derivations of the cult of Christ.[39] Yet, often as arguments for Jewish origins have been laid under contribution in defence of Christianity, they have also at times been welcomed by advocates of other causes. Thus Friedrich Engels applauded Bruno Bauer's identification of Philo as the real father of Christianity, and underlined the debt of early Christians to the book of Enoch.[40] Similarly, the historical argument for pre-Christian Jewish conceptions of an exalted divine agent can be related to apologetic argument for a divine messiah, but it was put to very different use by a proponent of the 'Christ-myth' theory like J. M. Robertson.[41] In the end, whatever use may be made of arguments about origins in defending or attacking Christianity, the continuities between early Christian and Jewish literature remain so prominent as to demand inquiry into the possible Jewish origins of Christian customs and tenets.

The general criticism sponsored by J. Z. Smith is perhaps most apt in the more restricted form which it was earlier given by B. A. Mastin, who suspected that suggestions of a Septuagintal background for the Johannine description of Christ as *theos* might have been given undue weight because of their acceptably biblical character, whereas the contemporary ruler-cult was *also* possibly influential.[42] In the present study it is urged that the gentile cults were indeed influential, but that their influence will have been indirect as well as direct, mediated through Jewish tradition as well as contemporary life. Among Jews before and during the rise of Christianity a king or the messiah could be praised in terms shared with contemporary ruler-cults, and the Christians inherited and developed this traditional Jewish practice, themselves continuing to draw on the contemporary vocabulary of royal praise.

It has been repeatedly asked, however, whether a Christ-cult could indeed have flourished among the earliest Judaean and Galilaean Christians, given Jewish opposition to idolatry and ruler-worship. The question is put or implied in various connections. The *doctrines* concerning Christ are the prime concern in M. Casey's contention that the heightening of christology is associated with the gentilizing of Christianity; the expulsions from the synagogue assembly reflected in the Fourth Gospel can be linked with Jewish perception of Johannine insistence on the deity of Christ as decisively non-Jewish, and the first apostles could not have shared this insistence.[43] The objection is most closely linked with the hymnic aspect of the cult considered here by G. Lindeskog; having followed the critical responses to Bousset outlined above, he still held that Christian Jews in the mother-country would not have given Christ the divine praises associated with the *Kyrios* of the Christ-hymns, for Paul, John and Hebrews represent a christology which is altogether different, in his view, from the 'messianology' of the first Christians.[44]

Such an objection can perhaps be countered in part by reference to the variety in the Judaism, and consequently in the Christianity, to be expected in Judaean cities like Joppa, Caesarea or Jerusalem (a point made especially strongly by M. Hengel).[45] More far-reaching, perhaps, is the consideration mentioned already: Christians at this period fully shared Jewish horror at idolatry and reservations on gentile ruler-cult, but they evidently did not regard their Christ-cult as inconsistent with these attitudes. Nevertheless, the strength of the argument sponsored by Lindeskog lies in its echo of the objections of Trypho the Jew, as envisaged by Justin Martyr in passages quoted with emphasis by Bousset: one of Justin's many blasphemies, says Trypho, with an echo of debate on the cult of Alexander the Great (chapter III, section 2, above), is his description of Christ as one who should receive obeisance – 'to be worshipped', *proskynetos*, but Jews worship the God who created even this Christ, and have no need of the confession or the worship of Christ (Justin Martyr, *Dial.* 38, 1; 63; 4–64, 1; cf. 8, 3).[46]

Probably, however, the Jewish rejection of the Christ-cult reflected in

Justin Martyr had gained in definition and importance as a result of opposition to Christian claims (chapter III, section 5, above), although it draws on elements in pre-Christian Judaism which also contributed to the Zealot position, and was already regarded as strong in the Fourth Gospel. The Christian exaltation of Christ will likewise have been intensified in controversy, among other contexts, but it is clearly rooted in Judaism. The search for Jewish origins for the Christ-cult seems justified, therefore, but the dissent which it has evoked perhaps arises partly because the connections between Jewish life and thought and the Christian phenomenon still seem loose, and much weight has to be placed on the Christian Jewish as well as the non-Christian Jewish links in the chain.

Thus, in Hurtado's careful work, Christians are said to take over 'the Jewish divine agency category', but to speak of this category involves some abstraction from the specific conceptions entertained by Christian Jews. Again, Hurtado stresses the formative character of early *Christian* religious experience, especially visions of the risen Christ such as that described in the first chapter of Revelation; here the importance of a specifically Christian factor is underlined (and Hurtado holds that it has been underestimated), but the Christ-cult then appears all the more strikingly as a specifically Christian phenomenon, especially as the direct Jewish antecedents of the Christian experience have been left in the generalized form of a divine agency tradition; and the connection between the cult of Christ and its Jewish origins seems therefore by no means close.[47] The formative influence of distinctive elements in the life and teaching of Jesus and in early Christian communal self-understanding should certainly be recognized, as C. F. D. Moule, once again, has stressed;[48] but the visions were an outcome as well as a stimulus of adherence to Christ, and the cult of Christ should also be related as closely as possible to the life and literature of the Jewish community whence the first Christians sprang.

2. Angel-christology and messianism

More satisfactory in this regard, at least in principle, is an approach which has been widely explored, that of angel-christology. It turns on the importance of expectations of angelic deliverers, and of beliefs that favoured mortals might be transformed into angels, such as were illustrated in chapter III, above. Further, particular attention has been given to the appearance in apocalypses and mystical texts of one exalted angel almost indistinguishable from God himself, like the 'angel of the Lord' in the Old Testament (compare the discussions of Exod. 23. 20 and Isa. 63. 9 in chapters II–III, above). It is suggested that these conceptions of God and a great angel offer a possible key to the exaltation of Christ manifested in the New Testament and associated with his cult.[49]

For interpretation of the titles and the cult of Christ it is also important, however, to view these conceptions against the broader background of the development of old Israelite notions of a pantheon or divine council into the later visualization of a host of angels, good and bad.[50] Thus vestiges of a pantheon appear in the Hebrew Bible, as noted in chapter I, section 2, above. The 'sons of El' or 'the host of heaven', in part identified with the sun, moon, and stars and the deities ruling the nations (Deut. 4. 19), include spirits who influence prophets (I Kings 22. 21–22). This heavenly host are seen together with the God of Israel in passages such as Deut. 32. 8–9; 33. 2; I Kings 22. 19–22; Pss. 29; 82 (divine council); 103. 20–21; 148. 2 (angelic praise); Job 1–2. These passages became central in the developing conceptions of the God of Israel as surrounded by angels which characterized the Second-Temple period. Such later understandings of the biblical traditions tended to emphasize the service given by the angels to the one God, but they were continuous with the earlier views of a company of sometimes turbulent deities, as emerges in the traditions concerning evil or rebellious angels.

The spirits of the heavenly host accordingly retained much of their demigod-like power in the thought of the later Second-Temple period, as was noted briefly in chapter III, section 5, above. Each nation is governed by an angel-prince (Ecclus 17. 17; Dan. 10. 13, 20–21); Tobit blesses God, his name and his angels, seven angels present the prayers of mortals to God (Tobit 11. 14; 12. 12–15), and the angels, whose personal names are sometimes given, as in Daniel and Tobit (Essenes swore to guard these names),[51] retain the old general biblical designations of 'spirit', 'god', and 'power'. This nomenclature, now amply attested in Hebrew through Qumran texts (see below), has also left traces in Septuagintal and New Testament Greek. Thus in Paul, when the Corinthians gather together with his own spirit and 'with the power of the Lord Jesus', or when Christ as 'last Adam' is 'a life-giving spirit', the messiah is probably viewed as an angel-like being (see the comments on Phil. 2. 5 in the previous section); and the chief evil angel seems to be indicated by the title 'the god of this world' (I Cor. 5. 4; 15. 45; II Cor. 4. 4).

From the time of Alexander the Great onwards the importance of these conceptions was marked by interpretative adaptation of divine titles from the Hebrew biblical books, to present the God of Israel as a lord of angels. Thus in the Greek Pentateuch the deity is addressed as 'God of the spirits and all flesh' (LXX Num. 16. 22; 27. 16, for Hebrew which may be rendered 'God of the spirits of all flesh'); the influence of this interpretation appears in a Hebrew composition in a well-known passage from the War Scroll quoted in chapter III, section 4, above: 'to raise up amongst the gods the princedom of Michael, and the dominion of Israel amongst all flesh' (1QM 17. 7). In Septuagintal and other texts from the Second-Temple period, compare the emphasis on angels in the titles 'God of the powers' (e.g. LXX Ps. 79. [80]. 5, 8, 15, 20), and 'lord of the powers' (e.g. LXX Ps. 23 [24]. 10) – these interpret 'YHWH Sabaoth', which sometimes elsewhere in the LXX, notably in Isaiah, was rendered *Kyrios Sabaoth* and was probably understood as 'Lord Sabaoth', as a special divine name; 'the ruler of the spirits and every power' (II Macc. 3. 24, variant 'lord of the spirits and ruler of every power'); 'lord of every spirit' (1QH xviii [x] 8); 'lord of spirits', used repeatedly in the Parables of Enoch (37. 2, etc.); and 'father of the spirits' (Heb. 12. 9).[52]

The title 'king of gods' appears in Greek, in a context where the place of the deities of the nations among the angels is important, and in Hebrew (*melekh elohim*), in the Qumran context of angelic liturgy (Esther's prayer in Esther 4. 17r LXX = Rest of Esther 14. 12; 4Q 400 2, 5). The Qumran hymnody in which the phrase is attested concentrates on praise uttered by the seven companies of angelic spirits or divinities (*elohim, elim*); the greater angels themselves are 'honoured in all the camps of the gods and feared by the companies of men' (4Q 400 2, 2).[53] Comparably, an inscribed Greek prayer for vengeance from about 100 BC begins, echoing LXX Numbers, 'I invoke and beseech the most high God, the lord of the spirits and all flesh', and ends 'O lord that seest all things, and the angels of God'.[54] With a similar echo, a Christian blessing formula at the end of the first century begins: 'May God the all-seeing, ruler of the spirits and lord of all flesh . . .' (I Clem. 64. 1). John the Divine's greeting, correspondingly, wishes grace and peace from God, 'and from the seven spirits that are before his throne, and from Jesus Christ' (Rev. 1. 4–5); and Justin Martyr, contesting the charge of atheism, stresses that 'We reverence and worship [God], and the Son, and the army of good angels, and the prophetic spirit' (*I Apol.* 6).

These expressions of invocation and reverence suggest that honour to angels was among the cultic practices inherited by Jews and Christians from the Judaism of the Second-Temple period. Its manifestation in hymns and prayers in connection with the cult of the God of Israel would have been encouraged by the lively conception of God as surrounded by angels which has just been illustrated from a series of divine titles and related texts. This suggestion is strengthened by Christian and pagan anti-Jewish charges of angelolatry, and internally-directed Jewish and Christian warnings against excessive honour to angels.[55]

A cult of angels therefore accompanied the development of the cult of

Christ. In both cases, as is clear from the references to Christ and the angels immediately after God in Justin's summary of Christian worship, honour was given within the general context of praise and prayer addressed to God. Irrespective of arguments for the influence of particular elements in angelology on christology, this point indicates one of the factors which will have contributed to the formation of a favourable Jewish environment for the Christ-cult.

Such arguments have a place, however, in discussion of the origins of the cult of Christ. This cult begins to look at home within ancient Judaism if Christ is being envisaged and honoured as an angelic figure. Hence for a while here the focus of attention must move from the cultic praise of Christ to the closely related but broader subject of the development of christology. An important place within this development was assigned to angel-christology in work done at the end of the nineteenth century, notably by Bousset and by his pupil Wilhelm Lueken in his book *Michael* (1898), discussed with regard to Daniel in chapter III, above. In writings from this period, angel-christology was held closely together with angel-messianism. Thus it was urged in well-known handbooks, for example by Bousset on Jewish religion and by Adolf Harnack on the history of dogma, cited above, that the Son of man in the Parables of Enoch is an angelic messianic figure, and that the Pauline conception of Christ as pre-existent yet subordinate to the Father indeed appears to be that of an angelic spirit; Bousset argued that a link between the two is formed by the understanding of Jesus as Son of man.[56] These views were developed especially by Martin Werner, of Berne, in part of his book translated as *The Formation of Christian Dogma* (1941, ²1954, ET 1957).[57] Werner underlined the importance of angel-christology in second- and third-century Christian writings, and urged that it was also characteristic of the New Testament; he treated it as leading naturally to Arian doctrine, on the lines suggested by Epiphanius's remark that Ebionites regard the Son as the ruler of angels and all creatures, but as himself a created archangel (Epiphanius, *Pan.* 30, 16, 4), and this understanding of the Son was taken as typical of Jewish-Christian angel-christology by H.-J. Schoeps.[58] These observations were soon complemented, however, by emphasis on the ambiguity of the depictions of Christ as an archangel, which could sometimes be interpreted in an 'Athanasian' as well as an 'Arian' sense.[59] M. Simonetti underlined the importance for historical inquiry of appreciating that angel-christologies which from the standpoint of later Christian doctrine may seem totally distinct, as incipiently 'Arian' or 'orthodox', respectively, were formed in the same intellectual setting.[60]

Later work included much concentration, as noted already, on the significance of the figure of the exalted angel for conceptions of God. It also received strong impulses from the vigorous revival of the study of ancient Jewish mysticism by G. Scholem and others. Attention therefore tended to move away from the association of angel-christology with angel-messianism which had been central from Bousset to Werner. Instead, the seemingly angelic features in depictions of the glorified Christ were set directly against the background of non-Christian Jewish depictions of the exalted angel.

C. Rowland derived these depictions in Jewish apocalypses from Israelite visualizations of the one God as two separated divine figures, exemplified in the treatment of the glory of the Lord in Ezekiel or the angel of the Lord in the Pentateuch; despite the monotheistic context of these descriptions, often emphasizing the monarchy of God, they could contribute to the notion of 'two powers' condemned in rabbinic teaching (for example Ber. R. 1. 7, on Gen. i 1, against the view that 'two powers' were involved in creating the world or giving the law).[61]

Interpretation of this incipiently binitarian kind seems likely to form part of the background against which Philo (*Conf.* 63) could speak of a 'second god' (*deuteros theos*), the Logos, and Justin Martyr (*Dial.* 55, 1) of 'another god beside the maker of the universe'; this deity was identified with the great angel of the patriarchs and the exodus in a line of thought which was fundamental for christology from Justin to Eusebius.[62] M. Barker, taking up especially Emerton, 'Origin' (see chapter I, section 2, above), has vividly shown how close this development of the later Second-Temple period seems to the ancient Israelite mythology in which a young deity (Yahweh) was paired with an old high god (El). She argues that a binitarian tradition continued in Judaism throughout the Persian, Greek and early Roman periods; Jesus was then seen by his followers as Yahweh, the son of God.[63] Despite the clear 'renaissance of mythology' in apocalypses such as Daniel, II Esdras and Revelation, the form in which this argument is put seems to underestimate the changes of the exilic and post-exilic and later period (these were stressed by Emerton, 'Origin'). Thus the identification of Yahweh and El which is attested in the Hebrew Bible (for example in Ps. 50. 1) was an important factor in the influential development towards confession of one God (Deut. 6. 3). The 'second god' or 'other god' of Philo and Justin certainly follows an existing thread of biblical interpretation, as Barker shows; but their conceptions of a heavenly court of angels and powers have been heavily influenced by post-exilic monotheistic trends in Israel, and by Platonic teaching on one transcendent God with subordinate powers and divinities.[64]

In accord with these explorations of the divinity of the exalted angel, the influence of angel-christology has been enhanced by observation of similarities between angelomorphism in ancient conceptions of Christ, and anthropomorphism in ancient Jewish mysticism.[65] The importance of angelology for christology is therefore widely brought out in various ways.[66] The likelihood that 'Son of man', as a title of Christ, indicated an angel-like messiah with particular angelic links is considered again.[67] Angel-christology is now often discussed, however, despite such exceptions, in some detachment from the Jewish messianism in which Werner and his predecessors found its origins.

The classical statements of early Christian angel-christology come not in the New Testament itself, but in the second century and later. They appear in the patristic treatment of the angel(s) who appeared to the patriarchs and guided the exodus and conquest (see chapter III, above) as manifestations of Christ, for example in Justin Martyr; and they are also found in the presentation of the Son as an angel in a range of apocrypha and other sources, some of which came to be classed as heretical.[68] Examples are the Ascension of Isaiah 9. 39, where Christ and the angel of the spirit together pray to God (this book still played a part in fourth-century christology);[69] the related interpretation of Isaiah's seraphim taught to Origen by a Christian Jew – one was the Son, the other the Spirit (Origen, *Princ.* 1, 3, 4); the vision of the Mesopotamian Elchasai at the time of Trajan's Parthian war (115–117), in which Christ appeared as a gigantic angel (Epiphanius, *Pan.* 30, 17, 6); Hermas's vision of a very tall man, 'glorious and great', identified as the Son of God (*Sim.* 9, 12, 8), the spirit who has earlier appeared, for the sake of Hermas's infirmity, in the form of a virgin, but is also 'the glorious angel' (*Sim.* 9, 1, 1–3); and also early eucharistic prayer, in a hint at the angel-like messiah of Isa. 9. 5 (6) LXX ('angel of great counsel'), discussed above in chapter III: 'through thy beloved child Jesus Christ, whom in the last times thou hast sent us as saviour and redeemer and angel of thy will'.[70]

The lack of clear evidence for an angel-christology in the New Testament books, as opposed to later sources, is the point which divides Werner's work from that of J. Barbel, *Christos Angelos*, just cited, which appeared in the same year 1941, and is devoted to a careful study of the later material. Barbel and G. Kretschmar, followed by Jean Daniélou, cited above, affirmed the great importance of Jewish angelology in early Christian doctrine; but they and many since have doubted the strength of the link alleged by Werner and others between Jewish views of angels and the very earliest Christian views of Christ.[71]

The link is probably there, however, but much speaks for locating it within the now somewhat neglected expectations of an angel-like messiah, rather than simply within the honour given to angels. The striking prevalence of conceptions of a 'spiritual messiah' was noted in the previous chapter, with reference to Septuagintal and later evidence including Isa. 9. 5 (6) and the messiah of the Parables of Enoch, II Esdras and Sib. 5. Christ, precisely in his capacity as messiah, could be considered an angelic spirit. That the term 'Son of man' had messianic associations at the time of Christian origins, for all its angelic aspects, is indicated by its links with Isa. 11 and the royal psalms in the sources just noted, together with the messianic use of other terms for 'man'.[72]

As the work of Bousset and Harnack suggested, a line would then lead from Jewish messianism to what has been classified as 'Spirit-christology', in which Christ is the 'holy spirit' and 'power of the highest' who over-shadowed the Virgin (Luke 1. 35 as interpreted by Justin, *I Apol.* 33; *Dial.* 105, 1).[73] Hermas envisaged 'that holy spirit which was before, which created all creation' as made to dwell in flesh (*Sim.* 5, 6, 5).[74] *Spiritus* was an important title of Christ for Tertullian, who speaks of him as 'power of God and spirit of God' (*Apol.* 23, 12, *dei virtus et dei spiritus*), and 'always spirit of God', even before he took flesh (*Marc.* 5, 8, 4, *semper spiritus dei*).[75] Origen was not far from this line of thought in his suggestion that the pre-existent soul of Christ became one spirit with the Logos and, having loved righteousness, was anointed as Christ (*Princ.* 2, 6, 3–7 and 4, 4, 4–5, quoting Ps. 45 [44]. 7).[76] Justin's view of Christ's spiritual pre-existence was in turn consistent with the belief shared by Justin, Tertullian, Origen and others that he appeared as an angel to the patriarchs, Moses and Joshua. With regard to the New Testament, such 'spirit-messianism' would account for the insistence on the superiority of the Son to the angels at the beginning of Hebrews, and for the Johannine assumption that the pre-existent Christ appeared before his birth; and it would provide a suitable background to the metamorphosis from divine to servile form, and subsequent superexaltation, celebrated in Phil. 2. 5–11, as suggested above.[77] It would also cohere with the expectation presupposed in the four Gospels that John the Baptist or Jesus might represent a pre-existent figure – a prophet or the messiah (Mark 8. 27–9), or the divine 'word' and 'light' identified with the messiah (John 1. 8, 17, 19–23). Origen again continued the line of Jewish thought reflected in these Gospel passages when he urged that John the Baptist was a pre-existent angelic spirit, on the basis of the presentation of Jacob as an incarnate angel in the apocryphal Prayer of Joseph (Origen, *Comm. in Joh.* 2, 30–31 [24–5], 180–192, on John 1. 6; chapter III, section 5, above).[78] The background of Jewish angelology is indeed of general importance for the understanding of ancient views of Christ, but the principal link with it will have been given initially by the acclamation of Christ as messiah.

It may then be urged that Jewish messianism deserves yet further attention in review of possible antecedents to the cult of Christ. Messianism was an important feature of pre-Christian Judaism, as was argued in chapters I–III; the Gospels are probably right in representing it as an important subject for the disciples and their master before the crucifixion; further, there are many points of resemblance between Christian depiction of the exalted Christ and the widely-attested Jewish traditions of a messiah with a spiritual and superhuman aspect, and these have now been illustrated here and in the previous chapter. It seems likely that messianism formed the principal medium through which angelology impinged on nascent christology, and that Christ, precisely as messiah, was envisaged as an angel-like spiritual being.

Inquiry specifically into messianism and the cult of Christ, however, now directs attention away from the overlapping subject of the development of beliefs about Christ, back towards literary material which is closely related to cult. The rich literary deposit of acclamations, titles and hymns offered to Christ was illustrated at the beginning of this chapter. These praises are biblically rooted, but they closely resemble the staple material and vocabulary of ruler-cult, and suggest a debt to it. It was also urged that the praises addressed to Christ had antecedents in Jewish praise of a king or messiah. This was illustrated in some biblical and post-biblical material considered in earlier chapters, for example, the LXX Pentateuch (chapter II, section 2, above).

On the other hand, it was recognized above that such praise might have seemed in danger of sounding out of tune with Jewish opposition to idolatry and ruler-worship. This opposition, so prominent in Herodian Judaea (chapter III, section 2, above) and in parts of the New Testament including Acts (12. 23; 14. 15, on the death of Agrippa I and the attempt to give Barnabas and Paul divine honours in Lystra), recalls the intense concentration on the kingdom of God and on God as sole saviour which was discussed in chapters II and III. The Christ-cult encountered an opposition which owed something to this existing tradition of zeal for God's sole rule, as is suggested by the criticism of the description of Christ as *proskynetos* which Justin ascribes to Trypho, and by the charge that Christ made himself god which the Fourth Gospel ascribes to Jewish opponents. An example already noted is offered by John 10. 33, where the charge is answered by what is probably a comparison with angels (chapter III, section 5, above).

The conceptions of a spiritual or angelic messiah which have now been illustrated, and are themselves not far from the conceptions surrounding the apotheosis of kings, help to show both how the Christians themselves judged the praises of Christ to be meet and right, and how these praises came to be expressed in the christological forms met in the Christian writings of the first and second centuries.[79] It remains desirable, however, to show the extent of the continuity between messianic praise and the praises of Christ. On a paradoxical yet biblically-inspired pattern which repeatedly appears, hostile rulers are condemned for their overweening divine pretensions, and gentile idolaters are mocked for neglecting the signs of the one God; but Jewish leaders, in a context of acknowledgement of the God of Israel, are envisaged as appropriately receiving the obeisance which might be withheld from a gentile king.

3. The praise of Jewish rulers and the worship of Christ

To what extent can the early Christian praise of Christ be interpreted by the praises of Jewish rulers, present and to come? The literary deposit of these praises survives in two interrelated forms. First, a biblically-centred tradition running through the Greek and Roman periods develops those praises of a present or coming king which are embodied in the Hebrew scriptures; this development is visible especially in the LXX, the pseud-epigrapha, the Targums, and rabbinic interpretation. Secondly, there are considerable traces of the praises which were offered to contemporary Jewish rulers in the Second-Temple period, often in some relation to the biblical tradition just mentioned; such traces appear especially in Ecclesiasticus, the books of the Maccabees, Philo and Josephus, and they recall the function of Jewish royal and messianic praise as a counterpart to gentile ruler-cult (chapter III, section 2, above). Both forms of this literary deposit have received illustration above, in argument for the prevalence and broad consistency of the expression of messianic hope. In the present con-text, however, each form is considered with the aim of picking out material which throws light on the links with the language of ruler-cult and on the cult of Christ in particular. The earliest Christian praise can then be located, despite its special features, within a continuum of Jewish praise which is related to contemporary ruler-cult and includes the theme of obeisance, *proskynesis*. Finally, the Christian praise itself is again made the centre of attention, as at the beginning of this chapter; and it is asked from this standpoint whether the chief titles associated with the cult of Christ take their place naturally in the series of messianic praises.

(a) Praises of Jewish rulers

(i) The LXX Pentateuch and Psalms render the biblical praise of Jewish rulers past and to come in the light of the royal praise of the Greek period, as noted already in respect of the Pentateuch (chapter II, section 2, above); the vocabulary of these Greek texts, shared with that of contemporary ruler-cult, includes words and phrases which are later taken up in the literature of the cult of Christ.

In both the Jewish and gentile sources praise often takes the form of prophecy.[80] Thus, to give a Ptolemaic example from near the time of the LXX Pentateuch, Callimachus in his fourth Hymn makes Apollo, still in the womb of his mother in the isle of Cos, prophesy for the people of Cos 'another god' (θεὸς ἄλλος, line 165) – king Ptolemy Philadelphus, who shall reign from sunrise to sunset. In the following century the importance of such oracles emerges at a popular level in the slave-revolt led by the sooth-saying Syrian Eunus, later styled king Antiochus, in Sicily (from 139 or 135 to 132 BC).[81] Under Augustus, oracular royal praise recurs in Roman poetry formed on Greek models, for example in the prophecies of Juno and Tiresias in Horace, *Od.* 3, 3; *Sat.* 2, 5, 62–64, in Anchises's speech in the underworld on the Roman future in Virgil's Sixth Aeneid,[82] and most famously in Virgil's Fourth Eclogue, later expounded as messianic prophecy by Lactantius and in the Oration of Constantine.[83] The gentile and Jewish interests mingle (see below) in the messianic praises of the Sibylline Oracles, a literature which in some form will have been known to Virgil and Horace, or in the oracle of Hystaspes on the fall of Rome cited by Lactantius as a prelude to a description of the Second Coming.[84] No great violence was in fact done to this kind of writing when Christian apologists like Lactantius and Eusebius set the oracles of Hystaspes, the Sibyl (classified as a gentile prophetess) and the Fourth Eclogue side by side with the messianic oracles of the Hebrew scriptures as prophecies of Christ.

In the Ptolemaic kingdom which nurtured the LXX, the contact between Jewish and gentile oracular praise is well illustrated by Sib. 3, 652–6, on the king to be divinely sent 'from the sun', ἀπ'ἠελίοιο; the phrase recalls the Egyptian Potter's Oracle in favour of a native Egyptian 'king from the sun' (compare also Ps.72 [71]. 17 LXX, 'before the sun his name shall endure', discussed in chapter III, section 5, above), and it is debated whether these Greek hexameters form a Jewish salute to a gentile ruler, Greek or Egyptian, or to a Jewish king – the interpretation which seems preferable in the light of the lines following in Sib. 3 on the temple of Jerusalem.[85] In the Roman period, similarly, contact between gentile and Jewish oracular praise of rulers is particularly clear when Josephus mentions an 'ambiguous oracle' from the Jewish scriptures to the effect that one from the Jews' country will rule the world, and Tacitus and Suetonius take it to have said that persons coming forth from Judaea would obtain power (Josephus, *BJ* 6, 312; Tacitus, *Hist.* 5, 13; Suetonius, *Vesp.* 4);

Josephus treats it as oracular praise supporting Vespasian's imperial claim, and this Roman application is accepted in Tacitus and Suetonius.

It is then by no means an isolated phenomenon when oracular praises of Jewish rulers in the Hebrew scriptures appear in the LXX rendering to have some contact with contemporary gentile royal praise. Some of their links with the language of ruler-cult are also anticipations of the literature of the cult of Christ. The following examples include illustration of both points.

Thus, first, in Jacob's oracle of the latter days, briefly considered in chapter II, above, the sayings on Judah and his offspring in the LXX come particularly close to the prophecy and praise of gentile kings. Judah, like a monarch with a ruler-cult, is to receive both praise and proskynesis from his brethren, on the lines noted above in connection with Alexander the Great (Gen. 49. 8, σὲ αἰνέσαισαν, προσκυνήσουσίν σοι). Compare also the 'praise' of Christ uttered by children in the temple, which was probably viewed as inspired acclamation (Ps. 8. 3 quoted in Matt. 21. 16; see below); and the *proskynesis* to Christ which is emphasized in such passages as Matt. 2. 11; Phil. 2. 10; Heb. 1. 6 (from Deut. 32. 43 LXX). Then, Judah is 'a lion's whelp' (Gen. 49. 9). The phrase recurs in the LXX Pentateuch (Deut. 32. 22), and is united in the New Testament with the prophecy of Isa. 11. 1 to make an oracle of messianic victory (Rev. 5. 5, cited in this connection in chapter II, section 2, above); but it is also applied in Hellenistic oracular praise, heard from the mouth of Cassandra in Lycophron's poem *Alexandra*, to founders of a nation which will gain the monarchy of land and sea (line 1233, on Romulus and Remus).

Similarly, in the LXX Genesis the ruler descended from Judah appears to be the great ruler expected in gentile prophecies like those of Cassandra and the Sibyl: '*he* (αὐτός) is the expectation (προσδοκία) of the gentile nations' (Gen. 49. 9–10). With the emphatic *he* compare later, from a student of the Sibyl, the emphatic *this* when Aeneas in Virgil's underworld is shown the promised Augustus Caesar; 'this is the man, this is he, whom you have often heard of as promised to you' (Virgil, *Aen.* 6, 791, '*Hic vir, hic est, tibi quem promitti saepius audis*'). Within the New Testament, compare the question to Christ in Q (Matt. 11. 3; Luke 7. 19), 'Are you the coming one, or do we expect (προσδοκῶμεν) another?' For the expectation of a messianic ruler over the gentiles in particular (Gen. 49. 10 LXX) compare Rom. 15. 12 on 'he that shall arise to reign over the gentiles' (from Isa. 11. 10 LXX), and Rom. 15. 18, on what '*Christos* has worked through me for the obedience of the gentile nations'. Finally, as noted already, the ruler descended from Judah is vividly portrayed as tying his colt to the vine, his clothing drenched with wine: 'his eyes are brilliant from wine, and his teeth are whiter than milk' (Gen. 49. 11–12 LXX). This portrait, here enhanced by the Septuagintal interpretation '*than* milk', became central in Christian as well as Jewish treatment of the beauty of the messiah (see the Targums quoted below, and compare chapter III, section 5 [*f*], above).

Secondly, development of the royal references in the material is exemplified in Balaam's oracles. The interpretation of 'the shout of a king' (Num. 23. 21) as a clear reference to the glory of earthly rulers has been noted already. Further, the mention of Israel's king and kingdom in the second part of Num. 24. 7 in the Hebrew becomes the governing theme of the first part of the verse in the LXX, so that the 'waters' there found twice in our Hebrew become first a royal 'man', and then his subject 'nations':

ἐξελεύσεται ἄνθρωπος ἐκ τοῦ σπέρματος αὐτοῦ
    καὶ κυριεύσει ἐθνῶν πολλῶν,
καὶ ὑψωθήσεται ἢ Γὼγ βασιλεία αὐτοῦ
    καὶ αὐξήθησεται ἡ βασιλεία αὐτοῦ.
A Man shall come forth from his seed,
    and shall lord it over many nations,
and his kingdom shall be higher than Gog
    and his kingdom shall be increased.[86]

At his 'advent' (ἐξέλευσις) he will 'lord it' (as *kyrios*) over the gentiles; the nouns given in brackets are not used here, but the verbs ἐξελεύσεται and κυριεύσει show that they could have occurred naturally, and these corresponding nouns and verbs belong both to Graeco-Roman court and cultic vocabulary, and to early Christian statements on Christ.[87] His kingdom can be called messianic, for it will be exalted over the enemy of the last days, Gog (for Agag in the Hebrew), and will be yet more increased – like David's kingdom in I Chron. 14. 2, where both the Hebrew and the Greek are close to the language of the Numbers oracle (see chapter II, section 1, above).[88] 'Increase' was later an important word in royal acclamations, as noted at the beginning of this chapter. This court usage as well as that of the Old Testament probably lies behind the passages on the increase of the body in Col. 2. 19; Eph. 2. 21; 4 15–16.

Thirdly, to move from oracles to a royal psalm, the mighty ruler addressed in divine terms in Ps. 45, whose portrayal merged with that of the ruler from Judah in Gen. 49. 11–12 to suggest the beauty of the messiah (see below), is in the LXX yet more clearly depicted as a king (v. 5 *rkb*, 'ride on', but LXX *basileue*, 'reign'); he is the *kyrios* of his bride (v. 12), but he receives *proskynesis* not from her, as in the Hebrew, but from the daughters of Tyre with their gifts, as the wealthy among the people make their entreaties (v. 13): the suppliant population of the Syrian cities fall down before him.

 The developments exemplified in these three passages mean that in the LXX the universal *proskynesis* to the Jewish monarch by the gentile kings and nations in Ps. 72. 11 (both Hebrew and Greek) appears still more clearly than in the Hebrew as typical of a widely-attested biblical conception. When later datings of the Hebrew psalms were common, the far-flung southerly imperial hopes of this psalm (compare in general Zech. 9. 9–11) led to the suggestion that the king in view at the time of composition must have been a Ptolemy, perhaps Philadelphus; this would then have been a Hebrew piece to set beside the court poetry of Callimachus and Theocritus.[89] Ps. 72 is more likely already to have been part of the Hebrew Psalter at the beginning of the Ptolemaic period, and, whenever it received its present literary form, to echo praises of the Israelite king from the pre-exilic age; but in its Greek version it can indeed stand as a Jewish counterpart to Alexandrian royal encomia – addressed to the Jewish, not the gentile king:

κοὶ προσκυνήσουσιν αὐτῷ πάντες οἱ βασιλεῖς,
    πάντα τὰ ἔθνη δουλεύσουσιν αὐτῷ.
And all kings shall do obeisance to him,
    all nations shall serve him.

In the Greek, the prominence of *proskynesis* brings to the fore an honour accorded to benefactors, especially kings, and debated, as already noted, because it could be taken as a sign of divinization. In the Jewish context *proskynein* was closely associated with the worship of the almighty God (e.g. LXX Gen. 22. 5 (mount Moriah); Neh. 8. 6 [LXX II Esdras 18. 6] (public reading of the law); Ecclus 50. 17 [19], 21 [23] (the Jerusalem temple); compare the Hebrew name *bet hishtahawot*, 'house of prostration', for a place of worship, in the Damascus Document (col. xi; 10.41), and the statement of the difference between Jewish and gentile custom – in a context where Jews are suspected of disloyalty to the Ptolemaic dynasty – as περὶ τῶν προσκυνήσεων καὶ τροφῶν διάστασις, 'a difference over prostrations and diets' (III Macc. 3. 7). In the LXX it was indeed also used, representing Hebrew השתחוה and somewhat as 'worship' was formerly used in English, for a humble salute to human authorities considered worshipful.[90] Nevertheless, it represents a salute close to homage, and can acquire among Jews in the Greek world some of its pejorative Greek overtones of barbaric or slavish self-abasement, as is clear when Philo, in a passage recalling his criticism of *proskynesis* to Gaius (*Legatio* 116), praises Joseph's brothers for hating the thought of doing obeisance (*proskynein*) to one who appropriates the honour of the immortal King (*Somn.* 2, 99–100).[91]

In Israelite custom as represented in the Hebrew Bible, however, it had been considered appropriate to use the same attitudes of respect for the earthly and the heavenly king, as when, in the imagined scene of David's offering for the temple, 'bowing the knee, they worshipped the Lord, and the king', κάμψαντες τὰ γόνατα προσεκύνησαν τῷ κυρίῳ καὶ τῷ βασιλεῖ (I Chron. 29. 20). The Greek renderings here and in Ps. 72 follow straightforward Hebrew, but in Ps. 45 the LXX interpretation extends the scope of the *proskynesis* and makes it into a definitely public event involving many of the king's subjects, with a reference to foreign homage recalling Ps. 72. The biblical topic of homage to the present or future Jewish monarch is therefore presented in these passages in language which highlights its resemblance to the disputed honours of gentile monarchs and to the worship of the Jewish God. Moreover, *proskynein* belongs, as noted already, to those antecedents of the praises of Christ which have already appeared in the royal vocabulary of the LXX.

Lastly, Psalm 72 (71). 17 is one of the passages which show special interest in the name of the king or the coming king (cf. Isa. 9. 6; Jer. 23. 6). 'Let his name be blessed for ever; before the sun his name shall abide, and all the tribes of the earth shall be blessed in it (*or* him). All the nations shall call him blessed.' Interest in the name was continued in rabbinic speculation on the name of the messiah, as noted in chapter III, section 5, above; but here the 'blessing' of the king's name is of note as a partial antecedent to the Christian practice of 'calling on the name' of Christ (I Cor. 1. 2 and elsewhere).

In the Greek period, then, the ancestral Jewish inheritance of kingship received the emphasis which the centrality of monarchy in Hellenistic political theory and practice naturally encouraged. A wide range of Jewish literature, including the Greek Pentateuch, bears this royal stamp. Messianic hopes were accordingly rooted in a political inheritance of kingship which was recognized by Jews themselves as ancestral, but which was also, a point less often noted, in touch with a central concern of the contemporary non-Jewish world. The convergence of Jewish and gentile concern meant that Jewish monarchy and the messianic kingdom were both envisaged in terms of the kingship of this period. Like the Hasmonaean and Herodian Jewish monarchies, Jewish messianism in many ways shared the ethos of the Greek kingdom. The praise and *proskynesis* envisaged in the Septuagint recall a Hellenistic royal court, and offer antecedents to the Christian praises and worship of Christ.

(ii) Against this background the exaltation of contemporary Jewish rulers by their subjects can now be recalled. It has many points of resemblance not only with descriptions of a king-messiah, but also with the treatment of past Jewish kings and leaders noted already in Chronicles, and apparent again in Daniel and Ezekiel the Tragedian. In Dan. 2. 46, as B. A. Mastin has shown, the ruler-cult is in view under its aspect as the acknowledgment of exceptional benefactions, and this, together with the effective satire constituted by a scene in which a gentile king abases himself before a Jew, helps to explain the striking presentation of Daniel as receiving divine honours with all serenity.[92] This presentation stands beside the Danielic vision of one like a son of man receiving 'dominion, and glory, and a kingdom' at the overthrow of the last gentile kingdom (7. 13–14), and the messianic allusion in Ben Sira's condemnation of royal claims (chapter II, section 3, above), as an indication that Jews envisaged the exaltation of their own leaders in a counterpart to gentile royal honours. The same conclusion can be drawn from the contrast implied in Ezekiel the Tragedian (second century BC) between Pharaoh and the enthroned Moses, who in a dream-vision receives homage from the stars of heaven (Ezekiel Tragicus 68–89). Correspondingly, in the Greek period, contemporary Jewish rulers were honoured by hymns of praise. The high priest evoked not only the messianic poem on a new priest in the Testament of Levi, where 'his star shall arise in heaven as a king's' (Test. Levi 18. 3, cited in chapter III, section 5 [*c*], above), but also the elaborate laudation of the officiating high priest presented in Ecclus. 50 with reference to Simon, son of Onias – a form of praise which was continued in the poetic celebration of the appearance of the high priest in the piyyutim of the Day of Atonement.[93]

Under the Hasmonaeans, as noted in chapter II, Judas Maccabaeus was 'the one who saved Israel' (I Macc. 9. 21), and poems in praise of Judas and Simon Maccabaeus were preserved (I Macc. 3. 3–9; 14. 4–15). The description of Hyrcanus I as king, priest and prophet in Josephus (*BJ* 1. 68–69; *Ant.* 13, 299–300), recalling the title of Simon Maccabaeus as prince (ἡγούμενος, cf. Gen. 49. 10 LXX) and high priest in I Macc. 14. 41, no doubt reflects Hasmonaean court theology which created a messianic atmosphere around a reigning king, somewhat as occurred later with Herod the Great and Bar Kokhba.[94]

(A Hebrew composition [4Q448] which has been interpreted as a prayer for a king Jonathan, identified as either Alexander Jannaeus or Jonathan Maccabaeus, would be to some extent comparable with this Greek material if that interpretation were correct. It seems more likely, however, that the proper name 'Jonathan' is not to be read in the relevant passages; the fragmentary text probably expresses hope for the future establishment of

God's kingdom in Jerusalem, rather than prayer for the particular king who now reigns.[95])

From the Herodian period, a series of Jewish royal acclamations are described by Josephus and Philo: notably, for Herod the Great's young Hasmonaean brother-in-law Aristobulus, a short-lived high priest, in the temple at the Feast of Tabernacles (Josephus, *Ant.* 15, 51–52, cited above; *BJ* 1. 437); for Archelaus, enthroned in the temple (*Ant.* 17, 200–12; cf. *BJ* 2. 1–9); for the supposed Alexander, son of Herod and Mariamme, in Rome (*Ant.* 17, 324–38; cf. *BJ* 2, 101–10); for Agrippa I in Alexandria (Philo, *Flacc.* 25–39), Jerusalem (Josephus, *Ant.* 17, 293–6, 299, cf. M. Sotah 7. 8), and Caesarea (Acts 12. 20–23; Josephus, *Ant.* 19, 343–50); and, modelled on these occasions, the king-like advent of Menahem, son of Judas the Galilaean, in Jerusalem and the temple in 66 (Josephus, *BJ* 2, 434, 444). With these should be associated the dedication of the rebuilt Jerusalem sanctuary on Herod the Great's accession day, and his speech to the people in the temple on the succession (Josephus *Ant.* 15, 423; 16, 132–5; cf. *BJ* 1, 457–66).[96] The mainly brief descriptions include notices of brilliant vesture (Aristobulus, Archelaus, Agrippa I, Menahem), enthronement (Archelaus in Jerusalem, Agrippa I at Caesarea) and acclamations (Aristobulus, Alexander, Archelaus, Agrippa I), sometimes with specific reference to titles (Archelaus, Agrippa I in Alexandria and Caesarea).

The familiarity and use of acclamation in the Jewish community is clear. A dramatically heightened form of such public appearances is presented by messianic epiphanies in Herodian apocalypses, notably the Parables of Enoch (48. 5; 62. 9, on obeisance before the revealed Son of man). Within the New Testament, the Transfiguration of Christ into a figure of dazzling brightness with glittering robes (Mark 9. 2–8 and parallels) is an epiphany partly comparable both with these appearances and with apocalyptic scenes; it is related to the messianic development of the enthronement and praise of the Israelite king, and it corresponds to the angelic appearance of the Son of man in the Parables of Enoch (46. 1).[97] Also comparable with the Jewish royal public appearances of this era as well as messianic tradition are the praise of Christ at his advent in Jerusalem and the temple, noted in section 1 of this chapter, above (see Mark 11. 9–10 and parallels, Matt. 21. 15); and the scene of universal obeisance and praise imagined in Phil. 2. 10–11, with concluding emphasis on the venerated royal name of Jesus and the titles of sovereignty 'Christ' (messiah) and 'Lord'.

Philo, who reports Agrippa I's enthusiastic welcome by Alexandrian Jews, is the most famous witness both to criticism and to sympathetic understanding of gentile ruler-cult on the part of the Jewish communities. He mocks Caligula's attempts to link himself with demigods and gods –

Heracles, Dionysus, the Dioscuri; Hermes, Apollo and Ares – and he represents Caligula as not satisfied with the time-honoured ὑπέρ formula of prayer on the king's behalf (*Leg. ad Gaium* 79–114; 356–7); on the other hand, he underlines Jewish readiness to give all the honours which the laws permit (*Flacc.* 97, cf. 48–9; *Leg. ad Gaium* 133), and expands without criticism on the exceptional honours, including temples, given to Augustus (*Leg. ad Gaium* 149–51, quoted above on the Augusteum honouring the emperor as sea-god). It is not surprising that the first-century Greek prose passages which have been taken to conceal communal hymns include Philo's panegyric on Augustus (*Leg. ad Gaium* 143–7). The representatively Jewish character of Philo's sympathy for these practices in the case of a monarch regarded as a Jewish benefactor is confirmed by the large-scale acclamations which the Jews of contemporary Rome and Alexandria offered to their own princes.

The accounts given above include reference to negative as well as positive reaction, on the lines discerned in the previous chapter (section 2) as followed among both gentiles and Jews with regard to ruler-cult. The negative reaction strikingly marks the tradition on Agrippa I. He could evoke enthusiastic demonstrations of Jewish loyalty, on the pattern of ruler-cult, as had happened in Alexandria (Philo, *Flacc.* 25–39, noted above, probably implying that Agrippa was hailed as *Marin*, 'our lord'); but his death was understood by many Jews as a punishment for accepting specifically divine praises in the theatre at Caesarea, an interpretation which appears in both Acts (12. 20–23, in general hostile to the king, who is regarded as a persecutor) and Josephus (*Ant.* 19, 343–50, in general more favourable). These sources should not be pressed for close accuracy on the acclamations, but it is likely that, as each source suggests in a different way, the acclamations offered to Agrippa were modelled closely on those currently offered to gentile rulers.[98] In Josephus, Agrippa's acclamation by courtiers 'addressing him as a god' (θεὸν προσαγορεύοντες) at the point when he shone out in his glittering robe at daybreak follows exactly the form which had been demanded shortly before by Agrippa's former patron Caligula (in Josephus's version of Claudius's letter, quoted above); and in Acts, the cry of the people 'the voice of a god, and not of a man' recalls the emphasis on the beauty and majesty of the ruler's voice which later became a famous aspect of Nero's court, but is more widely attested in ruler-cult.[99] Josephus ascribes the acclamation to misguided flattery, much as the divine praises of kings are treated in Wisdom (14. 17) and Plutarch and later on in Athenaeus, as cited above. Jews were divided on this matter, and on the merits of individual rulers, but all were familar with the idiom of royal praise, and many employed it enthusiastically for Jewish rulers of whom they approved.

Herodian ruler-cult in the larger sense offers, with all differences, a manifestation often comparable with the contemporary cult of Christ, honoured as 'king of the Jews' or 'king of Israel' (Matt. 2. 2; John 1. 41, etc.). The Herodian cult included the enthusiastic reception of Herodian princes in Rome and Alexandria, in Alexandria probably with the acclamation 'our lord' in Aramaic, which would fit other evidence for the Greek *kyrios* as a title of Herodian kings.[100] The same title, likewise attested both in Aramaic and Greek, deeply marks the contemporary New Testament literature of the cult of Christ (I Cor. 12. 3; 16. 22). For both Herod the Great and other Herodian kings and princes there is clear evidence for the celebration of birthdays and accession days. The dedication of the rebuilt Jerusalem temple on Herod the Great's accession day honoured the names of the heavenly and earthly king together; Archelaus on his accession was acclaimed and praised while enthroned in the temple (Josephus, *BJ* 2, 1; *Ant.* 17, 200–1, cited above); and Antipas's birthday involved a state banquet (Mark 6. 21). Correspondingly, it seems likely that 'Herod's Days', mentioned with their festal dinner by the Roman satirist Persius, under Nero, in a passage on the Jews (5, 179–84), were royal birthdays or accession days celebrated by the Jews of Rome.[101] As days dedicated to the ruler (*kyrios*) they would then offer an analogy to the early Christian 'Lord's Day' (Rev. 1. 10; Did. 14. 1), and 'Lord's Supper' (I Cor. 11. 20). Similarly, just as the rightful king was enthroned on a dais in the temple (Solomon, II Chron. 6. 13, so interpreted by Josephus, *Ant.* 8, 107; M. Sotah 7. 8; Archelaus followed this practice, Agrippa I sought favour by declining to sit), so his rival would enthrone himself there (II Thess. 2. 4). Herodian public life therefore exemplifies royal appearances, praises, days and meals which recall both the biblical royal and messianic traditions, and the literature and customs of the Christ-cult: the narratives of the Transfiguration and the entry into Jerusalem and the temple, the universal obeisance and acclamation imagined in Phil. 2. 10–11, the Lord's Day and the Lord's Supper.

(iii) Lastly, rabbinic and targumic biblical interpretation carries on this development, and confirms the continuing importance of its place in Jewish tradition. Treatments of the theme of homage to the messiah, in particular, present material for comparison with the literature of Christ-cult. First, the enthroned messiah receives tribute, in accordance with Pss. 45 and 72 and their Septuagintal interpretation, discussed above. Thus R. Hoshaiah (early third century) is said to have been pleased with a scriptural proof that 'all the gifts which Jacob our father gave to Esau, the nations of the world will give back to king messiah in the age to come'. This comfortable doctrine was inferred from Ps. 72. 10, 'an offering shall they bring *back*' (Ber. R. 78.

13, on Gen. 33. 10); it evidently presupposes that Ps. 72. 10 speaks of gifts to the messiah, but then suggests a new exegesis of *yashibu*, 'they shall bring back'. The age of the notion that the messiah will receive gifts is shown by its appearance in I Enoch 53. 1 (all who dwell on land, sea and islands will bring gifts and presents and offerings to the Chosen One). In the Targum, similarly, the 'lambs for the ruler of the land' to be brought to mount Zion from Petra are 'tribute for the messiah of Israel' (Targ. Isa. 16. 1). An ancient interpretation of the gifts, suggested by such passages as Isa. 60. 3–10, makes them the exiled Israelites themselves. This is already attested at Ps. Sol. 17. 31 (the nations shall come to see the messiah's glory, bringing Jerusalem's sons as gifts), and it appears again in the midrash, for example at Mid. Teh. 87. 6. Here 'I will remember Rahab and Babylon' (Ps. 87. 4) is explained, in the name of Judah b. Simon (early fourth century), as prophesying the restoration of exiled Israelites to Messiah son of David and Messiah son of Ephraim – 'a man and a man', as v. 5 can be rendered.

Secondly, the beauty and splendour of the messiah are celebrated. Here an interest in the outward appearance of the hero forms a link both with Greek and Roman cults and with the cult of Christ, as noted above. Thus in the LXX and the Targums the messiah becomes the subject of what G. A. Smith called 'perhaps the most voluptuous picture in the Old Testament' – the blessing of Judah as 'binding to the vine his foal, and to the choice vine his ass's colt; he washed his garments in wine, and his clothes in the blood of grapes; his eyes shall be red with wine, and his teeth white with milk' (Gen. 49. 11–12).[102]

'This might be the portrait of a Bacchus breaking from the vineyards of Sicily', as Smith memorably put it. In the LXX the details of the face were heightened, as already noticed, to give brilliant or joy-creating eyes and exceptionally white teeth. In the targums, development has gone much further, and combination with Ps. 45. 3 has presented a portrait of the messiah's beauty and royal majesty (compare chapter III, section 5, above). The rendering below is from the Fragment Targum on vv. 11–12, almost identical here with Pseudo-Jonathan and Neofiti.[103]

11. How fair is king messiah, who will arise from among those of the house of Judah! he girds his loins and goes out to war against his enemies, and will slay kings with their princes, reddening the mountains with the blood of their slain, and whitening the hills with the fat of their mighty ones. His clothes are rolled in blood, and he is like one who treads the grapes.

12. How fair are the eyes of king messiah to see, more than pure wine, not for beholding the uncovering of nakedness or the shedding of

innocent blood. His teeth are whiter than milk, not for eating what is gained by violence and robberies. His mountains are red with vines, and his presses with wine; his hills will be white from abundance of corn and flocks of sheep.

The figure portrayed here now brings vengeance and superabundance, gifts which would still suit Smith's Bacchic comparison, but in the context are to be understood as the benefits expected from a great king; so Trajan was praised for providing vengeance (*ultio*) against informers (Pliny, *Pan.* 35–36), St Paul commends the emperor as a 'revenger' against evil-doers (Rom. 13. 4), and Antichrist's plausibility partly consists in the fact that he pretends, like a good king, to offer vengeance (Irenaeus, *Haer.* 5, 37, 3). The figure of the avenger in the targums here was created by the combination of v. 11 with Isa. 63. 1–6, where the avenger in red-drenched garments is 'beautiful in his apparel' (Isa. 63. 1, LXX *horaios*); a messianic application of this passage already occurs at Rev. 19. 11–16, and it influences the rendering of Gen. 49. 11 in Neofiti, Ps. Jonathan and the Fragment Targum.

In Onkelos on this verse messianic victory remains the theme, but the note of vengeance is lacking; the messiah leads the people to the holy city, they build his temple, and then the righteous learn with him. Here the biblical portrait of the king as a bible-reader (Josh. 1. 8) is taken up.[104] The vividly pictorial character of the description remains. The messiah retains his red garments, imperial rather than drenched with wine or blood; 'let his raiment be of fine purple' and rich dye.

The picture of overflowing prosperity in v. 12, however, on vine-clad mountains and hills white with corn, is common to Onkelos and the other targums. It develops Old Testament passages on abundance under the messianic reign (e.g. Ps. 72. 16; 132. 15) into a form which is comparable with the expectations expressed by Jews and Christians at the end of the Second-Temple period; when the messiah reigns the vines will each have a thousand branches each bearing a thousand clusters (II Baruch 29. 5), or the clusters from vines ten times more fecund again will compete with one another in asking to be taken by the saints, saying 'Bless the Lord through me' (Papias, in Irenaeus, *Haer.* 5, 33, 3).[105] The corn-covered hills seem particularly to recall Ps. 72. 16. In the Targum 'there' or 'he' (the future king is the subject of the previous and the following verses) 'shall be a staff of bread in the land, on top of the mountains'; this seems likely to be an old interpretation, given the similar LXX 'there' or 'he' 'shall be a support in the land, on top of the mountains'. The psalm-verse is quoted to show that the last redeemer shall give bread like the first in a general comparison between Moses and the messiah, perhaps from the end of the third century (Eccl. R. 1, 9, 1; R. Berekiah, in the name of R. Isaac). Here the links between the messiah and bread taken up in John 6 and Didache 9–10 receive a comparable independent development.

Thirdly, the lofty exaltation of the messiah continues to be emphasized. In the midrash, in a famous interpretation of Isa. 52. 13, 'my servant . . . shall be exalted and lifted up, and shall be very high', the messiah is 'exalted' above Abraham, 'lifted up' above Moses, and 'high' above the ministering angels (Tanhuma Buber, Genesis, 70a, Toledoth 20).[106] The Targum here less startlingly but still emphatically has: 'my servant the messiah . . . shall be exalted, and increase, and be very strong.' The view presented in the midrash is consistent with the conceptions of a spiritual or heavenly messiah outlined from pre-rabbinic and rabbinic texts in chapter III, section 5, above. The subjugation of gentile kings is prominent in the theme of homage to the messiah, just noticed, both in rabbinic exposition and in its earlier appearance in apocalypses like the Parables of Enoch. Here, however, the messiah is exalted above all the angelic and human princes of the heavenly court. In the New Testament, a comparable implication can be drawn from the appearance of Moses and Elijah at the Transfiguration, and from the argument for the superiority of Christ to the angels in Heb. 1. 1–14.

Lastly, midrashic tradition preserves vestiges of hymns to the messiah in the homiletic midrash Pesikta Rabbathi (37. 7; ed. M. Friedmann, 164a; also found in PRK Suppl. VI 5). The passage belongs to a much discussed messianic section of Pes. R. (34; 36–37) which is given widely varying dates, in the third or the early seventh century, or later, but seems not to be strongly affected by Christian messianism; it can perhaps be ascribed in substance to the well-marked messianic expectations of the later third century.[107] This is suggested by the inclusion in the text of a teaching in the name of Simeon b. Pazzi: 'At that hour the Holy One, blessed be he, exalts the messiah to the heaven of heavens, and spreads over him the brightness of his glory because of the nations of the world, before the wicked Persians. He says to him, Ephraim, messiah of our righteousness, be judge over these, and do with them what your soul desires . . .' (Pes. R. 37, 3, 163a).[108]

The praises offered by Israel when the messiah is revealed in light run as follows (37, 7, 164a):[109]

Blessed is the hour in which he was created, blessed the womb from which he came forth, blessed the generation whose eyes see him, blessed the eye that waited for him; for the opening of his lips is blessing and peace, and his utterance is repose of spirit, the purpose of his heart is security and rest. Blessed is the eye that is worthy to see him, for his tongue has spoken forgiveness and pardon to Israel. His prayer is a sweet-smelling savour, his supplication is pure and holy. Blessed are his fathers, who are worthy of the good things of the world, which are hidden for ever.

These passages attest the continuation of the conceptions of a highly exalted messiah in glory, his designation as God's viceroy, and the offering of praise to him. Some of this material was cited by H. Riesenfeld to illustrate the messianic development of biblical enthronement texts with which the Transfiguration narrative is connected.[110] In the hymn concerning the messiah there is once again a pictorial element, but emphasis falls especially on the peace and pardon conveyed by his utterance (cf. Eph. 2. 17, echoing Isa. 57. 19) and his power as intercessor (cf. Rom. 8. 34). The New Testament depictions of Christ in state, at the Transfiguration and the entry into Jerusalem in the Gospels or in the scene of universal homage in Philippians, recall Herodian public life, as has just been shown; but they also belong within a continuum of messianic praise stretching from the LXX to the rabbinic literature.

(b) Titles of Christ and Jewish messianism

The praises and homage offered to Christ then seem to take their place naturally in the series of Jewish royal and messianic praises just considered. Would this be the case, however, if the early Christian material itself were made the starting-point? With this question in mind, finally, the titles most frequently given to Christ in the New Testament are briefly reviewed with an eye to their links with messianism as outlined above.

The titles are among the literary material closest to the cult, as noted already. Their number in the New Testament is already large; Vincent Taylor reviewed fifty-five.[111] Their collection and selection were important in ancient hymnody and doctrine, from the list in Justin Martyr, *Dial.* 34, 2 (King, Priest, God, Lord, Angel, Man . . .) to Latin treatises and hymns from late antiquity.[112] They continued to be important in worship, as appears in the mediaeval West from the Advent Antiphons, each beginning with a title of Christ, and from a sequence preserved in the Sarum Breviary and elsewhere, *Alma chorus Domini nunc pangat nomina summi*, 'Let the propitious choir now sound out the names of the highest Lord'; this hymn consists of fifty-three titles of Christ, many in transliterated Greek, beginning with Messias, Soter, Emanuel, and ending with Ysus (*Iesus*).[113]

The choice of titles to be considered in historical study of early christology often begins from those of the Synoptic tradition, which for the most part are also important in Paul and John. Thus F. Hahn dealt chiefly with five titles found in Mark: Son of man, Lord (*Kyrios*), Christ, Son of David, and Son of God; but on this basis he could write a general study of 'Christological titles of sovereignty: their history in early Christianity' (to quote his book-title).[114] The same titles are accordingly central in different types of investigation. G. Vermes, writing on Jesus and concerned with the relationship and contrast between titles and the thought of Jesus and the first disciples, picked out prophet, Lord, Messiah, Son of man, and Son of God (all attested in Matt. 16. 14–22); whereas C. F. D. Moule, writing on the origin of christology and arguing that titles show continuity and development in growth rather than shift and change under pressure, chose four from the same list: Son of man, Son of God, Christ, and Lord.[115] 'Christ' and 'Lord' each occur over two hundred times in the Pauline corpus; Son of God is far less common in Paul, significant though it is where it does occur, but deeply marks Johannine literature; Son of man, not in Paul, often appears in the Fourth Gospel. This approach from the Synoptic tradition thus brings under scrutiny titles which were very widely important, but those characteristic of John and Paul rather than the Synoptic Gospels can seem in danger of neglect. M. Hengel accordingly begins a short study of titles of Christ with the titles 'God' and 'Word' in John, only then considering others.[116]

The New Testament titles taken as representative here begin with the four chosen by Moule, which are important in the Synoptics, John and Paul: Christ, Lord, Son of man, Son of God. These four are supplemented by High Priest, Saviour and God, from Hebrews, Paul and John. At first glance the messianic traditions considered so far can be seen to embrace a number of these titles. Son of man, Christ and High Priest, together with Son of David from Hahn's list, clearly belong to Jewish tradition, however much further interpretation the Christians give them. V. Taylor regarded Christ, Son of man, and Son of God as messianic in origin, and he also recognized many less frequently used titles as messianic.[117] On the other hand, from the standpoint of a first-century observer, the group Son of God, Lord, Saviour and God most immediately recall the vocabulary of ruler-cult. Yet, attention has been drawn here to the long-standing inter-action between ruler-cult and the language of Jewish messianism, from the time of Alexander the Great onwards (chapter III, section 2; this chapter, section 1, above). Against this background, it has seemed likely that Son of God and Lord, which also belong to Old Testament royal vocabulary, reached the Christians through messianic tradition, and the same is probably true for Saviour and God (see below). As a group, therefore, the principal New Testament titles of Christ vividly attest the impact of Jewish messianism on the cult of Christ.

This general impression must now be substantiated by brief comment on individual titles.

(i) *Christ* might perhaps be thought problematic for the argument presented here, because already by the time of Paul – in whose writings more than half the *c.* 531 New Testament occurrences of the title are found – it was well on the way to being used simply as a surname.[118] In fact, however, this rapid development is a striking sign of the influence of messianism; Christian loyalty was given to one known simply as 'messiah', in line with the special Jewish usage of unqualified 'messiah' studied in chapter I, section 1, above. Correspondingly, the origin of the name *Christianos* (Acts 11. 26) has been plausibly connected with the politically disturbing proclamation of a messiah.[119] Moreover, the development of the title towards the status of a proper name by no means took away the specifically messianic associations of *Christos*, as can be seen in Paul.[120] Not only are these associations of the title connected with Pauline themes like the election of Israel, as C. E. B. Cranfield stresses, but the work of the messiah in deliverance and conquest underlies statements on redemption, for example at Gal. 1. 4; 5. 1 on *Christos* as delivering and setting free; moreover, there is a case for interpreting Paul's expectations of the future as including a messianic kingdom in Jerusalem, on the lines followed in the second century by Justin and Irenaeus.[121] These aspects of the Pauline epistles correspond in turn with the accusations said in Acts (17. 3, 7) to be brought against Paul's announcement of the messiah in Thessalonica.[122] Most important in all this, however, is the emergence of the messianic associations of *Christos* in connection with many different Pauline topics: Israel, the cross, resurrection appearances, redemption, gospel, apostleship, church, parousia.[123]

The continuation of these associations highlights the significance for the origins of the Christ-cult of the link between the title *Christos* and conceptions of the messiah as sovereign and worshipful. Precisely as messianic king, Christ would receive obedience, obeisance and acclamation. This point is illustrated by a wide range of New Testament sources. So in Matthew the wise men, having seen the star signalling 'the king of the Jews', and having occasioned an inquiry where 'the Christ' should be born, come to 'worship' him (Matt. 2. 2, 4, 8, 11). Similarly, in all the Synoptic Gospels, a major theme of the Transfiguration narrative is the epiphany of 'the Christ' whom Peter has confessed, and whom he now intends to honour with a tabernacle, along with Moses and Elijah (Matt. 17. 4 and parallels). In John, the unexpectedly successive phrases 'son of God, king of Israel' follow and correspond to *messias* (John 1. 41, 49); the two later phrases appear as equivalents, or perhaps even in ascending order, and their utterance by Nathanael expresses the fact that he 'believes'; comparably, in John 9, confession that Jesus is 'Christ' (in the probably editorial 9. 22) corresponds to expressed belief in 'the Son of man', which is followed by obeisance (9. 38); finally, in John it is explicitly 'the king of Israel' who is acclaimed with Hosanna at the entry into Jerusalem (12. 13, 15). In all these cases, then, 'Christ' and 'king of Israel' are titles of real eminence; for 'faith' in a royal leader compare the Pentateuchal faith in Moses (Exod. 14. 31, cf. Num. 21. 5).[124]

A famous but similarly unexpected succession of titles appears in Acts 2. 36, 'lord and Christ'; 'lord' arises from Ps. 110. 1, which has just been quoted, but it is evidently also or even more important to declare that Jesus is 'Christ', as is implied but not stated in Ps. 110. The speech in Acts including this phrase begins from the outpouring of the spirit on the disciples, and the messiah is perhaps envisaged as characteristically and pre-eminently endued with the spirit (Isa. 11. 2–4), and, so endued, as the anointed comforter of the afflicted with the oil of joy (Isa. 61. 1–4); this would be consistent with the depiction of Jesus in Luke 3. 22; 4. 1 (endued with spirit); 4. 17–19 (quoting Isa. 61. 1–2); Acts 10. 38 (anointed with the holy spirit and power; in a speech leading to another outpouring of the spirit).[125] The pre-eminence of the messiah in particular as bestowing the spirit on those who are his would then be in view.

In Paul, among the places where the messiah specifically is envisaged as receiving homage is Rom. 15. 7–12, on the gracious acceptance of gentiles as well as Jews by *Christos*; as noted already in discussion of the end of the greater Song of Moses (chapter III, section 3, above), Paul's quotation of 'Rejoice, O gentiles, with his people' from Deut. 32. 43 is particularly natural if he, like the writer to the Hebrews (Heb. 1. 6), takes it as prophesying homage to the messiah (Rom. 15. 11). The last of the little chain of texts which support Paul's exhortation mentions the messiah more explicitly: 'There shall be a root of Jesse, and he that shall arise to reign over the gentiles, in him shall the gentiles hope' (Rom. 15. 12, from Isa. 11. 10 LXX). The messiah here is king of the gentiles, who unite with the people of the circumcision to do him homage, and hope in him (compare the stress on hope in the praise of the emperor in the inscription of Tiberius Julius Alexander, cited in section 1, above).

The importance of homage specifically to the messiah in this instance underlines the eminence and weight of the title *christos* in two passages which more obviously suggest the importance of *kyrios*: II Cor. 4. 4–5 (the light of the gospel of the glory of the Christ . . .we preach *Christ* Jesus [as] Kyrios); Phil. 2. 5–11 (Christ Jesus . . . every tongue shall confess that Jesus

Christ is Kyrios). Lastly, in Hebrews the angels worship him who is called by God 'my son', namely, 'the Christ' (Ps. 2. 7 quoted in Heb. 1. 5; 5. 5). This is 'the Christ' who, being perfected, is the cause of everlasting 'salvation' for 'all who listen to him' (ὑπακούω), all his subjects; he receives from God himself the honorific address 'high-priest after the order of Melchizedech' (Heb. 5. 9–10). The verb προσαγορεύω, chosen here, is also used for giving honorific address to a king or emperor, as just noted from Josephus in connection with Caligula and Agrippa I. With this strikingly messianic vocabulary compare the use of 'obey' (πείθομαι) for the followers of Theudas and the Egyptian in Acts 5. 36–37 ('those who obeyed them'), and 'heaven and earth shall listen to his messiah' in 4Q521, fragment 2, ii 1 – probably implying the obedience of angels and humanity alike. Here in Hebrews Christ is again the messianic king who saves his obedient subjects; as Deut. 32. 6 shows, he is worshipped by angels; and as Ps. 110. 4 shows, he is also honoured by God himself, on the pattern of an earthly acclamation, with the title 'high priest' (see below). In a range of New Testament sources, therefore, it is envisaged that Christ rules and receives homage and acclamation precisely as messiah.

(ii) Against this background of the high and worshipful status of the messianic king it is possible to see the force of M. Hengel's statement that 'in early Christianity there was no Kyrios-theology which was not dependent on the messiahship of Jesus'.[126] *Lord* (*kyrios*) ranges downwards in application from its Septuagintal use to designate the supreme God, which has been taken as the main sense of the christological title by scholars including Fitzmyer and Hengel.[127] In the light of the vigour and loftiness of the title *Christos*, however, this inference seems open to question. It is perhaps more likely that *kyrios* too is a royal title. Indeed, the use of *kyrios* or the Aramaic equivalent *mara* as a substitute for the tetragram is a Jewish instance of a more widespread practice, also attested in pagan cultic vocabulary, whereby deities are given the titles of kings. Thus the 'lord Sarapis' was envisaged as a king, especially in Alexandria.[128] King-like deities can of course be viewed as the rivals of kings; compare the hostility of king Pentheus to Dionysus, and of Pharaoh to the God of Israel. Philo brings out the royal connotations of *kyrios* when he paraphrases Pharaoh's reply to Moses in Exod. 5. 2 by 'Who is this whom I ought to obey? I do not know this new so-called *kyrios*' (Philo, *VM* 1, 88). The application of *kyrios* and its Aramaic equivalent *mara* to earthly rulers, including Herodian kings, is well attested in usage contemporary with the New Testament, as noted above; and this usage has biblical antecedents, notably in the application of *adôn* (Greek *kyrios*) to the king in Ps. 110. 1 and the historical books. The related adjective *kyriakos*, used in the New Testament phrases 'Lord's

Supper' and 'Lord's Day', is also found in connection with rulers, for instance in the inscription of Tiberius Julius Alexander, as noted above (this chapter, section 1). To interpret *kyrios* as a title of Christ against this royal background in biblical and court usage seems most consistent with the development of *christos* just noted, and with the widespread New Testament importance of the concept of Christ as king.[129]

It is in fact likely that *kyrios* was already a title applied to the messiah. This is suggested by the occurrences of *christos kyrios*, 'Christ the lord', at Lam. 4. 20; Ps. Sol. 17. 32; Luke 2. 11 (p. 10, above). It has been suggested that the text of the first two passages should be emended to *christos kyriou*, 'the Lord's Christ', 'the messiah of the Lord', on the supposition that copyists familiar with the Lucan passage had mistaken or deliberately changed the final letter. This is not impossible, but familiarity with the Gospels would also have brought acquaintance with the phrase *christos kyriou* (Luke 2. 26, where no variant *-os* is recorded in the 27th edition of Nestle-Aland's Greek Testament); a Christian copyist would not necessarily be impelled to alter the form with *-ou* when writing out Old Testament books. Probably, then, Christians used *kyrios* as a royal title which was already associated with the messiah. This interpretation permits understanding of the development of the worship of Christ, in view of the exaltation accorded both to Israelite and to gentile kings, as noted above in discussion of ruler-cult.

(iii) *Son of man* develops, like *Christ*, from Jewish messianic usage (chapter II, section 3; chapter III, section 5, above). Its disuse as a title in Paul is probably due to the associations of lowliness which it acquired among Christians less acquainted with its messianic associations, but its strong representation in the four Gospels is a further attestation of the influence of Jewish messianism; the related *Man*, echoing texts including Num. 24. 7; Isa. 19. 20 LXX (chapter II, section 1, above), sometimes probably appears (John 19. 5; Acts 17. 31).[130]

(iv) *Son of God*, treated briefly above (this chapter, section 2), recalls that Psalms such as 2; 45; 89 and 110 envisaged the Israelite king as son of God or god.[131] The king is God's son in Pss. 2 and 89, and the description survives vestigially as a messianic title, and, once again, was prominent in gentile ruler-cult (this chapter, section 1). For its loftiness as a title of the messiah, corresponding to the eminence of *christos*, see the notice of Rom. 9. 5 under no. (vii), below.

(v) *High Priest* in Hebrews (2. 17, etc.), a title attested also in I Clement, is notable not so much for its reflection of the immense prestige of the high priest, in line with Ecclesiasticus, Philo and other Jewish authors, but rather because it does not reflect the dual constitution of high priest and king; 'for it is manifest that our lord arose from Judah' (Heb. 7. 14), yet he, the messianic king, rather than another, is identified as high priest with the help of Ps. 110 (compare 5. 5–9, discussed in connection with *christos*, above). In I Clement, somewhat comparably, this title of high-priest (36. 1; 'high-priest and patron', 61. 3; 64. 1) is evidently not viewed as incompatible with the title 'sceptre of God's greatness' (16. 1), which recalls the blessing of Judah as well as Ps. 110. 2. On the other hand, I Clement lacks the clear statement of descent from Judah given in Hebrews; 32. 2 ambiguously names Christ, among the descendants of Jacob, between the priests (descended from Aaron) and the kings (descended from Judah). In Hebrews especially, but also in I Clement, the impetus of the single messianic figure, noticed in chapter II, section 1, above, manifests itself strikingly through the title high priest.

In all these cases, then, the titles reflect the impression left on early Christians by Jewish messianism.

(vi) Is this also true of the famous royal title *Saviour* (σωτήρ), redolent of ruler-cult and often applied to Christ in the New Testament? A selective list of occurrences will show the wide distribution of the title: Luke 2. 11; John 4. 42; Acts 5. 31; 13. 23; Eph. 5. 23; Phil. 3. 20; at least five times in the Pastoral Epistles, including II Tim. 1. 10; Titus 2. 13; five times in II Peter, including 1. 11; I John 4. 14; Gospel of Peter 4. 13; Ignatius, Eph. 1. 1, and elsewhere; II Clem. 20. 5. 'The saviour' becomes a regular periphrasis for Christ in second-century writers, including Valentinians.[132]

Bousset, stressing the predominance of late sources in the attestation and the connection of *soter* with *epiphaneia* in II Tim. 1. 10, suggested that the title came late into Christian usage, from gentile ruler-cult; C. K. Barrett holds rather that the thought of salvation through Christ will have always been pressing the word into Christian use, but that pagan associations made its general acceptance late.[133] Yet it seems likely that Jewish association of the word with messianic deliverance, itself probably affected by ruler-cult, contributed to a Christian usage which, although its popularity came later, began early in the life of the church (Barrett's formulation seems to allow for this possibility).

Thus, first, some of the occurrences are in passages close to Jewish as well as Christian messianic hope, where debt to traditional material is possible: Luke 2. 11 (a saviour, Christ the lord, cf. Ps. Sol. 17. 32); Acts 5. 31 (exalted as *archegos* and saviour); 13. 23 (of David's seed a saviour); Phil. 3. 21 (saviour from heaven awaited).[134] Thus Wilfred Knox observed that the two occurrences in Acts recall the common rabbinic designation of the messiah as *goel*, 'redeemer', as in the First Benediction of the Amidah (Eighteen Benedictions) in the Babylonian recension: 'who rememberest the pious deeds of the Fathers, and bringest a redeemer to their children's children' (for the corresponding Aramaic *pariq* see Targ. Cant. 4. 5 on 'two redeemers', quoted in chapter I, section 1, above).[135]

Secondly, the Davidic king was linked in the psalter with divinely wrought salvation, Greek *soteria*, in the plural 'the salvations of his anointed' (Ps. 28. 8), LXX αἱ σωτηρίαι τοῦ χριστοῦ αὐτοῦ; compare II Sam. 22. 51 = Ps. 18. 51 on God's work in the 'salvations of his king' and 'loving-kindness for his anointed'.[136] This link will have contributed (perhaps together with gentile use of *soter*) to a rabbinic description of the messiah to arise from Judah as 'the one who saves Israel' (מושיע את ישראל), 'as it is said, And there shall come forth a rod from the stem of Jesse (Isa. 11. 1)' (Tanhuma Buber, Genesis, Wayehi, 12, 110a, on Gen. 49. 8). The phrase uses the participle which can stand independently as 'saviour' in references to 'saviours' in Judges and Neh. 9. 27 (see below).

Thirdly, the Septuagintal use of *soter* for a deliverer other than God seems to exhibit both limitation and development; these can perhaps be associated respectively with the mingled repulsion and attraction of the ruler-cult. Thus, sometimes the noun 'saviour' fails to occur where it might be expected (Obad. 21, LXX 'the saved' where the Massoretic pointing and the Targum prefer 'saviours'; I Macc. 9. 21, of Judas Maccabaeus, 'he who saves' [σῴζων] Israel, when the standard Greek royal application of *soter* itself would fit well). On the other hand, the corresponding verb appears in this context (Zech. 9. 9 LXX, a king 'righteous and saving', cf. I Macc. 9. 21; Isa. 19. 20 LXX, 'a man who shall save them', recalling the messianic 'man' of Num. 24. 7, 17 LXX, as noted in chapter II, section 1, above); compare the Hebrew description of the messiah quoted above. Moreover, the noun is in fact occasionally applied to human 'saviours' in the LXX (Judg. 3. 9, 15; Neh. 9. 27), and this usage also appears where it would not be expected on the basis of MT, at Isa. 42. 11 LXX, 'Say to the daughter of Zion, Behold, the saviour arrives for you' (see chapter II, section 1, above, on exilic hope for 'deliverers'); this verse is conflated with the similar Zech. 9. 9 at Matt. 21. 5, and the two verses were probably associated as prophecies of messianic advent to Zion.

Lastly, Jewish revision of the LXX introduced the noun in Isa. 19. 20, quoted in chapter II, section 1, above for its messianic elaboration and link with Balaam's prophecy in LXX; Aquila, Symmachus and Theodotion here unite in the more straightforward rendering 'saviour' (*soter*), confirming that the word could be used in a context understood as messianic (compare again the rabbinic description of the messiah quoted above).[137] As Theodotionic renderings were influential in New Testament times, this revision of the Greek Isa. 19. 20 suggests that by the time of Christian origins *soter* was regarded in the Jewish community as an acceptable messianic title. This christological title too, therefore, reflects the influence of a contemporary messianism already affected by ruler-cult, as well as the continuing ruler-cult itself.

(vii) The clearest New Testament occurrences of 'God' (*theos*) as a title of Christ are in the Fourth Gospel, and apply to the Logos (John 1. 1; 18) and the risen Christ (20. 28).[138] By implication this title appears in the opening verses of Hebrews (1. 8–9), through quotation of Ps. 45 (see below). On the question whether it occurs once in Paul (Rom. 9. 5) the probabilities are nicely balanced, but the scales seem to turn in favour of recognizing *theos* here as a title of Christ.[139] The relevant phrase in Rom. 9. 5, 'the Christ according to the flesh, he who is over all *theos*, blessed for ever', can be compared with Rom. 1. 3–4 'of David's seed according to the flesh, designated son of God in power'; 'son of God' indicates a share in divinity not only in gentile usage, as when Plutarch classes it with *theos* as an over-assertive royal title (chapter III, section 2, above), but also in its associations in Ps. 2. 7, some messianic interpretation of which survives (1QSa ii 11–12 and other material discussed in this chapter, section 2, above).[140] In both passages in Romans, then, messianic descent according to the flesh is contrasted with messianic divine power. *Theos* is freely used as a title of Christ in Ignatius (Smyrn. 1. 1, etc.), and some ambiguous occurrences of *theos* in later New Testament books (Titus 2. 13; II Peter 1. 1) should then probably be taken in this sense.

Yet again this title most immediately recalls ruler-cult. The solemn confession 'my lord and my God' by Thomas in John 20 has been linked specifically with Domitian's title 'lord and god'.[141] Once again, however, a connection with Jewish messianism is also likely, as G. Reim has urged. Comparing Ps. 45. 7, 'Thy throne, O God, is for ever and ever', an address to the king of Israel as a divine being (see above under *Son of God*) which is quoted in Heb. 1. 8 as an address to Christ, Reim notes that the Targum of Ps. 45 understands 'thou art fairer than the children of men' (v. 2) as spoken to the messiah in his beauty (see chapter III, section 5 [*f*], above); moreover (Reim adds), v. 7 is referred to the messiah's throne in the midrash (Ber. R. 99. 8 [10], on Gen. 49. 10, 'The sceptre shall not fail from Judah: this is the throne of kingship – Thy throne O God is for ever and ever, a sceptre of righteousness . . .').[142]

It is true that the Targum of Ps. 45 understands v. 7 itself as an address to the Lord God, not the king: 'The throne of thy glory, O LORD . . .' In another Targumic version the return from address to God in v. 7 to address to the messiah in v. 8 is specially marked by an addition at the beginning of v. 8; 'thy throne, O God, is in heaven for ever and ever . . .' (v. 7); 'and thou, king messiah, because thou hast loved righteousness . . .' (v. 8).[143] In both versions the Targumist probably takes v. 7 of the messiah's throne, considered 'the throne of the Lord', just as the Chronicler calls the throne of David and Solomon 'the throne of the kingdom of God over Israel' and 'the throne of the Lord' (I Chron. 28. 9; 29. 23; see chapter II, section 1, above). The same interpretation would fit the Hebrew text of Ps. 45. 7 with *elohim* as applied in the midrash, and the LXX and its Jewish revisions, all with forms of *theos*; Aquila rendered 'God' in v. 7 as a vocative, which is probably the sense intended by the nominative with article found in LXX, Symmachus and Theodotion. The Targumic interpretation of the vocative as an address to God is likely to be secondary, however, for it involves the awkward interpolation of this address in the middle of a passage (vv. 3–10) which the psalmist addresses consistently to the king, and the Targumist, apart from this verse, to the messiah. This suspicion is strengthened by another variant Targum of v. 7 quoted by P. Billerbeck, in which the change of person addressed occurs in the middle rather than at the end of this verse; only the first part is addressed to God, whereas the second part is explicitly addressed to 'king messiah'.[144]

Probably, therefore, in earlier Jewish interpretation the whole verse was taken as part of the address to the messiah, who would then be hailed as a divine being, *elohim*, *theos*. These words were applied in Qumran texts and in the LXX to angels, as noticed above, and Christ is being compared with angels when Ps. 45. 7 is quoted in Hebrews; closely comparable with the use of *theos* as a title of Christ implied at Heb. 1. 8 is the Qumran application of *elohim* also to Melchizedek active as deliverer, the *elohim* who stands up in Ps. 82 to judge the angels (11Q Melch ii 9–10, noted at the end of chapter III, above). Comparably again, Moses, a 'god' to Aaron and Pharaoh in Exodus (4. 16; 7. 1) and 'king in Jeshurun' in Deuteronomy (33. 5) was 'named god and king of the whole nation', according to Philo (*VM* 1, 158). In this last passage *theos* is envisaged precisely as a title. Heb. 1. 8, therefore, in the light of the Targum of Ps. 45. 3–10 as a whole, with 11Q Melchizedek and Philo, suggests that *theos* was used as a messianic title. The possibility that the LXX and the Greek renderings of Aquila and Theodotion could have been taken by Jews in this sense in Ps. 45. 7 is enhanced by the use of *soter* in Aquila, Symmachus, and Theodotion at Isa. 19. 20, discussed above. A broader background is formed by the concepts of a spiritual messiah discussed in chapter III, section 5, above; the title *theos* coheres with emphasis on the king or messiah as spirit (so Moses, 'holy and sacrosanct spirit', Ass. Mos. 11. 16, and 'mediator spirit', Ps.-Philo, *Ant. Bibl.* 9, 8, both discussed above; compare Solomon ('good' as pre-existent soul, Wisdom 8. 19–20). In this case too, therefore, the christological title reflects the influence of messianism affected by ruler-cult, as well as the influence of contemporary ruler-cult itself.

The principal New Testament titles of Christ, therefore, themselves suggest that messianism was an important factor in the rise of the cult of Christ. Those reviewed are all likely to have been connected with messianism as well as the cults of gentile rulers. They indicate that Christ was accorded obedience, worship and acclamation precisely in his capacity as messianic king.

The influence of Jewish on Christian messianism suggested above will not have been restricted to the earliest years of Christianity. Thus Vincent Taylor, excluding some titles treated as messianic above, still envisaged two waves of messianic influence, first in the ministry of Jesus, and then in the period 65–100 to which many New Testament books can be ascribed.[145] Comparably, on the related question of biblical testimonies, O. Skarsaune infers a Christian endeavour at the time of the later New Testament books to include the traditional testimonies current among contemporary Jews; he notes that Justin Martyr's proof-texts overlap far more closely than do those most prominent in the New Testament with texts commonly applied messianically in rabbinic literature.[146] A continuing second-century influence of Jewish messianism on Christians seems likely on other grounds.[147] Such influence, together with independent Jewish and Christian development of old common traditions in a shared Greek and Roman environment, is still probably a factor in the third-century resemblance and overlap between rabbinically-attested messianism and Spirit-christology. By the second century, however, the worship of Christ had long possessed its own impetus in the Christian community, and influence will probably have been effective mainly with regard to the accompanying conceptions.

Here it has been suggested that messianism constituted a major impulse towards the worship of Christ. Homage to the messiah was important in a Jewish messianism which formed a counterpart to gentile ruler-cult. Recognition of Christ as messianic king, beginning in the period of the ministry and becoming pervasive in the earliest Christian community, led directly to the scenes of acclamation and obeisance, the hymns and the titles preserved in the New Testament.

This suggestion has depended on the argument of chapters I to III for the importance of messianism in the Jewish community throughout the Second-Temple period. Chapters I and II therefore include reconsideration of some fundamental sources: evidence for the title 'messiah'; the messianism of the Old Testament as ultimately edited and collected;

biblical texts of the Persian period, the LXX Pentateuch in the third century, the Apocrypha of the Old Testament and some contemporary sources, and Qumran texts. Messianism then appears to have a more continuous history than is sometimes supposed, and to have formed a traditional element in biblical interpretation; it was indeed constantly in response to political developments, not least to contemporary ruler-cult, but it had its own life as a biblically-rooted tradition.

Yet, was it not too diverse to form a genuine tradition? Critical review of Bousset's vivid evocation of ancient Judaism as chaotic diversity, and recognition of the central importance of kingship as a focus of national mythology and hope, had led by the mid-twentieth century to greater recognition of the continuity and coherence of messianic expectation. H. Riesenfeld, one of those who took this view, also brought out the importance of homage to the royal messiah for New Testament interpretation. At the same time, however, a view like Bousset's was being developed again by historians who emphasized diversity in ancient Judaism. Moreover, on the other side, the chief modern exposition of unity in ancient Judaism, E. P. Sanders's monumental work *Judaism 63 BCE–66 CE*, retains a view of messianism in particular as marginal and varied. It has been urged above, however, that a good measure of unity and coherence in messianism can in fact be recognized, without neglect of the diversity which any lively tradition will present.

An element in this argument has been the presentation of a case for widespread attestation of a 'spiritual messiah' with superhuman characteristics. Recognition of this phenomenon tends to modify the sharp contrasts often drawn between a 'human' Jewish messiah and a 'divine' Christian figure. It is ironical that such contrasts largely depend on ancient Christian depictions of Jewish reaction to Christian messianic teaching: the Fourth Gospel, Justin's *Dialogue with Trypho*, and Hippolytus's *Refutation of All Heresies*. The present writer would not discount this Christian impression, but would set the Jewish attitude reflected by the Christian writers within the biblically-rooted tradition which rejects the exaltation of enemy rulers while endorsing the exaltation of the king of Israel. Here therefore the reconstruction offered above diverges from the view that the christology of the Fourth Gospel would necessarily have been perceived as radically non-Jewish. At the same time there seems to be a good case for understanding the title *theos* and the exaltation of Christ in the Fourth Gospel, like the christology of Paul, on the lines which were developed in Origen but were later considered subordinationist. The Johannine and Pauline conceptions can be interpreted as variations on a spirit-christology which continued and developed a spirit-messianism, and against a background of ruler-cult which influenced both Jewish and Christian developments.

Although conceptions and narratives of Christ are closely bound up with the cult of Christ, the cult itself has been the focus of attention here. It was not isolated within ancient Judaism and early Christianity, for the cult of the saints which developed in the church side by side with the cult of Christ had Jewish antecedents and contemporary parallels. In this respect too, as is argued more fully elsewhere, ancient Judaism presented a favourable environment for the growth of the Christ-cult.[148] Centrally important in this growth, however, will have been the messianism now outlined. As it had developed in the Second-Temple period, it included marked emphasis on homage to an exalted messiah of glory and beauty – an emphasis which does not wholly disappear from later Jewish messianic expectation. Messianism of this kind led to the titles, acclamations and worship illustrated in the New Testament, and forms the great link between the Judaism of the Herodian period and the Christian cult of the exalted Christ.

Bibliography

A. (R. E.) Agus, *The Binding of Isaac and Messiah*, Albany, New York 1988

R. Albertz, *A History of Israelite Religion in the Old Testament Period* ET (2 vols.), London 1994

P. S. Alexander, 'A Note on the Syntax of 4Q448', *JJS* 44, 1993, 301–2

J. Ashton, *Studying John: Approaches to the Fourth Gospel*, Oxford 1994

J. Assmann, 'Königsdogma und Heilserwartung. Politische und kultische Chaosbeschreibungen in ägyptischen Texten', in Hellholm, *Apocalypticism*, 345–77

M. Avi-Yonah, *The Jews of Palestine: A Political History from the Bar Kokhba War to the Arab Conquest*, ET Oxford 1976

W. Bacher, *Die Agada der Palästinensischen Amoräer* (2 vols.), Strassburg 1892, 1896

E. Badian, 'Alexander the Great between two thrones and Heaven', in Small, *Subject and Ruler*, 11–26

L. Baeck, 'Der Menschensohn', *MGWJ* 81, 1937, 12–24, repr. in *Aus drei Jahrtausenden*, Berlin 1938, cited here from ET 'The "Son of Man"' by W. Kaufmann in L. Baeck, *Judaism and Christianity*, Philadelphia 1958 repr. New York 1966, 23–38

—, 'The Faith of Paul', *JJS* 3, 1952, 93–110, cited here as reprinted in Baeck, *Judaism and Christianity*, 139–68

W. Baldensperger, *Das Selbstbewusstsein Jesu im Lichte der messianischen Hoffnungen seiner Zeit*, Strassburg ²1892

E. Bammel, *Judaica: Kleine Schriften* I, Tübingen 1986

—, *Judaica et Paulina: Kleine Schriften* II, mit einem Nachwort von Peter Pilhofer, Tübingen 1997

—, ΑΡΧΙΕΡΕΥΣ ΠΡΟΦΗΤΕΥΩΝ, reprinted from *TLZ* 79, 1954, cols. 351–6 in Bammel, *Judaica et Paulina*, 133–9

—, 'Die Zitate aus den Apokryphen bei Origenes', reprinted from *Origeniana Quinta*, ed R. J. Daly, BETL 105, Leuven 1991, 131–6, in Bammel, *Judaica et Paulina*, 161–7

R. S. Barbour (ed.), *The Kingdom of God and Human Society*, Edinburgh 1993

J. Barbel, *Christos Angelos*, Bonn 1941

J. Barclay and J. Sweet (eds), *Early Christian Thought in its Jewish Context*,

Cambridge 1996

M. Barker, *The Great Angel*, London 1992

—, *The Risen Lord: The Jesus of History as the Christ of Faith*, Edinburgh 1996

J. Barr, 'Messiah', in F. C. Grant and H. H. Rowley (eds), *Hastings' Dictionary of the Bible*, Edinburgh 1963, 646–55

C. K. Barrett, *A Critical and Exegetical Commentary on the Acts of the Apostles*, 1, Edinburgh 1994

D. Barthélemy and J. T. Milik, *Qumran Cave 1*, DJD I, Oxford 1955

H. N. Bate, *The Sibylline Oracles, Books III–V*, London 1918

R. J. Bauckham, 'The Worship of Jesus in Apocalyptic Christianity', *NTS* 27, 1981, 322–41

—, *The Climax of Prophecy: Studies on the Book of Revelation*, Edinburgh 1993

B. Bauer, 'Die messianischen Erwartungen der Juden zur Zeit Jesu', in B. Bauer, *Kritik der evangelischen Geschichte der Synoptiker* I, Leipzig 1841, 391–416

—, *Christus und die Caesaren. Der Ursprung des Christenthums aus dem römischen Griechenthum*, Berlin 1877

J. M. Baumgarten and J. T. Milik, with contributions from S. Pfann and A. Yardeni, *Qumran Cave 4, XIII: The Damascus Document, 4Q 266–273*, DJD 18, Oxford 1996

J. Becker, *Messiaserwartung im Alten Testament*, Stuttgart, 1977, ET by D. E. Green, *Messianic Expectation in the Old Testament*, Edinburgh 1980

P. Benoit, J. T. Milik and R. de Vaux, *Les grottes de Murabba'at*, DJD II, Oxford 1961

A. Bentzen, *King and Messiah*, ET London 1955

J. L. Berquist, *Judaism in Persia's Shadow*, Minneapolis 1995

G. Bertram, *Die Leidensgeschichte Jesu und der Christuskult*, FRLANT 32, Göttingen 1922

W. Beuken, S. Freyne, and A. Weiler (eds), *Messianism through History*, *Concilium* 1993/1, London and Maryknoll 1993

E. Bi(c)kerman, *Institutions des Séleucides*, Paris 1938

—, 'Consecratio', in den Boer, *Le culte*, 5–37

M. Black, in consultation with J. C. VanderKam, *The Book of Enoch or I Enoch*, Leiden 1985

G. J. Blidstein, 'The Monarchic Imperative in Rabbinic Perspective', *AJS Review* 7–8, 1982–3, 15–39

M. N. A. Bockmuehl, ' "The Form of God" (Phil. 2: 6). Variations on a Theme of Jewish Mysticism', *JTS* NS 48, 1997, 1–23

—, *Philippians*, London 1997

W. den Boer (ed.), *Le culte des souverains dans l'empire romain*, Entretiens Hardt, 19, Geneva 1973

P.-M. Bogaert, 'Relecture et refonte historicisante du livre de Daniel attestées par la première version grecque (Papyrus 967)', in R. Kuntzmann and J. Schlosser (eds), *Études sur le judaïsme hellénistique*, Paris 1984, 197–224

P. Borgen, ' "Yes," "No," "How Far?": the Participation of Jews and Christians in Pagan Cults', in T. Engberg-Pedersen (ed.), *Paul in His Hellenistic Context*, Edinburgh 1994, 30–59

B. Botte, *Le canon de la messe romaine*, Louvain 1935, repr. 1962

—, *La tradition apostolique de Saint Hippolyte*, Münster 1963

W. Bousset, *Der Antichrist in der Überlieferung des Judentums, des Neuen Testaments und der alten Kirche. Ein Beitrag zur Auslegung der Apokalypse*, Göttingen 1895; ET with a Prologue on the Babylonian Dragon Myth by A. H. Keane, *The Antichrist Legend. A Chapter in Christian and Jewish Folklore*, London 1896

—, 'Antichrist', *ERE* 1, 1908, 578–81

—, *Kyrios Christos*, Göttingen ²1921; ET Nashville 1970

—, *Die Religion des Judentums im späthellenistischen Zeitalter*, ed. H. Gressmann, Tübingen ³1926

G. W. Bowersock, 'Greek Intellectuals and the Imperial Cult', in den Boer, *Le culte*, 179–212

G. H. Box, *The Ezra-Apocalypse*, London 1912

R. Braun, *Deus Christianorum*, Paris ²1977

A. Brent, 'Luke–Acts and the Imperial Cult in Asia Minor', *JTS* NS xlviii, 1997, 411–38

M. Z. Brettler, *God is King: Understanding an Israelite Metaphor*, Sheffield 1989

R. E. Brown, *The Death of the Messiah: From Gethsemane to the Grave* (2 vols), New York 1994

P. A. Brunt, tr., *Arrian* (2 vols), Cambridge, Mass. and London 1976

R. Bultmann, *Theology of the New Testament*, ET (2 vols), London 1952, 1955

W. Burkert, *Greek Religion*, ET Oxford 1985

E. de W. Burton, *A Critical and Exegetical Commentary on the Epistle to the Galatians*, ICC, Edinburgh 1920

O. Camponovo, *Königtum, Königsherrschaft und Reich Gottes in den frühjüdischen Schriften*, Freiburg, Schweiz and Göttingen 1984

D. B. Capes, *Old Testament Yahweh Texts in Paul's Christology*, WUNT 2.47, Tübingen 1992

M. Casey, *From Jewish Prophet to Gentile God*, Cambridge 1991

[L. Cerfaux], *Recueil Lucien Cerfaux*, 1, BETL 6–7, Gembloux 1954

L. Cerfaux and J. Tondriau, *Un concurrent du christianisme: le culte des souverains dans la civilisation gréco-romaine*, Tournai 1957

H. Chadwick, 'Philo and the Beginnings of Christian Thought', in A. H. Armstrong (ed.), *The Cambridge History of Later Greek and Early Medieval Philosophy*, Cambridge 1967, corrected repr. 1970, 137–92

H. Chadwick and J. E. L. Oulton, *Alexandrian Christianity*, London 1954

G. Chalon, *L'édit de Tiberius Julius Alexander; étude historique et exégétique*, Olten 1964

R. H. Charles, *Religious Development between the Old and the New Testaments*, London 1914

J. H. Charlesworth, 'Christian and Jewish Self-Definition in Light of the Christian Additions to the Apocryphal Writings', in E. P. Sanders, with A. I. Baumgarten and A. Mendelson (eds), *Jewish and Christian Self-Definition*, Volume Two, *Aspects of Judaism in the Graeco-Roman Period*, London 1981, 27–55

—, (ed.) *The Old Testament Pseudepigrapha* (2 vols), London and New York 1983, 1985

—, (ed.), *The Messiah: Developments in Earliest Judaism and Christianity*, Minneapolis 1992

—, with F. M. Cross, J. Milgrom, E. Qimron, L. H. Schiffman, L. T. Stuckenbruck and R. E. Whitaker (eds), *Rule of the Community and Related Documents, The Dead Sea Scrolls*: Hebrew, Aramaic, and Greek texts with English translations, 1, Tübingen and Louisville 1994

M. P. Charlesworth, 'Some Observations on Ruler-Cult, Especially in Rome', *HTR* 37, 1935, 5–44

Andrew Chester, *Divine Revelation and Divine Titles in the Pentateuchal Targumim*, Tübingen 1986

—, 'Jewish Messianic Expectations and Mediatorial Figures and Pauline Christology', in M. Hengel and U. Heckel (eds), *Paulus und das antike Judentum*, Tübingen 1991, 17–89

—, 'The Parting of the Ways: Eschatology and Messianic Hope', in J. D. G. Dunn (ed.), *Jews and Christians: The Parting of the Ways AD 70 to 135*, Tübingen 1992, 239–313

M.-A. Chevallier, *L'Esprit et le Messie dans le Bas-Judaïsme et le Nouveau Testament*, Strasbourg 1958

M. Cimosa, *Il vocabolario di preghiera nel Pentateuco greco dei LXX*, Rome 1985

R. E. Clements, *Isaiah 1–39*, New Century Bible Commentary, Grand Rapids and London 1980

—, 'The Messianic Hope in the Old Testament', *JSOT* 43, 1989, 3–19

D. J. A. Clines (ed.), with J. Elwolde and others, *The Dictionary of Classical Hebrew*, Sheffield, 1, 1993; 2, 1995; 3, 1996 (in progress)

R. Coggins, A. Phillips and M. Knibb (eds), *Israel's Prophetic Tradition: Essays in Honour of Peter R. Ackroyd*, Cambridge 1982

J. J. Collins, 'Sibylline Oracles, Second Century BC–First Century AD: A New Translation and Introduction', in Charlesworth, *Pseudepigrapha*, 317–472

—, *Daniel*, Hermeneia Commentary, Minneapolis 1993

—, *The Scepter and the Star*, New York 1995

H. M. Cotton and A. Yardeni, *Aramaic, Hebrew and Greek Documentary Texts from Nahal Hever and Other Sites*, DJD 27, Oxford 1997

C. E. B. Cranfield, *A Critical and Exegetical Commentary on the Epistle to the Romans*, ICC (2 vols), Edinburgh 1977, 1979

J. A. Crook, 'Augustus: Power, Authority, Achievement', in A. K. Bowman, E. Champlin and A. Lintott (eds), *The Cambridge Ancient History*, Second Edition, X, *The Augustan Empire, 43 BC–AD 69*, Cambridge 1996, 113–46

O. Cullmann, *Christology of the New Testament*, ET, London ²1963

G. Dalman, *Aramäische Dialektproben*, Leipzig ²1927; reprinted, in one volume with Dalman, *Grammatik des jüdisch-palästinischen Aramäisch*, Darmstadt 1960

—, *Die Worte Jesu mit Berücksichtigung des nachkanonischen jüdischen Schrifttums und der aramäischen Sprache erörtert*, 1, Leipzig ²1930; ET of a revised form of the first edn, Leipzig 1898, Edinburgh 1909

J. Daniélou, *The Theology of Jewish Christianity*, ET by J. A. Baker, London 1964

—, *The Origins of Latin Christianity*, ET by D. Smith and J. A. Baker, London 1977

E. Dassmann, G. Stemberger, et al. (ed.), *Der Messias, Jahrbuch für biblische Theologie*, 8, Neukirchen-Vluyn 1993

W. D. Davies and D. C. Allison, *A Critical and Exegetical Commentary on the Gospel according to Saint Matthew*, ICC (3 vols), Edinburgh 1988, 1991, 1997

J. Day, *Psalms*, Sheffield 1990

A. Deissmann, *Licht vom Osten*, Tübingen ⁴1923; ET of second edn, Tübingen 1909, by L. R. M. Strachan, *Light from the Ancient East*, London 1910

H. J. de Jonge, 'BOTRYC BOHCEI. The Age of Kronos and the Millennium in Papias of Hierapolis', in M. J. Vermaseren (ed.), *Studies in Hellenistic Religions*, Leiden 1979, 37–49

M. de Jonge, 'The Use of the Word "Anointed" in the Time of Jesus', *NT* 8, 1966, 132–48

—, *Christology in Context. The Earliest Christian Response to Jesus*, Philadelphia 1988

—, 'Monotheism and Christology', in Barclay and Sweet, *Early Christian Thought in its Jewish Context*, 225–37

M. de Jonge and A. S. van der Woude, '11Q Melchizedek and the New Testament', *NTS* 12, 1965–6, 301–26

N. R. M. de Lange, *Origen and the Jews*, Cambridge 1976

Franz Delitzsch, *Die Psalmen*, Leipzig ⁵1894

L. Diez Merino, *Targum de Salmos. Edición Principe del Ms. Villa-Amil n.5 de Alfonso de Zamora*, Bibliotheca Hispana Biblica 6, Madrid 1982

D. Dimant, 'The Seventy Weeks Chronology, Dan. 9, 24–27, in the Light of New Qumranic Texts', in van der Woude, *Daniel*, 57–76

C.H. Dodd, *According to the Scriptures*, London 1952

F. J. Dölger, *Sol Salutis: Gebet und Gesang im christlichen Altertum*, ²1925, reprinted with foreword by T. Klauser, Münster 1972

S. R. Driver, *The Book of Genesis*, London 1904

J. D. G. Dunn, *Christology in the Making*, London 1980; second edn (text reprinted with new foreword, pp. xi–xxxix) London 1989

A. A. T. Ehrhardt, 'Jesus Christ and Alexander the Great', *JTS* 46, 1945, 45–51

J. D. Eisenstein, *Ozar Wikuhim*, New York 1928, reprinted in Israel 1969

J. A. Emerton, 'The Origin of the Son of Man Imagery', *JTS* NS 9, 1958, 225–42

—, 'Melchizedek and the Gods: Fresh Evidence for the Jewish Background of John x.34–36', *JTS* NS 17, 1966, 399–401

—, 'The Site of Salem, the City of Melchizedek', *SVT* 41, 1990, 45–71

C. W. Emmet, 'Messiah', *ERE* 8, Edinburgh 1915, 570–81

F. Engels, 'Bruno Bauer and Early Christianity', translated from contributions to *Der Sozialdemokrat*, 4 and 11 May 1882, in *K. Marx and F. Engels on Religion*, Moscow 1957, 193–203

—, 'The Book of Revelation', reprinted from *Progress*, II, London 1883, in *K. Marx and F. Engels on Religion*, Moscow 1957, 204–11

F. Field (ed.), *Origenis Hexaplorum quae supersunt* (2 vols), Oxford 1875

M. Finley, *Ancient Sicily*, revised edn, London 1979

M. Fishbane, *Biblical Interpretation in Ancient Israel*, Oxford 1985

D. Fishwick, *The Imperial Cult in the Latin West: Studies in the Ruler Cult of the Western Provinces of the Roman Empire*, I. 1, I. 2, II 1–2, Leiden, New York and Cologne 1987, 1991, 1992

—, 'Prayer and the Living Emperor', in R. M. Wilhelm and H. Jones (eds), *The Two Worlds of the Poet: New Perspectives on Vergil*, Detroit 1992, 343–55

J. A. Fitzmyer, *Luke*, Anchor Bible Commentary (2 vols), Garden City, New York 1981, 1983

W. Foerster, κύριος, *TWNT* 3, 1938, 1038–56, 1081–98 (ET in *TDNT* 3, 1965, 1039–58, 1081–98)

J. E. Fossum, *The Name of God and the Angel of the Lord*, Tübingen 1985

—, review of M. Barker, *The Great Angel*, in *JTS* NS 45, 1994, 187–91

—, *The Image of the Invisible God. Essays on the Influence of Jewish Mysticism on Early Christology*, NTOA 30, Freiburg, Schweiz and Göttingen 1995

R. Lane Fox, *Pagans and Christians in the Mediterranean World from the Second Century AD to the Conversion of Constantine*, London 1986

P. M. Fraser, *Ptolemaic Alexandria* (3 vols), Oxford 1972

R. A. Freund, 'From Kings to Archons: Jewish Political Ethics and Kingship

Passages in the LXX', *SJOT* 2, 1990, 58–72

M. Friedmann (ed.), *Pesikta Rabbati*, Vienna 1880

S. B. Frost, *Old Testament Apocalyptic, Its Origins and Growth*, London 1952

A. von Gall, ΒΑΣΙΛΕΙΑ ΤΟΥ ΘΕΟΥ, *eine religionsgeschichtliche Studie zur vorkirchlichen Eschatologie*, Heidelberg 1926

F. García Martínez, 'Esperánzas mesiánicas en los escritos de Qumrán', in id. and J. Trebolle Barrera, *Los hombres de Qumrán*, Madrid 1993, 187–222

C. Geertz, 'Centers, Kings and Charisma: Reflections on the Symbolics of Power', reprinted from J. Ben-David and T. N. Clark (eds), *Culture and Its Creators*, Chicago 1977, in C. Geertz, *Local Knowledge: Further Essays in Interpretive Anthropology*, New York 1983, 120–46

J. van der Geest, *Le Christ et l'Ancien Testament chez Tertullien*, Latinitas Christianorum Primaeva 22, Nijmegen 1972

J. Geffcken, 'Euhemerism', *ERE* 5, 1912, 572–3

A. Gelin, 'Messianisme', *Dictionnaire de la Bible, Supplément* V, 1957, 1165–212

C. Gianotto, *Melchisedek e la sua tipologia*, Brescia 1984

Arnold Goldberg, *Erlösung durch Leiden. Drei rabbinische Homilien über die Trauernden Zions und den leidenden Messias Ephraim, PesR 34. 36. 37*, Frankfurter Judaistische Studien 4, Frankfurt am Main 1978

—, 'Die Namen des Messias in der rabbinischen Traditionsliteratur. Ein Beitrag zur Messiaslehre des rabbinischen Judentums', *Frankfurter Judaistische Beiträge* 7, 1979, 1–93

Judah Goldin, '"Not by Means of an Angel and not by Means of a Messenger"', in Neusner (ed.), *Religions in Antiquity*, 412–24

A. S. F. Gow (ed.), *Theocritus*, (2 vols), Cambridge ²1952

J. D. Grainger, *Hellenistic Phoenicia*, Oxford 1991

G. B. Gray, *A Critical and Exegetical Commentary on the Book of Isaiah I–XXVII*, ICC, Edinburgh 1912

J. Gray, *The Biblical Doctrine of the Reign of God*, Edinburgh 1979

H. Gressmann, *Der Ursprung der israelitisch-jüdischen Eschatologie*, FRLANT 6, Göttingen 1905

—, 'The Sources of Israel's Messianic Hope', *AJT* 17, 1913, 173–94

—, *Der Messias*, FRLANT 43, Göttingen 1929

J. Gwyn Griffiths, 'Apocalyptic in the Hellenistic Era', in Hellholm, *Apocalypticism*, 273–93

H. Gross, *Die Idee des ewigen und allgemeinen Weltfriedens im alten Orient und im Alten Testament*, Trierer Theologische Studien 7, Trier 1956

I. Gruenwald, S. Shaked and G. G. Stroumsa (eds), *Messiah and Christos: Studies in the Jewish Origins of Christianity Presented to David Flusser*, Tübingen 1993

W. Grundmann, F. Hesse, M. de Jonge and A. S. van der Woude, χρίω,

TWNT 9, 1973, 482–576 (ET in *TDNT* 9, 1974, 493–580)

H. Gunkel, *Schöpfung und Chaos in Urzeit und Endzeit. Eine religions-geschichtliche Untersuchung über Gen 1 und Ap Joh 12*, Göttingen, 1895

J. Habermann, *Präexistenzaussagen im Neuen Testament*, Europäische Hoch-schulschriften Reihe 23, Theologie 362, Frankfurt a. M. 1990

C. Habicht, *Gottmenschentum und griechische Städte*, Munich ²1970

F. Hahn, *Christologische Hoheitstitel*, FRLANT 83, Göttingen 1963; fifth enlarged edn, Göttingen 1995; ET with substantially curtailed notes, *The Titles of Jesus in Christology*, London 1969

R. Hanhart, 'Die Septuaginta als Interpretation und Aktualisierung: Jesaja 9: 1 (8: 23)–7(6)', in A. Rofé and Y. Zakovitch (eds), *Isaac Leo Seeligmann Volume*, III, Jerusalem 1983, 331–46

—, 'Die Bedeutung der Septuaginta für die Definition des "Hellenistischen Judentums"', in J. A. Emerton (ed.), *Congress Volume: Jerusalem, 1986*, SVT 40, Leiden 1988, 67–80

M. Harl, *La Bible d'Alexandrie, 1, La Genèse*, Paris 1986

A. Harnack, *Lehrbuch der Dogmengeschichte*, I, *Die Entstehung des kirchlichen Dogmas*, Freiburg i. B. and Leipzig ³1894, ET by N. Buchanan, *History of Dogma*, I, London and Edinburgh ²1897

M. J. Harris, *Jesus as God: The New Testament Use of Theos in References to Jesus*, Grand Rapids 1992

R. D. Hecht, 'Philo and Messiah', in Neusner, Green and Frerichs, *Judaisms*, 139–68

K. Heim, 'The Perfect King of Psalm 72: An Intertextual Enquiry', in Satterthwaite, Hess and Wenham, *The Lord's Anointed*, 223–48

D. Hellholm (ed.), *Apocalypticism in the Mediterranean World and the Near East*, Tübingen 1983

M. Hengel, *The Son of God*, ET London 1976

—, 'Erwägungen zum Sprachgebrauch von Χριστός bei Paulus und in der "vorpaulinischen" Überlieferung', in M. D. Hooker and S. G. Wilson (eds), *Paul and Paulinism: Essays in Honour of C. K. Barrett*, London 1982, 135–59

—, 'Messianische Hoffnung und politischer "Radikalismus" in der "jüdisch-hellenistischen Diaspora": zur Frage der Voraussetzungen des jüdischen Aufstandes unter Trajan, 115–117 n. Chr.', reprinted from Hellholm, *Apocalypticism*, 655–86, in Hengel, *Judaica et Hellenistica*, 314–43

—, *Between Jesus and Paul*, ET London 1983

—, 'Das Christuslied im frühesten Gottesdienst', in *Weisheit Gottes – Weisheit der Welt: Festschrift für Joseph Kardinal Ratzinger*, St Ottilien, 1987, 1, 357–404

—, 'Christological Titles in Early Christianity', reprinted from Charlesworth, *The Messiah*, 425–48, in Hengel, *Essays in Early Christology*, 359–89

—, *Essays in Early Christology*, Edinburgh 1996

—, *Judaica et Hellenistica*, Kleine Schriften I, Tübingen 1996

—, 'Präexistenz bei Paulus?', in C. Landmesser, H.-J. Eckstein and H. Lichtenberger (eds), *Jesus Chistus als die Mitte der Schrift*, Berlin 1997, 479–518

—, J. H. Charlesworth and D. Mendels, 'The Polemical Character of "On Kingship" in the Temple Scroll: An Attempt at Dating 11Q Temple', *JJS* 37, 1988, 28–39

M. Hengel, with C. Markschies, *The 'Hellenization' of Judaea in the First Century after Christ*, ET London 1989

M. Hengel and A. M. Schwemer (eds), *Königsherrschaft Gottes und himmlischer Kult im Judentum, Urchristentum und in der hellenistischen Welt*, Tübingen 1991

A. Henrichs, 'The Sophists and Hellenistic Religion: Prodicus as the Spiritual Father of the Isis Aretalogies', *HSCP* 88, 1984, 139–58

O. Hofius, 'Ist Jesus der Messias? Thesen', in Dassmann and Stemberger, *Der Messias*, 103–29

S. H. Hooke (ed.), *Myth, Ritual, and Kingship: Essays on the Theory and Practice of Kingship in the Ancient Near East and in Israel*, Oxford 1958

—, 'Myth and Ritual: Past and Present', in Hooke, *Myth, Ritual, and Kingship*, 1–21

W. Horbury, 'Suffering and Messianism in Yose ben Yose', in W. Horbury and B. McNeil (eds), *Suffering and Martyrdom in the New Testament*, Cambridge 1981, pp. 143–82

—, 'The Aaronic Priesthood in the Epistle to the Hebrews', *JSNT* 19, 1983, W. Horbury and C. C. Rowland [eds], *Essays in Honour of Ernst Bammel*, 43–71

—, 'The Messianic Associations of "the Son of Man"', *JTS* NS 36, 1985, 34–55

—, 'The Twelve and the Phylarchs', *NTS* 32, 1986, 503–27

—, 'Constitutional Aspects of the Kingdom of God', in R. S. Barbour (ed.), *The Kingdom of God and Human Society*, Edinburgh 1993, 60–79

—, 'Land, Sanctuary and Worship', in Barclay and Sweet, *Early Christian Thought in its Jewish Setting*, 207–24

—, 'Messianism among Jews and Christians in the Second Century', *Augustinianum* 28, 1988, 71–88

—, 'Herod's Temple and "Herod's Days"', in William Horbury (ed.), *Templum Amicitiae*, Sheffield 1991, 103–49

—, 'Septuagintal and New Testament Conceptions of the Church', in M. Bockmuehl and M. B. Thompson (eds), *A Vision for the Church*, Edinburgh 1997, 1–17

—, *Jews and Christians in Contact and Controversy*, Edinburgh 1998

—, 'Antichrist among Jews and Gentiles', in M. Goodman (ed.), *The Jews in the Roman Empire*, Oxford 1998

—, 'The Cult of Christ and the Cult of the Saints', *NTS* 44, 1998

—, see also Krauss

W. Horbury and D. Noy, *Jewish Inscriptions of Graeco-Roman Egypt*, Cambridge 1992

A. Hultgård, *L'eschatologie des Testaments des Douze Patriarches* (2 vols), Uppsala 1977 and 1982

L. W. Hurtado, *One God, One Lord*, Philadelphia and London 1988

H. Jacobson, *A Commentary on Pseudo-Philo's* Liber Antiquitatum Biblicarum, AGJU 31 (2 vols), Leiden 1996

J. Jeremias, 'Nochmals: Artikelloses *Christos* in I Cor 15 3', *ZNW* 60, 1969, 214–19

A. R. Johnson, *Sacral Kingship in Ancient Israel*, Cardiff ²1967

—, 'Hebrew Conceptions of Kingship', in Hooke, *Myth, Ritual, and Kingship*, 204–35

P. Joyce, 'The Kingdom of God and the Psalms', in Barbour, *The Kingdom of God and Human Society*, 42–59

D. Juel, *Messianic Exegesis*, Philadelphia 1988

J. Juster, *Les juifs dans l'empire romain* (2 vols), Paris 1914

M. Karrer, *Der Gesalbte: die Grundlagen des Christustitels*, FRLANT 151, Göttingen 1990

J. N. D. Kelly, *Early Christian Doctrines*, London ⁵1977

E. Kiessling and W. Rübsam, *Wörterbuch der griechischen Papyrusurkunden*, Suppl. 1, 1940–66, Amsterdam 1969

G. D. Kilpatrick, 'Acts vii. 52 ΕΛΕΥΣΙΣ', *JTS* 46, 1945, 136–45

J. Klausner, *The Messianic Idea in Israel from Its Beginning to the Completion of the Mishnah*, three parts, 1902, 1909, 1921; ET of revised edn, London 1956

M. L. Klein, *The Fragment-Targums of the Pentateuch* (2 vols), Rome 1980

W. Knox, *St Paul and the Church of the Gentiles*, Cambridge 1939

—, *The Acts of the Apostles*, Cambridge 1948

L. Koep, 'Consecratio II, Kaiserapotheose', *RAC* 3, 1957, cols. 284–94

H. Kraft, *Die Entstehung des Christentums*, Darmstadt 1986

W. Kramer, *Christ, Lord, Son of God*, ET London 1966

S. Krauss, *Griechen und Römer*, Monumenta Talmudica 1, Vienna and Leipzig 1914, reprinted Darmstadt 1972

— and W. Horbury, *The Jewish-Christian Controversy*, 1, *History*, Tübingen 1996

L. J. Kreitzer, *Jesus and God in Paul's Eschatology*, *JSNT* Supplement Series 19, Sheffield 1987

P. Kuhn, *Gottes Trauer und Klage in der rabbinischen Überlieferung, Talmud und Midrasch*, AGJU 13, Leiden 1978

A. Laato, *Who is Immanuel? The Rise and the Foundering of Isaiah's Messianic Expectations*, Åbo 1988

—, *Josiah and David Redivivus: the Historical Josiah and the Messianic Expectations of Exilic and Postexilic Times*, Stockholm 1992

G. W. H. Lampe (ed.), *A Patristic Greek Lexicon*, Oxford 1961, repr. 1968

K. J. A. Larkin, *The Eschatology of Second Zechariah*, Kampen 1994

S. H. Levey, *The Messiah: An Aramaic Interpretation, the Messianic Exegesis of the Targum*, Cincinnati 1974

I. Lévi, 'Le ravissement du Messie à sa naissance', *REJ* 74, 1922, 113–26; 77, 1923, 1–11

—, 'Le ravissement du messie-enfant dans le *Pugio Fidei*', *REJ* 75, 1922, 113–17

M. Lichtheim, *Ancient Egyptian Literature*, 1, *The Old and Middle Kingdoms*, Berkeley, Los Angeles and London 1975

S. Lieberman, *Greek in Jewish Palestine*, New York 5702–1942

H. Lietzmann, *Der Weltheiland*, Bonn 1909, reprinted in H. Lietzmann, *Kleine Schriften* 1, TU 67, Berlin 1958, 25–62

O. Limor, 'Beyond Barcelona', *Jewish History* 9, 1995, 107–12

G. Lindeskog, *Das jüdisch-christliche Problem. Randglossen zu einer Forschungsepoche*, Stockholm 1986

S. Loesch, *Deitas Jesu und Antike Apotheose*, Rottenburg a. N., Württemberg 1933

R. Loewe, 'Apologetic Motifs in the Targum to the Song of Songs', in A. Altmann (ed.), *Biblical Motifs*, Cambridge, Mass. 1996, 159–96

W. Lueken, *Michael. Eine Darstellung und Vergleichung des jüdischen und der morgenländisch-christlichen Tradition vom Erzengel Michael*, Göttingen 1898

J. Lust, 'Messianism and Septuagint', in J. A. Emerton (ed.), *Congress Volume: Salamanca, 1983*, Leiden 1985, 174–91

M. Mach, *Entwicklungsstadien des jüdischen Engelglaubens in vorrabbinischer Zeit*, TSAJ 34, Tübingen 1992

—, 'Christus Mutans: Zur Bedeutung der "Verklärung Jesu" im Wechsel von jüdischer Messianität zur neutestamentlichen Christologie', in Gruenwald, Shaked and Stroumsa, *Messiah and Christos*, 177–97

J. Maier, 'Der Messias', in P. Sacchi (ed.), *Il giudaismo palestinese: dal 1 secolo a.C. al 1 secolo d.C.*, Associazione Italiana per lo Studio del Giudaismo, Testi e Studi 8, Bologna 1993, 157–86

T. W. Manson, 'Miscellanea Apocalyptica', *JTS* 46, 1945, 41–5

J. Marcus, *The Way of the Lord: Christological Exegesis of the Old Testament in the Gospel of Mark*, Edinburgh 1993

A. Marmorstein, 'Ra'yon ha-ge'ullah be-aggadat ha-tanna'im veha-amora'im', reprinted from *Sinai* 5, 7, 8 (1942, 1943, 1944), in A. Marmorstein, *Studies in Jewish Theology*, London 1950, part 2, 17–76

B. A. Mastin, 'The Imperial Cult and the Ascription of the Title Θεός to Jesus,

John xx.28', in E. A. Livingstone (ed.), *Studia Evangelica* 6, TU 112, Berlin 1973, 352–65

—, 'Daniel 2[46] and the Hellenistic World', *ZAW* 85, 1973, 80–93

—, 'A Neglected Feature of the Christology of the Fourth Gospel', *NTS* 22, 1975, 32–51

J. P. Meier, *A Marginal Jew: Rethinking the Historical Jesus*, 1, New York 1991; 2, New York 1994

B. M. Metzger, 'The Punctuation of Rom. 9:5', in B. Lindars and S. S. Smalley (eds), *Christ and Spirit in the New Testament: Studies in Honour of Charles Francis Digby Moule*, Cambridge 1973, 95–112

A. Mirsky, *Yosse ben Yosse: Poems*, Jerusalem 1977

A. Moenikes, 'Messianismus im Alten Testament, vorapokalyptische Zeit', *ZRGG* 40, 1988, 289–306

—, *Die grundsätzliche Ablehnung des Königtums in der hebräischen Bibel*, Bonner Biblische Beiträge 99, Weinheim 1995

G. F. Moore, *Judaism* (3 vols), Cambridge, Mass., 1–2, 1927; 3, 1930

C. R. A. Morray-Jones, 'Transformational Mysticism in the Apocalyptic-Merkabah Tradition', *JJS* 43, 1992, 1–31

C. F. D. Moule, *The Origin of Christology*, Cambridge 1977

—, review of Dunn, *Christology in the Making*, *JTS* NS 33, 1982, 258–63

S. Mowinckel, *Psalmenstudien, II. Das Thronbesteigungsfest Jahwäs und der Ursprung der Eschatologie*, Oslo 1922, repr. Amsterdam 1966

—, *He That Cometh*, ET by G. W. Anderson, Oxford 1956

B. Murmelstein, 'Adam, ein Beitrag zur Messiaslehre', *WZKM* 35, 1928, 242–75; 36, 1929, 51–86

O. Murray, 'Aristeas and Ptolemaic Kingship', *JTS* NS 18, 1967, 337–71

G. Mussies, 'The Interpretatio Judaica of Sarapis', in M. J. Vermaseren (ed.), *Studies in Hellenistic Religions*, Leiden 1979, 189–214

A. Neubauer, S. R. Driver, E. B. Pusey, *The Fifty-third Chapter of Isaiah according to the Jewish Interpreters* (2 vols), 1876, repr. with Prolegomenon by R.Loewe, New York 1969

J. Neusner, *Messiah in Context*, Philadelphia 1984

—, *Judaism and Christianity in the Age of Constantine: History, Messiah, Israel, and the Initial Confrontation*, Chicago 1987

—, 'Mishnah and Messiah', in Neusner, Green, and Frerichs, *Judaisms and Their Messiahs*, 265–82

J. Neusner, W. S. Green and E. S. Frerichs (eds), *Judaisms and Their Messiahs at the Turn of the Christian Era*, Cambridge 1987

C. Newsom, *Songs of the Sabbath Sacrifice: a Critical Edition*, Harvard Semitic Studies 27, Atlanta 1985

V. Nikiprowetzky, 'Réflexions sur quelques problèmes du Quatrième et du Cinquième livres des Oracles sibyllins', *HUCA* 43, 1972, 29–76

A. D. Nock, 'Early Gentile Christianity and its Hellenistic Background', reprinted from A. E.J. Rawlinson (ed.), *Essays on the Trinity and the Incarnation*, London 1928, in A. D. Nock, *Essays on Religion and the Ancient World* (2 vols), Oxford 1972, 1, 49–133

E. Norden, *P. Vergilius Maro, Aeneis Buch VI*, Berlin ²1916

D. E. Noy, *Jewish Inscriptions of Western Europe*, 1, *Italy, excluding the City of Rome, Spain and Gaul*, Cambridge 1993

—, see also Horbury

G. S. Oegema, *Der Gesalbte und sein Volk: Untersuchungen zum Konzeptualisierungsprozess der messianischen Erwartungen von den Makkabäern bis Bar Koziba*, Göttingen 1994

W. O. E. Oesterley, *The Evolution of the Messianic Idea. A Study in Comparative Religion*, London 1908

J. C. O'Neill, *Paul's Letter to the Romans*, Harmondsworth 1975

—, *The Bible's Authority: A Portrait Gallery of Thinkers from Lessing to Bultmann*, Edinburgh 1991

—, 'The Man from Heaven: *SibOr* 5.256–259', *JSP* 9, 1991, 87–102

—, *Who did Jesus think he was?*, Leiden 1995

M. Ottosson, *Josuaboken: En programskrift för davidisk restauration*, Uppsala 1991

E. Pax, ΕΠΙΦΑΝΕΙΑ. *Ein religionsgeschichtlicher Beitrag zur biblischen Theologie*, Münchener Theologische Studien I. 10, Munich 1955

M. Perez Fernandez, *Tradiciones mesiánicas en el Targum Palestinense*, Valencia and Jerusalem 1981

R. F. Person, *Second Zechariah and the Deuteronomic School*, Sheffield 1993

M. Pesce, *Dio senza mediatori*, Brescia 1979

E. Peterson, *Heis Theos*, FRLANT 41, Göttingen 1926

K. E. Pomykala, *The Davidic Dynasty Tradition in Early Judaism, Its History and Significance for Messianism*, Atlanta 1995

J. R. Porter, *Moses and Monarchy*, Oxford 1963

—, 'The Succession of Joshua', in J. I. Durham and J. R. Porter (eds), *Proclamation and Presence*, London 1970, 102–32

S. R. F. Price, *Rituals and Power: The Roman Imperial Cult in Asia Minor*, Cambridge 1984

—, 'Gods and Emperors: The Greek Language of the Roman Imperial Cult', *JHS* 104, 1984, 79–95

E. Puech, *La croyance des Esséniens en la vie future: immortalité, résurrection, vie éternelle?* (2 vols), Paris 1993

P. A. Rainbow, 'Melchizedek as a Messiah at Qumran', *Bulletin for Biblical Research*, 1997

O. S. Rankin, *Jewish Religious Polemic*, Edinburgh 1956

G. Reim, *Jochanan. Erweiterte Studien zum alttestamentlichen Hintergrund des*

Johannesevangeliums, Erlangen 1995

—, 'Jesus as God in the Fourth Gospel: the Old Testament Background', reprinted from *NTS* 30, 1984, 158–60 in Reim, *Jochanan*, 348–51

H. Graf Reventlow, *Problems of Biblical Theology in the Twentieth Century*, ET London 1986

J. M. Reynolds and R. Tannenbaum, *Jews and Godfearers at Aphrodisias*, Cambridge Philological Society Supplementary Volume 12, Cambridge 1987

H. Riesenfeld, *Jésus transfiguré: l'arrière-plan du récit évangélique de la Transfiguration de Notre-Seigneur*, Acta Seminarii Neotestamentici Upsaliensis 16, Copenhagen and Lund 1947

J. J. M. Roberts, 'The Old Testament's Contribution to Messianic Expectations', in Charlesworth, *The Messiah*, 39–51

J. M. Robertson, *Pagan Christs*, London ²1911

A. Rofé, 'The Battle of David and Goliath: Folklore, Theology, Eschatology', in J. Neusner, B. A. Levine and E. S. Frerichs (eds), *Judaic Perspectives on Ancient Israel*, Philadelphia 1987, 117–51

—, 'Qumranic Paraphrases, the Greek Deuteronomy and the Late History of the Biblical *nasi*', *Textus* 14, 1988, 164–74

—, 'Isaiah 59:19 and Trito-Isaiah's Vision of Redemption', in J. Vermeylen (ed.), *The Book of Isaiah, le Livre d'Isaïe: les oracles et leurs relectures, unité et complexité de l'ouvrage*, BETL 81, Leuven 1989

—, 'The Piety of the Torah-disciples and the Winding-up of the Hebrew Bible: Josh 1: 8; Ps 1: 2; Isa 59: 21', in H. Merklein, K. Müller, and G. Stemberger (eds), *Bibel in jüdischer und christlicher Tradition: Festschrift für Johann Maier zum 60. Geburtstag*, Bonner Biblische Beiträge 88, Frankfurt am Main 1993, 78–85

C. C. Rowland, *The Open Heaven*, London 1982

H. H. Rowley, *The Servant of the Lord and Other Essays on the Old Testament*, London 1952

H. E. Ryle and M. R. James (eds), *Psalms of the Pharisees, commonly called the Psalms of Solomon*, Cambridge 1891

E. P. Sanders, *Judaism: Practice and Belief, 63 BCE – 66 CE*, London 1992

—, 'Paul', in Barclay and Sweet, *Early Christian Thought in its Jewish Context*, 112–29

P. E. Satterthwaite, R. S. Hess and G. J. Wenham (eds), *The Lord's Anointed: Interpretation of Old Testament Messianic Texts*, Carlisle 1995

P. Schäfer, 'Die messianischen Hoffnungen des rabbinischen Judentums zwischen Naherwartung und religiösem Pragmatismus', reprinted from C. Thoma (ed.), *Zukunft in der Gegenwart*, Bern and Frankfurt a.M. 1976, 95–125 in P. Schäfer, *Studien zur Geschichte und Theologie des rabbinischen Judentums*, Leiden 1978, 214–43

P. Schäfer et al., *Synopse zur Hekhalot-Literatur*, TSAJ 2, Tübingen 1981

J. Schaper, 'Psalm 47 und sein "Sitz im Leben" ', *ZAW* 106, 1994, 262–75

—, *Eschatology in the Greek Psalter*, Tübingen 1995

S. Schechter, *Aspects of Rabbinic Theology*, New York and London, 1909, repr. New York 1961

L. H. Schiffman, 'Messianic Figures and Ideas in the Qumran Scrolls', in Charlesworth, *The Messiah*, 116–29

G. Schimanowski, *Weisheit und Messias: die jüdischen Voraussetzungen der urchristlichen Präexistenzchristologie*, WUNT 2. Reihe 17, Tübingen 1985

W. H. Schmidt, *The Faith of the Old Testament*, ET Oxford 1983

W. M. Schniedewind, 'King and Priest in the Book of Chronicles and the Duality of Qumran Messianism', *JJS* 45, 1994, 71–8

H. J. Schoeps, *Theologie und Geschichte des Judenchristentums*, Tübingen 1949

G. Scholem, *The Messianic Idea in Judaism and Other Essays on Jewish Spirituality*, ET London 1971

E. Schürer, *Geschichte des jüdischen Volkes im Zeitalter Jesu Christi*, Leipzig ³⁻⁴1901–9; ET of second edn, 1886–90, *The History of the Jewish People in the Age of Jesus Christ*, Edinburgh 1890–91; ET of third-fourth edn, revised by G. Vermes, F. Millar, M. Black, M. Goodman and P. Vermes, Edinburgh, I, 1973; II, 1981; III. 1, 1986, III. 2, 1987

S. Schwartz, 'On the Autonomy of Judaea in the Fourth and Third Centuries BCE', *JJS* 45, 1994, 157–68

A. M. Schwemer, 'Gott als König und seine Königsherrschaft in den Sabbatliedern aus Qumran', in Hengel and Schwemer, *Königsherrschaft Gottes und himmlischer Kult*, 45–118

—, 'Irdischer und himmlischer König: Beobachtungen zur sogenannten David-Apokalypse in Hekhalot Rabbati 122–126', in Hengel and Schwemer, *Königsherrschaft Gottes und himmlischer Kult*, 309–59

K. Scott, 'Plutarch and the Ruler Cult', *TAPA* 60, 1929, 117–35

—, 'Humor at the Expense of the Ruler Cult', *CP* 27, 1932, 317–28

I. L. Seeligmann, *The Septuagint Version of Isaiah: A Discussion of its Problems*, Mededelingen en Verhandelingen van het Vooraziatisch-egyptisch Genootschap 'Ex Oriente Lux' 9, Leiden 1948

A. F. Segal, *Two Powers in Heaven*, Leiden 1978

M. Z. (H.) Segal, *Sepher Ben Sira ha-shalem*, Jerusalem ²1958

M. Simon, *Verus Israel*, cited from ET, Oxford 1986 of second edn with Post-Scriptum, Paris 1964

M. Simonetti, 'Cristologia giudeocristiana: caratteri e limiti', *Augustinianum* 28, 1988, 51–69

O. Skarsaune, *The Proof from Prophecy, A Study in Justin Martyr's Proof-Text Tradition: Text-Type, Provenance, Theological Profile*, Suppl. to *NT* 56, Leiden 1987

A. Small (ed.), *Subject and Ruler: The Cult of the Ruling Power in Classical Antiquity*, Journal of Roman Archaeology Supplementary Series 17, Ann Arbor 1996

G. A. Smith, *The Historical Geography of the Holy Land*, Edinburgh 41897

J. Z. Smith, *Drudgery Divine. On the Comparison of Early Christianities and the Religions of Late Antiquity*, London 1990

Morton Smith, 'What is Implied by the Variety of Messianic Figures?', repr. from *JBL* 78, 1959, 66–72, in Smith, *Studies*, 1, 161–7

—, 'The Work of George Foot Moore', repr. from *Harvard Library Bulletin* 15, 1967, 169–79, in Smith, *Studies*, 1, 201–10

—, ed. S. J. D. Cohen, *Studies in the Cult of Yahweh* (2 vols), Leiden, New York and Cologne 1996

W. Speyer, 'Religiöse Betrüger', reprinted from *Falschungen im Mittelalter*, Monumenta Germaniae Historica, Schriften Bd 33.5, 1988, in W. Speyer, *Frühes Christentum im antiken Strahlungsfeld*, Tübingen 1989, 440–62

J. E. Stambaugh, *Sarapis under the Early Ptolemies*, Leiden 1972

E. Stauffer, *New Testament Theology*, ET London 1955

—, 'Agnostos Christos: Joh. 2. 24 und die Eschatologie des Vierten Evangeliums', in W. D. Davies and D. Daube (eds), *The Background of the New Testament and its Eschatology*, Cambridge 1954, 281–99

G. C. Stead, 'Arius in Modern Research', *JTS* NS 45, 1994, 24–36

—, *Philosophy in Christian Antiquity*, Cambridge 1994

M. E. Stone, *Fourth Ezra*, Hermeneia Commentary, Minneapolis 1990

H. L. Strack and P. Billerbeck, *Kommentar zum Neuen Testament aus Talmud und Midrasch*, Munich I, 1922; II, 1924; III, 1926; IV. 1, 1928; IV. 2, 1928; index volumes by K. Adolph and J. Jeremias, V, 1956; VI, 1961

G. G. Stroumsa, *Savoir et salut*, Paris 1992

L. T. Stuckenbruck, *Angel Veneration and Christology*, WUNT 2. 70, Tübingen 1995

A. Stuiber, 'Christusepitheta', *RAC* 3, 1957, cols. 24–9

R. Syrén, *The Blessings in the Targums: A Study on the Targumic Interpretations of Genesis 49 and Deuteronomy 33*, Åbo 1986

Justin Taylor, S.M., *Les Actes des deux Apôtres*, V, *Commentaire historique (Act. 9, 1–18, 22)*; VI, *Commentaire historique, Act. 18, 23–28, 31*, Paris 1994, 1996

—, 'Why were the Disciples first called "Christians" at Antioch? Acts 11, 26', *RB* 101, 1994, 75–94

V. Taylor, *The Names of Jesus*, London 1953

J. Theodor and C. Albeck (eds), *Bereschit Rabba mit kritischem Apparat und Kommentar* (4 vols), Berlin 1912, 1927, 1929, 1931, reprinted in 3 vols, Jerusalem 1965

M. E. Thrall, *A Critical and Exegetical Commentary on the Second Epistle to the Corinthians* 1, Edinburgh 1994

P. R. Trebilco, *Jewish Communities in Asia Minor*, SNTS Monograph Series 69, Cambridge 1991

J. Tromp, 'Taxo, the Messenger of the Lord', *JSJ* 21, 1990, 200–9

—, *The Assumption of Moses: a Critical Edition with Commentary*, Studia in Veteris Testamenti Pseudepigrapha 10, Leiden, New York and Cologne 1993

J. VanderKam, 'Righteous One, Messiah, Chosen One, and Son of Man in I Enoch 37–71', in Charlesworth, *The Messiah*, 169 91

G. Vermes, *Jesus the Jew*, London 1973

—, 'Qumran Forum Miscellanea I', *JJS* xliii, 1992, 299–305

—, 'The Oxford Forum for Qumran Research: Seminar on the Rule of War (4Q285)', *JJS* 43, 1992, 85–90

—, 'The So-Called King Jonathan Fragment', *JJS* 44, 1993, 294–300

—, *The Complete Dead Sea Scrolls in English*, London 1997

B. L. Visotzky (ed.), *Midrash Mishle*, New York 1990

P. Volz, *Die Eschatologie der jüdischen Gemeinde*, Tübingen ²1934, reprinted Hildesheim 1966

F. W. Walbank, 'Monarchies and Monarchic Ideas', in Walbank, Astin, Frederiksen and Ogilvie, *The Hellenistic World*, 62–100

F. W. Walbank, A. E. Astin, M. W. Frederiksen and R. M. Ogilvie (eds), *The Cambridge Ancient History*, Second Edition, VII. 1, *The Hellenistic World*, Cambridge 1984

J. Weiss, *Die Predigt Jesu vom Reiche Gottes*, Göttingen ²1900

—, ed. R. Knopf, *Das Urchristentum*, Göttingen, 1917; ET *Earliest Christianity* (2 vols), New York 1937

J. Wellhausen, *Prolegomena zur Geschichte Israels*, Berlin and Leipzig ⁶1905; ET of second edn, Berlin 1883, by J. S. Black and A. Menzies, *Prolegomena to the History of Israel*, Edinburgh 1885

—, *The Book of Psalms*, Polychrome Bible, London 1898

P. Welten, 'Königsherrschaft Jahwes und Thronbesteigung. Bemerkungen zur unerledigten Fragen', *VT* 32, 1982, 297–310

M. Werner, *The Formation of Christian Dogma*, ET London 1957

G. Widengren, 'Early Hebrew Myths and Their Interpretation', in Hooke, *Myth, Ritual and Kingship*, 149–203

M. F. Wiles, 'Eternal Generation', *JTS* NS 12, 1961, 284–91

—, *The Divine Apostle*, Cambridge 1967

R. D. Williams, *Arius: Heresy and Tradition*, London 1987

H. G. M. Williamson, 'The Dynastic Oracle in the Books of Chronicles', in A. Rofé and Y. Zakovitch (eds), *Isaac Leo Seeligmann Volume*, III, Jerusalem, 1983, 305–18

H. Windisch, *Die Orakel des Hystaspes*, Verhandelingen der koninklijke Akademie van Wetenschappen te Amsterdam, Letterkunde, NR XXVIII. 3,

Amsterdam 1929

M. O. Wise, *A Critical Study of the Temple Scroll from Qumran Cave 11*, Chicago 1990

H. W. Wolff, 'Herrschaft Jahwes und Messiasgestalt im Alten Testament', *ZAW* 54, 1936, 168–202

A. S. van der Woude (ed.), *The Book of Daniel in the Light of New Findings*, BETL 106, Leuven 1993

—, see Grundmann

N. T. Wright, *The Climax of the Covenant*, Edinburgh 1991

Notes

Introduction

1. Rankin, *Polemic*, 191; Eisenstein, *Ozar Wikuhim*, 90 (*'eyn ha-din veha-mishpat she-lanu 'iqqaro be-mashiah*).

2. Nahmanides is set in the context of more widespread reluctance to recognize messianic belief as a principle of Judaism, even by writers who are concerned with messianism in other contexts, e.g. by M. Kellner, *Dogma in Medieval Jewish Thought*, Oxford 1986, 214–16.

3. On Nahmanides's formulation as not only a polemical response influenced by Christianity, but also itself subsequently influential among Christians as well as Jews, see Limor, 'Beyond Barcelona', 111–12. Protests against undue limitation of the significance of messianism in rabbinic teaching and the Judaism influenced by it were made by Schechter, *Aspects of Rabbinic Theology*, 101 n.2, 345–6; Scholem, *Messianic Idea*, 8–10.

4. These views are exemplified in Becker, *Messiaserwartung*; the volumes of essays edited by Neusner, *Judaisms*; Charlesworth, *The Messiah*, and Beuken, Freyne and Weiler, *Messianism*; Sanders, *Judaism*, 295–8; Brown, *Death*, 1, 473–5.

5. Karrer, *Der Gesalbte*, 22–3, 30–4, 88–9; Brown, as cited in the previous note; earlier, Charles, *Religious Development between the Old and the New Testaments*, 1914, 74–90 and Dodd, *According to the Scriptures*, 1952, 114.

6. For criticism on lines often differing from those followed below see O'Neill, *Jesus*, 23–54. A. Laato, *A Star is Rising*, University of South Florida 1997, has reached me too late for consideration here.

7. Weiss, *Predigt Jesu*, 158–9, and *Das Urchristentum*, 22–3 (ET 1, 31–3), held that belief in God's vindication of Jesus evoked from the disciples a clear Yes to the messianic question which had been central among them before his death; it confirmed that in the ministry he had been called to be messiah, and signified that he had now become messiah. For Bultmann, *Theology*, 1, 27, however, these texts mainly show that Jesus's messiahship was dated from the resurrection (similarly, Knox, *Acts*, 74–6; Barrett, *Acts*, on 2. 36; on the background and influence of this view, O'Neill, *Jesus*, 8–12). The implication drawn by Bultmann does not necessarily follow from the texts (O'Neill, *Romans*, 27, on 1. 4), and is questioned by the likelihood that Christians held

Jesus to have been messiah during the ministry (Moule, *Christology*, 31–5).

8. De Jonge, 'Monotheism and Christology', 224–5.

9. See especially Horbury, 'The Messianic Associations of "the Son of Man"', 'Messianism among Jews and Christians in the Second Century', and 'Herod's Temple and "Herod's Days"'.

10. Horbury, 'The Cult of Christ and the Cult of the Saints'.

I. Messianism and the Old Testament

1. The title of a lecture given in Cambridge by J. V. M. Sturdy, Dean of Caius College, Cambridge, in January 1995.

2. So for example Dalman, *Worte*, 237 (ET 289); Gressmann, *Der Messias*, 1; Rowley, *Servant*, 61 n.3; Hesse, *TDNT* 9, 505; Schmidt, *Faith*, 198–9; Roberts, 'The Old Testament's Contribution to Messianic Expectations', 39–41; but in the psalter the title can be applied both to the reigning and to the ideal king (so H. H. Rowley, *The Faith of Israel*, London 1956, 188, n.1), and the understanding of the relevant psalms and prophecies during and after the exile should also be reckoned with in description of Old Testament usage (see below).

3. Becker, *Messianic Expectation*, 37–82.

4. For examples of such lists see Charles, *Religious Development*, 75–6; Dalman, *Worte*, 243 (ET 296); Emmet, 'Messiah', 575–6 ('Books where the Messianic hope is ignored'); von Gall, BASILEIA, 376–7; Bousset and Gressmann, *Die Religion des Judentums*, 222; Frost, *Old Testament Apocalyptic*, 66–7; Mowinckel, *He That Cometh*, 280; Becker, *Messianic Expectation*, 79; Hofius, 'Thesen', 109–10.

5. Reventlow, *Problems of Biblical Theology*, 49.

6. Clements, 'Hope', 2.

7. Gelin, 'Messianisme', 1165–6.

8. Brettler, *God is King*, 126–31, 133–4.

9. Karrer, *Gesalbte*, 209–13, 265–7, 293–4, 313, 406–9 (dissociating Christian origins from royal usage); for royal interpretation of Ps. 105. 15 see F. Brown, S. R. Driver and C. A. Briggs, *A Hebrew and English Lexicon of the Old Testament*, corrected reprint, Oxford 1953, 603b; and compare chapter III, below, on the kingship of Abraham in Gen. 23. 6 MT and LXX.

10. Jeremias, 'Nochmals', and van der Woude, *TDNT* 9, 509–10 and n.71, offer valuable material but are not directed to this particular question.

11. For discussion see the commentary by J. J. Collins, *ad loc.*

12. See Dalman, *Words*, 293–4.

13. See J. M. Baumgarten, on the basis of transcriptions by J. T. Milik, with contributions by S. Pfann and A. Yardeni, *Qumran Cave 4, XIII, The Damascus Document (4Q266–273)*, DJD 18, Oxford 1996, 72–4.

14. Text edited by D. Barthélemy in Barthélemy and Milik, *Qumran Cave 1*, 110, and again by J. H. Charlesworth and L. T. Stuckenbruck in Charlesworth

and others, *Rule of the Community and Related Documents*, 116.

15. Casey, *From Jewish Prophet*, 41–4, 79; his assertions that in non-Christian Jewish documents of the Second-Temple period the term is not commonly used of a future redeemer, and that unqualified 'Messiah' is not found (42), need qualification.

16. On the expectation in general, see Stauffer, 'Agnostos Christos'; on Isa. 32. 2 LXX in this connection, see Horbury, 'Messianic Associations', 50–1.

17 This inference is sometimes drawn from the grand total of under thirty instances of 'anointed' in Jewish literature between 200 BC and AD 100, reckoned by de Jonge, 'The Use of the Word "Anointed" in the Time of Jesus'. Note, however, besides the consideration mentioned in the text above, that both the New Testament and the rabbinic literature (not included in de Jonge's data) independently suggest the familiarity of the term 'messiah'.

18. Inconsistency even within particular groups or writings was influentially exhibited by Morton Smith, 'What is Implied by the Variety of Messianic Figures?'; but the differences do not exclude broad agreement in messianic expectation, as is indeed suggested by the inclusion of varied material within single writings like II Esdras.

19. See Bauer, 'Erwartungen', and *Christus und die Caesaren*, 292–8.

20. The studies mentioned below are not reassessed in the relatively short treatments by Becker, *Messianic Expectation*, and Roberts, 'The Old Testament's Contribution'.

21. Wellhausen, *Prolegomena*, 412–15: 414 (ET 414–17: 416).

22. Wellhausen, *Psalms*, 184, 201–2, on Psalms 47, 92, 97.

23. Clements, *Isaiah 1–39*, ad loc., citing H. Barth, *Die Jesaja-Worte in der Josiazeit*, Neukirchen-Vluyn 1977.

24. The quotation is from the study of Wellhausen's critique of this book by O'Neill, *Authority*, 236–8.

25. Gunkel, *Schöpfung*, 198–200; the text from Lam. R. was edited, with reference also to the Talmudic version, by Dalman, *Aramäische Dialektproben*, 14–15, and Gunkel's view was taken up and developed by Lévi, 'Le ravissement'.

26. See the warm tribute to Gunkel in Bousset, *Antichrist Legend*, 5–16.

27. Gressmann, *Ursprung*, especially 260, 285, 293–5, 300–1, 334–65.

28. Oesterley was also indebted to the anthropological writing of Robertson Smith and J. G. Frazer, and, like Gressmann himself, to H. Gunkel on mythology; but Gressmann's own influence emerges not only in citations (Oesterley, *Evolution*, 83, 125) but also in long quotations (ibid., 101, 258–9). This point modifies the impression of Oesterley's independence which can be gained from Clements, 'Messianic Hope'.

29. E. Meyer, *Die Israeliten und ihre Nachbarstämme*, Halle 1906, 451–5.

30. Gressmann, *Der Messias*, 230–2, 431 (citing E. Meyer), 445.

31. Gressmann, *Der Messias*, 10*, 415.

32. Mowinckel, *Thronbesteigungsfest*, 297–314; *He That Cometh*, 125–33, 159–62, 181–6.

33. H. Gunkel, *Ausgewählte Psalmen*, Göttingen 1904, 162, quoted by Gressmann, *Ursprung*, 295.

34. Mowinckel, *Thronbesteigungsfest*, 14, 297–8; Delitzsch, *Die Psalmen*, 602, on Ps.93, spoke of two parallel series of prophecies, on the kingdom of God and the kingdom of the messiah, respectively, which in the Old Testament converge without meeting.

35. Wolff, 'Herrschaft Jahwes und Messiasgestalt im Alten Testament'.

36. So in Roberts, 'The Old Testament's Contribution', 43, 51.

37. von Gall, BASILEIA, 173, 175–88.

38. von Gall, BASILEIA, 9–16; Mowinckel, *He That Cometh*, especially 127–8.

39. See for example Welten, 'Königsherrschaft Jahwes und Thronbesteigung', with comment on the history of the study of the enthronement psalms; the tendency towards dating them late in their present form and questioning their treatment as a group is also illustrated by Brettler, *God is King*, 145–58 (93; 95–99 can be grouped because of common vocabulary and theme, but 47 and 81 should be treated separately, and no specific festival is to be presupposed as a setting); Joyce, 'The Kingdom of God and the Psalms', 52 (envisaging the possibility that language about the Lord as king only came to the fore after the demise of Davidic monarchy at the beginning of the sixth century, but leaving the question open); Schaper, 'Psalm 47' (this psalm is post-exilic in its present form, finds parallels in texts like Isa. 52. 9; Obad. 18–21; and Zech. 9. 9, and offers no basis for reconstructing a festal setting).

40. von Gall, BASILEIA, 48–82, surveying the material in a critique directed mainly at Meyer and Lietzmann; Gross, *Die Idee des ewigen und allgemeinen Weltfriedens*, 14–16, against Gressmann.

41. Mowinckel, *Thronbesteigungsfest*, 299; *He That Cometh*, 15, 181–6.

42. Thus Egyptian influence is recognized in the ninth–seventh century BC monolithic tombs of Silwan, overlooking the Kidron valley, and the large tombs of a similar date at St Stephen's basilica on the north hill of Jerusalem. See G. Barkai, A. Mazar and A. Kloner, 'The Northern Cemetery of Jerusalem in First Temple Times', *Qadmoniot* 8, 1975, 71–6 (a plate at p.74 illustrates the head-rests in the shape of the Hathor wig); D. Ussishkin, *The Village of Silwan: The Necropolis from the Period of the Judean Kingdom*, Jerusalem 1993, 317–18 (the main, though not the only, source of inspiration was Egypt).

43. von Gall, 81; these writings are treated as apocalyptic compositions by J. Gwyn Griffiths, 'Apocalyptic in the Hellenistic Era', as non-apocalyptic works containing apocalyptic motifs by J. Bergman, 'Introductory Remarks on Apocalypticism in Egypt', and as political prophecies by J. Assmann, 'Königsdogma und Heilserwartung', in Hellholm, *Apocalypticism*, 273–93, 51–60, and 345–77, respectively. Fishbane, *Biblical Interpretation*, 474–6, compares them with the 'mantological exegesis' found in Daniel.

44. These two texts are translated and introduced by Lichtheim, *Ancient Egyptian Literature*, 1, 139–45, 215–22; for comment in connection with prophecy see Assmann, 'Königsdogma', 357–61 and nn. 5, 103, and Bergman, 'Remarks', 53–5.

45. See Welten, 'Königsherrschaft Jahwes', 297 ('ein gewisser Horror vor der Kühnheit der Väter').

46. On Scandinavia and Britain see, respectively, Widengren, 'Early Hebrew Myths', and Johnson, 'Hebrew Conceptions of Kingship', with Hooke, 'Myth and Ritual: Past and Present'.

47. Bentzen, *King and Messiah* (see below); Riesenfeld, *Jésus transfiguré*; Mowinckel, *He That Cometh*; Johnson, *Sacral Kingship* (see below).

48. Favourable British reaction to Mowinckel on the enthronement psalms is exemplified by Johnson, *Sacral Kingship*, 61–2, n.1; Emerton, 'The Origin of the Son of Man Imagery', 230; Gray, *The Biblical Doctrine of the Reign of God*, 7–71; Day, *Psalms*, 67–87.

49. Frost, *Old Testament Apocalyptic*, 32–70, 249–53 (67 n.32 on Hooke).

50. Johnson, *Sacral Kingship*, 8, 59, 61–2 n.1, 134–6, 143–4; quotation from his 'Hebrew Conceptions of Kingship', 234–5.

51. Johnson, *Sacral Kingship*, 31–2, 85–90, 92–5.

52. For what follows see Emerton, 'Origin', and Collins, *Daniel*, 286–94.

53. Bentzen, *King and Messiah*, 74–5.

54. Emerton, 'Origin'.

55. Bentzen, *King and Messiah*, 11–20, 77–80.

56. For a comment on the non-dynastic interpretation of such passages by K. E. Pomykala see p. 43, below.

57. Perez Fernandez, *Tradiciones mesiánicas*, 113 and n.189, noting the striking Mishnaic regulation (Meg. 4. 10) that, despite its content, this chapter is read aloud and translated when the Torah is publicly read.

58. Person, *Second Zechariah and the Deuteronomic School*; see especially 85–104.

59. Isa. 66. 7 on the birth of the man child is echoed messianically at 1QH xi (formerly iii) lines 7–10, in association with titles from Isa. 9. 5 (6), and at Rev. 12. 2, 5, in association with Ps. 2. 8–9; later, at Ber. R. 85. 1, on Gen. 38. 1, it is likewise referred to the birth of the 'last redeemer'. The Targum 'before trembling shall come upon her . . . her king shall be revealed' therefore probably also refers to the messiah. Isa. 66. 20 is correspondingly applied to the coming Davidic king in Ps. Sol. 17. 34 (31), discussed in chapter III, section 5, below.

60. This understanding of the prince in Lev. 4. 22 appears in Mishnah, Horayoth 3, 3, discussed with other evidence by Horbury, 'Phylarchs', 518–19.

61. See the following chapter for discussion of the suggestion that it is further reflected in Chronicles.

62. Porter, *Moses and Monarchy*; 'The Succession of Joshua'.

63. Horbury, 'Septuagintal and New Testament Conceptions of the Church'.

64. This aspect of Moses tends to fall out of sight in the examination of his role by F. Crüsemann, *Die Tora*, Munich 1992; he concentrates on Moses as lawgiver rather than leader of the exodus.

65. Juel, *Messianic Exegesis*, 121–2.

66. On Zech. 9–14 in Mark see Marcus, *Way*, 154–64.

67. On Messiah ben Joseph, Moore, *Judaism* II, 370–1; Agus, *Binding*, 207–8, 218–20.

68. Oegema, *Der Gesalbte und sein Volk*, 70–3, 229–32.

II. The Prevalence of Messianism in the Second-Temple Period

1. Schürer, *History*, ET 1890, 135–6.

2. Karrer, *Der Gesalbte*, 11–47.

3. Charles, *Religious Development between the Old and the New Testaments*, 1914, 74–90; Dodd, *According to the Scriptures*, 1952, 114.

4. Frost, *Old Testament Apocalyptic*, 66–7; Collins, *Scepter*, 31–8, 40.

5. Gressmann, *Der Ursprung*, 294–301.

6. Horbury, 'Yose', 165, 175, on Yose ben Yose, *'anusah le-'ezrah*, lines 60–64; the poem in question incorporates the biblical *shofaroth* texts inserted in the Tefillah at New Year (see Mishnah Rosh ha-Shanah 4. 6), and ends with a couplet introducing the quotation of Zech. 9. 14–15.

7. These sayings are discussed, in the context of a collection of comparable passages, by Kuhn, *Gottes Trauer*, 254–7; comparing Old Testament and rabbinic treatments of divine grief (ibid., 474–89, 510–11), he contrasts rabbinic anthropomorphism with the relative reserve of biblical texts, without perhaps allowing sufficiently for the anthropomorphism of biblical theophany texts such as those noted in connection with Gressmann in the text above.

8. Strack and Billerbeck, *Kommentar zum Neuen Testament aus Talmud und Midrasch*, I, 68, on Matt. I 21; historical explanation of the variation is exemplified by A. Marmorstein, 'Ra'yon ha-ge'ullah', 54, suggesting that in the fourth century rabbinic emphasis fell on redemption by God alone partly because of the failure of messianic movements, partly because of the growth of Christianity. The latter reason is also envisaged by Loewe, 'Apologetic Motifs in the Targum to the Song of Songs' and '"Salvation" is not of the Jews'.

9. von Gall, BASILEIA, 173, 175–88; this point is emphasized again by Albertz, *A History of Israelite Religion*, 2, 424–6, 456–7.

10. von Gall, BASILEIA, 214–57, 291, 374–7.

11. Collins, *Scepter*, 40–1; Sanders, *Judaism*, 295.

12. Note especially Porter, 'The Succession of Joshua'; Ottosson, *Josuaboken*, 38–42, 263, 274, 280.

13. Albertz, *A History of Israelite Religion*, 2, 456–7.

14. Moenikes, 'Messianismus', 305; *Ablehnung*, 218–21.

15. On these Pseudo-Clementine and rabbinic passages see Schoeps, *Theologie und Geschichte des Judenchristentums*, 242–7; at Sifre Deut. 156 the

critical statement seems to be that of Nehorai rather than that of Judah b. Ilai, cited by Schoeps.

16. The application to the deity is adopted, after a sensitive discussion, by Larkin, *Second Zechariah*, 76; but the resemblances to Gen. 49. 10 and Ps.72. 8 which she notes, following M. Fishbane, point rather towards a messianic interpretation.

17. So for example Berquist, *Judaism in Persia's Shadow*, 63–73, doubts Zerubbabel's claim to Davidic descent (because his father is Shealtiel in Haggai, but in I Chron. 3. 17–19 Shealtiel's brother Pedaiah; in either case, however, according to the Chronicles pedigree, Jehoiachin would be Zerubbabel's grandfather); Berquist understands the oracles as an affirmation of his position as a governor appointed by Persia. The Chronicles tradition of Davidic descent can well be understood, however, as a later reflection of claims made at the time about Zerubbabel, for Hag. 2. 23 on the signet seems to echo Jer. 22. 24, an oracle concerning Jehoiachin. Moreover, Haggai's messianism is bound up in other ways with the pre-exilic Jerusalem court tradition, as noted by R. A. Mason (in Coggins et al., *Israel's Prophetic Tradition*, 143). Similarly, the title 'branch' given to Zerubbabel in Zech. 3. 8; 6. 12 echoes Jer. 23. 5–6, 'I will raise up to David a righteous branch', cf. Jer. 33. 15–16. For a recognition of the politically explosive character of the claims made for Zerubbabel see Albertz, *A History of Israelite Religion*, 2, 452–4 and n.4.

18. Pomykala, *The Davidic Dynasty Tradition*, 38–41, 61–3, 66–7, 104–11.

19. See Rofé, 'Battle', 139–44.

20. Rofé, 'Qumranic Paraphrases', 169–74.

21. A comparable transition to hopes for the end of the present world-order, rather than for imminent change within it, is situated at this point by Albertz, *A History of Israelite Religion*, 2, 454–8, also with reference to Trito-Isaiah. The present writer would not distinguish so sharply as Albertz and Rofé between the hopes envisaged in Haggai and Zechariah, on the one hand, and Trito-Isaiah and Daniel, on the other; in all cases a this-worldly change in rulers is arguably central.

22. See Rofé, 'Isaiah 59:19'; he proposes the pointing *ṣir* in v. 19, rendering 'for an envoy will come'. This proposal seems probable (for the word, compare Isa. 18. 2, and 63. 8 following LXX); but, even if it is rejected, his explanation of *go'el* in v. 20 can stand.

23. Rofé, 'Battle', 139–44.

24. On the Chronicler's belief in the eternal establishment of the Davidic dynasty see H. G. M. Williamson, 'The Dynastic Oracle in the Books of Chronicles', in A. Rofé and Y. Zakovitch (eds), *Isaac Leo Seeligmann Volume*, 3, Jerusalem 1983, 305–18; he prefers to avoid the word 'messianic' (which might imply expectation of one unique eschatological monarch), but understands the Chronicler to expect the re-emergence of a ruling Davidic house-hold in post-exilic Judah. This interpretation is followed by Albertz, *A History of Israelite Religion*, 2, 554–5.

25. Schniedewind, 'King and Priest in the Book of Chronicles and the Duality of Qumran Messianism'; as argued in the previous chapter, a more important antecedent for the dual constitution was probably Num. 27. 15–23, on the ordination of Joshua.

26. For this translation of I Enoch 49. 2 and 4 see M. A. Knibb in H. F. D. Sparks (ed.), *The Apocryphal Old Testament*, Oxford 1984, 230.

27. Aramaic is likely to have been the common language of most Judahites in the fourth century, but Hebrew is used in many of the bullae and seals from this period found near Jerusalem; see Schwartz, 'On the Autonomy of Judaea in the Fourth and Third Centuries BCE', 159–60.

28. For a dismissal of claimed evidence for Jewish rebellion, and discernment of popular resistance to foreign rule in Sidon and Tyre, see Grainger, *Hellenistic Phoenicia*, 22–37.

29. The importance of the constitutional aspect of messianic oracles and interpretations is emphasized from different points of view by Horbury, 'Aaronic Priesthood' and 'Constitutional Aspects'; Maier, 'Der Messias'; Oegema, *Der Gesalbte und sein Volk*.

30. Murray, 'Aristeas and Ptolemaic Kingship'; Hengel, Charlesworth and Mendels, 'The Polemical Character of "On Kingship" in the Temple Scroll'; Wise, *A Critical Study of the Temple Scroll from Qumran Cave 11*, 101–21, 228–31.

31. See in general Porter, *Moses and Monarchy*: Deut. 33. 5 was probably understood to mean that Moses was king.

32. Thus the Ptolemaic setting is viewed as possibly discouraging interest in messianism by H. B. Swete, *Introduction to the Old Testament in Greek*, Cambridge 1902, 259 (on the absence of Jer. 33. 14–26 from the Greek), and Lust, 'Messianism', 179–80, and as having a similar influence on translation of passages on Jewish kingship by Hanhart and Freund, as cited below. LXX passages suggesting both the restraint and the accentuation of messianism are collected by M. Harl in G. Dorival, M. Harl and O. Munnich, *La Bible grecque des Septante*, Paris 1988, 219–22.

33. Z. Frankel, *Ueber den Einfluss der palästinischen Exegese auf die alexandrinische Hermeneutik*, Leipzig 1851, repr. Farnborough 1972, 50–1, 182–5 (on Gen. 49. 10; Num. 24. 7, 17, 23–24).

34. So Rofé, 'Qumran Paraphrases', 169–74; he suggests that the purpose of the change would have been to defend the place of God as the sole king over against any earthly ruler.

35. The rendering ἄρχων here contrasts with the use of βασιλεύς in I Samuel = I Kingdoms (including passages critical of kings); Hanhart, 'Die Bedeutung der Septuaginta für die Definition des "Hellenistischen Judentums"', 72–4, suggests that the former, inoffensively legitimizing Jewish authorities subordinate to the Greek kings, was deliberately chosen in the Pentateuch, while the rendering in I Kingdoms sharpened Jewish criticism of Greek kingship. Ἄρχων was indeed probably favoured as a flexible word (see

Horbury, 'The Twelve and the Phylarchs', section II), but in Deut. 17 and in Gen. 49. 10; Num. 23. 21; Deut.33. 5, connected below with Deut. 17, it would have primarily suggested the Jewish kings to a Jewish hearer; the future king David is ἄρχων (Ezek. 37. 22–25), and the word also rendered Hebrew *nasi*, an equivalent of *melekh* in post-exilic Hebrew (Ezek. 37. 25; with reference to the law of the king, CD v 1). The retention of βασιλεύς in the translation of I Samuel need not imply criticism of Greek kings, given the positive Pentateuchal uses of the word in Jewish connections noted immediately below. Paradoxically, Samuel's δίκαιωμα τοῦ βασιλέως (I Kgdms 8. 9, 11; 10. 25) may sometimes have been taken positively, as in *Didasc*. 2. 34, where I Kgdms 8. 10–17 sets out the people's duties to the bishop (similarly, without the full quotation, *Ap. Const*. 2. 35). Freund, 'From Kings to Archons', took a similar view of the Pentateuchal rendering, without reference to Hanhart; adding a survey of further passages, he found hope for a non-kingly Davidic ruler, and a general reserve on kingship which was continued (he urged) in Philo and Josephus, and contrasts with Hebrew and Aramaic messianic interpretation. Freund does not discuss the implications of Exod. 19. 6; 22. 23 LXX, and Philo on Moses as king, or Camponovo's treatment of kingship in the LXX (see the following note); these seem considerably to modify his thesis.

36. For interpretation of the verses in this sense see Camponovo, *Königtum, Königsherrschaft und Reich Gottes in den frühjüdischen Schriften*, 386–7; note in addition the apparent adaptation of Deut.33. 5 LXX to Ps. 46 (47). 10 LXX, implying a reference to an eschatological gathering of gentile rulers which strengthens Camponovo's view that a messianic king is envisaged in Deut. 33. 5 LXX.

37. On Deut. 17. 15 understood as a commandment to make a king see Blidstein, 'The Monarchic Imperative in Rabbinic Perspective', citing among other texts Ps.-Philo, *Ant. Bibl*. 45. 1–3 (in the time of Samuel the people were too hasty in their wish to fulfil Deut. 17. 15, which was more truly fulfilled when David succeeded).

38. βασίλειον ἱεράτευμα will have been understood as two nouns; the LXX is taken in this way in II Macc. 2. 17 and Philo (*Abr*. 56; *Sobr*. 66), and Exod. 19. 6 is so understood in Jub. 16. 18; Rev. 1. 6; 5. 10; Symmachus, Theodotion, Peshitta and Targums (see Camponovo, 384–6, 411). Judah is chosen for the 'kingship' (βασίλειον) at I Chron. 28. 4 LXX (Hebrew נגיד 'prince').

39. For ῥάβδος in this sense, cf. Pss. 45 (44). 7; 110 (109). 2 LXX.

40. Further material in Horbury, 'Septuagintal and New Testament Conceptions of the Church', 5–6, 8–9; Exod. 4. 20 is quoted in Midrash Tehillim on Ps. 21. 2 (ed. S. Buber, f.89b) to show that, although in the case of an earthly king others may not use his sceptre (Mishnah, Sanh. 2. 5), Moses used God's sceptre.

41. For these connections see Harl, *La Genèse*, 308–9, and Horbury, 'Messianic Associations', 39–40.

42. On the Targums of Numbers and 'man' as a messianic title, see Perez

Fernandez, *Tradiciones mesiánicas*, 220–86; for other instances of a messianic 'man' and other messianic interpretations of Num. 24. 7, 17 see Horbury, 'Messianic Associations', 49–52 (written without knowledge of the work of Perez, who argues on similar lines).

43. The LXX is interpreted in this way by Camponovo, *Königtum, Königs-herrschaft und Reich Gottes*, 386–7, 413–14, with quotation of the Targums; he notes that this was also the view of Z. Frankel.

44. This view is defended in Horbury, 'The Christian Use and Jewish Origins of the Wisdom of Solomon'; *Contact and Controversy*, 29–33 (here with reference to M. Hengel's proposal that the LXX book collection is essentially of Christian origin).

45. Emmet, 'Messiah', 575.

46. On the tradition of hagiographical portraits of the high priest see Horbury, 'The Aaronic Priesthood in the Epistle to the Hebrews', 59–66.

47. The LXX form of Isa. 9. 6–7 is associated with Maccabaean Davidic expectation by Hanhart, 'Die Septuaginta als Interpretation', 345–6.

48. The Parthian threat to Jerusalem, as reflected in I Enoch 56, would well suit the time of the Parthian interventions in Judaea just before the reign of Herod the Great. For this interpretation of Dan. 7 in the Parables see Horbury, 'Messianic Associations'.

49. This and other suggestions, in the names of tannaitic teachers active before the Bar Kokhba war, are collected in a baraitha found in Babylonian Talmud, Sanhedrin 99a, and elsewhere.

50. For surveys see Schiffman, 'Messianic Figures and Ideas'; García Martínez, 'Esperanzas mesiánicas'; Collins, *Scepter*.

51. For discussion of these two texts see Collins, *Scepter*, 136–72, and (on 4Q246) chapter IV, below.

52. 'Firstborn son' is referred to a ruler in the edition by H. W. Attridge in H. Attridge et al., *Qumran Cave 4.VIII*, DJD XIII, Oxford 1994, 356–9; but context, and comparison with 4Q503, suggest that the allusion is to Israel as 'my son, my firstborn' (Exod. 4. 22).

53. For fuller discussion of this scene see Horbury, 'Antichrist among Jews and Gentiles'.

54. For text and discussion see G. Vermes and R. P. Gordon in Vermes, 'Seminar on the Rule of War from Cave 4 (4Q285)'.

55. J. M. Allegro, *Qumrân Cave 4*, i, DJD V, Oxford 1968, 13–15, and Plate v; translation also in F. García Martínez, *The Dead Sea Scrolls Translated*, ET by W. G. E. Watson, Leiden 1994, 186.

56. *'w]ybw* (line 18) is taken by Allegro and García Martínez as a defectively written plural and rendered 'his enemies', but the more straightforward rendering 'his enemy', in the singular, seems preferable against the background sketched above. Vermes and Gordon do not discuss this question in their comments on 4Q161 in Vermes, 'Seminar on the Rule of War from Cave 4 (4Q 285)'.

57. According to the Greek of Codex Vaticanus (B), Ecclus. 48. 17b, on Hezekiah, runs 'and he led Gog into their midst'. Γώγ is probably an inner-Greek corruption of Γίων, 'Gihon' (see J. H. A. Hart, *Ecclesiasticus: the Greek Text of Codex 248*, Cambridge 1909, 219–20), but it suggests knowledge of the link in Jewish thought between Hezekiah and the messiah; see pp. 66–67, and above Bar Kappara's saying in Sanh. 94a (p. 195, n. 13, below). As Hezekiah's captive, Gog is the messianic adversary.

58. So J. T. Milik in Barthélemy and Milik, *Qumrân Cave 1*, 82.

59. Mirsky, *Yosse*, 108; the context is summarized in Horbury, 'Yose', 151.

60. Seeligmann, *The Septuagint Version of Isaiah*, 118–20 ['Nowhere does the rendering of biblical images into Greek terminology transpose the content of the text into the Hellenistic sphere of thought more markedly than in the case of this Messianic figure' (in 9. 6; 11. 2–4, conceived as bringer of peace and ecstatic; but it is not clear that 7. 14 was influenced by mysteries, as thought by R. Kittel, *Die hellenistischen Mysterienreligionen und das Alte Testament*, Stuttgart 1924, 14, 23–4]; J. Lust, 'Messianism and Septuagint', in J. A. Emerton (ed.), *Congress Volume: Salamanca, 1983*, Leiden 1985, 174–91.

III. The Coherence of Messianism

1. Bousset and Gressmann, *Religion*, 222–33, 259–68; on studies of ancient Judaism in general which have modified Bousset's emphasis on diversity see Horbury, *Jews and Christians*, 3–7.

2. Riesenfeld, *Jésus transfiguré*, 54–83.

3. Chevallier, *L'esprit et le messie*, 49–50 (quotation translated from 50).

4. The arguments for the centrality and coherence of messianic hope put forward by Riesenfeld and Chevallier are not considered by contributors to Neusner, Green and Frerichs, *Judaisms*, and Charlesworth, *Messiah*.

5. Harl, *Genèse, ad loc.*; the material is surveyed by S. R. Driver, *The Book of Genesis*, London 1904, 410–15, and Perez Fernandez, *Tradiciones mesiánicas*, 127–35.

6. E. P. Sanders, stressing that the 'branch of David' is not envisaged in the battle-scenes of the War Scroll, speaks of 'the non-appearance of a Davidic messiah' in this work (*Judaism: Practice and Belief*, 296–7); this passage, however, seems to reflect Davidic expectation in the form attested in other Qumran texts.

7. This Hebrew and Aramaic composition, preserved in Hekhaloth Rabbathi, the Midrash of the Ten Martyrs and elsewhere, is studied by Schwemer, 'Irdischer und himmlischer König' (322, mentioning the assembly of kings); the passage in question, paragraph 126 in P. Schäfer, with M. Schlüter and H. G. von Mutius, *Synopse zur Hekhalot-Literatur*, Tübingen 1981, 62–3, can also be seen in Ad. Jellinek, *Bet ha-Midrasch*, V, Vienna 1872, repr. Jerusalem, 1967, 168, and G. Reeg, *Die Geschichte von den Zehn Märtyrern*, Tübingen 1985, 59*.

8. This point is noted with regard to Hezekiah by Mach, *Entwicklungs-stadien*, 80 n.34.

9. For text and translation see Dimant, 'The Seventy Weeks Chronology (Dan 9,24–27) in the Light of New Qumranic Texts', 72–6.

10. Ezekiel Tragicus 36–41, 68–89; Philo, *Mos.* 1, 148–62 (ὠνομάσθη γὰρ ὅλου τοῦ ἔθνους θεὸς καὶ βασιλεύς, 158); Targum Ps.-Jonathan on Deut. 33. 5; Midrash Tehillim 1. 2, on Ps. 1. 1 (Moses, like David, was king of Israel and Judah, as Deut. 33. 5 shows); for other evidence see p. 179 n. 39 above and L. Ginzberg, *The Legends of the Jews*, VI, Philadelphia 1956, nn. 170, 918.

11. See for example I Kings 11. 34; Ezek. 34. 24; 37. 25 (the past and future Davidic king); M. Horayoth 3. 1–3, where the offering of the 'prince' (Lev. 4. 22) is understood as that of 'the king' rather than a tribal prince. See chapter II, above, on the significance of the LXX rendering *archon*.

12. Gianotto, *Melchisedek*, 117–18 so interprets the LXX, following F. Parente; already in Gen. 14. 18 Salem is probably used to refer to Jerusalem, as in Ps. 76. 3 (Emerton, 'The Site of Salem, the City of Melchizedek', reviewing the ancient evidence).

13. So, on Roman imperial cult and Christianity, Loesch, *Deitas Jesu und antike Apotheose*; Hengel, *The Son of God*, 30 ('at best a negative stimulus, not a model').

14. Hultgård, *L'eschatologie des Testaments des Douze Patriarches*, 1, 326–81, finds strong influence from the language of ruler-cult, with special reference to coins and inscriptions.

15. G. S. Oegema's argument that messianic figures are depicted on the model of contemporary rulers, gentile as well as Jewish, points in the same direction (Oegema, *Der Gesalbte und sein Volk*, cited at the end of chapter I, section 4, above).

16. Bousset and Gressmann, *Religion*, 225–6.

17. For distinction between broader and narrower views of ruler-cult see Crook, 'Augustus: Power, Authority, Achievement', 134.

18. This point, expounded by Geertz, 'Centers, Kings, and Charisma: Reflections on the Symbolics of Power', is applied to ancient ruler-cult by Price, *Rituals and Power*.

19. For this see especially Charlesworth, 'Some Observations on Ruler-Cult, Especially in Rome', and Bi(c)kerman, *Institutions des Séleucides*, 257, and in den Boer, *Le culte*, 26, 28, 210 (Greek 'ruler cult' honoured benefactors, not rulers as such).

20. Nock in *Cambridge Ancient History* X, Cambridge 1934, 481–9 (481 quoted above), modified by Price, *Rituals and Power*, 15–16; similarly, Fishwick, *Imperial Cult*, I. 1, 44–5 (the cult can properly be called a religion); compare discussion of spontaneous veneration in den Boer, *Le culte*, 11–14, 30–7, 208–11.

21. Bickerman, 'Consecratio', 5–6; similarly, Fishwick, 'Prayer and the Living Emperor', 343–4; but with the differing view taken in the text above

compare C. Habicht, modifying K. Thraede's stress on the sheerly literary conditioning of Horace's verse on this theme, in den Boer, *Le culte*, 305.

22. Thus Domitian's official use of the title 'lord and god', *dominus et deus*, is denied by Hengel, *Studies in Early Christology*, 366 n.22, following J. R. Fears; but its use in court poetry suggests that it may still have been part of the imperial honours known to Jews and Christians.

23. Bickerman, 'Consecratio', 11–14 (distinguishing from religion of mental and emotional conviction as defined by Augustine); Price, *Rituals*, 11–15, 247.

24. Price's condemnation of the impact of Christian criticism on historiography *(Rituals*, 11–15) could perhaps have been complemented by notice of the extent to which this criticism implicitly recognizes elements in ruler-cult which he himself is highlighting.

25. Gow, *Theocritus*, on *Id.* 17, 30; Walbank, 'Monarchies and Monarchic Ideas', 85–6; Fraser, *Ptolemaic Alexandria*, I, 203–4, with nn.717–8; Nisbet and Hubbard on Horace, *Od.* I, 12, 50 (on Augustus and Jupiter).

26. This point is made by Geffcken, 'Euhemerism' (here following P. Wendland) and by Fraser, *Ptolemaic Alexandria*, I, 289–94; see also Henrichs, 'The Sophists and Hellenistic Religion', 145–52, on predecessors of Euhemerus, including Hecataeus of Abdera.

27. Price, *Rituals*, 14–15.

28. Arrian, *Anabasis*, 4. 9, 9 – 12, 7; for Alexander's probable belief in his descent from heroes (Heracles, Perseus, Achilles) and his claim to divine filiation from Zeus-Ammon, see appendixes IV and V in Brunt, *Arrian*, I, 464–80; he judges the debate on obeisance to reflect not Alexander's intention but late fourth- or early third-century argument over deification.

29. For different views see Brunt, *Arrian*, I, 538–41 (appendix XIV) (Alexander wanted to gain conformity to Persian custom, not to claim divine honour); Badian, 'Alexander the Great between two thrones and Heaven' (Alexander at first wanted *isotheoi timai* only, but later sought deification itself).

30. Habicht, *Gottmenschentum*, 213–21, 270–1 (on late fourth-century criticism of the cults of Alexander the Great and Demetrius Poliorcetes in Athens).

31. So Walbank, 'Monarchies and Monarchic Ideas', 89–90, 95–6 (noting Callisthenes's objection to Alexander's claim as invoking the difference between gods and mortals).

32. See Walbank, Astin, Frederiksen and Ogilvie, *The Hellenistic World*, 160 (E. G. Turner on petitions), 556 (petitionary papyri collected by O. Guéraud, ΕΝΤΕΥΞΕΙΣ, Cairo, 1931–2); Chalon, *L'édit de Tiberius Julius Alexander*, 27 line 10.

33. For example by C. Habicht in den Boer, *Le culte*, 33; to the contrary, Price, 'Gods and Emperors', 91–3, citing a series of texts overlapping with those quoted below. Fishwick, 'Prayer and the Living Emperor', comments that the verse need not reflect cultic usage, but that prayer to the emperor by Alexandrians is reliably attested in Philo and Suetonius on Augustus as sea god (cited below). It may be added that, as noted from Virgil below, in this case

poetic praise does indeed correspond to cultic practice.

34. On 'dear' as often found in invocations of gods see Burkert, *Greek Religion*, 274.

35. Martial, 7. 60, ending '*te pro Caesare debeo rogare;* | *pro me debeo Caesarem rogare*'; 8. 24, 5–6 '*qui fingit sacros auro vel marmore vultus* | *non facit ille deos; qui rogat, ille facit*'.

36. The debt of this passage to peculiarly Jewish emphasis on the need to worship one deity exclusively may then not be so strong as is suggested by Collins, *Daniel*, 267. Badian, 'Alexander', 13–17, documents fifth-century Greek impressions of the superhuman and godlike status of the Persian king.

37. Suetonius, *Aug.* 98. 2 (they sang that 'through him (*per illum*) they lived, through him they sailed the sea, through him they enjoyed liberty and good fortune'); the repeated *per illum* reflects the style of acclamation.

38. This language, with its emphasis on the distinction between the gods and humanity, is traced to an Augustan formula by C. Habicht, following M. P. Charlesworth, in den Boer, *Le culte*, 76–80.

39. Other comparable passages in Plutarch are noted by Charlesworth, 'Ruler-Cult', 14 (*Dem.* 12), 38–9, and Scott, 'Plutarch and the Ruler Cult' and 'Humor at the Expense of the Ruler Cult'; Scott views Plutarch as implying criticism of the contemporary imperial cult, an interpretation denied by Bowersock, 'Greek Intellectuals and the Imperial Cult', in den Boer, *Le culte*, 187–91, 207–8.

40. Athenaeus 6, 250a (from Timaeus of Tauromenium), 253e (from Duris of Samos; discussed by Walbank, 91–2).

41. *AP* 9, 355, line 3 = D. L. Page, *Further Greek Epigrams*, Cambridge 1981, line 1984, Διὸς εὖνι.

42. '. . . *deus, qui flectit habenas* | *orbis, et humanos propior Iove digerit actus*.'

43. Valerius Maximus, I, *praef.* (the divinity of other gods is envisaged by thought, but yours is attested by present witness, '*praesenti fide*'); Pliny, *Pan.* 80, 5–6 (Trajan fulfils Jupiter's role, '*vice sua*', on earth); panegyric to Maximian translated in Price, *Rituals and Power*, 247.

44. Most of the passages discussed below are surveyed by Hengel, *Zealots*, 99–110, and *Judaism and Hellenism*, I, 285 and n.179; ruler-cult is here thought to have been less important than Hengel suggests as a source of resentment against Antiochus IV, but Hengel's judgment that otherwise the issue became burning in Judaea only in the Roman period is followed.

45. The absence of reference to the royal cult in III Maccabees is noted (as a difficulty for arguments for a date in the imperial period) by H. Anderson in Charlesworth, *Pseudepigrapha* 2, 511; the possible allusions noted by Hengel, *Zealots*, 99 n.121 (II, 29, 31), seem more naturally to refer to the Dionysiac cult favoured by the king. Beaujeu, 'Apologètes', in den Boer, *Le culte*, 105 n.1, justly stresses that I, II and III Maccabees are silent on ruler cult.

46. So F. Millar, 'The Imperial Cult and the Persecutions', in den Boer, *Le culte*, 145–75, followed by Price, *Rituals*, 221.

47. Krauss, *Griechen und Römer*, 90. For similar nonchalance in the East, note that according to rabbinic tradition in Babylonia, great teachers of the early third century AD highly esteemed an ancient synagogue in Nehardea, despite the fact that there was a statue there (RH 24b = AZ 43b, discussed by A. Oppenheimer, with B. Isaac and M. Lecker, *Babylonia Judaica in the Talmudic Period*, Wiesbaden 1983, 278, 290–1).

48. See *CIJ* 1440 (Schedia) and *CPJ* III, no.1532A (Crocodilopolis) (= Horbury and Noy nos. 22, 117), with comments by Fraser, *Ptolemaic Alexandria*, 1, 116, 226–7, 282–3.

49. The First Commandment according to Josephus, *Ant.* 3, 91, teaches 'that God is one' and that he only must be worshipped. The repetition of Deut. 4. 45 at Deut. 6. 4 in LXX and the Nash Papyrus shows how closely Decalogue and Shema were linked.

50. Josephus paraphrases the Third Commandment as 'not to swear by God on any frivolous matter' (*Ant.* 3, 91), and Philo too takes it as a warning on oaths (*Decal.* 84–95). Instances of Jewish oaths by the king or emperor are noted below.

51. Juster, *Juifs*, I, 344 n.6; papyri surveyed by H. M. Cotton in Cotton and Yardeni, *Aramaic, Hebrew, and Greek Documentary Texts*, 177–9.

52. H. M. Cotton in Cotton and Yardeni, *Aramaic, Hebrew, and Greek Documentary Texts*, 179. For varying attitudes to pagan cult compare Borgen, 'Yes'; Reynolds and Tannenbaum, *Jews and Godfearers*, 56–67.

53. Pesce, *Dio senza mediatori*, 203–5, judges that they seek to secure Israel's direct contact with her God, and to exclude emphasis on the importance of angels, Moses, or, implicitly, a messiah.

54. Sanders, *Judaism: Practice and Belief*, 297.

55. Midrash Tehillim 36, f.125b, on Ps. 36. 6; on the theme of messianic light taken up here see further section 5, below.

56. Schäfer, *Studien*, 21 (quoting N. N. Glatzer); 'Hoffnungen', 224–5.

57. For lively expressions of hope ascribed to him see Avi-Yonah, *The Jews of Palestine*, 130, 132.

58. Hofius, 'Thesen', 109–10.

59. Chevallier, *L'esprit et le messie*, 42–4; Neusner, 'Mishnah and Messiah'.

60. Neusner, *Constantine*, 4–7, 59–80.

61. Horbury, *Jews and Christians*, 212–14.

62. For example, Mekilta, Pisha, Bo, 7, on Exod. 12. 12 (not by angel or legate); PRK 1. 2; 5. 8 (on this occasion the Israelites saw God in Egypt); Targ. Ps.-Jonathan on Exod. 12. 12, 'I will be revealed . . . in the Shekhinah of my Glory' (contrast Neofiti, 'I will pass through in my Memra'), with discussion of Targums on Exod. 12. 12, 23; 11. 5 by Chester, *Divine Revelation and Divine Titles in the Pentateuchal Targumim*, 144–9, 154–5 (on Ps.-Jonathan's closeness to rabbinic texts). In the seventeenth century, Abraham Cowley's poem 'The Tenth Plague', inspired especially by the Wisdom of Solomon, takes the destroyer to be the archangel Michael.

63. Occurrences of the formula are discussed by Goldin, '"Not by Means of an Angel and not by Means of a Messenger"', and by Pesce, *Dio senza mediatori*.

64. The possibly messianic implications of the quotation of Deut. 32. 35–36 in Heb. 10. 30–31 are not noted in the commentaries on Hebrews by A. Nairne, H. Moffatt, H. Braun and H. W. Attridge; however, the interpretation given above is supported not only by the ensuing quotation of Hab. 2. 3–4, but also by the slightly earlier reference in Hebrews to the approaching Day (10. 25), which is that of the appearance of Christ (9. 28).

65. Pesce, *Dio senza mediatori*, 194–6 (on Deut. 32. 8–9), 203–5.

66. III Enoch 48 A in H. Odeberg, *3 Enoch*, Cambridge 1928, reprinted with Prolegomenon by J. C. Greenfield, New York 1973, 63–6 (Hebrew), 157–60 (translation and commentary); paragraphs 69–70=935–6 in Schäfer, *Synopse*, 34–5, 292–3; translation and notes by P. S. Alexander in Charlesworth, *The Old Testament Pseudepigrapha*, 1, 301–2.

67. Traditions on these figures are gathered and compared by Morray-Jones, 'Transformational Mysticism in the Apocalyptic-Merkabah Tradition', 10–15, 18–19, and viewed in the broader context of the transformation of the righteous into angels or stars by Mach, *Entwicklungsstadien*, 163–73.

68. So Box, *The Ezra-Apocalypse*, 283–4; N. Schmidt, A. Lacoque and J. J. Collins (Michael), and Z. Zevit (Gabriel), discussed by M. Casey, *Son of Man*, London 1979, 31–2 and P. R. Davies, *Daniel*, Sheffield 1985, 105–6; Rowland, *The Open Heaven*, 181–3 (Michael), see Collins, *Daniel*, 310 and pp. 33–4, above. The figure is indeed 'with clouds', like the divinity in biblical theophanies, and man-like, as angels are elsewhere in Daniel (3. 25; 8. 15; 10. 5, 18); but the bestial opponents are explained as kings or kingdoms (7. 17, 23–24), not the angel-princes of the nations who would be expected to resist Israel's angel-patron (10. 13, 20–21), and the figure was early interpreted messianically in books in which angels remain important (the Parables of Enoch, II Esdras).

69. The passages are discussed, together with the treatment of Dan. 7 in Justin, *Dialogue* 32, in Horbury, 'Messianic Associations', 36, 40–8.

70. Exod. R. 32. 1–9, on 23. 20 (unnamed angel); Sanh. 38b; III Enoch 12. 5 (Metatron); for the continuing ambiguity of the passage, see Ibn Ezra on v. 20 (the emissary is not the book of the law or the ark, but an angel, to be identified as Michael).

71. Lueken, *Michael*, 25 (Michael); T. W. Manson, 'Miscellanea Apocalyptica', *JTS* 46, 1945, 41–5 (Elijah); J. Tromp, 'Taxo, the Messenger of the Lord', *JSJ* 21, 1990, 200–9 (a human messenger, Taxo the Levite; Tromp compares Ass. Mos. 11. 17, '*magnus nuntius*', of Moses).

72. Bousset, *Antichrist*, 227–8; Lueken, *Michael* (n. 68), 26–7; Rowland, as cited above; Fossum and Barker (pp. 123–4 and nn. 63, 66, below).

73. 'Keine menschliche Macht hilft dazu, kein Messias; die Rettung ist eine rein himmlische That; Michael steht an der Stelle des Messias' (Lueken,

Michael, 26). Bousset, *Antichrist,* 228 had urged that Michael here acquires messianic significance. In Hermas the same glorious angelic figure seems at one point to be Michael (*Sim.* 8, 3, 3), at another to be Christ (*Sim.* 9. 12, 8).

74. This point does not figure in the informative discussion of angelic-human intermingling by Collins, *Daniel,* 304–19.

75. In Lev. R. 1. 1, followed by Rashi on Numbers, *ad loc.,* and Maimonides, *Guide,* 2, 6 and 42, this is taken to be one of the places where מלאך means prophet, and referred to Moses (compare the varying interpretations of Exod. 23. 20–21, noted above).

76. A few letters from this clause are attested in 4Q 266, 3 ii line 5 and 4Q 267, 2 line 1; see Baumgarten and Milik, with contributions from Pfann and Yardeni, *Qumran Cave 4, XIII: The Damascus Document,* 41, 97.

77. Those (including L. Cohn, E. R. Goodenough and H. A. Wolfson) who have interpreted the vision (165) as a reference to the messiah would then be right in their understanding of the passage as a whole, but would have rejected an angelic interpretation of the vision of 165 through neglect of the co-ordination of angelic and human guidance in the Exodus narrative; F. H. Colson, *Philo* 8, London 1939, *ad loc.,* cites and questions Cohn's judgment, well comparing *Mos.* 1, 66; 2, 254, on the burning bush and the cloudy pillar. On Goodenough see Schürer, Vermes, Millar and Black, *History* II, 508 n.26; Hecht, 'Philo and Messiah', 143 and n.13, also discussing Wolfson.

78. On these lines, Bousset and Gressmann, *Religion,* 222–33, 259–68 (treating the 'messiah' in a chapter on the national hope, the 'mythical depiction of the messiah' in a separate chapter on apocalyptic); Billerbeck in Strack and Billerbeck, *Kommentar* II, 352; Klausner, *Messianic Idea,* 289, 385–6, 465–6, 520; Frost, *Old Testament Apocalyptic,* 249–53; Collins, *Scepter,* 37–8. Moore, *Judaism,* II, 344, 349, likewise stresses the humanity of the messiah in rabbinic sources, but adds that the apparently superhuman figure of II Esdras and II Baruch is also fully human; similarly, Vermes, *Jesus the Jew,* 139. Mowinckel's view, related but allowing for the regularly-attested overlap between the two differentiated conceptions, is summarized in the text below.

79. Schürer, *History,* II. 2 (ET 1890), 160–2; *Geschichte* II (3–41907), 615–19; Schürer, revised by Vermes, Millar and Black, *History* II 1979, 519–23; Mowinckel, *He That Cometh,* 280–6.

80. Riesenfeld, *Jésus transfiguré,* 62–5.

81. For the messiah as dead compare II Esdras 7. 28–9; as slain, the messiah son of Joseph or Ephraim, e.g. at Targ. Zech. 12. 10. The notion of the death of the sole messiah seems to have become exceptional ('not generally accepted in Jewish thought', according to Levey, *The Messiah,* 108; similarly, Stone, *Fourth Ezra,* cited below).

82. Contrast between 'pre-existence' in Jewish and early Christian sources was strongly stressed, for example, by P. Billerbeck, in a passage quoted below from the end of his full discussion, in Strack and Billerbeck, *Kommentar* II, 352; similarly, G. Vermes, *Jesus the Jew,* 138–9. Goldberg, *Erlösung,* 48, speaks

only of a contrast between ante-mundane creation in rabbinic thought and pre-existence from eternity in Christian teaching; but this is debatable with regard to teaching like that of Origen, cited in the text below. The texts reviewed below overlap with those discussed by Schimanowski, *Weisheit und Messias*, 107–205; he justifiably urges that Billerbeck's argument for a merely ideal pre-existence of the messiah in Jewish thought should be modified.

83. Wiles, *Divine Apostle*, 77–80; see in general Wiles, 'Eternal Generation'.

84. Horbury, 'Land, Sanctuary, and Worship', 210–11.

85. The midrash understands *nakhôn* here as 'ready', with the LXX; compare the LXX presentation of the sanctuary as 'ready', divinely prepared, just noted. Variation in order is further illustrated by the textual tradition of Midrash Mishle 8, in which the messiah can be either first or last on the list (Visotzky, *Midrash Mishle*, 59, note on 8, lines 26–34).

86. See Lampe, *A Patristic Greek Lexicon*, 311, s. γεννάω.

87. 'The idea of eternal generation as it stands in Origen's scheme of thought as a whole does not really have any effective anti-subordinationist significance at all' (Wiles, 'Eternal Generation', 288).

88. The angelology of the LXX and extra-biblical writings is described and investigated, without special reference to divine titles, by Mach, *Entwicklungsstadien*, 65–278.

89. See further Horbury, 'The Cult of Christ and the Cult of the Saints', section 3, part 2.

90. Puech, *La croyance des Esséniens en la vie future*, 1, 213–15, interprets Josephus as speaking of resurrection under the guise of transmigration; but against the background of general Jewish concern with angels and spirits it seems better to give fuller value to the prominence of the soul in these passages as a reflection of Jewish opinion.

91. Differing examples of this interpretation include Gressmann, *Ursprung*, 349–65, and Mowinckel, *He That Cometh*, 346–450, both noted in chapter I, section 2, above; Box, *Ezra-Apocalypse*, 282–4; Schürer, revised by Vermes, Millar and Black, *History*, II, 519–23; Harnack, *Lehrbuch der Dogmengeschichte*, I, 98–9 (ET 102–3), modified and enlarged by a strong contrast between Hebraic and Hellenic views at 755–64 (ET 318–32); Baldensperger, *Selbstbewusstsein*, 85–94; Bousset and Gressmann, *Religion*, 262–8; Volz, *Eschatologie*, 204–8; Baeck, 'Son of Man', 31–6, and 'Faith of Paul', 148–52; Emerton, 'Origin', 234–42.

92. Horbury, 'Messianic Associations', 40–8; for the Parables of Enoch, a similar conclusion is reached in the fresh review of biblical allusions by VanderKam, 'Righteous One, Messiah, Chosen One, and Son of Man'.

93. Bousset and Gressmann, *Religion*, 264–5.

94. Gray, *Isaiah I–XXVII*, 173; he rightly stresses that Hebrew *el*, used here, regularly refers to the almighty God, but the importance in the Old Testament of its use in the sense of a divinity or angel from the divine assembly, probably reflected here, has since been underlined by Qumran

writings (see Clines, *Dictionary*, 1, 253–4, sv. *'el*). For Gray's assessment of this passage compare Gressmann's, discussed in chapter 1, section 2, above.

95. Gospel of the Ebionites in Epiphanius, *Pan.* 30, 13, φῶς μέγα; Old Latin texts of Matthew, for instance g¹, *lumen magnum*; an echo of Isa. 9. 1 (2) seems likely, even with the caution urged by Chevallier, *L'Esprit et le Messie*, 67 n.2, on account of the currency of a parallel tradition of fire rather than light (Justin Martyr, *Dial.* 88, 3).

96. Hanhart, 'Die Septuaginta als Interpretation und Aktualisierung. Jesaja 9: 1 (8:23) – 7 (6)', taking up the characterization of the passage by Seeligmann, *The Septuagint Version of Isaiah*, 118–19.

97. Seeligmann, *The Septuagint Version of Isaiah*, 119.

98. Gen. 6. 3 is here thought to foretell Moses, an interpretation also found in the midrash (*PRE* 32 and other passages cited by Jacobson, *Commentary*, 1, 415–16); the understanding of *mediator spiritus* as applied to him, followed here, is encouraged by the probable reference to his soul or spirit a few lines earlier (9. 8, 'I will light my lamp for him which shall dwell in him'; see Jacobson, *Commentary*, 1, 413 for the possibility that the lamp here is the soul, cf. Prov. 20. 27) and by the comparable Ass. Mos. 11. 15, quoted in the text above.

99. His name in this form is known from contemporary documents; see for instance contracts of the year 133 in the papyrus Mur 24, edited by J. T. Milik in Benoit, Milik and de Vaux, *Les grottes de Murabba'at*, 124, 128, 131.

100. Goldberg, *Erlösung durch Leiden*, 13*–14* (text), 154–5 (translation); the rendering 'my light' above represents the Yalkut reading (preferred by M. Friedmann [ed.], *Pesikta Rabbati*, Vienna 1880, f.162b) rather than Goldberg's text, to be rendered 'his light'; cf. Yalkut Shimeoni on the Prophets, no. 499. The passage is introduced in the text as a tradition from the Tannaitic period (before c. AD 200), but this perhaps means only that it was already identified as an old piece when it reached the compiler of Pesikta.

101. For example, the 'Julian star', '*Iulium sidus*', Horace, *Od.* 1, 12, 46, cf. '*Caesar's star*', '*Caesaris astrum*', Virgil, *Ecl.* 9. 47; discussed with reference to coins of Caesar and Augustus, the star in Hellenistic ruler-cults, and Test. Levi 18. 3, 'his star will arise in heaven, as a king's', by Hultgård, *L'eschatologie des Testaments des Douze Patriarches*, 1, 326–81.

102. Daniélou, *Latin Christianity*, 278–9, also including the blessing of the Prince of the Congregation in this series (see the following note).

103. 'For God has raised you up as sceptre over rulers' (lines 27–8) recalls Num. 24. 17, 'And there shall rise up a sceptre,' somewhat more closely than Gen. 49. 9–10, 'Who shall raise him up? There shall not depart a sceptre . . .', which was clearly also influential, the question at the end of v. 9 probably being applied to the messianic figure; this point helps to confirm the identification of allusions to both passages, without discussion of Gen. 49. 9, by Milik in Barthélemy and Milik, *Qumran Cave 1*, 128–9.

104. On these passages in the context of Philo's thought see Chadwick,

'Philo', 143–5 (stressing Philo's assumption that the Logos-conception was well known, and the anticipations of christology in his language); Chester, 'Jewish Messianic Expectations and Mediatorial Figures', 48–50.

105. See J. Armitage Robinson, *St Irenaeus, The Demonstration of the Apostolic Preaching*, London 1920, 19–22, on attestations in Iren., *Dem.* 43 (where these texts are attributed to Jeremiah), Justin, and later anti-Jewish writing; Skarsaune, *Proof*, 234–42, makes a strong case for the view that the source was the lost *Controversy of Jason and Papiscus concerning Christ* mentioned by Celsus (Origen, *Cels.* 4, 52).

106. Theodoret, *Ps.* 71. 17 (PG 80, 1440) comments on this longer text, which may already have influenced Justin, *Dial.* 76, 7.

107. On early stages in the messianic interpretation of Ps. lxxii, with special reference to verses other than those considered here, see Heim, 'The Perfect King of Psalm 72'.

108. Possible contacts are reviewed by Skarsaune, *Proof*, 266, 381.

109. Ber. R. 1. 4, on Gen. 1. 1, and Targ. Micah 5. 1; Zech. 4. 7, both with 'whose name was spoken from of old' (Micah, '. . . from of old, from the days of eternity'), are among many comparable texts collected and discussed by P. Billerbeck in Strack and Billerbeck, *Kommentar*, I, 335, on John 1. 1, and Goldberg, 'Die Namen des Messias', 76–80.

110. This point is urged with regard to v. 17 in the light of the Targum by Schaper, *Eschatology in the Greek Psalter*, 93–6.

111. Goldberg, 'Die Namen des Messias', 77.

112. Volz, *Eschatologie*, 204–5; Schaper, *Eschatology in the Greek Psalter*, 101–7 (with a critique of the exclusion of a temporal sense of 'before' by Schimanowski, *Weisheit und Messias*, 139–41). P. Billerbeck, in Strack and Billerbeck, *Kommentar*, II, 334, had counted Ps. 110 (109). 3 LXX among passages attesting the messiah's 'ideal pre-existence' in the mind of God.

113. Horbury, 'Land, Sanctuary, and Worship', 210–11.

114. On these texts see Horbury, 'Antichrist among Jews and Gentiles', arguing that the Sibylline passage alludes in the first place to the Samaritans rather than the line of the Augusti, especially Nero (the latter view is represented by J. J. Collins, 'Sibylline Oracles', 360).

115. F. Field (ed.), *Origenis Hexaplorum quae supersunt*, II, Oxford 1875, 162, 266.

116. See M. D. Goodman in Schürer revised, *History*, III. 1, 501–4.

117. Irenaeus, *Haer.* 3, 19 (20), 2, cited with other passages by Horbury, 'Messianism among Jews and Christians in the Second Century', 75 n.16.

118. Schürer, *History*, II. 2 (ET 1890), 160; *Geschichte* II (3–41907), 616; Schürer, revised by Vermes, Millar and Black, *History* II, 1979, 519.

119. Ryle and James, *Psalms of Solomon*, 149–50, on 18. 6, found pre-existence to be suggested by ἄναξις, but they rejected this interpretation because they could find no hint of it in Ps. Sol. 17; such hints seem to be given, however, by 17. 23 and 42, discussed in the text above. In 18. 6 the later

conjecture ἀνάδειξις (Manson, 'Miscellanea Apocalyptica', 41–2) equally suggests a hidden period, on earth or in heaven.

120. Barthélemy in Barthélemy and Milik, *Qumran Cave 1*, 110, 117; Vermes, *Complete Dead Sea Scrolls in English*, 159; Charlesworth and L. T. Stuckenbruck in Charlesworth, *Rule of the Community and Related Documents*, 116–17.

121. So Chester, 'Jewish Messianic Expectations and Mediatorial Figures', 23.

122. Johnson, *Sacral Kingship*, 1–2, 120–1.

123. It is transmitted side by side with sayings of the fourth-century Judah b. Simon, and in the name of Abba of Serungin, which was south of Tiberias; see Y. Tsafrir, L. Di Segni and J. Green, *Tabula Imperii Romani: Judaea. Palaestina*, Jerusalem 1994, 228.

124. Passages are collected by P. Billerbeck in Strack and Billerbeck, *Kommentar*, I, 161–2, on Matt. 4. 16; II, 346, 348 n.2, on John 1. 1; and 428, on John 3. 19.

125. For the soul as light, compare Ber. R. 17. 8, on 2. 21: 'Why was the precept of the sabbath lights given to woman? Because she extinguished Adam's soul (נשמתו).'

126. Perez Fernandez, *Tradiciones mesiánicas*, 113, following R. Bloch.

127. The same was said of the messiah as the descendant of Nahshon (Num. R. 13. 12, on 7. 13). Further midrash on (the son of) Perez includes the comparable suggestion that Gen. 2. 4 and Ruth 4. 18, verses in both of which *tôlᵉdôt*, 'generations', is written fully, together indicate that death will be swallowed up in the days of the son of Perez, as promised in Isa. 25. 9 (Exod. R. 30. 3, on Exod. 21. 1, in an interpretation beginning with teaching ascribed to the late third-century Abbahu of Caesarea). Perez is also linked with 'the breaker' of Micah 2. 13 (Ber. R. 85. 14, on Gen. 38. 29, where in Targ. Ps.-Jon. he shall similarly 'inherit the kingdom'). See Goldberg, 'Die Namen des Messias', 49–51.

128. Midrashic passages on the correspondence between Adam and the messiah, including Ber. R. 12. 6; Num. R. 13. 12, are brought together with patristic teaching on Adam and Christ by Murmelstein, 'Adam, ein Beitrag zur Messiaslehre' (on light, 255–6 n.3).

129. Theodor and Albeck, *Bereschit Rabba*, II, 233, with parallels and interpretation; this understanding of 'spirit' was adopted by Rashi and is viewed as possible by Bacher, *Die Agada der Palästinensischen Amoräer*, II, 172–3, n.5.

130. For the influence of Septuagintal interpretation on third-century Galilaean rabbinical teaching compare the exegesis of II Sam. 6. 20, 'vain fellow' as 'dancer', in agreement with LXX, in the name of Abba bar Kahana (jSanh. 2. 4, 20b, discussed by Lieberman, *Greek in Jewish Palestine*, 33); also Mid. Teh. on Ps. 93. 3, discussed above.

131. Tertullian, *Hermog*. 32. 2, quotes the verse shortly after Amos 4. 13, discussed above, on the spirit and the Christ; it seems likely that this is one of

the many places where he speaks of Christ as spirit (see the following chapter, section 2), and that accordingly he interprets the spirit in Isa. 57. 16 messianically.

132. So also Mid. Teh. 139. 5; Ber. R. 8. 1, on 1. 26 (where, as at Lev. R. 14. 1, on Lev. 12. 2, 'king messiah' is found in the traditional text, probably by contamination from Ber. R. 1. 4, quoted above).

133. Schoeps, *Theologie und Geschichte des Judenchristentums*, 100–11, discusses this passage together with *Hom. Clem.* 17. 4, 3, on the series Adam, Enoch, Noah, Abraham, Isaac, Jacob, Jesus.

134. For a similar view of third-century rabbinic teaching, with a stress on resemblances to Origen, see de Lange, *Origen and the Jews*, 27, 126.

135. The passages from II Esdras and the Parables of Enoch are summarized and discussed by Schürer, revised by Vermes, Millar and Black, *History*, II, 519–23.

136. Horbury, 'Messianic Associations', 44–5, on allusions to passages including Isa. 11. 4; Dan.7. 13, 22; Zech. 6. 12; Ps. 110. 2.

137. With Sib. 5. 108, Chester, 'The Parting of the Ways: Eschatology and Messianic Hope', 243, compares Sib. 3. 286 ('the celestial God will send a king'), 652 ('from the sun God will send a king'), justly noting that all three passages might be referred solely to an earthly career; but this is hardly the most natural interpretation, given the allusions to the sky and the sun in these lines from book 3, and the king who is sent θεόθεν in Sib. 5. 108 seems more likely to come from the skies, like the sceptred man in Sib. 5. 414–15.

138. Sib. 5. 158 is interpreted in this way, with reference to the star-oracle of Num. 24. 17, by Chester, 'The Parting of the Ways: Eschatology and Messianic Hope', 243.

139. Sib. 5. 256–9 are widely considered Christian in part (so Charlesworth, 'Christian and Jewish Self-Definition in Light of the Christian Additions to the Apocryphal Writings', 48–9; Chester, 'The Parting of the Ways: Eschatology and Messianic Hope', 241–2) or as a whole (so Bate, *Sibylline Oracles*, 105). The latter judgment seems preferable, despite justified scholarly emphasis on the Jewish qualities of most (so Chester) or all (Nikiprowetzky, 'Reflexions', 58–65; O'Neill, 'The Man from Heaven'); the four lines together present a consistent view of Joshua as inspired by the pre-existent spirit of the crucified (so Justin Martyr, *Dial.* 113. 4, quoted by O'Neill). This version of the rabbinic and earlier Jewish conception of a pre-existent spiritual messiah who could inspire Adam and other biblical figures appealed especially to Christians because Jesus had the same name as Joshua, and it can be compared in general with the Christian view illustrated in (*h*), above, from *Hom. Clem.* 3. 20, 1.

140. Box, *Ezra-Apocalypse*, 283; Billerbeck in Strack and Billerbeck, *Kommentar*, I, 68; Emerton, 'Origin', 236–8.

141. Other messianic developments of Isa. 66 were noted under (*g*) above, and in chapter I, section 3, above.

142. See for instance Capes, *Old Testament Yahweh Texts in Paul's*

Christology (without attention to this aspect of the background).

143. Schürer, *History*, II. 2 (ET 1890), 160–2; *Geschichte* II ³⁻⁴1907, 615–19 (judging that superhuman depictions were played down among Jews after the rise of Christianity); Schürer, revised by Vermes, Millar and Black, *History* II, 1979, 519–23 (with changes including a later dating of the Parables of Enoch and the removal of this opinion). The material cited above suggests that the humanity of the messiah could indeed be stressed by Jews in argument, on the lines followed by Trypho according to Justin Martyr, but that many traces of the superhuman aspect survived, especially through the continuing influence of the interpretations known from the Greek scriptures and other writings of the Second-Temple period, as passages in Targum and midrash show.

144. Billerbeck in Strack and Billerbeck, *Kommentar*, II, 333–52, on John 1. 1 (351–2).

145. Moore, *Judaism* II, 337–8, 343–9: 349. Moore's book is judged to exemplify its author's own adherence to a noble form of American 'Pharisaic Puritanism' by Smith, 'Moore', 210.

146. Vermes, *Jesus the Jew*, 139.

147. Stone, *Fourth Ezra*, 216, on 7. 29, judges that 'the idea of the death of the Messiah seems to have no precise parallels in its explicitness' (compare Levey, *The Messiah*, 108, cited above). Perhaps the closest parallels are Zech. 13. 7; Dan. 9. 26 as probably understood in the late Second Temple period (see chapter I, section 4 [*d*], above), and Hippolytus, *Ref.* 9, 30, 8, cited p. 87 above.

148. Compare Stone, *Fourth Ezra*, 210, on critics who have thought the notions of Davidic descent and pre-existence expressed in II Esdras to be mutually inconsistent, but in his view have been applying 'categories of logic and consistency that are too rigid'.

149. The phrase is from Schürer, revised by Vermes, Millar and Black, *History*, 519, retaining Schürer's original judgment and expression (Schürer, *History*, II. 2 [ET 1890], 160; *Geschichte* II, ³⁻⁴1907, 616 (he appears here 'ganz und gar als menschlicher König').

150. See for example Emerton, 'Melchizedek and the Gods: Fresh Evidence for the Jewish Background of John x.34–36', discerning the argument as: if the angels rebuked in Ps. 82. 6 are there called gods, how much more worthy of the title 'son of God' is Jesus, sanctified and sent by his Father. Grounds for doubting this interpretation have included the objection that Johannine christology is little concerned with angels (de Jonge and van der Woude, '11Q Melchizedek and the New Testament', 314); but Ashton, *Studying John*, 71–89, convincingly argues that the divine sending of Christ in John treats him implicitly as an angelic spirit.

151. For a short summary of developments leading to fourth-century concentration on the two natures of Christ, viewed against the contemporary philosophical background, see Stead, *Philosophy in Christian Antiquity*, 187–201.

IV. Messianic Origins of the Cult of Christ

1. Dölger, *Sol Salutis*, 107–17, urged that *carmen* represents 'formula', not hymn, for Christians will have been charged with using spells (*carmina*); but the context combines with Pliny's not unsympathetic tone to indicate the less damaging sense, 'hymn'. For *dicere*, here rendered 'recite', in the sense of 'sing', see Dölger, *Sol*, 129 n.2, and, for use with *carmen*, Horace, *Saec*. 8, '*dicere carmen*'; compare Greek *legein* with *hymnos* (Eusebius, *HE* 2, 17, 22; Dölger, *Sol*, 131 n.1) and Hebrew *lomar ymnon* (below). In a late-Roman Jewish epitaph at Venosa, 'they spoke laments' (*dixerunt*) probably signifies chanting (Noy, *Italy*, no. 86 = *CIJ* 611).

2. 'Ye servants of God, your master proclaim', verse 4 in the text printed in John Wesley, *A Collection of Hymns for the Use of the People called Methodists*, with a New Supplement, London 1896, p.257, no. 859.

3. On the problem of reconstructing Paul of Samosata's teaching, which probably embraced exegesis of the divine praise offered to the righteous Anointed in Ps. 45, see Williams, *Arius*, 159–62; Stead, 'Arius in Modern Research', 34–5.

4. The verb αὔξειν, 'increase' or 'praise', perhaps designedly recalls the popular acclamation 'increase' discussed by Peterson, *Heis Theos*, 181–3, with examples including Ovid, *Fasti* 1, 611, '*augeat imperium nostri ducis, augeat annos*', 'may he increase the sway of our leader, increase his years'.

5. Compare Origen's disapproval of the addressing of prayer (*proseuche*) to Christ, rather than to the Father through Christ (*Orat*. 15, 1–3, translated and discussed by J. E. L. Oulton in H. Chadwick and J. E. L. Oulton [eds], *Alexandrian Christianity*, London 1954, 269–71, 346–7). On the widespread patristic application of Rom. 9. 5 to Christ see Wiles, *Divine Apostle*, 83–4.

6. See *Hymns Ancient and Modern*, New Edition, London 1904, iii–iv.

7. Discussion is summarized by M. Hengel, 'Hymns and Christology' (1980), in Hengel, *Between Jesus and Paul*, 78–96; Hurtado, *One God, One Lord*, 101–4; on Pliny and hymn-like New Testament passages, M. Hengel, 'Das Christuslied im frühesten Gottesdienst', in *Weisheit Gottes – Weisheit der Welt: Festschrift für Joseph Kardinal Ratzinger*, 1, 357–404: 382–404, translated in Hengel, *Studies in Early Christology*, 227–91: 262–91.

8. So Bertram, *Leidensgeschichte*, 96–9, 101 (but he dates the cultic evaluation of Jesus from the first confession of him as risen, not from the time of the ministry).

9. 'Hier war des Kultkyrios Bild, hier seine Geschichte zu finden' (Bertram, *Leidensgeschichte*, 98; cf. 101).

10. Horbury, 'Messianism', 74–8, with further texts.

11. Morton Smith, 'What is Implied by the Variety of Messianic Figures?'; de Jonge, 'The Use of the Word "Anointed" in the Time of Jesus'.

12. Sanders, 'Paul', 113–15, referring to Dunn, *Christology in the Making*, 33–5, 114. Comparably with Sanders here, but differing in viewpoint from him

and one another, Hengel, *Son of God*, 58–9, and *Studies in Early Christology*, 109, stresses that early christology did not merely reproduce Jewish material, and that there were no fixed Jewish 'Messiah dogmatics'; and De Jonge, 'Christology and Monotheism', urges that christology drew not (just) on messianism, but on a range of Jewish hopes for divine intervention, with or without intermediaries.

13. For this name for Ps. 2 see Ber. 10a (Abbahu of Caesarea, in the name of Johanan), discussed with Lev. R. 27. 11; Sanh. 94a (further third-century applications of Ps. 2 to the messiah and Gog-and-Magog) by Horbury, 'Antichrist among Jews and Gentiles'; earlier, Ps. 2 was used to depict the messiah punishing the gentiles and their kings in Ps. Sol. 17. 23–24; with Ps. 110 and Dan. 7, in the Parables of Enoch (45. 3; 46. 3–6; 48. 10) and perhaps (allusion to 'my son' on mount Zion, cf. Ps. 2. 6–7) in II Esdras 13. 6–7, 32, 35–38, 52 (see Horbury, 'Messianic Associations', 44–5). Ps. 2. 7 'I, this day, have begotten you' seems to be echoed in 1QSa=1Q28 ii 11–12, 'when God engenders the messiah', quoted in the previous chapter, section 5 (*g*).

14. For interpretation on these lines, rather than from the related but different background suggested by Bockmuehl, 'Form', see further n. 77, below.

15. Horbury, 'Land, Sanctuary, and Worship', 220–2.

16. Bousset, *Kyrios Christos*, 91–101, 258 (ET 138–48, 330–1).

17. For translation in the context of other rabbinic passages on acclamation, see Krauss, *Griechen und Römer*, 103, no. 221; for the rendering 'sing' compare n. 1, above.

18. Hullin 139b, attributed to R. Kahana, and probably therefore current in third-century Tiberias, a Herodian foundation; a dissenting dove who coos *Kyrie cheirie* ('Lord, slave') is put to death.

19. For the currency of the saying in both settings see Davies and Allison, *Matthew*, I, 713; in the present writer's view, in the ministry it would have reflected Jesus's corrective response to his followers' messianic fervour, comparably with Mark 10. 37–40 (Horbury, 'The Twelve and the Phylarchs', 525; 'Constitutional Aspects', 73–4).

20. Bousset, *Kyrios Christos*, 91–7, 150–2 (ET 138–44, 206–7).

21. Inscribed on the propylon of the temple of Hibis near al-Kharga in the Great Oasis; see Deissmann, *Light*, 362–3 (photograph of lines 1–46); Bousset, *Kyrios Christos*, 94 (ET 140–1); Chalon, *L'édit de Tiberius Julius Alexander* (photographs), lines 13, 18, pp.27–8.

22. See the comments by Chalon, *L'édit de Tiberius Julius Alexander*, 97–8.

23. On these two words in Ptolemaic and later ruler-cult see Pax, ΕΠΙΦΑΝΕΙΑ, 16–18, 49–57.

24. Ehrhardt, 'Jesus Christ and Alexander the Great'.

25. Bousset, *Kyrios Christos*, 156–7 (ET 213–15).

26. The centrality of the conception of the 'present god' was picked out in the brief sketches of Greek and Roman ruler-cult by P. Wendland, *Die*

hellenistisch-römische Kultur. Tübingen 1907, 75, 93.

27. The apologists are surveyed by J. Beaujeu, 'Les apologistes et le culte du souverain', in den Boer, *Le culte des souverains dans l'empire romain*, 103–42.

28. Horbury, 'The Cult of Christ and the Cult of the Saints', section i.

29. Tertullian, *Apol.* 39, 15–16 (Tiberius); Chrysostom, *Hom. in Ep. ii ad Cor.*, 26, 4 (PG 61, 580–1) (Pilate); Orosius 7, 4, 5–6. Koep, 'Consecratio II', 290, suggests that the story found in the last two sources may have arisen in the early third century under Alexander Severus, reputed to number Christ – together with some deified emperors, Apollonius of Tyana, Abraham, Orpheus and others – among his domestic deities (HA Severus Alexander29, 2); but its occurrence in Tertullian suggests that it was already current in the second century. In the apocryphal 'Delivery of Pilate', connected with the Acts of Pilate, Tiberius writes to his eastern governor Licianus that the Jews forced Pilate to crucify 'a god named Jesus', θεόν τινα λεγόμενον Ἰησοῦν (*Paradosis Pilati*, 6; Tischendorf, *Evangelia Apocrypha*, 453).

30. Bousset, esp. 99–101 (ET, 146–8); Bultmann, *Theology*, 1, 51 (section 7).

31. For continuity between the associations of Maranatha, formally an invocation, and the acclamation of Jesus as *Kyrios* see Moule, *Origin*, 36–43.

32. J. Weiss, *Das Urchristentum*, 26–7 (ET I, 37–8); L. Cerfaux, 'Le titre Kyrios et la dignité royale de Jésus', and '"Adonai" et "Kyrios"', reprinted from *Revue des sciences philosophiques et théologiques* 11, 1922, 40–71; 12, 1923, 125–53 and 20, 1931, 417–52 in *Recueil Lucien Cerfaux*, 1, 3–63, 136–72; E. Meyer, *Ursprung und Anfänge des Christentums*, 3, Stuttgart and Berlin 1923, 218 n.1; W. Foerster in *TWNT* 3, 1938, 1038–56, 1081–98, s.v. *kyrios* etc., followed with qualifications by O. Cullmann, as cited below, and by Hahn, *Hoheitstitel* , 68–125 (ET 68–114); F. C. Burkitt, *Christian Beginnings*, London 1924, 44–52; Nock, 'Early Gentile Christianity and its Hellenistic Background', 71–7.

33. See, for example, Vermes, *Jesus the Jew*, 83–222; Hengel, *The Son of God* ; Segal, *Two Powers in Heaven* ; Chester, 'Jewish Messianic Expectations and Mediatorial Figures and Pauline Christology' (literature).

34. Stuiber, 'Christusepitheta'; Kramer, *Christ, Lord, Son of God*; Hahn, *Hoheitstitel.*

35. Weiss, *Das Urchristentum*, 25–8 (ET I, 35–40).

36. Dunn, *Christology in the Making*, reviewed by Moule in *JTS* NS 33, 1982, 258–63 (he argues that Dunn has misunderstood Pauline passages on Christ's pre-existence; Dunn responds to criticism on this point in *Christology in the Making*, second edn, xvii–xxii); de Jonge, *Christology in Context* and 'Monotheism and Christology'.

37. Cullmann, *Christology*, 195–237 (especially 205–15); Hengel, 'Hymns and Christology' (1980), ET in id., *Between Jesus and Paul*, London 1983, 78–96; Bauckham, 'The Worship of Jesus in Apocalyptic Christianity' (1981), revised and reprinted in Bauckham, *The Climax of Prophecy*, 118–49; Hurtado, 93–124.

38. Bauckham, 'Worship', 323–31, 334–5, revised as *Climax*, 120–40, 147–9. The apocalypses contrast with earlier sources in which obeisance is not disapproved, for instance Josh. 5. 14; I Chron. 21. 16.

39. Smith, *Drudgery Divine*, 66–84, 134–43.

40. Engels, 'Bruno Bauer and Early Christianity' (1882), and 'The Book of Revelation' (1883). Philo is of course here envisaged as an integrator of Jewish and Greek thought, but Engels urges that both Philo and Enoch represent a Judaism to which Christianity was immediately and deeply indebted.

41. Robertson, *Pagan Christs*, 85–92, 163–4, 223–8.

42. Mastin, 'The Imperial Cult and the Ascription of the Title Θεός to Jesus (John xx.28)', 353–4, 365.

43. Casey, *From Jewish Prophet to Gentile God*, 34–40, 156–9, 169–70.

44. Lindeskog, *Das jüdisch-christliche Problem*, 122–36.

45. Hengel, with Markschies, *The 'Hellenization' of Judaea in the First Century after Christ*, 3–5.

46. Bousset, 251 (ET 323).

47. Hurtado, 98–9, 117–23.

48. Moule, *Origin*, especially 6–10.

49. Jewish sources relevant to each of the three points are expounded with special reference to angel-christology by Rowland, *Open Heaven*, 94–113; Chester, 'Jewish Messianic Expectations and Mediatorial Figures and Pauline Christology', 47–65.

50. On the angels of the Hebrew Bible and the LXX see Mach, *Entwicklungsstadien*, 10–113.

51. Josephus, *BJ* 2, 142; the angels whose names they kept were perhaps regarded as the spirits of their prophets (*BJ* 2, 159).

52. The LXX rendering of the Hebrew title in Num. 16. 22; 27. 16, when added to the material surveyed by Black, *Enoch*, 189–92, suggests that, despite his doubts in some cases, all these passages refer to angels; the Targums of Numbers (see Chester, *Divine Revelation and Divine Titles*, 358, nos. 77–80) strikingly avoid exegesis on the lines of the LXX, probably in order to exclude thoughts of angels. The title in LXX Numbers is also echoed at Rev. 22. 6, 'the God of the spirits of the prophets' (the angels who inspire them).

53. Text and comment in Newsom, *Songs of the Sabbath Sacrifice*, 110–15; line 2 is noted for its contribution to evidence for the honouring of angels by Schwemer, 'Gott als König', 100 n.153, and Stuckenbruck, *Angel Veneration*, 156–64.

54. CIJ 725 (Rheneia, off Delos); see Deissmann, *Light*, 423–35; F. Millar in Schürer revised, III.1, 70.

55. So for example Lueken, *Michael*, followed by Charles, *Revelation*, 2, 224–5, on the angel's refusal of obeisance in Rev. 22. 9, and Simon, *Verus Israel*, 345–7; Stuckenbruck, *Angel Veneration and Christology*, 47–203, reviewing the material now available, affirms veneration of angels, but avoids the term 'cult'.

56. Bousset and Gressmann, *Die Religion des Judentums*, 263–5; Harnack, *Dogmengeschichte*, I, 97–101, 181–90 (ET 102–5, 189–99); Bousset, *Kyrios Christos*, 264 (ET 337). See chapter III, section 5, above.

57. Werner, *Formation*, 120–61; the interest of this aspect of the work was noted in the review of the second edition of the original (1954) by H. Chadwick, *JTS* NS 6, 1955, 325.

58. Werner, *Formation*, 134; Schoeps, *Theologie*, 78–82.

59. So Daniélou, *Jewish Christianity*, 118 n.3, taking up work by W. Michaelis and G. Kretschmar.

60. Simonetti, 'Cristologia giudeocristiana', 55.

61. Rowland, *Open Heaven*, 96–8, 111–12; Segal, *Two Powers*; Theodor, *Bereschit Rabba*, 4.

62. Chadwick, 'Philo', 143–4, on *Conf.* 63 and comparable passages; Skarsaune, *Proof from Prophecy*, 206–13, 409–24, on Justin Martyr, *Dial.* 55–62, 75, 126–129.

63. Barker, *The Great Angel: A Study of Israel's Second God*, reviewed by J. Fossum, *JTS* NS 45, 1994, 187–91.

64. Chadwick, 'Philo and the Beginnings of Christian Thought', 141–3, 163.

65. So for example Stroumsa, *Savoir et salut*, 65–84 (revised version of 'Form(s) of God: some Notes on Metatron and Christ', *HTR* 76, 1983, 269–88); Bockmuehl, ' "The Form of God" (Phil. 2: 6). Variations on a Theme of Jewish Mysticism' (arguing that, for the visionary Paul, the pre-existent Christ had the majestic beauty of the body of God as envisaged by ancient Jewish mystics).

66. In addition to work cited in this section already, see Fossum, *The Name of God and the Angel of the Lord* (1985) and *The Image of the Invisible God* (1995); Barker, *The Risen Lord* (1996); Morray-Jones, 'Transformational Mysticism in the Apocalyptic-Merkabah Tradition' (1992), cited in chapter III, above; Mach, 'Christus Mutans' (1992), and *Entwicklungsstadien*, 287–91; Ashton, *Studying John* (1994), 71–89. I have not seen C. H. T. Fletcher-Louis, *Luke–Acts: Angels, Christology and Soteriology*, WUNT 2, Tübingen 1997. Work on these lines is surveyed by Chester, 'Jewish Messianic Expectations and Mediatorial Figures and Pauline Christology', 62–5, and set in a longer perspective by Fossum, *Image*, 1–11.

67. Mach, *Entwicklungsstadien*, 288 n.24.

68. Daniélou, *Jewish Christianity*, 117–46, gives a selection of examples; most of those noted in the text below are discussed in a broader christological context, and brought together with 'Spirit-christology', by Simonetti, 'Cristologia giudeocristiana', 52–6.

69. Williams, *Arius*, 41, 146–7.

70. *Gratias tibi referimus, Deus, per dilectum puerum tuum Jesum Christum, quem in ultimis temporibus misisti nobis salvatorem et redemptorem et angelum voluntatis tuae*, from the bishop's prayer at the offering of bread and cup in the

Latin version of the Egyptian Church Order ('Apostolic Tradition'), in Botte, *La tradition apostolique*, 12. For the argument that in the later Roman canon, somewhat similarly, Christ himself is the 'holy angel' by whose hands the oblations are carried up to the altar on high, as some mediaeval interpreters of the prayer *Supplices te rogamus* thought, see Barbel, *Christos Angelos*, 279–84; against this interpretation, Botte, *Le canon de la messe romaine*, 66–7, and J. A. Jungmann, *Missarum Sollemnia* III, Paris 1954, 153–4.

71. For such doubts see Hengel, *Studies in Early Christology*, 221–2, 376–7.

72. Horbury, 'Messianic Associations'.

73. Harnack, *Lehrbuch der Dogmengeschichte*, I, 183–5 n.1 (ET I, 192–3 n.1); Kelly, *Early Christian Doctrines*, 142–5.

74. Harnack, *Lehrbuch der Dogmengeschichte*, I, 182 n.1, cf. 185 n.1 (ET I, 191 n.1, cf. 193 n.1).

75. Braun, *Deus Christianorum*, 283–9, 587–91; van der Geest, *Le Christ et l'Ancien Testament chez Tertullien*, 237–8.

76. On this teaching of Origen, and its relation with Jewish angelology, see Williams, *Arius*, 144–7.

77. On John, Reim, *Jochanan*, 487–534; in Phil. 2, to envisage the 'form' of an angel-like messiah rather than (with Bockmuehl, 'Form') the one God himself seems better suited to the subordination of the Son in Paul as a viceroy (I Cor. 15. 28) who is 'sent' (Gal. 4. 4). With messianism in view, Christ's pre-existence need not be taken (with Habermann, *Präexistenzaussagen*, 421–3) as a specifically Christian notion.

78. Williams, *Arius*, 146, following R. Lorenz, *'Arius judaizans?'*, Göttingen 1978, 211–19, 223–4; for Origen's background in widespread Christian apocryphal reading, and his reliance on the Prayer of Joseph as support, see Bammel, 'Die Zitate aus den Apokryphen bei Origenes'.

79. In the case of the Fourth Gospel this is argued by Ashton, *Studying John*, 71–89 (acknowledging J. A. Bühner's work on these lines), with reference simply to the exalted angel, not to the messiah as an angelic being.

80. Jewish and gentile prophecy is compared by Knox, *Gentiles*, 8–25 (noting dynastic themes); Hengel, *Judaism and Hellenism*, I, 184–6, and nn. 516–25 (also stressing differences).

81. Hengel, *Judaism and Hellenism*, I, 185–6; II, 125 n.523; Finley, *Ancient Sicily*, 139–44, notes the absence of ruler-worship from his kingdom (but is this an argument from the silence of the fragmentary sources?), whereas W. Speyer thinks (with fair probability, in the present writer's view) that he could have considered himself a 'divine man' (Speyer, 'Religiöse Betrüger', 449–50).

82. The background in royal encomia is brought out by Norden, *Aeneis Buch VI*, on lines 752 ff.

83. The present writer (see below) views this exposition as less alien to the spirit of the Fourth Eclogue itself than is suggested by Lane Fox, *Pagans and Christians*, 649–52.

84. Lactantius, *DI* 7, 15, 19: before the foundation of the Trojan race,

Hystaspes prophesied 'that the empire and name of Rome would be taken away from the world', '*sublatum iri ex orbe imperium nomenque Romanum*'; the saying is compared with oracles of the fall of Rome reported in Phlegon (second century AD) from the historian Antisthenes (second century BC), and identified as gentile rather than Jewish, by Windisch, *Die Orakel des Hystaspes*, 52–5.

85. See the parallels noted by Bate, *The Sibylline Oracles*, 76–7; for the differing views see J.J. Collins, 'Sibylline Oracles', 354–6; *Scepter*, 38–9 (a Ptolemaic rather than an Egyptian king); Bousset, *Religion*, 225–6 (the messiah, associated with the sun in the *Hofstil* of Graeco-Roman royal hymnody); Chester, 'The Parting of the Ways and Messianic Hope', 243 n.1 (probably a Jewish messianic figure).

86. On the rendering of the first part of the verse see Horbury, 'Messianic Associations', 49–50.

87. On advents Kilpatrick, 'Acts vii. 52 ΕΛΕΥΣΙΣ', compare n. 23, above; and Latin *adventus* for royal or divine arrivals, e.g. Lucretius, 1, 7 (Venus), Pliny, *Ep.* 10, 10, 2 (Trajan). For ἐξελεύσεται see also LXX Isa. 11. 1; 57. 16 (chapter III, section 5, above); Micah 5. 2; probably Num. 24. 7 has been conformed to these messianic passages. On κύριος as a royal title see Foerster, *Kyrios*, especially 1048–9 (ET 1049–50); his finding that its application to kings becomes widely current from the first century BC (note his Herodian examples) is borne out in the further material surveyed by Kiessling and Rübsam, *Wörterbuch der griechischen Papyrusurkunden*, Suppl. I, 330–6.

88. The resemblance between the parallel II Sam. 5. 12 and Num. 24. 7 is slightly less close both in Hebrew (ממלכה for מלכות) and in Greek (part of ὑψόω for part of αὐξάνω).

89. So Wellhausen, *Psalms*, 193–4.

90. Cimosa, *Il vocabolario di preghiera nel Pentateuco greco dei LXX*, 68.

91. See the excursus on obeisance in Moule, *Christology*, 175–6 (citing Philo, *Legatio*, 116, among other passages); Cimosa, *Vocabolario*, 66, noting *Somn.* 2, 99. The representation of Jesus as receiving obeisance in the Gospels, particularly Matthew, seems likely to reflect not only his personal presence, as Moule suggests, but also the treatment of him as a king, beginning among his followers during the ministry and taken for granted in the first-century church.

92. Mastin, 'Daniel 2[46] and the Hellenistic World'.

93. Horbury, 'Aaronic Priesthood', 61.

94. Bammel, ΑΡΧΙΕΡΕΥΣ, 133–6.

95. This is the view of Alexander, 'A Note on the Syntax of 4Q448'; by contrast, one occurrence of 'Jonathan' is accepted, and it is referred to Jonathan Maccabaeus rather than Alexander Jannaeus, by Vermes, 'The So-Called King Jonathan Fragment' (with discussion of earlier study). Vermes notes, however, that J. Strugnell did not read the name 'Jonathan' in either of the two passages in which it has later been identified.

96. Horbury, 'Herod's Temple and "Herod's Days"', 109–14.

97. Riesenfeld, *Jésus transfiguré*, 223–5, 265–72 (enthronement); Mach,

'Christus Mutans', 190–2 (angelic appearance).

98. The differing details of the praises in Acts and Josephus are regarded as probably independent redactional developments of a common source by Taylor, *Les Actes*, 5, 122–3, 125 (citing other source-critical attempts).

99. Tacitus, *Ann.* 16, 22 (Thrasea Paetus never sacrificed 'for the celestial voice'), with other evidence discussed by Loesch, *Deitas Jesu und antike Apotheose*, 18–24.

100. Foerster, 'Kyrios', 1048–9.

101. Horbury, 'Herod's Temple and "Herod's Days" ', 114–15, 123–46.

102. The quotations of Smith here and in the following sentence are from G. A. Smith, *Historical Geography*, 308.

103. For text (from MS. Vat. ebr. 440) and translation see Klein, *The Fragment-Targums of the Pentateuch*, I, 158–9; II, 119; the translation below is my own.

104. Rofé, 'The Piety of the Torah-disciples and the Winding-up of the Hebrew Bible: Josh 1: 8; Ps 1: 2; Isa 59: 21'; on this feature in the messianic portrait of Targ. Cant. 7. 14 (13)–8. 2, Loewe, 'Apologetic Motifs', 171–3.

105. Papias's report reflects Jewish expectation influenced by myths of the superabundance of the age of Cronus (H. J. de Jonge, 'BOTRYC BOHCEI').

106. Also printed and translated from the quotation in Yalkut, 2, 571 in Neubauer, Driver, and Pusey, *Fifty-Third Chapter*, 1, 9; 2, 9; this passage often received comment from mediaeval and later Jewish exegetes (Neubauer, Driver, and Pusey, *Fifty-Third Chapter*, 2, 'Prolegomenon', 17–18 (R. Loewe); xlii–xliv (Pusey).

107. For these against the political background see Avi-Yonah, *Jews of Palestine*, 128–33.

108. Goldberg, *Erlösung*, 291 shows that the reference to the Persians, which could suit periods including the third or the early seventh century, is probably a later insertion; he suggests that the passage is close to II Esdras 13, on the messiah ruling and destroying foes from the top of Zion.

109. Translation, commentary and re-edited text in Goldberg, *Erlösung*, 274, 319–31, 19*–21*.

110. Riesenfeld, *Jésus transfiguré*, 200, 225.

111. Taylor, *Names*, 169.

112. Stuiber, 'Christusepitheta', cols. 28–9.

113. Reprinted in *Hymnale secundum usum . . .Sarum*, Littlemore 1850, 74–5.

114. Hahn, *Hoheitstitel*, 9–10 (ET 11–12).

115. Vermes, *Jesus the Jew*, 84–5; Moule, *Origin*, 9–10; Marcus, *Way*, 6–8.

116. Hengel, 'Christological Titles'; compare Dunn, *Christology* (Son of God, Son of man, and then the less strongly titular headings Adam, Spirit, Wisdom, Word).

117. Taylor, *Names*, 67–74.

118. For statistics see Hengel, 'Erwägungen', 135.

119. Taylor, *Les Actes*, 5, 69, 82–3; more fully, 'Why were . . . ?'.

120. See for example Burton, *Galatians*, 396; Cranfield, *Romans*, 2, 836–7; Hengel, 'Erwägungen'; Wright, *Climax*, 41–4; Thrall, *II Corinthians*, 1, 81–2 (on the formula 'Christ Jesus').

121. Horbury, 'Land', Sanctuary, and Worship', 219–22.

122. Taylor, *Les Actes*, 5, 278–9; agreeing with this element in Taylor's reconstruction, I would allow more credit than he does to the description of Jewish opposition in Acts 17. 5–9, given the probably divisive character of this announcement within the Jewish community (see further Horbury, *Jews and Christians*, 16 and n.41).

123. Hengel, 'Erwägungen', 141–3. Wright, *Climax*, stresses this point (41–9), perhaps without fully allowing for the spiritual and worshipful character of the messiah (96).

124. Horbury, 'Septuagintal and New Testament Conceptions of the Church', 5–6, 15.

125. Ps. 68. 19, 'Thou hast gone up on high, thou hast received gifts' (not quoted in Acts), is possibly echoed at Acts 2. 33 (Barrett, *Acts* 1, 149–50 judges this likely); such an echo would suit the prominence of 'Christ' in 2. 36, but the more explicit links of spirit and messiah in Isaiah are perhaps still more likely to be important, given the quotation of Isa. 61 in Luke 4.

126. Hengel, 'Erwägungen', 141 and 154 n.54.

127. Fitzmyer, *Luke*, 1, 202; Hengel, 'Christological Titles', 380–2. Marcus, *Way*, 40, compares Fitzmyer's conclusion that Christ was likened to but not identified with God with the view that, according to Mark, God acts in Christ.

128. Stambaugh, *Sarapis*, 55–6, 68–74; Jewish association of Sarapis with Joseph (Tertullian, *Nat* 2. 8; AZ 43a, in the name of Judah b. Ilai) likewise implies a regal Sarapis (Mussies, 'Sarapis').

129. It therefore also seems inappropriate to envisage an early period of non-messianic Kyrios-theology (so for example Kraft, *Entstehung*, 56–7).

130. Horbury, 'Messianic Associations'.

131. The problems of interpreting the probably vocative *elohim* in Ps. 45. 6 are summed up by J. Day, *Psalms*, Sheffield 1990, 103–5; the present writer thinks that it was a court address to the king as a divine being, comparable (as Day suggests) with Isa. 9. 7, and that it will have been so understood in the Persian period.

132. Lampe, *A Patristic Greek Lexicon*, 1368b–1369a, s. v.; Bousset, *Kyrios Christos*, 240–1 (ET 310–11).

133. Bousset, *Kyrios Christos*, 240–4 (ET 310–15); Barrett, *Acts*, 1, 290, on v. 31.

134. On the last passage in relation with messianic hope in Paul see Horbury, 'Land, Sanctuary, and Worship', 219–22; Bockmuehl, *Philippians*, 235.

135. Knox, *Acts*, 79.

136. The last two words of 'the stronghold of the salvations of his anointed'

(Ps. 28. 8) could be picked out together, as shown by the title of one of Isaac Abravanel's treatises on messianic redemption, *Yeshu'oth Meshiho* (end of fifteenth century; notice in Krauss and Horbury, *Controversy*, 204–5).

137. Field, *Origenis Hexaplorum quae supersunt*, II, 464.

138. For surveys of usage see Bousset, *Kyrios Christos*, 246–59 (ET 317–32); Cullmann, *Christology*, 306–14; Mastin, 'A Neglected Feature', 32–4 (an instructive survey of surveys); Hengel, 'Christological Titles', 366–7; Harris, *Jesus as God*.

139. Metzger, 'Punctuation'; Casey, *Prophet*, 135; Hengel, 'Präexistenz', 491, quoting Harris, *Jesus as God*, 143–72, as likewise finding some uncertainty.

140. On Son of God, Marcus, *Way*, 70–1; Bousset, *Kyrios Christos*, 249 n.5; 256–7 (ET 321 n.305; 329–30, noting the association of 'son of God' and 'God' also in Celsus, e.g. Origen, *c. Cels.* 2. 30; compare 8. 14, quoted in this chapter, section 1, above).

141. Bousset, *Kyrios Christos*, 246–7 (ET 317–18); Mastin, 'The Imperial Cult', and 'A Neglected Feature', 46.

142. Reim, 'Jesus as God in the Fourth Gospel'; Targum translated with comment in Levey, *The Messiah*, 109–13; midrash on Gen. 49. 10 and Ps. 45. 7 in Theodor and Albeck, *Bereschit Rabba*, 3, 1280 (noting other MSS where it occurs at 97. 8), and in Tanhuma, Wayehi 10, 77a.

143. Diez Merino, *Targum de Salmos*, 110.

144. Billerbeck in Strack and Billerbeck, *Kommentar*, I, 979, on Matt. 25. 31, quotes from a Munich MS an Aramaic text which may be rendered: 'Thy throne, O God, is in the heavens for ever and ever: a righteous kingdom is the sceptre of thy kingdom, O king messiah.'

145. Taylor, *Names*, 67–8, 170–3.

146. Skarsaune, *Proof*, 260–2.

147. Horbury, 'Messianism among Jews and Christians in the Second Century'.

148. Horbury, 'The Cult of Christ and the Cult of the Saints'.

Index of References

Page numbers in italic indicate references to the Septuagint

Old Testament

Genesis	28, 59
1.1	190 n.109
1.2	91, 101, 113
1.14	95
1.26	192 n.132
1.26–27	101
1.27	88, 94
2.4	100, 191 n.127
2.7	94
5.1	100
6.3	92, 189 n.98
11.2	*94*
14.18	68, 182 n.12
15.13	58
22.5	*131*
22.11	68
23.6	*49, 68*, 172 n.9 (MT and LXX)
33.11	62
35.11	49
38	28, 100
38.1	100, 175 n.59
38.29	191 n.127
42.15	*77*
49	28, 49
49.1	48
49.8	*129*, 147
49.8–12	111
49.9	*50, 129*, 189

	n.102
49.9–10	50, *129*, 189 n.102
49.10	11, 25, 27, 45, *48*, 49, 50, *50*, 58, 66, 66 (Peshitta), *66*, 67, 93, *129, 133*, 177 n.15, 178 n.32, 179 n.34, 203 n.142
49.11	*31*, 51, 111, 138
49.11–12	*50, 111*, *129–30*, 130, 137
49.12	138–9
50.24–26	28
Exodus	7
3.2	84, 85
4.1–9	*31, 49*
4.5	*31, 49*
4.8	*31, 49*
4.9	*31, 49*
4.16	149
4.20	*31, 49, 179* n.40
4.22	180 n.52
5.2	144
7.1	149

11.4	80
11.5	185 n.62
12.12	80, 81, 185 n.62
12.23	80, 185 n.62
14.14	81
14.19	84
14.31	31, 49, 142
14.31–15.18	83
15	27, 54
15.1–18	37, 38
15.3	38–9
15.6	82
15.16	82
15.17	54, *88*, 97
19.6	49, *56, 179* n.35, 179 n.38
21.1	191 n.127
22.23	*179 n.35*
22.27	*76*
23.20	84, 119, 186 n.70
23.20–21	84, 85, 187 n.75
23.22	49
26.15	62
32.11	31
32.32	31
32.34	84, 85
33.2	84, 85
34.13	76
40.9–11	7

Leviticus 7, 28
4.3–5 9
4.22 30, 175
n.60, 182
n.11
8.12 9
12.1–2 101
12.2 192 n.132
24.1–4 99
26 28
26.24–25 82

Numbers 30, 61, *121*
3.3 9
7.13 191 n.127
11.26 61
16.22 *89*, 102, 120,
197 n.52
20.16 84
21.5 143
23.10 *89*
23.21 *48, 50, 51*,
130, 179
n.35
24.7 29, 30, 43,
44, 45, 50,
61, 85, 101,
102, 130,
145, 147,
178 n.33,
179–80
n.42, 200
n.87, 200
n.88
24.14 50
24.17 27, 34, *45,
50*, 66, 85,
92, 93, 96,
102, 147,
178 n.33,
179–80
n.42, 189
n.103, 192
n.138
24.23–24 178 n.33
27.15–23 67, 178 n.25

27.16 30, *120*, 197
n.52

Deuteronomy
28, 29, 49,
68
4.19 92, 120
4.45 185 n.49
6.3 123
6.4 *185 n.49*
10.17 89
12.2–3 76, 77
17 179 n.35
17.14 42
17.14–20 *48*, 49
17.15 *48*, 179 n.37
20.1 82
20.4 82
20.9 82
26.8 80
27–28 28
30.3–5 28
32 54, 55, 81
32.6 144
32.8–9 120, 186
n.65
32.22 *129*
32.35 81
32.35–36 79, 80, 81,
186 n.64
32.36–43 37, 38
32.38 54
32.41–43 54, 79, 81
32.43 81, *81*, 104,
129, 143
32–33 27
33.2 120
33.4–5 *48, 50*
33.5 31, 49, *51*,
55, 68, 149,
178 n.31,
179 n.35,
179 n.36,
182 n.10

Joshua 37
1.8 201 n.104

1.9 138
5.13–15 84–5
5.13–6.2 85
5.14 197 n.38
10.14 82
10.42 82

Judges 42, 44, 147
2.16–18 43
3.9 43, *147*
3.15 43, *147*
8–9 42

Ruth
4.18 100, 191
n.127
4.18–22 100

*I Samuel (LXX I
Kingdoms)*
32, 42–3,
44, *178 n.35*
2.10 7, 27
8 42
8.6 42
8.7 14
8.9 *179 n.35*
8.10–17 *179 n.35*
8.11 *179 n.35*
8.20 42
10 42
10.25 *179 n.35*
12 42
12.6–11 43
16–17 43
16.1–13 12
16.14–23 32
17 44
17.47 54
24.6 7

*II Samuel (LXX II
Kingdoms)* 31
2.4 7
5.3 7
5.12 200 n.88,
200 n.88
6.20 191 n.130

7.14	113	29.22	45	18.51	147
14.17	84, *91*	29.23	45, 149	20	32
14.20	84, *91*			20.7–9	82
19.28	84, *91*	**II Chronicles**		21.1–7	85
21.17	99	6.5–6	32, 45	21.2	179 n.40
22	27, 31–2	6.13	136	21.13	85
22.51	147	6.42	57	21–22	32
23.1	34	9.8	45	22	32
23.1–7	27, 32	13.3–4	82	22.21	85
23.2	7	13.8	45, 83	23 (24).10	*121*
23.2–4	*91*	13.8–11	45	28	38
		13.12	82	28.8	*147*, 202–3
I Kings		20.15	54, 82		n.136
1.34	7	20.29	82	29	120
1.45	7	35.25	21	35.1–6	39
8.16	32			35.5–6	85
11.34	182 n.11	**Ezra**	26	36.6	78, 185 n.55
19.16	7			45	97, 111,
22.19	92	**Nehemiah**	26		*130–1, 132,*
22.19–22	120	4.20	82		136, 145,
22.21–22	120	8.6	131(= LXX		148, 194 n.3
			II Esdras	45.2	148
II Kings	28		18.6)	45 (44).2–3	111
9.3	7	9.20	44	45.3	111, 137
9.6	7	9.27	43, 147, *147*	45 (44).4	97
11.12	7			45.5	*130*
23.30	7	**Job**		45.6	202 n.131
		1–2	120	45.7	148, *149,*
Chronicles	26, 37, 42,				203 n.142
	43, 45, 46,	**Psalms**		45 (44).7	125, *179*
	51, 79, 100	1.1	50, 182 n.10		*n.39*
		1.2	201 n.104	45.12	*130*
I Chronicles		2	22, 27, 58,	45.13	*130–1*
1.1–4	68		96, 113, 145,	46	22
2.3–15	45, 100		195 n.13	46 (47).10	179 n.36
3	43	2.2	7	47	174 n.39
3.17–19	177 n.17	2.4–9	85	47.6–9	54
5.2	45, 50	2.6–7	195 n.13	47.8	38
14.2	45, 130	2.7	17, 98, 113,	48	22
16.18–29	32		144, 148,	50.1	123
16.22	7		195 n.13	54	32
21.16	197 n.38	2.8 (7)	*95–6*	57	32
28.4	32, *179 n.38*	2.8–9	175 n.59	59	32
28.5	45, 82–3	3	32	60	32
28.9	149	8.3	129	62	32
28.12	32	16.8–11	32	68	32, 62
28.19	32	18	22, 27, 31–2		
29.20	*132*	18.50	85		

68.19	202 n.125
68.30–31	62
72	14, 17, 22, 27, 67, 94 (71), 96, 96 (71), 99, 102, 111, 131, *132*, 136, 190 n.107
72 (71).5	94, 95, 96
72.8	177 n.16
72.10	62, 136–7
72.10–11	62
72.11	131, *131*
72.16	138
72 (71).17	94, 95, 96, *128*, 132
76	22
76.3	182 n.12
78.40	39
78.49–50	39
78.65	39
78.68	32
79 (80).5	*121*
79 (80).8	*121*
79 (80).15	*121*
79 (80).20	*121*
80 (79).5	*89*
80.18	34
82	120, 149
82.6	193 n.150
86	32
87.4	137
87.5	137
89	27, 32, 43, 145
89.20–21	32
89.22	82
89.26–27	113
89.39	33
89.52	11
90.15	58, 95
91	32
93	174 n.34
93.3 (2)	88, 188

	n.85, 191 n.129
94	80
95.3	54
95.10–11	39
96	54
97.5	103
103.20–21	120
104.32	103
105.15	7, 9
110 (109)	14, 22, 27, 34, 58, 67, 94 (109), 96, 99, 111, 113, 143, 145, 146, 195 n.13
110.1	10, 32, 143, 144
110.2	146, 191 n.136
110 (109).2	179 n.39
110.3	17, 58, 68, 96
110 (109).3	94, *95*, *96*, 97, *113*, *190 n.112*
110.4	144
118	22
118.27	78
122.1	99
122.3	99
132	27, 43
132.15	138
132.17	99
139.5	101
142	32
145	32, 37
145.13	45
146	76
148.2	120
149	76
151	32, 43, 53, 57

151.6–7	*32 (151.4–5)*

Proverbs
8.22	88
20.27	189 n.98

Ecclesiastes 26, 47

Isaiah	21, 25, 28, 38, 40, 41, 42, 44, *45*, *53*, 55, 78, *78*, 79, 80, 90, 177 n.21, *181 n.60*
7	27
7.14	181 n.60
9	16, 24, 27, 34
9.1 (2)	90, 94, 96, 99, 189 n.95
9.1–6	20, 22
9.5	16, *90*, *113*
9.5 (6)	*84*, *89*, *89–90*, *91*, *92*, *96*, *99*, 107 (MT), *124*, *125*, *175* n.59
9.5–6	*57*
9.6	90, 132, *181 n.60*
9.6 (5)	94
9.6–7	*180 n.47*
9.7	202 n.131
10	60
10.33	61
10.33–11.5	61
10.34	61
10.34–11.1	29
10.34–11.5	61
11	27, 33, 43, 58, 125

11.1	*50, 101*, 129, 147, *200 n.87*	54.11	*97*	66.7	55, 99, 175 n.59
11.1–2	*92–3*, 93, 96	55.1–5	33	66.14–16	54
		55.3–5	27, 43	66.18–20	103
11.2	101	57.16	100, *101*, 191–2	66.20	62, 175 n.59
11.2–4	90, 143, *181 n.60*		n.131, *200 n.87*	66.24	54
11.4	60, *60*, 61, 62, 65, *91*, 93, 103, 192 n.136	57.19	140	*Jeremiah*	25, 27, 28, 44, 46, 53
		59.10	43	10.19	39
		59.16–18	38, 44, 80	20.1	8
		59.16–20	81	22.24	177 n.17
		59.17	38	23.5	27, 28, 32, 94
11.10	*129, 143*	59.19	177 n.22		
16.1	62, 137	59.19–20	44	23.5–6	177 n.17
16.5	27, 62	59.20	42, *55*, 177 n.22	23.6	132
18.2	*177 n.22*			25.30	39
19.20	43, 44, *44*, 45, *50, 102*, *145, 147*, *147–148*, *149*	59.20–23	38	30.8–9	43
		59.21	201 n.104	30.9	27, 32
		60	54	33.14–26	178 n.32
		60.1–3	92, 103	33.15	28
		60.3–10	137	33.15–16	177 n.17
		60.19–20	103	33.17–22	57
24.21–23	38	60–62	42		
24.23	38	61	202 n.125	*Lamentations*	
24–25	38	61.1	7, 42, *91*, 92, 101	4.20	*10*, 91–2, *91–2, 145*
24–27	38				
25.6	38	61.1–2	81, 143		
25.9	191 n.127	61.1–4	143	*Ezekiel*	25, 27, 28, 29, 30, 44, 46, 53, 123
26.21–		61.2	81		
27.1	38	62	39	34.15	82
32.1–2	*12*, 15	62.11	42, *43, 44*, *55*	34.23	32, 82
32.1–3	27			34.23–24	43
32.2	*173 n.16*	63.1	*138*	34.24	27, 182 n.10
33.17	111	63.1–6	38, 44, 138	36	28–9
35.4	*80*	63.3–5	80	37.22–25	179 n.35
35.6–12	38	63.7–64.11		37.23–25	43
42.11	*147*	(12)	43	37.24	27
45	97	63.8	*177 n.21*	37.24–26	67
51.4–5	*101*	63.9	*80*, 119	37.25	32, 179 n.35, 182 n.10
51.9	83	63.9–11	84		
52.1–12	33	63.10–11	85		
52.9	174 n.39	63.11	31		
52.13	11, 139	63.11–14	43	38.5	61
53	33, 34, 41	63.12	82		
53.2	83	66	192 n.141	*Daniel*	16, 20, 26, 34, 39, 41,
54	33	66.5–24	62		
54.5	78				

	45, 52, 53, 58, 74, 75, 85, 123, 174 n.43, 177 n.21
2	34
2.22	99
2.46	75, 133
3	*74, 75*
3.25	186 n.68
3.86	*89*
4.32	45
4.34	45
6	75
6.7	45
6.8–10 (7–9)	72
7	23, 33, 34, 41, 58, 84, 85, 86, 107, 113, 180 n.48, 186 n.69, 195 n.13
7.9	84
7.13	192 n.136
7.13–14	133
7.17	34, 186 n.68
7.22	192 n.136
7.23–24	34, 186 n.68
8.15	186 n.68
9	9
9.24	7, 7 (Peshitta)
9.24–27	182 n.9
9.25	8
9.25–26	8
9.26	8–9, 33, 59, 193 n.147
10.5	186 n.68
10.13	34, 120, 186 n.68
10.18	186 n.68
10.20–21	34, 120, 186 n.68
11	26

12	86
12.1	34, 84, 86
12.3	33
Hosea	25, 29, 44, 46
3.5	27, 32, 43
11.10	39
Amos	25, 29
4.13	*61, 91, 101,* 191 n.131
7.1	*61, 91*
9.11	27, 43, 91
9.11–15	61
Obadiah	
18–21	38, 174 n.39
21	43, 82, *147*
Micah	
1.3–4	103
2.13	191 n.127
5	16, 24, 27, 34
5.1	58, 95
5.1 (2)	89
5.1–4	22
5.2	*200 n.87*
Nahum	
1.2–8	80
Habakkuk	
2.3	*29*
2.3–4	81, 186 n.64
3	38
Zephaniah	
3.14–20	38
Haggai	2, 6, 25, 26, 28, 37, 43, 177 n.20
2.20–23	25
2.23	177 n.17
Zechariah	25, 26, 29,

	37, 43, 177 n.21
1–8	43
3	28
3.6	28
3.8	25, 33, 177 n.17
3.9 (8)	*94*
4.6–10	25
6	28
6.12	11, 25, 28, 34, 94, 96, 177 n.17, 192 n.136
9–14	28, 43, 176 n.66
9.9	33, 43, *147*, 174 n.39
9.9–11	131
9.14	38
9.14–15	176 n.6
9.14–17	38
12–14	28
12.10	187 n.81
12.10–14	10
13.7	33, 193 n.147
14	40
14.1–9	38
Malachi	29
3	84
3.1	43
3.20 (4.2)	93

Apocrypha

I Esdras	52, 53
9.40	56
II Esdras (=IV Ezra)	10, 12, 16, 17, 23, 24, 34, 46, 52, 53, 55, 58, 60, 62, 63, 77, 78, 84,

	86, 89, 98,
	102, 104,
	105, 105–6,
	107, 123,
	125, 173
	n.18, 186
	n.68, 187
	n.78, 193
	n.148
3–14	30, 58, 59,
	62, 83
7	33, 58
7.26–29	96
7.28–29	187 n.81
7.29	105
7.33	58
7.99	89
12.11	58
12.31–32	96
12.32	10, 102
12.34	58
12.42	98
13	113, 201
	n.108
13.1–13	62
13.1–53	58
13.3–4	103
13.6–7	195 n.13
13.13	62
13.25–16	96
13.26	83, 102
13.29	83
13.32	195 n.13
13.35	58
13.35–38	195 n.13
13.39–40	55
13.52	195 n.13
14.9	102
14.52	10
Tobit	52, 53, 54,
	79
1.19–20	54
2.8	54
11.14	120
12.12–15	120

13	79
13–14	54
13.1	54
13.6	54
13.7	54
13.9ff.	54
13.10	54
13.11	54
13.15	54
Judith	52, 53, 54,
	74, 75, 79
3.8	54
4.6–15	56
6.2	54
9.8	54
9.13	54
10.8	54
13.4	54
15.8	56
15.9	54
16.2–17	54
16.17	79, 83
16.18–20	54
Rest of Esther	52, 53, 54,
	74, 75
(Greek Esther, Additions to Esther)	
13.9	54
13.12–14	54
13.15	54
14.3	54
14.8–12	54
14.12	
(4.17r)	89, 121
14.17	54
14–15	54
Wisdom of Solomon	47, 52, 54,
	74
2	33
3–5	57
3.1	89
5	33

5.16–23	38
7–9	56
7–10	57
7.22	88
7.25–26	88
8.19–20	89, 149
9.8	97
14	76
14.17	135
18.14–16	80
18.20–25	56
Ecclesiasticus	
	52, 53, 57,
	57–8, 63,
	74, 75, 127,
	133, 145,
	181 n.57
I	133
11.12–13	33
17.17	120
36	57
45.1–26	56
45.25	57
47.1–11	57
48.17b	181 n.57
50.1–21	56
50.17 (19)	131
50.21 (23)	131
Baruch	52, 53, 54,
	79
1.1–3.8	52
4–5	54, 79
Epistle of Jeremy	52, 53
Prayer of Manasses	52–3
I Maccabees	
	47, 52, 53,
	54, 60, 63,
	74, 127, 184
	n.45
2.49–70	57
2.57	57, 58

3.3–9	56, 133
4.30	56
5.62	56
9.21	56, 133, 147
14.4–15	56, 133
14.41	133

II Maccabees

	52, 53, 54, 56, 74, 79, 184 n.45
1.24–29	79
1.25–29	54–5
2.10	9
2.17	179 n.38
2.17–18	49, 56
3	9, 56
3.24	121
4.8	71
4.10	9
6–7	53–4
11.8–10	82
15	9, 56

Pseudepigrapha

Letter of Aristeas 47

Ascension of Isaiah

4.1–18	97
9.39	124

Assumption of Moses 81, 84

9.7–10.7	81
10.2	84
11.15	92, 189 n.98
11.16	89, 149
11.16–17	84
11.17	186 n.71

II Baruch 10, 12, 30, 53, 60, 62, 66, 77, 78, 105, 106, 187 n.78

29.3	10, 98
29.5	138
30.1	98, 106
40	61
56–74	106
61	66
63	66
66	66
70–73	66

I Enoch 16, 17, 84, 117, 197 n.40

22.9	89

I Enoch 37–71 (= Parables of Enoch) 22, 23, 34, 45–6, 53, 58, 89, 95, 98, 104, 113, 122, 125, 186 n.68, 188 n.92, 193 n.143

37–71	53
37.2	121
39.6–7	102
45.3	195 n.13
46.1	96, 134
46.1–4	102
46.3–6	195 n.13
48.3	95, 102
48.5	134
48.6	96, 102
48.10	11, 195 n.13
49.2	178 n.26
49.2–4	46, 102
49.4	178 n.26
52.4	11
52.6	103
53.1	137
56	180 n.48
62.7	96, 102
62.9	134
91.14	59

III Enoch

12.5	186 n.70
48A	186 n.66

Ezekiel the Tragedian 31, 49, 68, 75

36–41	182 n.10
68–89	133, 182 n.10

Jubilees 53, 79

16.18	179 n.38
31	40
49.2–4	80

III Maccabees 74, 184 n.45

2.29	70
3.7	131

IV Maccabees 74

Psalms of Solomon 10, 23, 30, 47, 53, 55, 59, 63, 90, 97, 98, 102, 106

17	95, 97, 98, 190 n.119
17–18	40, 98
17.4	32
17.21	32
17.23 (21)	97, 190 n.119
17.23–24	93, 195 n.13
17.26	55
17.27	93
17.31	137
17.32	145, 146
17.32 (36)	10
17.32–37	57
17.34 (31)	175 n.59
17.34–35 (31–32)	103

17.42	III, 113, 190 n.119	*Testament of Levi*	47	*Luke*	45–6
17.42–44	55	18.3	133, 189 n.101	1.32	32
17.46 (51)	83			1.35	125
17.47 (42)	97, 98	18.3–4	93	1.69	32
18.6 (5)	97, 98, 190–91 n.119			1.78–79	94
				1.79	90
18.31	62	**New Testament**		1.80	98
				2.11	10, 145, 146
				2.26	145
Sibylline		*Matthew*		2.30–31	98
Oracles	20, 26, 30, 47, 102, 104, 106, 128	1.21	176 n.8	3.22	143
		2.2	III, 136, 142	3.36–38	68
		2.4	142	4	202 n.125
3	53, 61	2.8	142	4.1	143
3.47–49	83	2.11	129, 142	4.17–19	143
3.63–74	97	3.16	90	6.46	114
3.286	192 n.137	4.16	90, 191 n.124	7.19	129
3.319–21	61			9.29	112
3.652	192 n.137	7.21	114	9.34	112
3.652–56	128	11.3	129	23.2	9
5	34, 53, 58, 60, 62, 77, 78, 89, 90, 102, 103, 107, 125	16.14–22	141	23.35	46
		17.4	142		
		18.10	84	*John*	22, 105, 119, 151, 199 n.79
		21.5	147		
5.108	103, 192 n.137	21.15	109, 134	1.1	148, 190 n.109, 191 n.124, 193 n.144
5.158	103, 192 n.138	21.16	129		
		22.43	32		
5.256	103	25.31	203 n.144	1.6	125
5.256–59	192 n.139			1.8	125
5.414–15	102–3, 103, 192 n.137	*Mark*	176 n.66	1.17	125
		1.2	84	1.18	148
5.414–33	84, 113	2.25–26	32	1.19–23	125
5.420–28	103	6.14–16	89	1.41	136, 142
6.18–19	88	6.21	136	1.42	8, 10
		8.27–29	125	1.49	115, 142
Testaments of the Twelve Patriarchs		8.28	89	3.19	191 n.124
		8.29	10	4.25	8, 10
	30, 40, 53, 67	9.2–8	134	4.42	146
		9.3	III	5.18	115
Testament of		10.37–40	195 n.19	5.22–23	109, 115
Judah	47	10.45	33	6	139
		11.9–10	109, 134	7.41–42	10
24	93	11.10	32	7.42	32
		12.35	10	9.22	143

9.38   143
10.33   126
10.34–36   193 n.150
10.36   115
11.27   115
12.13   143
12.15   143
14.28   110
19.5   111–12, 145
19.7   115
20   148
20.28   148, 197 n.42
20.31   115

Acts   45–6
2.30   32
2.33   202 n.125
2.36   2, 10, 143, 202 n.125
5.31   146
5.36–37   144
7.35   85
7.52   200 n.87
8.32–33   33
9.22   10
10.38   143
10.40–42   2
10.42   46
11.26   142
12.15   84
12.20–23   134, 135
12.23   126
13.23   146
13.33   2
14.15   126
17.3   142
17.5–9   202 n.122
17.7   142
17.31   145
19.34   114
26.33   10

Romans
1.3–4   2, 148
1.4   113

1.23   75
6.3   110–11
8.34   140
9.5   110, 148, 194 n.5
10.9   109, 110–11
11.26   81
12.19   81
13.4   138
15.7–12   143
15.11   81, 104, 143
15.12   129, 143
15.18   129

I Corinthians
1.2   110–11, 132
2.10   99
4.5   99
5.4   120
8.5   114
8.6   115
11.20   110–11, 115, 136
12.3   109, 136
14.12   89
14.32   89
15.24–28   106
15.28   199 n.77
15.45   120
16.22   110–11, 116, 136

II Corinthians
3.18   111
4.4   120
4.4–5   143
4.6   111

Galatians
1.4   142
4.4   199 n.77
5.1   142

Ephesians   22
2.17   140
2.21   130

4.15–16   130
5.23   146

Philippians
2   113, 199 n.77
2.5   120
2.5–11   115, 125, 143–4
2.6   111, 112, 198 n.65
2.6–11   110
2.10   129
2.10–11   134, 136
2.11   109
3.20   146
3.21   146

Colossians   22
1.15   88
2.19   130

I Thessalonians
2.19   115

II Thessalonians   60, 62
1.7–8   81
2.1   55
2.4   136
2.8   115

I Timothy
2.1   71

II Timothy
1.10   146

Titus
2.13   146, 148

Hebrews
1.5   144
1.6   81, 104, 129, 143
1.8   148, 149

1.8–9	148
1.11–14	139
2.17	145
5.5	144
5.5–9	146
5.9–10	144
7.14	67, 146
9.28	186 n.64
10.25	186 n.64
10.30	80–1
10.30–31	81, 186 n.64
10.35–39	81
11.28	80
12.9	89, 121
12.23	89

I Peter
1.4	98

II Peter
1.1	148
1.11	146

I John
2.22	10
4.14	146

Jude
14	68

Revelation   15, 24, 53, 62, 123
1	119
1.4–5	121
1.6	179 n.38
1.10	115, 136
5.5	50, 129
5.9–12	109
5.9–14	109
5.10	179 n.38
7.10	109
12	15
12.2–5	175 n.59
12.5	55
12.7–12	86
12.10	86

15.3	109
19.11–16	138
22.6	197 n.52
22.9	197 n.55
22.16	93

New Testament Apocrypha

Gospel of Peter
4.13	146

Paradosis Pilati
6	196 n.29

Philo   30, 31, 49, 68, 75, 84, 85, 86, 117, 127, 145, 149, 179 n.35, 183 n.33, 197 n.40

Abr.
56	179 n.38

Conf.
60–63	94
62	101
63	123
146	94, 101
173	89
174	89

Dec.
6–9	75
66–76	75
76–80	76

Decal.
84–95	185 n.50

Flacc.
25–39	134, 135
48–49	135
97	135

Gig.
6–18	89

Leg. ad Gaium
79–114	134–5
116	131–2, 200 n.91
118	75
133	75, 77, 135
134–37	75
139	76
143–47	135
149	47
149–51	135
151	72
162–64	76
200–203	76
346	75
356–57	134–5

Mos.   47
1.66	187 n.77
1.88	144
1.148–62	182 n.10
1.158	149
2.254	187 n.77

Praem.
95	85
165	85, 187 n.77

Qu. Gen.
1.4	94

Sobr.
66	179 n.38

Somn.
2.99	200 n.91
2.99–100	132

Josephus 2, 6, 47, 67,
          68, 75, 127,
          144, 179
          n.35

BJ
1.68–69   133
1.414   72
1.437   134
1.457–66   134
2.1   136
2.1–9   134
2.57   111
2.101–110   134
2.142   197 n.51
2.159   197 n.51
2.163   89, 188 n.90
2.169–71   75
2.195   75
2.434   134
2.444   134
3.374   89, 188 n.90
6.312   128
7.418–19   76

Ant.
1.80   68
1.83–88   68
3.91   185 n.49,
             185 n.50
4   47
4.201   76
4.207   76–77
4.297   82
8.107   136
11.331–39   75
13.76   77
13.299–
  300   56, 133
15.51   111
15.51–52   134
15.329–30   75
15.423   134
16.132–35   134
17.200–
  201   136

17.200–12   134
17.293–96   134
17.299   134
17.324–38   134
18.23   14
18.55   75
18.258   76
18.264–67   75
18.271   75
19.284   76
19.343–50   134, 135

Vita
2   47

Ap.
2.74–75   76
2.76–77   77
2.218   89, 188 n.90

Secular Authors

Antisthenes
             199–200
             n.84

Aristophanes
Birds   26

Arrian   71
Anabasis
4,9.9–12.7   183 n.28

Athenaeus 73, 74, 135
Deip.
6.250a   184 n.40
6.253e   71, 184 n.40

Callimachus
Hymns
1.8–9   70
1.165–89   70
2.26–27   70
2.26–28   70
4.165   128

Iambi
12.16 (fragment 202)
             70

Cassius Dio
51.20.1   114

Euhemerus
             71–2, 183
             n.26

Hecataeus
of Abdera 183 n.26

Historia Augusta
Severus Alexander
29.2   196 n.29

Horace   73
Ep. 2.1.5–
  17   70, 73

Od.
1.12.46   189 n.101
1.12.50   183 n.25
3.3   128
3.3.9–12   70, 73
3.3.12   111
3.5.1–3   73
4.5.31–36   70
4.5.33   71–2

Saec. 8   194 n.1

Sat. 2.5.62–64
             128

Pseudo–
Hystaspes 26, 128,
             199–200
             n.84

Leonides of
Alexandria 73
AP 9.355.3 184 n.41

Lucretius
1.7   200 n.87

Lycophron
Alexandra
line 1233   129

Martial   72, 73
7.60   184 n.35
8.24.5–6   184 n.35

Ovid
Fasti 1.611 194 n.4

Persius
5.179–184 136

Philo of
Byblos   21, 23

Pseudo–
   Philo   68, 86
Biblical Antiquities
9.8   92, 149, 189
              n.98
25.2   67, 85
25.5   67
27.10–12   85
45.1–3   179 n.37
59.4   32
60.2   32
63.9   32

Phlegon   199–200
              n.84

Pliny   74, 194 n.7
Ep.
10.10.2   200 n.87
10.96.7   109

Pan.
35–36   138
80.5–6   184 n.43

Plutarch   74, 135, 148
Alex.Virt.
   1.8   115

De laude ipsius
12.543
   D–E   72, 114

Statius
Silvae 5.1.
   37–38   73, 184 n.42

Suetonius   72, 183 n.33
Aug. 98.2 184 n.37

Vesp. 4   128–9

Tacitus
Ann. 16.22 201 n.99

Hist. 5.13 128–9

Theocritus
Id. 17.130 70, 183 n.25

Valerius Maximus
73–4
I, *praef.*   184 n.43

Virgil   183 n.33
Aeneid
6   128
6.791   129

Eclogues
4   128, 199
              n.83
9.47   189 n.101

Georgics   70
1.29–30   72

Christian Authors

Apostolic Fathers

I Clement   145
16.1   146
32.2   67, 146

36.1   146
61.3   146
64.1   121, 146

II Clement
14.1–2   88
20.5   146

Ignatius
Eph. 1.1   146
Smyrn. 1.1 148

Hermas
Sim.
5.6.5   125
8.3.3   187 n.73
9.1.1–3   114
9.12.8   114, 187
              n.73

Vis.
1.3.4   88
2.4.1   88

Didache
9–10   139
14.1   136

Apostolic Constitutions
2.35   179 n.35

Arnobius
Adversus Gentes
1.36–42   115

Chrysostom
Hom. in Ep. ii ad Cor.
26.4 (PG 61, 580–1)
              196 n.29

Clement of Alexandria
              110

Pseudo–Clementines
              42, 176 n.15
Hom. Clem.
3.20.1   101, 192
              n.139
17.4.3   192 n.133

Rec.Clem.
1.38   42

Commodian
Carm.apol.
291   93

Didasc.
2.34   179 n.35

Epiphanius
Pan.
30.3   101
30.13   189 n.95
30.16.4   122
30.17.6   124

Eusebius of
Caesarea   4, 104, 128
HE
2.17.22   194 n.1
4.6.2   92
5.28.5–6   110
7.30.10–11   110

Hippolytus
Refutation of
All Heresies 151
9.30.7–8   87
9.30.8   193 n.147

Irenaeus
Dem. 43   190 n.105

Haer.
1.1.1   88
3.19(20).2   190 n.117
5.33.3   138
5.37.3   138

Justin
Martyr   33, 104, 126,
    150, 190
    n.105
I Apol.
6   121
13.2–9   33
21–22   115

31   92
32.12–13   93
33   125

Dialogue   34, 105, 151,
    193 n.143
8.3   117, 118
32   186 n.69
32.1   107
33–34   67
34.2   140
38.1   117, 118
45.4   94
49.1   87, 105
55–62   198 n.62
55.1   123
63.4–64.1   118
75   198 n.62
75.1–2   84
76.7   94, 190
    n.106
88.3   189 n.95
89.2–90.1   33
105.1   125
106.4   94
113.4   192 n.139
126–29   198 n.62

Lactantius 128
DI
7.15.19   199–200
    n.84

Origen   4, 88, 104,
    108, 110,
    188 n.82,
    188 n.87,
    192 n.134,
    199 n.78
c.Cels.
2.30   203 n.140
3.22–44   115
4.52   190 n.105
8.12   116
8.12–15   115
8.14   110, 203
    n.140

Comm. in Joh.
2.30–31
    (24–5)   125
2.180–92   125
2.188–90
    (31)   89

Hexapla   95–6, 97

Orat.
15.1–3   194 n.5

Princ.
1.2.9–10   88
1.3.4   124
2.6.3–7   125
4.4.4–5   125

Orosius
7.4.5–6   196 n.29

Theodoret
Ps.
71.17 (PG 80.1440)
    190 n.106

Tertullian
Apol.
23.12   125
39.15–16   196 n.29

Hermog.
32.2   191–2 n.131

Marc.
5.8.4   125
5.9.7   96

Nat. 2.8   202 n.128

Qumran Texts
    12

1Q16   62

1QapGen   59 (=4Q369
    see below)
on Gen.
    14.18   68

1QH(Hymns)
59
xi (iii) 55
xi (iii) lines
7–10 98–9, 175
n.59
xviii(x) 8 121

1QM (War Scroll)
34, 38, 39,
59, 66, 79,
85, 86, 181
n.6
v 1 66, 85
xi 1–7 66, 82, 85
xi 8 7
xii 11–12 38
xv 2 61
xvii 7 85
xvii 7 121

1QS (Rule of the
Community)
59, 60
ix 11 10, 60

1QSa (Rule of the Con-
gregation, = 1Q28a)
30, 59, 60,
98, 106
ii 11–12 10, 98, 148,
195 n.13
ii 11–22 98
ii line 12 30
ii 20–21 10

1QSb (Blessings, =
1Q28b)
59, 60, 61,
93
v 93
v lines
24–25 61
v lines
27–8 189 n.103

4Q161 61, 61–2,
180 n.56
line 5 61
fragments 8–10, line 8
61–2
line 8 61
lines
16–18 61
line 20 61

4Q174(Florilegium)
59
line 11 113

4Q246 74

4Q252
fragment 2 50

4Q266 30
3 ii line 5 187 n.76
fragment 10 i
line 12 10

4Q267
ii line 1 187 n.76

4Q285 (Rule of War)
29–30, 32,
61, 180
nn.54, 56
fragment 5 61

4Q369
fragment 1,
col. ii 59

4Q390 [Pseudo–Moses
Apocalypse]
fragment 1, lines 2–5
67–8

4Q400
ii 121
ii 2 121
ii 5 89
v 121

4Q426 59, 180 n.50

4Q448 (King Jonathan
Fragment) 59, 133

4Q491
fragment
11 59

4Q503 180 n.51

4Q521 (Messianic
Apocalypse)
53, 59, 60
fragment 2, ii 1
9, 11, 144

4QPatriarchal Blessings
11 (on Gen.
49.10)

4QPBless 66

4QTestim (Testimonia)
59

11QMelchizedek
59
ii 9–10 149
ii 13 81

11QPsa (Psalms
Scroll) 91
xxvii 32, 91

11QTemple (Temple
Scroll) 47
lvii–lix 47

CD (Damascus
Document)59, 60
i 17 82
v 1 179 n.35
v 17–18 85
vii 19 66
xi 22 131
xii 23–xiii
1 10
xiv 9 10

xix 13   82

Targums

12, 138 (*Onkelos*)
            197 n.52 (of
            Numbers)

Targum Onk. Gen.
49.10   11, 66
49.11   138

Targum Ps.–J. Gen.
38.29   191 n.127
49.11   111, 138
49.11–12   137–8

Targum Neof. Gen.
49.10   66
49.11   138
49.11–12   137–8

Frag. Targ. Gen.
49.10   66
49.11   138
49.11–12   137–8

Targum Ps.–J. Exod.
12.12   185 n.62
40.9–11   7

Targum Neof. Exod.
11.4   80
12.12   80, 185 n.62

Targum Onk. Num.
24.17   93

Targum Ps.–J. Num.
24.17   93

Targum Neof. Num.
11.26   61

Frag. Targ. Num.
11.26   61

Targum Ps.–J. Deut.
33.4–5   50
33.5   182 n.10

Targum Neof. Deut.
33.4–5   51

Frag. Targ. Deut.
33.4–5   51

Targum Isaiah
11.1   93
16.1   62
52.13   11
61.1   137

Targum Micah
5.1   190 n.109

Targum Zech.
4.7   190 n.109
6.12   11
12.10   187 n.81

Targum Ps.
45   148
45.3–10   149
72.17   95, 190
            n.110

Targum Sheni on Esther
            76

Targum Cant.
4.5   10, 147
7.14(13)–
8.2   201 n.104

Mishnah   12

Ber.
1.5   11, 79

Rosh ha-Shanah
4.6   176 n.6

Meg.
4.10   175 n.57

Sotah
7.8   134, 136
9.15   11

Sanh.
2.5   179 n.40

Horayoth
3.1–3   182 n.11
3.3   175 n.60

Babylonian Talmud

Ab. Z.
43a   202 n.128
43b   185 n.47

Ber.
3a   39
10a   195 n.13
28b (Joh. b. Zaccai)
            66–67

Pes.
54a   88, 95
118b   62

Sukkah
52a   10

Rosh ha-Shanah
24b   185 n.47

Hag.
14a   84

Yeb.
63b   100

Sanh.
38b   84, 186 n.70
94a   181 n.57,
            195 n.13

97a   11
98b   11, 81, 139
99a   180 n.49
99b   95

Hullin
139b   195 n.18

Aboth de Rabbi Nathan

B31   76–7

Jerusalem Talmud
(Yerushalmi)

Ber.
2.3.5a   15

Kil.
32b   11

Taanith
2.8.69d   92

Ket.
35a   11

Sanh.
2.4.20b   191 n.130

Midrash

Mekilta
Pisha, Bo, 7 (on Exod.
12.12)   185 n.62

Sifre Deut.
156   42, 176 n.15
325 (32.35
  –36)   80
344   89

Ber. R.
1.4 (on Gen. 1.1)
             190 n.109

1.4 (on Gen. 1.2)
             101, 192
             n.132
1.6 (on 1.1)
             99
1.7 (on Gen. 1.1)
             123
2.4 (on Gen. 1.2)
             113
8.1 (on 1.26)
             192 n.132
12.6 (on Gen. 2.4)
             100, 191
             n.128
24.4 (on Gen. 5.1)
             100
55.7 (on Gen. 22.1)
             68
78.12   62
78.13 (on Gen. 33.10)
             136–7
85.1 (on Gen. 38.1)
             100, 175
             n.59
85.14 (on Gen. 38.29)
             191 n.127
97.8   203 n.142
99.8 (10)
(on Gen. 49.10)
             148

Exod. R.
15.6 (on 12.2)
             89
30.3 (on 21.1)
             191 n.127
32.1–9 (on 23.20)
             186 n.70
35.5 (on 26.15)
             62

Lev. R.
1.1   187 n.75
14.1 (on Lev. 12.2)
             192 n.132
27.11   195 n.13
31.11   99

Num. R.
13.12 (on 7.13)
             191 n.127,
             191 n.128
16.8 (on 13.2)
             99

Lam. R.   173 n.25
1.16   99
1.51 (on 1.16)
             15, 99

Eccl. R.
1.9.1   139

Cant. R
8.6.1   99

Midrash Mishle
8   188 n.85

Midrash Tehillim
1.2 (on Ps. 1.1)
             50, 182 n.10
21.2
  (f.89b)   179 n.40
36 (f.125b) (on Ps. 36.6)
             185 n.55
87.6   137
87.6 (on verse 4)
             62
90.17 (on Ps.90.15)
             95
93 (on Ps. 93.3[2])
             88
93.3   191 n.130
139.5   192 n.132

Pes. R.
34   139
36–37   139
36.12   92, 99
37.3.163a   139
37.7.164a
(= PRK Suppl. VI 5)
             139, 139–40

Pesikta de–Rab Kahana
38–9
on Exod. 15.3
             38–9
1.2   185 n.62
5.8   185 n.62
5.17   39
22.5   39
Supplement VI 5
             39, 81, 139

Tanhuma
Genesis 77a, Wayehi 10
             203 n.142

Tanhuma Buber
Genesis
70a, Toledoth 20
             139
110a, Wayehi 12
             147

Exodus
30b, Beshallah 13
             114

Leviticus
16b,
   Tazria 2 101

Pirqe de–Rabbi Eliezer
32   189 n.98

Yalkut Shimeoni
2.571   189 n.100,
             201 n.106

Jewish Liturgy

Amidah (Eighteen
Benedictions =
Tefillah)   23, 30, 55,
             57, 79, 176
             n.6
First Benediction
             146–7
Fourteenth Benediction
             11

Yose ben Yose
'anusah le 'ezrah
line 23   62
lines 60–64 176 n.6

Passover
Haggadah   80

Egyptian Literature

Neferti, Prophecies of
             20–1

Oracle of
the Lamb   20

Papyrus
Westcar   20

Potter's
Oracle   20, 26, 128

Inscriptions

CIJ 611 = Noy, *Italy*,
no. 86   194 n.1

CIJ 725 (Rheneia)
             197 n.54

CIJ 1440 (Schedia) =
Horbury and Noy no.
22   185 n.48

CPJ III, no. 1532A
(Crocodilonpolis)=
Horbury and Noy no.
117   185 n.48

Papyri

CPJ II, no. 153, p. 40 =
P.Lond. 1912, col iii,
lines 50–51
             72

CPJ II no. 427 = BGU
1068   77

Mur 24   189 n.99

P Col.967   9

P. Yadin
   16   77

XHev/Se
   61   77

Index of Authors

Abravanel, Isaac, 202–3 n.136
Agus, A. (R. E.), 176 n.67
Albeck, Ch., 191 n.129, 203 n.142
Albertz, R., 42, 176 nn.9, 12, 177
  nn.17,21,24
Alexander, P. S., 186 n.66, 200 n.95
Allegro, J. M., 180 nn.55, 56
Allison, D. C., 195 n.19
Anderson, H., 184 n.45
Ashton, J., 193 n.150, 198 n.66, 199
  n.79
Assmann, J., 174 n.43, 175 n.44
Astin, A. E., 183 n.32
Attridge, H. W., 180 n.52, 186 n.64
Avi-Yonah, M., 185 n.57, 201 n.107

Bacher, W., 191 n.129
Badian, E., 183 n.29, 184 n.36
Baeck, L., 188 n.91
Baldensperger, W., 188 n.91
Bammel, E., 199 n.78, 200 n.94
Barbel, J., 124, 198–9 n.70
Barkai, G., 174 n.42
Barker, M,. 123, 186 n.72, 198 nn.63,
  66
Barrett, C. K., 146, 171 n.7, 202
  nn.125,133
Barth, H., 173 n.23
Barthélemy, D., 98, 172–3 n.14, 181
  n.58, 189 n.103, 191 n.120
Bate, H., 192 n.139, 200 n.85
Bauckham, R. J., 116–17, 196 n.37, 197
  n.38
Bauer, Bruno, 14, 36, 117, 173 n.19,
  197 n.40
Baumgarten, J. M., 172 n.13, 187 n.76

Beaujeu, J., 184 n.45, 196 n.27
Becker, J., 5, 171 n.4, 172 nn.3, 4, 173
  n.20
Benoit, P., 189 n.99
Bentzen, A., 21, 23, 24, 175 nn.47,.53,
  55
Bergman, J., 174 n.43, 175 n.44
Berquist, J. L., 177 n.17
Bertram, G., 111, 194 nn.8, 9
Beuken, W., 171 n.4
Bickerman, E., 69, 182 n.19, 182–3
  n.21, 183 n.23
Billerbeck, Paul, 39, 105, 106, 107, 149,
  176 n.8, 187 nn.78, 82, 188 n.82, 190
  nn.109, 112, 191 nn.124, 140, 193
  n.144, 203 n.144
Black, M., 187 nn.77, 79, 188 n.91, 190
  n.118, 192 n.135, 193 nn.143,149,
  197 n.52
Blidstein, G. J., 179 n.37
Bloch, R., 191 n.126
Bockmuehl, M. N. A., 195 n.14, 198
  n.65, 199 n.77, 202 n.134
den Boer, W., 182 nn.19, 20, 182–3
  n.21, 183 n.33, 184 nn.38, 39, 45, 46,
  196 n.27
Borgen, P., 185 n.52
Botte, B., 198–9 n.70
Bousset, Wilhelm, 15, 39, 64, 65, 69,
  90, 114, 114–15, 115, 116, 118, 122,
  123, 125, 146, 151, 172 n.4, 173 n.26,
  181 n.1, 182 n.16, 186 n.72, 186–7
  n.73, 187 n.78, 188 nn.91, n.93, 195
  nn.16, 20, 21, 25, 196 n.30, 197 n.46,
  198 n.56, 200 n.85, 202 n.132, 202
  nn.133, 138, 203 nn.140, 141

Bowersock, G. W., 184 n.39
Box, G. H., 186 n.68, 188 n.91, 192 n.140
Braun, H., 186 n.64, 199 n.75
Brettler, M. Z., 172 n.8, 174 n.39
Briggs, C. A., 172 n.9
Brown, F., 172 n.9
Brown, R. E., 111, 171 nn.4, 5
Brunt, P. A., 183 nn.28, 29
Buber, S., 179 n.40
Bühner, J. A., 199 n.79
Bultmann, Rudolf, 2, 116, 171–2 n.7, 196 n.30
Burkert, W., 184 n.34
Burkitt, F. C., 116, 196 n.32
Burton, E. de W., 202 n.120

Camponovo, O., 179 nn.35, 36, 38, 180 n.43
Capes, D. B., 192–3 n.142
Casey, M., 12, 118, 173 n.15, 186 n.68, 197 n.43, 203 n.139
Cerfaux, L., 116, 196 n.32
Chadwick, H., 189–90 n.104, 194 n.5, 198 nn.57, 62, 64
Chalon, G., 183 n.32, 195 nn.21, 22
Charles, R. H., 37, 171 n.5, 172 n.4, 176 n.3, 197 n.55
Charlesworth, J. H. 98, 171 n.4, 172–3 n.14, 178 n.30, 181 n.4, 184 n.45, 186 n.66, 191 n.120, 192 n.139
Charlesworth, M. P., 182 n.19, 184 nn.38, 39
Chester, A., 185 n.62, 189–90 n.104, 191 n.121, 192 nn.137, 138, 139, 196 n.33, 197 nn.49, 52, 198 n.66, 200 n.85
Chevallier, M. A., 65, 181 nn.3, 4, 185 n.59, 189 n.95
Cimosa, M., 200 nn.90, 91
Clements, R. E., 6, 172 n.6, 173 nn.23, 28
Clines, D. J. A., 188–9 n.194
Coggins, R., 177 n.16
Cohn, L., 187 n.77
Collins, J. J., 34, 37, 41, 172 n.11, 175

n.52, 176 nn.4,11, 180 nn.50, 51, 184 n.36, 186 n.68, 187 nn.74, 78, 190 n.114, 200 n.85
Colson, F. H., 187 n.77
Cotton, H. M., 77, 185 nn.51, 52
Cowley, Abraham, 185 n.62
Cranfield, C. E. B., 142, 202 n.120
Crook, J. A., 182 n.17
Cross, F. M., 98
Crüsemann, F., 176 n.64
Cullmann, O., 116, 196 nn.32, 37, 203 n.138

Dalman, G., 172 nn.2, 4, 12, 173 n.25
Daniélou, J., 189 n.102, 198 nn.59, 68
Davies, P. R., 186 n.68
Davies, W. D., 195 n.19
Day, J., 175 n.48, 202 n.131
de Jonge, H. J., 201 n.105
de Jonge, M., 2, 112, 116, 172 n.8, 173 n.17, 193 n.150, 194 n.11, 194–5 n.12, 196 n.36
de Lange, N. R. M., 192 n.134
Delitzsch, F., 18, 174 n.34
Deissmann, A., 114–15, 195 n.21, 197 n.54
Diez Merino, L., 203 n.143
Dimant, D., 182 n.9
Di Segni, L., 191 n.123
Dodd, C. H., 37, 171 n.5, 176 n.3
Dölger, F. J., 194 n.1
Dorival, G., 178 n.32
Driver, S. R., 172 n.9, 181 n.5, 201 n.106
Dunn, J. D. G., 116, 194–5 n.12, 196 n.36, 201 n.116

Ehrhardt, A. A. T., 195 n.24
Eisenstein, J. D., 171 n.1
Eissfeldt, O., 23
Emerton, J. A., 23, 123, 175 nn.48, 52, 54, 181 n.60, 182 n.12, 188 n.91, 192 n.140, 193 n.150
Emmet, C. W., 52, 172 n.4, 180 n.45
Engels, Friedrich, 117, 197 n.40

Fears, J. R., 183 n.22
Field, F., 190 n.115, 203 n.137
Finley, M., 199 n.81
Fishbane, M., 174 n.43, 177 n.16
Fishwick, D., 182 n.20, 182–3 n.21,
    183–4 n.33
Fitzmyer, J. A., 144, 202 n.127
Fletcher-Louis, C. H. T., 198 n.66
Foerster, W., 116, 196 n.32, 200 n.87,
    201 n.100
Fossum, J. E., 186 n.72, 198 nn.63, 66
Fox, L., 199 n.83
Frankel, Z., 48, 178 n.33, 180 n.43
Fraser, P. M., 183 nn.25, 26, 185 n.48
Frazer, J. G., 173 n.28
Frederiksen, M. W., 183 n.32
Frerichs, E. S., 181 n.4
Freund, R. A., 178 n.32, 179 n.35
Freyne, S., 171 n.4
Friedmann, M., 139, 189 n.100
Frost, S. B., 22, 24, 37, 172 n.4, 175
    n.49, 176 n.4, 187 n.78

Gall, A. von, 19–20, 24, 39–42, 172
    n.4, 174 nn.37, 38, 40, 43, 176 nn.9,
    10
García Martínez, F., 180 nn.49, 54, 55
Geertz, C., 182 n.18
van der Geest, J., 199 n.75
Geffcken, J., 183 n.26
Gelin, A., 6, 172 n.7
Gianotto, C., 182 n.12
Ginzberg, L., 182 n.10
Glatzer, N., 185 n.56
Goldberg, A. M., 95, 187–8 n.82, 189
    n.100, 190 nn.109, 111, 191 n.127,
    201 nn.108, 109
Goldin, J., 186 n.63
Goodenough, E. R., 187 n.77
Goodman, M. D., 190 n.116
Gordon, R. P., 180 nn.53, 55
Gow, A. S. F., 183 n.25
Grainger, J. D., 178 n.28
Gray, G. Buchanan, 90, 107, 188–9
    n.94
Gray, J., 175 n.48

Green, J., 191 n.123
Green, W. S., 181 n.4
Greenfield, J. C., 186 n.66
Gressmann, H., 6, 15–26, 38, 41, 172
    nn.2, 4, 173 nn.27, 28, 30, 31, 174
    nn.33, 40, 176 nn.5, 7, 181 n.1, 182
    n.16, 187 n.78, 188 nn.91, 93, 188–9
    n.94, 198 n.56
Griffiths, J. Gwyn, 174 n.43
Gross, H., 19, 20, 174 n.40
Guéraud, O., 183 n.32
Gunkel, H. 15–18, 23–5, 39, 173 nn.25,
    26, 28, 174 n.33

Habermann, J., 199 n.77
Habicht, C., 182–3 n.21, 183 nn.30, 33,
    184 n.38
Hahn, F., 141, 196 nn.32, 34, 201
    n.114
Hanhart, R., 90, 178 nn.32, 35, 179
    n.35, 180 n.47, 189 n.96
Harl, M., 178 n.32, 179 n.41, 181 n.5
Harnack, Adolf, 122, 125, 188 n.91,
    198 n.56, 199 nn.73,.74
Harris, M. J., 203 nn.138, 139
Hart, J. H. A., 181 n.56
Hecht, R. D., 187 n.77
Heim, K., 190 n.107
Heinrichs, A., 183 n.26
Hellholm, D., 174 n.43
Hengel, M., 116, 118, 141, 144, 178
    n.30, 180 n.44, 182 n.13, 183 n.22,
    184 nn.44, 45, 194 n.7, 194–5 n.12,
    196 nn.33, 37, 197 n.45, 199 nn.71,
    80, 81, 201 nn.116, 118, 202 nn.120,
    123, 126, 127, 203 nn.138, 139
Hesse, F., 172 n.2
Hofius, O., 172 n.4, 185 n.58
Holtzmann, H. J., 36
Hooke, S. H., 21, 22, 175 nn.46, 49
Hooker, M. D., 3
Horbury, W., 172 nn.9, 10, 173 n.16,
    175 nn.60, 63, 176 n.6, 178 n.29,
    178–9 n.35, 179 nn.40, 41, 179–80
    n.42, 180 nn.44, 46, 48, 53, 181
    nn.59, 1, 185 nn.48, 61, 186 n.69,

188 nn.84, 89, 92, 190 nn.113, 114, 117, 192 n.136, 194 n.10, 195 nn.13, 15, 19, 196 n.28, 199 n.72, 200 nn.86, 93, 96, 201 n.101, 202 nn.121, 122, 124, 130, 134, 202–3 n.136, 203 nn.147, 148
Hubbard, M., 183 n.25
Hultgård, A., 182 n.14, 189 n.101
Hurtado, L. W., 116, 119, 194 n.7, 196 n.37, 197 n.47

Ibn Ezra, 186 n.70
Isaac, B., 185 n.47

Jacobson, H., 189 n.98
James, M. R., 190 n.119
Jellinek, A., 181 n.7
Jeremias, J., 172 n.10
Johnson, A. R., 21–5, 175 nn.46, 47, 48, 50, 51, 191 n.122
Joyce, P., 174 n.39
Juel, D., 176 n.65
Jungmann, J.A., 198–9 n.70
Juster, J., 185 n.51

Karrer, Martin, 7, 36, 171 n.5, 172 n.9, 176 n.2
Kellner, M., 171 n.2
Kelly, J. N. D., 199 n.73
Kiessling, E., 200 n.87
Kilpatrick, G. D., 200 n.87
Kittel, R., 181 n.59
Klausner, J., 187 n.78
Klein, M. L., 201 n.103
Kloner, A., 174 n.42
Knibb, M. A., 178 n.26
Knox, W., 146, 171 n.7, 199 n.80, 202 n.135
Koep, L., 196 n.29
Kraft, H., 202 n.129
Kramer, W., 196 n.34
Krauss, S., 185 n.47, 195 n.17, 202–3 n.136
Kretschmar, G., 146, 198 n.59
Kuhn, P., 176 n.7

Laato, A., 21, 171 n.6
Lacoque, A., 186 n.68
Lampe, G. W. H., 188 n.86, 202 n.132
Larkin, K. J. A., 177 n.16
Lecker, M., 185 n.47
Levey, S. H., 187 n.81, 193 n.147, 203 n.142
Lévi, I., 173 n.25
Lichtheim, M., 175 n.44
Lieberman, S., 191 n.130
Lietzmann, H., 16, 174 n.40
Limor, O., 171 n.3
Lindeskog, G., 118, 197 n.44
Loesch, S., 182 n.13, 201 n.99
Loewe, R., 39, 176 n.8, 201 nn.104, 106
Lorenz, R., 199 n.78
Lueken, W., 39, 84, 86, 122, 186 nn.71, 72, 186–7 n.73, 197 n.55
Lust, J., 178 n.32, 181 n.60

Mach, M., 182 n.8, 186 n.67, 188 n.88, 197 n.50, 198 nn.66, 67, 200–1 n.97
Maier, J., 178 n.29
Maimonides, 187 n.75
Manson, T. W., 98, 186 n.71, 190–1 n.119
Marcus, J., 176 n.66, 201 n.115, 202 n.127, 203 n.140
Markschies, C., 197 n.45
Marmorstein, A., 176 n.8
Mason, R. A., 177 n.17
Mastin, B. A., 117–18, 133, 197 n.42, 200 n.92, 203 nn.138, 141
Mazar, A., 174 n.42
Mendels, D., 178 n.29
Metzger, B. M., 203 n.139
Meyer, E., 17, 116, 173 nn.29, 30, 174 n.40, 196 n.32
Michaelis, W., 198 n.59
Milik, J. T., 98, 172 n.13, 172–3 n.14, 181 n.57, 187 n.76, 189 nn.99, 103, 191 n.120
Millar, F., 184 n.46, 187 nn.77, 79, 91, 190 n.118, 192 n.135, 193 nn.143, 149, 197 n.54

Mirsky, A., 181 n.58
Moenikes, A., 42, 176 n.14
Moffatt, H., 186 n.64
Moore, G. F., 105, 106, 107, 176 n.67, 187 n.78, 193 n.145
Morray-Jones,, C. R. A. 186 n.67, 198 n.66
Moule C. F. D., 3, 116, 119, 141, 171–2 n.7, 196 nn.31, 36, 197 n.48, 200 n.91, 201 n.115
Mowinckel, S., 6, 15–24, 41–2, 87, 172 n.4, 174 nn.32, 34, 38, 41, 175 nn.47, 48, 187 nn.78, 79, 188 n.91
Munnich, O., 178 n.32
Murmelstein, B., 191 n.128
Murray, O., 178 n.30
Mussies, G., 202 n.128
Mutius, H. G. von, 181 n.7

Nahmanides, 1, 171 nn.2, 3
Nairne, A., 186 n.64
Neubauer, A., 201 n.106
Neusner, J., 171 n.4, 181 n.4, 185 nn.59, 60
Newsom, C., 197 n.53
Nikiprowetsky, V., 192 n.139
Nisbet, R. G. M., 183 n.25
Nock, A. D., 69, 116, 117, 182 n.20, 196 n.32
Norden, E., 199 n.82
Noy, D., 185 n.48, 194 n.1

Odeberg, H., 186 n.66
Oegema, G. S., 34, 176 n.68, 178 n.29, 182 n.15
Oesterley, W. O. E., 16, 173 n.28
Ogilvie, R. M., 183 n.32
O'Neill, J. C., 171 nn.6, 7, 173 n.24, 192 n.139
Oppenheimer, A., 185 n.47
Ottosson, M., 176 n.12
Oulton, J. E. L., 194 n.5

Page, D. L., 184 n.41
Parente, F., 182 n.12
Pax, E., 195 n.23

Perez Fernandez, M., 175 n.57, 179–80 n.42, 181 n.5, 191 n.126
Person, R. F., 175 n.58
Pesce, M., 78, 81, 185 n.53, 186 nn.63, 65
Peterson, E., 194 n.4
Pfann, S., 172 n.13, 187 n.76
Pomykala, K. E., 43, 175 n.56, 177 n.18
Porter, J. R., 31, 175 n.62, 176 n.12, 178 n.31
Price, S. R. F., 182 nn.18, 20, 183 n.23, 24, 27, 33, 184 nn.43, 46
Puech, E., 188 n.90
Pusey, E. B., 201 n.106

Rad, G. von, 28
Rankin, O. S., 171 n.1
Rashi, 187 n.75, 191 n.129
Reeg, G., 181 n.7
Reim, G., 148, 199 n.77, 203 n.142
Reventlow, H. Graf, 172 n.5
Reynolds, J., 185 n.52
Riesenfeld, H., 21, 23, 24, 65, 87, 140, 151, 175 n.47, 181 n.2, 181 n.4, 187 n.80, 200–1 n.97, 201 n.110
Roberts, J. J. M., 172 n.2, 173 n.20, 174 n.36
Robertson, J. M., 117, 197 n.41
Robinson, J. Armitage, 190 n.105
Rofé, A., 44, 177 nn.19, 20, 21, 22, 23, 24, 178 n.34, 201 n.104
Rowland, C. C., 123, 186 nn.68, 72, 197 n.49, 198 n.61
Rowley, H. H., 172 n.2
Rübsam, W., 200 n.87
Ryle, H. E., 190 n.119

Sanders, E. P., 44, 78, 112, 112–13, 151, 171 n.4, 176 n.11, 181 n.6, 185 n.54, 194 n.12
Schäfer, P., 181 n.7, 185 n.56, 186 n.66
Schaper, J. L. W., 96, 174 n.39, 190 n.110, 190 n.112
Schechter, S., 171 n.3
Schiffman, L. H., 180 n.49

Schimanowski, G., 187–8 n.82, 190 n.112

Schlüter, M., 181 n.7

Schmidt, N., 186 n.68

Schmidt, W. H., 172 n.2

Schniedewind, W. M., 178 n.25

Schoeps, H.-J., 122, 176–7 n.15, 192 n.133, 198 n.58

Scholem, G., 123, 171 n.3

Schürer, E., 36, 87, 98, 104, 104–5, 105, 176 n.1, 187 nn.77, 79, 188 n.91, 190 nn.116, 118, 192 n.135, 193 nn.143, 149, 197 n.54

Schwartz, S., 178 n.26

Schwemer, A. M., 181 n.7, 197 n.53

Scott, K., 184 n.39

Seeligmann, I. L., 90–1, 181 n.59, 189 nn.96, 97

Segal, A. F., 196 n.33, 198 n.61

Simon, M., 197 n.55

Simonetti, M., 122, 198 nn.60, 68

Skarsaune, O., 150, 190 nn.105, 108, 198 n.62, 203 n.146

Smith, G. A., 137, 138, 201 n.102

Smith, J.Z., 117, 197 n.39

Smith, M., 111, 173 n.18, 193 n.145, 194 n.11

Smith, Robertson. 173 n.28

Sparks, H. F. D., 178 n.26

Speyer, W., 199 n.81

Stambaugh, J. E., 202 n.128

Stauffer, E., 173 n.16

Stead, G. C., 193 n.151, 194 n.3

Stone, M. E., 187 n.81, 193 n.147, 193 n.148

Strack, H. L., 176 n.8, 187 n.78, 187–8 n.82, 190 nn.109, 112, 191 n.124, 192 n.140, 193 n.144, 203 n.144

Strauss, D. F., 14

Stroumsa, G. G., 198 n.65

Strugnell, J., 200 n.95

Stuckenbruck, L. T., 98, 172–3 n.14, 191 n.120, 197 n.53, 197 n.55

Stuiber, A., 196 n.34, 201 n.112

Sturdy, J. V. M., 5, 172 n.1

Styler, G. M., 3

Swete, H. B., 178 n.32

Tannenbaum, R., 185 n.52

Taylor, J., 201 n.98, 202 nn.119, 122

Taylor, V., 141, 150, 201 nn.111, 117, 203 n.145

Theodor, J., 191 n.129, 198 n.61, 203 n.142

Thraede, K., 182–3 n.21

Thrall, M. E., 202 n.120

Tischendorf, C., 196 n.29

Tromp, J., 186 n.71

Tsafrir, Y., 191 n.123

Turner, E. G., 183 n.32

Ussishkin, D., 174 n.42

VanderKam, J., 188 n.92

Vaux, R. de, 189 n.99

Vermes, G., 98, 105, 105–6, 106, 141, 180 n.54, 180 n.56, 187 nn.77, 78, 79, 187–8 n.82, 188 n.91, 190 n.118, 191 n.120, 192 n.135, 193 nn.143, 146, 149, 196 n.33, 200 n.95, 201 n.115

Visotzky, B. L., 188 n.85

Volz, P., 96, 188 n.91, 190 n.112

Walbank, F. W., 183 nn.25, 31, 32, 184 n.40

Watson, W. G. E., 180 n.54

Weiler, A., 171 n.4

Weiss, Johannes, 2, 116, 171 n.7, 196 nn.32, 35

Wellhausen, J., 14–17, 23–4, 34, 173 nn.21, 22, 24, 200 n.89

Welten, P., 21, 174 n.39, 175 n.45

Wendland, P., 69, 183 n.26, 195–6 n.26

Werner, Martin, 122, 123, 124, 198 nn.57, 58

Wesley, Charles, 109

Wesley, John, 194 n.2

Widengren, G., 175 n.46

Wiles, M. F., 188 nn.83, 87, 194 n.5

Williams, R. D., 194 n.3, 198 n.69, 199 nn.76, 78

Williamson, H. G. M., 177 n.23

Windisch, H., 199–200 n.84
Wise, M. O., 178 n.29
Wolff, H. W., 18, 23, 24, 41, 174 n.35
Wolfson, H. A., 187 n.77
van der Woude, A. S., 172 n.10, 193
　n.150

Wright, N.T., 202 nn.120, 123
Yardeni, A., 172 n.13, 185 n.51, 185
　n.52, 187 n.76

Zakovitch, Y., 177 n.23
Zevit, Z., 186 n.68

Subject Index

Aaron, 30, 44, 45, 56, 57, 66, 80, 85, 86, 99
  Messiah of, 10, 30, 60, 82, 113
Abraham
  as king, 9, 49, 68
Acclamation and cult
  of a deity as king, 19, 132, 144–5
  of angels, 119–22
  of Christ
    angel-cult derivation of, 121–2
    as angel, 122
    Christian derivation of, 111, 116, 118–19
    Gentile derivation of, 113–15, 117–18, 144–5
    Jewish (messianic) derivation of, 3, 113, 116–19, 126, 134–6, 142–8, 149–50
    resemblance to ruler cult of, 111–12
  of Jewish king, 22, 127, 133–6
  in rabbinic literature, 136–40
  in Targums, 137–40
  Jewish and Christian employment of Gentile motifs of, 112, 134–5, 137–8
  of Jesus Christ, 109–19, 122, 135, 140
  with focus on physical appearance, 111–12, 137–8
  see also Praise, Ruler cult
Agrippa I, 134, 135, 136, 144
Angel(s)
  as divine council, 120
  as gods, 120–1
  christology, 90–1, 105, 119–27

in connection with binitarian concepts, 123
spirit-christology, 125
  as derivative from spirit-messianism, 124–5, 151
cult of, 121–2
embodied, as messiah, 2, 39, 86–7
messianism, 34, 64, 80–5, 88–90, 120, 122–4, 125, 148–9
  as related to earthly messianism, 83–6
  as (un)distinguishable from divine deliverance, 80–3
  in Psalms of Solomon, 97–8
  in apocalyptic literature (including Sibyllines), 102–7
  in rabbinic literature, 99–102, 105, 139
  in Septuagint, 90–7
  in Qumran texts, 93, 98–9
  in Targums, 93, 139
Anoint(ed)
  as a special term, 7–13
  see also Messiah, Messianism
Antichrist, 15
  see also Gog
Apocrypha, 52–9
  narrative works, 53–6
  wisdom books, 57–8
Augustus, 70, 71, 72, 73–4, 75, 83, 114, 135

Balaam
  oracles of, 27, 48–9, 50, 61, 130, 147
  see also Index of References, Num.23.21; 24.17

Barcelona Disputation, 1
Bar Kokhba, 7, 30, 67, 79, 92, 95, 133

Christ cult
  see Acclamation and cult
Christology, 112–13, 116, 118
  pre-existence, 86, 87–9, 90–1, 94–6,
    98, 101–2, 103–4, 106–8, 113,
    120, 122, 123–4, 149
  titles of Christ, 120, 126, 140–50
    evidence of impact of Jewish
      messianism on, 141–2
    evidence of impact of ruler cult
      on, 146, 148
  see also Angel(s)-christology

David, 9, 28, 56, 66
  as messianic figure, 25, 27, 31–3, 34,
    37, 42, 45–6, 54, 67, 82, 84, 91
  branch of, 29–30, 32, 43, 50
  choice/covenant of, 42–3, 57, 102
  in Chronicles, 45–6
  kingdom of, 11, 14, 27, 29, 32, 40,
    45–6, 57–8
  last words of, 27
  messiah of, 10, 17, 22, 25, 27, 30, 44,
    51, 60, 66–7, 87, 92–3, 99, 113,
    137, 147
  son of, 9, 10, 25, 98, 137, 141
  song of, 27
Deliverance
  see Saviour
Demetrius the chronographer, 47

Eleazar, 30, 53, 66, 67, 85
Enthronement festival, 17, 18

Gabriel, 84
Gog (and Magog), 50, 61, 113, 130, 181
  n.57, 195 n.13

Hezekiah, 66–7

Isaac, 9
Israel, 66
  messiah of, 10, 30, 60, 82

Jacob, 9
  blessings of, 27, 28, 48–9, 50, 51, 66,
    67, 129–30
Jehoshaphat, 54, 82
John Hyrcanus, 7, 56
John the Baptist, 84
Joshua, son of Josedech, 8, 26, 28, 30
Joshua, son of Nun, 30, 37, 42, 57, 64,
  66, 67, 82, 84, 85, 86, 125
Josiah, 24, 41, 56, 66
  model of ideal king, 15, 21
Justus of Tiberias, 47, 68

King
  as divine, 70–1, 148
  as God's representative, 14–15, 17,
    45–6, 73
  as saviour, 66, 147
  faith in, 143
  gods styled as, 70, 144
  God as, 15, 19, 37–9, 43, 44, 50–1,
    54
    portrayed anthropomorphically,
      38–9
    in messiah's place, 14, 37–9,
      78–83, 126
    fulfilling messiah's role, 38, 40, 44,
      87–8
  see also Ruler cult
Kingdom
  of God, 37–46, 54
    anticipation of, 40
    as depreciative of human
      kingdoms, 42–4
    as excluding kingdom of messiah,
      18, 19, 37–8, 39–41, 55, 78–83,
      87
    as legitimizing human kingdom,
      14, 42–3
    v. kingdom of messiah, 18, 19, 24
    as linked with prosperity, 16
  see also Monarchy

Levi, 51, 57, 66

Maccabees, 56–7
Melchizedek, 64, 68, 84, 81, 144, 149

Messiah
    as a term, 1, 2, 7–13, 30–1, 59–60,
        142
    as God's human representative,
        14–15
    as God's servant, 33
    pre-existence of, 58, 86–108, 120–4,
        139
    prototypes, 31–5, 55–6
        David, 31–2, 34
        Moses, 31, 34
        Servant of Isaiah 53, 33, 34, 41
        Smitten shepherd of Zechariah
          13.7, 33, 34
        Son of Man of Daniel 7, 33–4, 41
    royal, 5–6, 30, 66–7, 145–6
    see also David; Moses
Messianism
    viewed by some as peripheral to the
        New Testament, 1, 2, 6
    Christian, 6, 87
    defined, 6–7
    influence of Christian on Jewish, 79,
        109
    influence of Jewish on Christian, 12,
        15, 94–5, 101–2, 140–50
    influence of pagan on Christian, 15
    prevalence in Second-Temple period
        of, 9, 12, 22, 36–63, 43–4
    relevance to Judaism of, 1, 2, 36–63
    royal, 30–1, 34, 45–6, 60, 64–8,
        145–6
    spirit, *see* Messiah, pre-existence of
    varieties, 6–7, 64–5
        dual, 29–30, 60, 67
          in Mosaic constitution, 30
        unitary, 30–1, 66, 67–8, 145–6
    see also Acclamation and cult
Michael, 34, 39, 84, 85–6, 121
Monarchy
    as category overlapping with
        messianism, 5, 11, 25, 66–8
    as conceived in Psalms, 22, 130–2
    as promoted in Pentateuch, 48, 49
    in Israel, 49
    in Old Testament, 25–6

    in the ancient Near East, 16, 21, 23,
        25, 26, 47
    Jewish views on, 75
    see also Kingdom; Ruler Cult
Moses, 44, 56, 64, 76, 85, 86, 125
    as king, 30, 31, 42, 49, 50–1, 56, 68,
        75, 83, 133
    as messianic figure, 31, 37, 42, 80,
        82, 84
    Blessings of, 27, 28, 48–9, 50–1, 55
    faith in, 31, 143
    Songs of, 27, 28, 37–8, 39, 54, 55,
        81, 104, 143
Myth and Ritual School, 21, 25, 65

Nahmanides, 1
Nicolas of Damascus, 47

Old Testament, 5–35
    as edited and collected, 5, 25–31
        creating thematic link between
          Pentateuch and Prophets,
          28–30
        influencing interpretation of
          oracles, 26–7
        integrating Davidic and non-
          Davidic kingship, 26–7
        producing messianic prophecies,
          29, 37
        reflecting monarchic traditions
          and aspirations, 25–6
        reflecting interest in national
          eschatology, 28, 29
    theology, 1, 5–6, 37–41
    theocracy, 14–15, 17–18
Onias, 8, 56
Origins of messianism, 13–25, 34–5
    after exile, 19–20, 22
    in Canaanite influence, 21, 23
    in Egyptian influence, 16–17, 19–21
    in Greco-Roman influence, 23–6,
        40–2
    in Persian influence, 19–20, 23, 26,
        37–46
    in pre-exilic royal ideology, 14–15,
        17–19, 26

in pre-exilic ancient Near Eastern
    mythology, 15–17, 18–21, 23
in relation to Psalms, 22–3

Pentateuch
    as promoting monarchy and
        priesthood, 48–9
    as understood in relation to Prophets
        and Psalms, 26–9, 50–1, 93
    eschatological theme of, 35
    messianic theme of, 37
Phinehas, 56, 57
Praise
    contact between Jewish and Gentile,
        128–30
    in ruler cult, 71–4
    of Christ as influenced by Gentile
        royal praise, 117–18, 127
    of Jewish rulers
        as anticipating praise of Christ,
            129
        in Septuagint Pentateuch, 127–32
        in Septuagint Psalms, 127–32
    oracular
        Gentile, 128–30
        Jewish, 128–30
        as influenced by Gentile royal
            praise, 127–8, 129–30
    see also Ruler cult
Prophecy
    as affirmation of an ideal, 14, 15
    as prediction of deliverance, 14
    Messianic, Old Testament, 27–8
        of Davidic Messiah, 27–8, 37–9,
            45–6
        paralleled in non-Israelite
            prophecy, 26
Prophets
    as understood in relation to
        Pentateuch and Psalms, 26–9,
        50–1, 93
    eschatological theme of, 35
Psalms
    as linked with Pentateuch and
        Prophets, 26–9
    enthronement, 14, 15, 16, 18, 19, 21,

22–3, 38, 40–1, 54
linking king with salvation, 147
messianic, compared with ruler
    cults, 14
royal, 14, 16, 17, 18, 19, 22–3, 24,
    25, 75, 97, 130
    as oracles, 27
    in relation to messianism, 16, 18,
        19, 22–3, 25
    in relation to ruler cult literature,
        14
Zion, 22–3, 24

Qumran Texts, 59–63
    dual messianism of, 66, 67–8, 85
    messiah of Aaron, 9–10, 30, 60, 82
    messiah of Aaron and Israel, 60, 82
    messiah of David, 50
    messiah of Israel, 9–10, 30, 60, 82
    messianic interpretation
        of the Pentateuch, 48, 66
        of Jacob's blessing, 50
    messianism in, 59–60, 81, 93
    Prince of the Congregation, 9, 29,
        30, 60, 61, 66
    theme of vengeance on great
        adversary in, 60–3
    unitary messianism in, 30–1

Rabbinic literature
    as related to New Testament, 15
    Davidic messianism in, 30, 66–7
    deliverance by God without messiah
        in, 38, 80–1, 105
    impact of Christian messianism on,
        79
    messiah son of Ephraim, 10, 33, 137
    messiah son of Joseph, 10, 33
    messianism in, 10–11, 79, 99–102,
        136–40
    relevance to study of Second Temple
        Judaism of, 3
    royal messianic interpretation of the
        Pentateuch in, 48, 50–1
    theme of judgment on great
        adversary in, 62

Ras Shamra (Ugarit), 21, 23
Ruler cult
  as cult of 'present god', 24, 73–4, 115
  recognition of benefaction, 69
  as relating king to the entire world,
    69
  as religion, 69–70
  central premise of, 115
  compatibility with ancestral religions
    of, 69–71
  compatibility with Judaeo-Christian
    views of, 70, 74–5
  conflicts with other pieties of, 71–4
  familiarity to Jews of, 72
  fostering exercise of power through
    its rites, 69
  Hasmonean, 14
  Hellenistic, 68, 69, 70, 71, 73, 74, 75,
    77, 128–9
  Herodian, 114, 134–6
  impinging on honour of gods, 71–4
  in context of Jewish loyalty, 74–5,
    76–7
  influence on content of messianism
    of, 24, 69, 71, 106, 117–18,
    127–8, 137, 149–50
  influence on cult of Christ of,
    113–15, 127–8, 129–30, 134,
    137, 140, 146, 148–50
  influence on praise of Jewish kings
    of, 68–9, 127–8, 129–30, 131–2
  Jewish manifestation of, 23, 112,
    127–40
  Jewish opposition to, 68, 74, 75–6,
    77, 134–5
  Jewish sympathy with, 77, 134–5
  Ptolemaic, 14, 20, 34, 70, 71, 74, 76,
    106, 128, 131
  Roman, 34, 69, 70, 71, 72, 73, 74,
    75, 76, 77, 106, 114–15, 128–9,
    134–5, 137–8
  see also Acclamation and cult, Praise

Saviour (Deliverance)
  as aspect of messianism, 43–5, 55,
    56, 146–8

  as king, 66, 147
  God as, 37–8, 55, 64, 78–83
    apart from messianic agent, 2,
      78–83, 126
    in Christian messianism, 55
    in narrative apocrypha, 54, 56
Scandinavian school of Old Testament
    study, 25, 65
Septuagint
  as developing royal messianism, 48,
    50–1, 55, 130–1
  as exalting Jewish monarchy, 49,
    131–2
  as supporting pre-existent
    messianism, 90–6
  deliverance by God apart from agent
    in, 80
  emphasis on angels of, 90–7, 121
  introducing messianic
    interpretation, 29–31, 37, 53,
    147–8
  introducing ruler cult motifs, 129,
    147
  Pentateuch, 46–51, 127–32
  Psalms, 127–32
Silence on messianism, 5, 38, 41,
    78–83, 112
  in apocrypha, 5, 38, 41, 52, 53,
    55–6
  in Mishnah, 11, 79
  in (portions of) Old Testament, 5, 41
  in pseudepigrapha, 5, 38
Solomon, 45, 47, 56, 66, 67, 82–3, 149
  kingdom of, 14, 27
Spirit(s), Spirit-christology
  see Angel(s)

Targums, 40
  expectations of messianic age in, 138
  messianic interpretation of the
    Pentateuch in, 48, 66
  messianism in, 51, 55, 79, 93, 136–40
  on royal messiah, 30–1, 148–9
  relevance to study of Second Temple
    Judaism of, 3
  theme of judgment in, 61

Vengeance
  as aspect of messianism, 54, 55,
    60–3, 137–8
  in Christian messianism, 55
  in narrative apocrypha, 54

taken by God, 38

Zerubbabel, 7, 8, 25, 26, 28, 30, 40, 42,
  43, 44, 46, 56